OGDEN NASH

OGDEN NASH

The Life and Work of
America's Laureate of Light Verse

DOUGLAS M. PARKER

With a Foreword by Dana Gioia

IVAN R. DEE

Chicago 2005

www.ivanrdee.com

Library of Congress Cataloging-in-Publication Data:
Parker, Douglas M., 1935–
   Ogden Nash : the life and work of America's laureate of light verse / Douglas M. Parker ; with a foreword by Dana Gioia.
     p. cm.
   Includes bibliographical references and index.
   ISBN 1-56663-637-X (alk. paper)
     1. Nash, Ogden, 1902–1971. 2. Poets, American—20th century—Biography.
   3. Humorous poetry, American—History and criticism. I. Title.

PS3527.A637Z79 2005
811'.52—dc22
[B]

2004059912

For Angela

and

Heather and Melissa

CONTENTS

ACKNOWLEDGMENTS

MY INTENTION has been to capture much of the life and work of Ogden Nash in his own words, words not only from his poetry but from his voluminous correspondence with family, friends, and colleagues. This approach was made possible by Ogden Nash's daughters, Linell Nash Smith and Isabel Nash Eberstadt, who have generously permitted me to quote from Nash's published and unpublished writings. They also provided access to their private papers, were freely available for interviews, and were a constant source of support and encouragement without ever seeking to control what was to be included or omitted, or my interpretation of events. My gratitude to them is boundless.

I am also indebted to Linell Nash Smith for her own 1990 book, *Loving Letters from Ogden Nash*, which published many of Nash's letters to his family along with her biographical commentary. The book was an extraordinarily helpful starting place and a valuable resource throughout.

Another important asset was George Crandell's *Ogden Nash: A Descriptive Bibliography*. Nash published an enormous number of poems in magazines and books, and without Crandell's compilation, attempts to keep track of Nash's work or to locate particular poems would have been far more difficult.

The largest single repository of Nash's papers is the Harry Ransom Humanities Research Center at the University of Texas, which purchased them from Nash in 1968. Large numbers of Nash's papers were also found in the collections of his agent, Curtis Brown Ltd., and Dan Longwell at Columbia University, and in the files of Nash's publisher, Little, Brown & Co. The Nash Collection at Dartmouth College was assembled by Nash's friend from Baltimore, David Woods, and includes tape recordings and transcripts of interviews of Nash friends and colleagues conducted by Woods within a few years after Nash's death in 1971. The collection of *The New Yorker* at the New York Public Library includes not only letters from Nash but letters to Nash from the staff of the magazine, which it has graciously permitted me to quote. My sincere thanks to each of these firms and institutions.

Thanks are also due to numerous libraries and other institutions that made available Nash material, including Canaday Library, Bryn Mawr College; Kroch Library, Cornell University; Georgia Historical Society; Houghton Library, Harvard University; Haverford College Library; Library of Congress; Princeton University Library; Radcliffe College Library; Rye Historical Society; Syracuse University Library; University of North Carolina Library; and Music Library and Beinecke Library, Yale University. I also wish to thank the Snow Library in Orleans, Massachusetts, which helped me track down secondary sources.

I am particularly grateful to family, friends, and associates of Nash who made themselves available for interviews. In addition to Linell Nash Smith and Isabel Nash Eberstadt, the family members included Linell Smith, Frances Smith, Brigid Robins, Frederick Eberstadt, Nicholas Eberstadt, Fernanda Eberstadt, Juanita Rogers, and Charlton Rogers, III. Nash's friends and colleagues included Roger Angell, Dr. Ben Bagley, D. Angus Cameron, Tom Glazer, Al Hirschfeld, Emilie Jacobson, Perry Knowlton, Naomi Burton Stone, and Robert and Kay Southworth. Records, pictures, and other information about Nash's days at St. George's School were provided by its headmasters, Charles Hamblet and Eric F. Peterson; its archivist, Jack Doll; its historian, Dr. George Taverner; and William Rogers. David Goodrich shared information concerning Nash's friendship with Goodrich's aunt and uncle, the screenwriters Albert and Frances Hackett.

Finally, I am greatly indebted to my wife, Angela, who not only did much of the early typing before I reached an uneasy alliance with the computer, but also made valuable suggestions throughout. Without her patience and support the book could not have been completed.

D. M. P.

South Orleans, Massachusetts
January 2005

FOREWORD

by Dana Gioia

MY MOTHER, a working-class woman of Mexican descent, never went beyond high school, but like millions of ordinary Americans half a century ago, she loved poetry. My mother especially liked reading it aloud or reciting it from memory. She knew a surprising number of famous poems by heart as well as a remarkable selection of obscurities. Her taste ran mostly to those anthology favorites that publishers and editors back then still credibly termed as "beloved." Inspired by some turn of events, however trivial, in the day's business, she would recite a passage or poem from Poe, Whittier, Longfellow, Kipling, Service, Byron, or Shakespeare. I loved her impromptu recitations, and I have often looked back on those occasions with both personal affection and a certain scholarly curiosity about how poetry once reached an enormous nonliterary audience.

There was only one living poet in my mother's repertory—Ogden Nash. When she swatted some fly in the kitchen, she would intone with mock solemnity:

God in his wisdom made the fly
And then forgot to tell us why.

The appearance of either chocolate or alcohol would often elicit the remark that:

Candy
is dandy

But liquor
is quicker.

Did someone suggest danger? Mom would reply, "If called by a pan-
ther / don't anther." And no one could mention termites in our home without hearing the sad story of Cousin May, who "fell through the parlor floor
today." On those rare occasions when my mother, who worked nights at the
phone company, read to her children at bedtime—what a special treat it
seemed—she inevitably included "The Tale of Custard the Dragon." I
have often read this same ballad to my sons, enviously savoring its delicious
wordplay. What poet would not covet the brilliant rhyme in which the cat
Ink and mouse Blink flee the pirate?

Ink trickled down to the bottom of the household,
And little mouse Blink strategically mouseholed.

Nash was present elsewhere in my childhood, even if I didn't always
recognize his authorship. "Speak Low" and "Foolish Heart" were songs I
heard innumerable times before I ever learned who wrote their urbanely
romantic but irresistibly world-weary lyrics. The LP of Camille Saint-
Saëns's *A Carnival of Animals* at the public library had hilarious English
texts by you-know-who. I even found an album of sheet music called *Ogden Nash's Musical Zoo* by Vernon Duke among the piano music left behind by my dead uncle. I grew up knowing very little about contemporary
literature, but even I, a West Coast Latin prole, understood that Nash was
America's unchallenged champion of comic verse.

I have often wondered how Nash's work made its way into my childhood home. No copy of *The New Yorker* or respectable anthology of modern verse had ever entered our household. In fact, I don't recall seeing any
adult neighbor or relation, except my mother, ever read a book. One of the
many virtues of Douglas Parker's exemplary biography of Ogden Nash is
that he so clearly documents and chronicles how this singular poet won a
vast and appreciative readership during an era when American poets were
universally declared to be unpopular.

Nash's literary career was sui generis. What other American poet of the
Modernist era published best-selling collections of verse, collaborated in
Hollywood screenplays, authored Broadway lyrics, recited his work on radio variety shows, and served as a television game show panelist—all the
while writing poems on contract for several of America's biggest maga-

zines? A few poets might qualify on one of these categories. Carl Sandburg and Langston Hughes wrote screenplays. Robert Frost appeared on television talk shows. And T. S. Eliot wrote—unintentionally—the lyrics for a posthumous hit musical. But no other American poet ever had a life quite so closely associated with popular entertainment and media celebrity. If Nash's life was the exception to the rule of modern poetry's marginality to American mass culture, it also demonstrates the many missed opportunities of poetry to find a meaningful place in contemporary society.

At the center of Nash's unique literary life was a paradox. Although his commercial success and personal eagerness to please his large audience defied the general assumptions of a modern poet's career, Nash was in his odd way a product of Modernism. He was an inveterate experimentalist— a congenial one, to be sure, but also a wildly inventive artist. In terms of technical experimentation, his work sits comfortably beside that of his critically acknowledged revolutionary contemporaries like Lorine Niedecker, Louis Zukofsky, Kenneth Rexroth, Laura Riding, and Kenneth Fearing. A comic poet eager to get a laugh, Nash was no alienated visionary, but however accessible his tone and subject matter, he was endlessly innovative in his versification and diction. Many of his poems are rhymed free verse. Some consist of ingeniously rhymed prose. His rhymes were not merely amusing but often revelatory—playing on the differences between speech and writing or brilliantly contrasting levels of diction, shades of etymology, or arbitrary features of English like the inconsistency of our language's spelling and pronunciation:

> I would live all my life in nonchalance
> and insouciance
> Were it not for making a living, which
> is rather a nouciance.

Nash ultimately belongs to the neglected but important line of what I have called elsewhere Populist Modernists, those poets who adopted experimental techniques but rejected the uncompromising but elitist standards of High Modernism. These Populist Modernists include Vachel Lindsay, Carl Sandburg, Langston Hughes, Robinson Jeffers, Archibald MacLeish, and Robert Penn Warren. They constitute a lesser tradition than the High Modernism of T. S. Eliot, Wallace Stevens, Ezra Pound, and others, but their legacy remains a vital part of twentieth-century American poetry. Their poetry and Nash's has never lacked readership, even though it has rarely received much support from academic critics or literary tastemakers.

Douglas Parker's intelligent, informative, and engaging new biography fills a significant scholarly need in presenting the life and times of this neglected but important American poet. There is no comparable study not only of Nash's life but also of the role that poetry, especially comic verse, played in modern American literary culture. But beyond its considerable scholarly importance, Parker's book also movingly conveys the human story of an enormously gifted comic writer who often found himself at odds with his own era and yet found ingenious ways to match his talent to the times. It is a story long overdue in the telling.

OGDEN NASH

INTRODUCTION

On August 19, 2002, a large crowd, sitting and standing under a brilliant summer sun, filled the spacious backyard of a comfortable Baltimore home. The home was one in which Ogden Nash and his family had lived for many years, and the visitors were present to observe the dedication of an Ogden Nash postage stamp on the centennial of his birth. Colors were presented, speeches made, and Nash poems read by, among others, the political satirist Mark Russell as well as Nash's daughter, Linell Smith, his grandson, Nick Eberstadt, and his great-granddaughters, Isabel and Katie Eberstadt. The jazz singer Ethel Ennis sang the classic ballad "Speak Low," which Nash had written with Kurt Weill. Although video cameras whirred, it was a scene that might have been better captured by Norman Rockwell.

The stamp recognized Ogden Nash's accomplishments as a poet and his place in American culture. It was the eighteenth issuance in the Literary Arts Series that had begun in 1979 by honoring John Steinbeck. The Nash stamp, like Nash's poetry, is unique. The face of the stamp bears six short Nash verses that are actually readable by anyone with very sharp eyes or, for the rest of us, a good magnifying glass.

The odyssey that brought this recognition to Ogden Nash began in 1930 with the appearance of his verse in *The New Yorker*. By the time the magazine had published several of his poems, Nash had become a favorite of the editor, Harold Ross, and of Katharine White, one of Ross's editors, and he was soon recognized as one of the writers whose work defined the character of the magazine. While *The New Yorker* would always remain Nash's favorite outlet, his verse was published in dozens of other magazines and filled more than thirty volumes of poetry (including several children's books, a sideline that he took up in his fifties).

Nash once said that when he found he could not write successfully in the manner of classic poets, he decided to become "a good bad poet, rather than a bad good poet." The result was poetry unique in both style and subject matter: tortured spelling that created novel rhymes, and elongated lines that seemed to mock conventional meter, were well suited to the humorous perspectives that he brought to his verse. Nevertheless, beneath the humor a telling point would often be found. Robert Burns had once written, "Oh wad some power the giftie gie us/ To see oursels as others see us." Nash had that very gift and the added talent of being able to share it. Thus his poems not only conveyed shrewd observations about himself; his portrayals of the "minor idiocies of humanity" gave many of his readers a pretty good idea of how they sometimes looked to others. One of Nash's favorite subjects was families—husbands, wives, parents, children, and grandchildren—and even Nash's wife, Frances, for whom his devotion was endless, was not exempt from his gentle satire.

Despite Nash's self-deprecating assessment, there are ample grounds to argue that he was not a "good bad poet" after all but simply a good poet with a knack for writing poems that appealed to a remarkably broad range of people. While Nash was no doubt beloved by some who read little other poetry, he has long been appreciated by distinguished poets and critics as well. In the thirties, W. H. Auden wrote to a friend that Nash was "one of the best poets in America," and an admiring essay by the Poet Laureate Billy Collins recently observed that Nash's work revealed "the most essential of a poet's credentials, a crazed affection for the language."

Although Nash's poetry is the bedrock of his reputation, his career was remarkably varied. Despite extraordinary success in writing light verse, he made repeated efforts to escape the bounds of that genre and to find other outlets for his talents. Early on, he became fascinated with show business, and at different times he wrote scripts for Hollywood and songs for musicals on and off Broadway—with results that ranged from exhilarating triumph to embarrassing failure. Although he always denied being a performer, he frequently turned up in that role, and when he did, he carried it off with style: in lecture halls, on radio and television, and on the concert stage, reading verses with major orchestras. Nash's ventures in show business led him to work closely with a wide range of talents and personalities that included the broadcasting stars Edgar Bergen and Guy Lombardo, the composers Kurt Weill and Vernon Duke, the satirist and play-wright S. J. Perelman, the actresses Mary Martin and Bette Davis, and the conductor Andre Kostelanetz. Despite the continuing lure of show business, however, Nash always returned to writing verse.

Nash's verse gave many glimpses of his life and personality, but it gave little hint of the many serious challenges that he faced: issues of financial stability, professional disappointment, serious illness, and bouts of depression. He met his problems with varying measures of controlled exasperation and wry good humor, fortified by quiet determination. He never gave in, and he never relinquished for long an underlying sense of optimism.

In the 1960s, Nash struggled to cope with a variety of issues—including the difficulty of writing light verse amid the rising conflicts and tensions spawned by the Vietnam War. After a 1969 visit to the relative calm of London, and a tour of England and Scotland, had provided a welcome respite, a journalist asked Nash whether he might consider living abroad. "No," he replied firmly, "I am a part of this country, and it is a part of me." Nash found the strength to continue writing until his death in 1971. More than three decades later, he and his verse remain very much a part of us.

THE EARLY INFLUENCES

Ogden Nash was born Frederick Ogden Nash, after his great-grandfather, Frederick Nash, who had been chief justice of the Supreme Court of North Carolina. Although Nash would adopt the less formal Ogden, or sometimes Og, he did have a strong sense of ancestry. A personal profile included in Nash's first book of poetry, *Hard Lines* (1931), proudly noted that he had "ten thousand cousins in North Carolina, his great-great-grandfather was revolutionary governor of the state, and the latter's brother, General Francis Nash, gave his name to Nashville, Tennessee." While the estimate of Nash cousins was exaggerated, the connection with the governor and the general (as well as the chief justice) was factual. Indeed, that heritage was a matter of considerable family pride, and one that usually found its way into newspaper reports of family weddings, births, and deaths.

The governor, Abner Nash, had been born in Virginia, where his parents had immigrated from Tenby, Wales. His mother, Ann Owen Nash, was the daughter of Sir Hugh Owen, second baronet of Orielton (a heritage that would also be noted in family announcements). Abner Nash and his younger brother Francis, the future general, left Virginia in 1762 for Hillsborough, North Carolina, a town that would be a home to Nashes for several generations. (Reflecting his own interest in family history, Ogden Nash passed along to his children the explanation that the Nash brothers had left Virginia "because of their bad relations with their step-mother and disputes about inheritance.")

Within a few years Abner Nash was elected to the North Carolina House of Commons, and after the start of the Revolutionary War he became the second governor of the new state. His experience as governor, however, was a troubled one. Opposition from Loyalists and from some of his own colleagues made it impossible for him to govern effectively and took a toll on his health. Moreover, the British seized and burned Pembroke, the plantation he had established on the River Trent near New Bern. As Nash's son, Frederick, later wrote of his father, "He went into the War of the Revolution a wealthy man and came out of it worth nothing—the latter I *know* by painful experience."

Abner Nash declined a second term as governor in 1781 but served in the Continental Congress from 1782 to 1786, attending as regularly as his health would allow until his death from "consumption" during a session of the Congress in New York. It was an example of resilience and determination that was arguably a more valuable legacy to his descendants than the honor of his brief term as governor.

Despite a promising start, the fate of Abner's brother, Francis, proved to be even more unfortunate. Francis Nash entered the war as a lieutenant colonel and by February 1777 had been promoted to brigadier general. Only eight months later, however, he was killed while commanding the North Carolina brigade in action against the British near Philadelphia. Nash was nonetheless considered a hero of North Carolina, and two years later, when settlers from that state built a log stockade overlooking the Cumberland River in Tennessee, they called it Fort Nashborough. When the settlement was renamed Nashville in 1784, Francis's place in history was secure.

Meanwhile, Abner Nash's son, Frederick—Ogden's great-grandfather—had been born in 1781 at the governor's palace at New Bern. He grew up at Pembroke, after its recovery from the British, and despite the ruin of the plantation and the family fortunes, he was able to graduate from Princeton before returning to study law. As a young lawyer, Nash followed in his father's footsteps by serving in the state legislature, but after the loss of his first child he left New Bern for Hillsborough, seeking a healthier climate away from the coast.

In Hillsborough, Frederick Nash reestablished a successful law practice and was later appointed to the Supreme Court of North Carolina. He became chief justice in 1852 and served in that capacity until his death in 1856. Frederick and his wife had seven children, of whom the fourth was Henry Kollock Nash. Henry also became a successful lawyer in Hillsborough, though he never reached the eminence enjoyed by his father and grandfather. Henry and his wife, Mary Simpson Nash, had five children, of whom the youngest was Ogden's father, Edmund Strudwick Nash.

Edmund, born in 1854, grew up in Hillsborough and retained strong memories of the town throughout his life. He enjoyed recounting tales of his boyhood, and Ogden once told an interviewer that at the close of the Civil War his father had "patrolled the grounds of the family estate with a shotgun to protect his mother and sisters from stragglers and looters." Another family story, perhaps apocryphal, had it that Edmund, having watched Yankee soldiers make off with the family silver, was served with the same silver decades later at a dinner party in New York City. According to the story, he was too tactful to remark upon the irony in the presence of his host.

While Edmund's older brother, Frederick, had followed the family tradition and become a lawyer, that did not appeal to Edmund. Disdaining higher education, he left Hillsborough in 1877 to seek his fortune in New York City. He soon took a job with Patterson, Downing and Company, a firm in the business of buying and selling naval stores, chiefly turpentine and rosin. The company had offices in Europe and Russia, and young Nash did a good deal of traveling. In 1882 he wrote his father a long letter from London describing his experiences and outlining his business itinerary: "Antwerp thence to Amsterdam & Rotterdam, Mainz, Berlin and Cologne. Then Hamburg, Stetin, Danzig, Warsaw, Riga, St. Petersburg & Moscow—leaving there I will go to Southern Europe, then to Paris, England again, Scotland and *home*. That is quite a trip isn't it?"

And in February 1884, Edmund wrote his mother from St. Petersburg, describing his life there with evident delight:

> I wish I could for amusement and entertainment send you a
> picture of my daily life here. In the morning my agent calls for
> me in his sleigh and we visit the small firms with whom my
> business brings me in contact. I then lunch—in the afternoon I
> proceed in due state, enveloped in fur like an esquemaux, to the
> Royal Exchange where I parade, doffing and being doffed at every
> step, as solemnly as tho this was the chief business in life.

Edmund's merry insouciance is eerily similar to the tone that Ogden struck in letters nearly fifty years later, when the son was also delighted by sudden success at an early age.

As Edmund Nash's career progressed, he found time for occasional vacations, and he proceeded one year to a resort at White Sulphur Springs, West Virginia. There he met a beautiful young girl from Kentucky, Mattie Chenault, who would soon become his wife. While Edmund Nash could claim distinguished forebears, Mattie too came from a highly respected family, and she had an educational background that would later prove important.

The Chenaults were believed to have been descended from Etienne Chenault, a French Huguenot, who had immigrated to America in 1701. Mattie's father, Jason, was an educator who had been born in Danville, Kentucky, and raised at Millwood, a farm outside Danville that had once been visited by Harriet Beecher Stowe and later became the setting for her novel *Uncle Tom's Cabin*. Although Jason attended Harvard for a year, he graduated from Centre College in 1861 and then took up the study of law. Conditions after the Civil War, however, made it difficult to establish a law practice, and Jason took a teaching position in Richmond, Kentucky. It was there, in 1868, that Mattie was born.

After returning to Centre College to earn a master's degree, Jason joined its faculty. In 1875, however, he moved to Louisville and founded a prep school that became highly successful. Under her father's guidance, Mattie's own academic accomplishments won admission to Wellesley at the precocious age of fourteen. Although she dropped out of Wellesley before graduating, Mattie had become well prepared for the time when she would participate in the education of her own children. Long after his mother's death, Ogden noted that she "came from a very scholarly family" and spoke of how important her tutoring had been to him in his boyhood.

Edmund Nash and Mattie Chenault were married on December 10, 1889, at Mattie's home in Louisville. The wedding was lavishly covered by the *Louisville Courier-Journal*. Headlines proclaimed that the Chenault drawing room had been "Made to Represent a Chapel With Picturesque Appointments" and that the ceremony had been witnessed by a "Brilliant Assemblage." The ensuing report described Mattie Chenault as "one of the belles of the city"—"beautiful, bright and accomplished." Continuing in the same breathless voice, it was noted that "society had been on the qui vive for weeks" and that "the spacious parlors, reception rooms and halls" of the Chenault home had been "crowded with a representative Louisville society gathering." The account of the wedding ceremony was flawed only by an amusing typographical miscue: the ceremony was conducted by two clergy, the first of whom, it was said, "made the anti-nuptial address." (It was the kind of "news break" that Ogden Nash's colleague on *The New Yorker* in 1931, E. B. White, would have gleefully quoted with a comment such as "But the ceremony went ahead anyway.")

The *Courier-Journal* story also included a brief account of Edmund Nash's business success, noting that he was responsible for management of his firm's branches in Europe. In aid of those responsibilities, the paper said, the newlyweds would spend the winter in St. Petersburg and would then reside in London. St. Petersburg in the winter might not be every bride's idea of a place to honeymoon, but the Nashes were unquestionably off to a glamorous start.

By some time in 1890 the Nashes had returned and established themselves in Greenwich, Connecticut, where a first child, Shirley Gwendolyn, "Gwen," was born on December 8, almost exactly one year after her parents' wedding. Two years later, Mattie went home to Louisville for the birth of the Nashes' next child, Eleanor. The Nashes' first son, Edmund Witherell, "Ted," was born in 1896 in Savannah, Georgia, where much of the naval stores business was conducted and where the Nashes had a winter residence. The Nashes' home in Savannah was a stately house on Lafayette Square rented from Juliette Low, founder of the Girl Scouts of America. (Since 1928 the house has been occupied by the Georgia Society of Colonial Dames. For many years the Society has published a cookbook to which Ogden Nash obligingly contributed an introductory poem. It began, "Pilgrim's Progress is a good book, and so, I'm told is Deuteronomy / But neither is to be compared with this epic of gastronomy.")

In the meantime, Edmund's career continued to flourish, though not without some bumps along the way. In times of adversity, nothing was more important to Edmund than the love and support of his wife. In a letter written in 1894 to his children (then only Gwen and Eleanor, aged four and two), he asked that, if they should marry, they read two letters from Mattie to "learn how to give that comfort and strength which it is in the power of a good wife to bestow." Some years later, continuing the letter to his children, Edmund explained that Mattie's letter had been written at a time when his business had been "struggling through the deep waters." He had, Nash continued, "emerged strong and buoyant" to enjoy "many years of abounding prosperity."

By the time Ogden was born, on August 19, 1902, the Nashes had moved from Greenwich to Milton Point in Rye, New York. The move made it more convenient for Mattie to visit her sister, Shirley, who, with her husband, Franklin Watkins, lived at Ramaqua, a large estate in Rye. Franklin Watkins was a friend of Edmund Nash, and according to his daughter, Shirley Watkins Steinman, he had acted in a "John Alden" role in Nash's initial courtship of Mattie at White Sulphur Springs. Later, Edmund and Mattie reciprocated by introducing Watkins to Shirley Chenault, and the families had a close relationship. Sometime after Ogden was born, they drew even closer when the Nashes moved to Rockledge, a home adjacent to Ramaqua. But as Edmund Nash's fortunes continued to improve and those of Franklin Watkins declined, the Watkins family left Ramaqua and rented it to the Nashes. Ogden was joined by a younger brother, Aubrey, born in 1904, and Ramaqua became the place of their most vivid childhood memories.

The house at Ramaqua was a three-story structure, sometimes described as "Victorian-Italian," or, as Ogden later put it, "grotesque Victorian." Its most distinguishing feature was a tower where, according to legend, a former owner, a Mr. Loder, had hanged himself, and where his ghost would appear, clad in dressing gown and slippers. Aubrey Nash, however, always maintained that he was the only family member who had ever seen the ghost. Another story held that the house had once been connected to Long Island Sound by way of an underground tunnel used by smugglers, and Ogden and Aubrey spent many hours searching for it without success. The legends were less important to Edmund and Mattie than the fact that the house was well suited to the kind of gracious entertaining they enjoyed. (Describing life in Rye at the turn of the century, a 1955 history of the town noted that "The society columns contained frequent references to the Edmund Nash family. . . .")

The surrounding grounds were even grander than the house and were spread over more than fifty acres along the Boston Post Road. On the other side of the property lay the tracks of the New York, New Haven and Hartford Railway—whose commuter train would make a special stop to let Edmund off at the foot of his property. Rolling lawns led to woods, fruit trees, stables, and a carriage house. It was, in short, a wonderful place for young boys to explore and and to do all the sorts of things that young boys like to do. Ogden, it appears, developed an instinct for mischief at an early age; Aubrey would later recall a variety of pranks and adventures that he claimed his brother Og had instigated. Similarly, a youthful playmate of

Ogden's remembered how he had tricked her into hitting a hornet's nest and showed no sympathy when she sought refuge from the angry hornets by plunging into a nearby pond. (The victim apparently forgave Nash. She recounted the incident in a letter requesting an autograph of one of his books for her son.)

Ogden's own favorite memory of Ramaqua was sitting on the estate wall with Aubrey while identifying and counting the cars on the Post Road ("If we counted eight or ten we had a very high mark to be chalked up on the calendar"). Some sixty years later, Nash wrote a poem, "From an Antique Land," that recalled the names of the early cars, including his family's Royal Tourist and Pope Hartford. It also recalled an annual road race in Savannah that, Nash said, was a great event in his life and gave him the ambition—never pursued—to be a racing driver.

As Ogden and Aubrey were growing up, Edmund Nash was no longer the jaunty young man who had written of exploits in St. Petersburg. Now in his fifties, he was an established businessman but remained an imposing figure, standing six feet three inches and sporting a bushy mustache. He was also a man of some seriousness: it was, for example, his practice to begin the day by gathering his family and the servants in the drawing room for a brief morning prayer. Still, he had not entirely lost his sense of fun, and he would sometimes take Ogden and Aubrey out in the early morning for "mushroom creeping" on the lawn—picking mushrooms to be taken inside, immediately cooked in a chafing dish, and eaten. It was necessary to creep up on the mushrooms, Edmund told the boys, because if they were not very, very careful, the mushrooms would go back underground. In the evening, Edmund and Mattie would enjoy a cocktail together and, as the boys grew older, Aubrey recalled, it was Og's idea for them to partake surreptitiously of the "last little drippings" of the shaker. It was, he said, their first taste of "the good life."

Mattie was the family disciplinarian, but as very young children Ogden and Aubrey saw more of their nurse, Jane Hamilton, than of their mother. Ogden's closest relationship with his mother would not come until a few years later when she became his tutor. Meanwhile, Ogden relied greatly on the care and companionship of his sister, Gwen, twelve years older, to whom he sometimes referred as "Momma Number Two." Ogden's daughter Linell has described Gwen as "her father's darling and her mother's strong right arm." Even after her marriage, Gwen and her home outside Baltimore were a "safe haven" for family members who might be experiencing a difficult time. According to Linell, her father's devotion to Gwen was "unfailing."

Even while Nash was growing up at Ramaqua and in Savannah, early signs of his instinct for writing began to appear. At the wedding of Gwen in Savannah, ten-year-old Ogden recited a poem he had written, beginning "Beautiful spring at last is here!/ And has taken my sister, I sadly fear." Decades later, lecturing at the University of North Carolina, Nash observed that "these lines displayed an early aptitude for the inaccuracy that has come to distinguish what I have come to think of as my more mature work, because the marriage was in January." Nash went on to recall, "There followed some twelve or fourteen stanzas, equally emotional, equally philosophical, equally beautiful, and equally poetic. And it concluded with a tribute to my mother and my sister and the affection which they had maintained for each other: 'the mother of the playful cat/ Is always anxious on her behalf.'"

Two and a half years after Gwen's wedding, Ogden wrote to her on the birth of her second child and enclosed his "two latest poems." The first, "The Song of the Wanderer," had a rather mournful tone ("I must wander, I must wander,/ Through forest, field and plain,/ And not until I leave this earth,/ Can I ever rest again"), but the second, "The Devil," may have foreshadowed Nash's later affinity for poetic humor:

> The devil is a bad man,
> He has horns both sharp and strong
> And his tail is very long.
>
>   *   *   *   *
>
> I went to see the devil
> And the devil said to me
> "Be bad, young Tommy Simpson,
> Or I'll lay you cross my knee."
>
> I replied, "you old red devil,
> I will do no such thing,"
> And started to talk back at him,
> But then—I woke up—"Bing."

The letter to Gwen also enclosed a letter to Ogden's infant nephew, welcoming him into the world: "It is a cold and cruel world sometimes, but at others it is hot and kind."

In fact the Nashes had begun to experience the cold and cruel side of the world a year before, with an event that changed all of their lives. As Ogden described it many years later, "When I was twelve or thirteen my father's business began to rock due to a series of lawsuits brought by the government, so our lives were disturbed as the financial situation changed. I was too young to realize exactly what was going on, but I knew that things were not as they used to be or should be." Indeed, Edmund's business had not merely begun to rock but had suffered an abrupt collapse.

In 1903, Edmund Nash had become president of Patterson, Downing and Company and had led the firm into a merger with the S. P. Shotter Company to form American Naval Stores Company. Spencer P. Shotter was chairman of the new company and Edmund Nash its president. The company quickly became a major force within the naval stores industry and prospered accordingly—perhaps too well. In April 1908 the United States government brought an indictment against the company and several of its officers, including Shotter and Nash, under the then relatively new and untested Sherman Anti-trust Act. The indictment charged a conspiracy in restraint of trade and a conspiracy to monopolize trade. A year later, after a trial of several days, the jury returned a guilty verdict and the court imposed sentences: Spencer Shotter and J. F. C. Meyers, a vice president, were given the maximum fine of $5,000 and sentenced to three months in jail; Edmund Nash was fined $3,000; two other officers were fined lesser amounts.

Savannah was stunned by the verdict. The *Savannah Morning News* reported it as "a surprise both to those who heard the evidence and those who read it in the newspapers." The paper acknowledged that there had been evidence of "irregularities" at the company's facilities in Brooklyn, New York, and Jacksonville, Florida, but it questioned the jury's inference of a conspiracy. The *Savannah Press* was even more outspoken, suggesting that "Perhaps no case has ever been tried in Savannah in which the result caused such surprise and disappointment." The paper noted that the defendants had received "letters from banks and others expressing their unabated confidence in them," and assured the defendants that the verdicts would not do them "the slightest harm in the community where they live, and in the business world with which they deal."

For many months the optimism of the Savannah newspapers appeared to have been justified: appeals were taken and the company continued to operate profitably. In 1912, however, the government filed a second suit, now seeking the dissolution of the company, and on Monday, March 17,

1913, American Naval Stores made the startling announcement that it had been forced to suspend operations. The company's statement was issued by its secretary, in the absence of Edmund Nash, who was traveling in Europe with his family. The statement said that the existence of the pending government actions had made it impossible to secure new capital and that its existing resources, though "large and valuable," were no longer adequate. A meeting with creditors to devise a workout plan had been scheduled for Friday of the same week.

If the management of the company had hoped for agreement on a plan that would allow them to remain in charge of its operations, they were quickly disappointed. On March 22 the *Savannah Morning News* reported that a committee of five bankers, selected by creditors, had taken over the company. The committee, it was said, would seek the resignation of all the company's officers and would then determine whether to accept them. If that appeared to leave the door open a crack, it was a very narrow crack indeed, and the pressure from the government was unremitting. The United States attorney, who had been invited by the chairman of the creditors' committee to attend the meeting, observed that if the officers resigned and assets were administered for the benefit of creditors, the government would not "pursue a phantom."

None of the company's officers was retained, liquidation proceeded, and Nash returned to Savannah on May 2 to find his company effectively gone. The liquidation, however, had proceeded with remarkably successful results for the creditors. A headline in the *Savannah Weekly Naval Stores Review* of June 7, 1913 declared, "American Working Out in Magnificent Shape." The *Review* then set forth a report by the creditors' committee. Not only would all creditors be satisfied, the *Review* reported, but of the company's capital of $3.2 million, as much as $1.7 million might be available for distribution to stockholders. It had not been necessary to dispose of the company's inventory at sacrifice prices, and over $3 million of indebtedness had been discharged, the remainder to be liquidated within the next few weeks.

Given the optimistic financial report of the creditors' committee, one may wonder whether liquidation had really been necessary in the first place. The irony was compounded almost immediately when on June 9 the United States Supreme Court reversed the convictions of Nash, Shotter, and the other officers. An opinion by Justice Holmes rejected the defendants' attacks on the Sherman Act, including the claim that it was unconstitutionally vague, but did find a fatal flaw in the instructions of the court to the jury. The instructions, Holmes held, had obscured the fact that several key charges had been abandoned by the government.

The Supreme Court's decision was heralded in Savannah and elsewhere. A *Naval Stores Review* headline trumpeted, "Vindication Comes to Mr. Spencer P. Shotter." Satisfying as such "vindication" may have been to Shotter, Nash, and the other defendants, it can only have increased their bitterness to read in a separate story in the paper that officials of the Justice Department now sought to minimize the significance of the Supreme Court decision by saying that "They never considered that they had a strong case."

Over the years the collapse of Edmund Nash's company took on something of a mythic character within the Nash family. Ogden, it was understood, would always hold a disparaging view of Theodore Roosevelt, whose trust-busting policies were thought to have inspired the prosecution. But there was also a theory that speculation with the company's assets by one of its principals had contributed to its financial problems. Although the possibility cannot be excluded, there is no evidence of such speculation in the contemporaneous accounts. Still, apart from such theories, puzzling questions remain. Did Edmund Nash realize his company's precarious financial position when he left for Europe with Mattie, Eleanor, and Aubrey at the beginning of March? If so, why did he not cancel or postpone the trip? Why did Shotter apparently do nothing to try to preserve the company or at least to delay its demise until the Supreme Court had an opportunity to rule? Were the company and Nash in communication by cable during his absence? Under the circumstances, it may be that Nash could have done nothing more than Shotter even if he had been on hand throughout.

At this distance, the full measure of the financial impact of the debacle on the Nash family is hard to assess. A part of the family story is that Edmund Nash took it upon himself to make good on the company's debts, but from the accounts in the *Naval Stores Review*, that does not appear to have been necessary. On the other hand, the creditors' committee indicated that it would require repayment of company loans to officers totaling almost $600,000, a portion of which was presumably owed by Nash. In any event, the collapse of the company left Nash without employment, and a new position at the age of sixty would not be easy to come by. Shirley Watkins Steinman later suggested that Edmund, like her own father, had become a victim of Ramaqua itself—a curse of Mr. Loder's ghost. However that might be, one consequence of Edmund's financial problems was its impact on the course of Ogden's education.

Even before his father's financial ruin, Ogden's early schooling had been eclectic. At the outset, Ogden and Aubrey had a tutor in Savannah who, according to Aubrey, "had a crush on my sister, Eleanor, and for that reason didn't last very long." Later, after attending day school in Rye, Ogden was sent to the Shaw School in Groton, Connecticut, when he was ten. It was a very small school—a capacity of only eight boys—that served as preparation for the Groton School itself, where Ogden's brother Ted was enrolled. Nash thoroughly enjoyed the Shaw School. It was, he said, where he "learned some Latin—began my rather serious study of Latin, a language I've found very useful." On the other hand, Nash admitted that he also "spent a good deal of time riding a bicycle through the New England countryside." Nash's letters home in the fall of 1912 confirm both his academic progress and his enjoyment of the outdoors. The letters routinely reported that he was considerably ahead of his classmates in both arithmetic and Latin, and in addition to bike riding ("Tell Aub he ought to see some of the hills I go up"), he wrote of impromptu games of football and ice hockey. Nash's affection for the school surfaced more than fifty years later when he was visiting Concord, Massachusetts, and was delighted to run into Mrs. Shaw, now over ninety. He found her "spry as a cricket, sound as a nut, clear as a bell, sharp as [a] hound's tooth," and full of anecdotes. Nash was so entertained that he dashed off a note to his editor at *The New Yorker* suggesting that the magazine do a story about her.

Despite his success at the Shaw School, Nash did not return the following year, nor would he go on to attend Groton. He had encountered difficulty with his eyesight that greatly disturbed his mother. Believing that Ogden's condition would grow progressively worse, she took two actions: she had her son take a course in touch-typing ("which proved invaluable until my fingers curled up on me in later life"), and she took him out of school to study at home. Nash did a great deal of reading with his mother and would later claim that much of his "real education" was gained from her tutoring. A large diet of reading would seem to be a curious prescription for someone with eye problems, and it may be that financial considerations were a factor in Nash's withdrawal from school. In any event, there is little doubt that, once his eyesight had stabilized, financial constraints prevented his return to boarding school.

After the spring of 1913 the Nashes gave up their home in Savannah and lived at Ramaqua year round. A diary Nash kept in 1916 offers glimpses of his life at Ramaqua that year. By then Mattie had turned over the tutoring reins to a Miss Filkins, and Nash records a variety of social activities, including sledding parties and snowball fights with several other boys and girls who may also have been her pupils. In addition, he spent afternoons with his mother, who was ill at the time, and sometimes played pool with his father in the evening. Finally, the diary notes the engagement and marriage of Ogden's sister Eleanor. (Although the wedding was attended only by the immediate families, it was reported in the *New York Times* of April 5, 1916, which obligingly, if somewhat inaccurately, described Eleanor as a "descendant of the Nashes of Nashville" and a "granddaughter of Sir Hugh Owen of Wales.")

The following year, Nash's educational path took another detour. On a visit from her home in Baltimore, Gwen came down with polio at Ramaqua. As a precaution, Ogden and Aubrey were sent off to Mattie's sister, Nell, in Nashville, where Ogden attended Wallace University School. By the spring of 1917, financial pressures finally forced the Nashes to give up Ramaqua, and many of their furnishings from the house were auctioned off. Edmund, Mattie, and Aubrey moved into an apartment in New York City while Ogden went to stay temporarily with his brother Ted on Long Island. But Ogden did leave Rye with something to remember him by. The United States had declared war against Germany on April 6, and the July 21 issue of the *Rye Chronicle* carried on its front page a poem entitled "The Scrappy U.S. Sammy." In the fifth and final stanza, the poem concluded:

> So the Kaiser may as well recall his U-boats
> And the Hohenzollerns start to say good night
> From now on they will sink but mighty few boats
> For our scrappy U.S. Sammy's in the fight.

It was signed, Ogden Nash, Cedarhurst, L.I.

Just as affairs seemed to be at a low point for the Nashes, Ogden's father was at last successful in finding a new position as president of the Rosin and Turpentine Export Company. Two years later Edmund Nash would write, "After four years of patient waiting, Fortune withdrew her frown and I was offered a livelihood and an opportunity of which I have taken full advantage. New friends have replaced the old—the present is secure and the future is full of promise." For Ogden it meant that his education would take yet another direction.

If the idea had been for Ogden to follow his brother Ted to Groton, that plan had long since been set aside. Now, when boarding school had again become financially feasible, admission to Groton on short notice would probably have been difficult. Another opportunity, however, soon appeared. In February 1917, Ted had married Esther Auchincloss; her father, Hugh, had served on the board of trustees of St. George's School in Newport, Rhode Island, until his death in 1913, and her mother had been the principal donor of a gymnasium for the school. So it was that in the fall of 1917, Ogden enrolled at St. George's. The school had a good reputation, but it was not as well established as some of the other New England boarding schools. Perhaps for that reason it may have been more willing to take on a new student with a modest record of formal education.

St. George's had been founded in 1896 by an Episcopal clergyman, the Reverend John Byron Diman, and it occupied a Georgian manor house set on a hilltop with sweeping views of the ocean. When Nash arrived in 1917, the school had 14 faculty members and a student body of 140, a new high. Circumstances at St. George's, however, were a bit unsettled on two counts. The founding headmaster, the Reverend Diman, who had presided over the school's remarkable growth, had resigned unexpectedly at the beginning of the year; a faculty member, Stephen P. Cabot, had been appointed headmaster. In addition, the impact of the world war was clearly being felt. Even before the entry of the United States into the war, the school had formed a "Battalion of Infantry" for military drill, students had rolled bandages for the Red Cross, and several alumni had joined the Canadian Forces or the Lafayette Escadrille. Now some of the older boys would be tempted to leave school and enlist in either the military or ambulance services. As the historian of the school, George Y. Taverner, later wrote, "The boys' imaginations were stirred to write war stories, brimming with military action. Alumni serving in France sent back diaries and accounts of battles further stimulating support of the War by the boys and masters." Fortunately the new headmaster proved well suited to the position, and with a firm hand he kept the school running in as normal a fashion as could be hoped.

As customary with boarding schools, St. George's was divided into forms from one through six, corresponding to grades seven through twelve. Ogden entered the fourth form, or tenth grade, which meant that he was joining a group in which many friendships had already been made.

Nonetheless he was quickly accepted by his classmates and began what he would look back on as "three very happy years." Academically, his scattered preparation turned out to be more than adequate, and by the time he graduated he was awarded the Binney Prize, the school's highest award for scholastic achievement.

The masters at St. George's were a dedicated group, several of whom would spend their entire careers at the school. Nash found that the masters in history, Latin, and English were "extremely stimulating," and throughout his life he kept in touch with the English master, Arthur Roberts. Writing to Roberts on the latter's ninetieth birthday, Nash earnestly expressed his gratitude for Roberts's "patient understanding of the lazy evasive stray who was the bane of your English classes from the fall of 1917 through the spring of 1920." It was Roberts's grounding in correct usage, Nash said, that later enabled him to "hit upon the conscious employment of incorrect usage for my own devious ends." It was, he continued, "the love for the mother tongue that you instilled in me which enabled me to tease it and flirt with it to the limits of decency." Even allowing for some hyperbole on a festive occasion, Nash's regard for Roberts was obviously genuine. And he enjoyed the other masters as well: a poem written for the school's fiftieth anniversary celebration in 1946 vividly recalled them all and affectionately portrayed the idiosyncrasies of each.

Nash was not a natural athlete, and his eyesight required glasses, but he was an eager participant in football, basketball, and baseball at various levels. Still, his talents in other areas were more obvious. He became president of the Civics Club and was elected to the boards of *The Dragon*, the school's newspaper and literary magazine, and *The Lance*, the school yearbook. He was a prolific contributor of a variety of short stories and poems to *The Dragon*. These included at least two rather macabre horror stories, a genre with which he would occasionally experiment long after he had become a successful poet. The poems, on the other hand, were almost all serious in form and content, and while quite competent work for a schoolboy, did not suggest that their author was likely to become a latter-day Keats or Shelley or Tennyson. They were nevertheless an essential step in Nash's progress to his eventual conclusion that he would "rather be a good bad poet than a bad good poet."

When Nash graduated in June 1920, his further education seemed assured. While he had earlier indicated an intention to attend Princeton, he was now planning to attend Harvard along with his close friend and classmate, Eugene Reynal. A year later, after Nash's first year at Harvard, things looked quite different. Rosin and Turpentine had been sold by its parent corporation and, with the sale, Edmund Nash's employment had once again disappeared. At that point, Nash later confessed, he lacked the intellectual curiosity, physical vigor, or ambition to work his way through his remaining three years, having decided that "three years at St. George's had to make do for four years at Harvard." But what was he to do?

Remarkably enough, Nash returned to St. George's, which agreed to take him on as a French instructor. Despite his brilliant record at St. George's, this was surely a daunting assignment for a college dropout who had left the school little more than a year before. And it is not clear how the school was persuaded to hire him. As Taverner commented in 1996, "The mystery of Nash's returning to the School in 1921 as a Harvard dropout remains unsolved. The [headmaster] Stephen Perkins Cabot who would have brought Nash on, was a strong, progressive educator. His appointing Nash seems totally out of character for the man." Possibly one of the faculty had left abruptly, creating a vacancy that needed to be quickly filled. Or perhaps the Auchincloss influence had once again been helpful. In any event, Nash had a safe harbor for a few months while trying to figure out his next move.

The most difficult aspect of his tenure on the faculty, Nash would later say, was officiating in the dining hall, where he claimed to have "lost [his] entire nervous system carving lamb for a table of fourteen-year-olds." (It may be that Nash suffered from a comparison—his or the boys'—with the headmaster who, it was said, had the "unusual ability to carve a roast with one hand standing at table in King Hall straight as a Prussian soldier.") On the other hand, there is some evidence that Nash's classroom performance was at least adequate. In 1963, when Nash was on the lecture circuit, one of his hosts wrote to St. George's seeking some background information on the scheduled speaker. A tongue-in-cheek reply from a faculty member, George Wheeler, noted that Wheeler himself had been instructed by Nash in French, and continued by remarking that he could not say whether Nash's "stimulating teaching" had led to his own appointment as head of the French Department many years later.

Nevertheless it was clear that without further education Nash would have no future on the faculty at St. George's or anywhere else. So, at the end of the school year, Nash left the school, not to return to college but to make his way in New York City—very much as Edmund Nash had done in 1877.

2

GETTING STARTED

Manhattan in the 1920s was the centerpiece of the revolution in manners and mores that accompanied the postwar boom. Women's skirts had long since climbed "far beyond any modest limitation," and as skirts had risen, morality, in the eyes of many, had declined just as rapidly. Young men and women were drinking cocktails, smoking cigarettes, and "in darkened rooms or in parked cars [engaging in] the unspeakable practice of petting and necking." Such demeanor, vividly described in Scott Fitzgerald's 1920 novel *This Side of Paradise*, showed no sign of abating. In New York the advent of Prohibition had done nothing to diminish the fun. Manhattan boasted "thousands of speakeasies," with clubs "lining the streets of the forties and fifties between Fifth and Sixth Avenues."

It was also a time of ferment in the literary world. In 1923, H. L. Mencken launched the iconoclastic *American Mercury* magazine, championing such writers as Theodore Dreiser, Sherwood Anderson, Willa Cather, and Sinclair Lewis, and "[pouring] critical acid upon sentimentality and evasion and academic pomposity in books and in life." In New York the round table at the Algonquin hotel became celebrated for the repartee of the literati who gathered around it, including Alexander Woollcott, Heywood Broun, Franklin P. Adams, Robert Benchley, George S. Kaufman, Marc Connelly, Robert Sherwood, Harold Ross, and Dorothy Parker.

Against that stimulating if sometimes frantic backdrop, Nash set out on the modest and prosaic course of becoming a bond salesman. He arrived on Wall Street with little enthusiasm but because friends of his family had been able to give him a job. He reasoned, no doubt, very much as had a character in another Fitzgerald novel, *The Great Gatsby*, "Everybody I knew was in the bond business, so I supposed it could support one more single man." Nash, however, did not find much success on Wall Street. He began in the mail room of a prominent brokerage firm, Dillon Reed, working from four in the afternoon to twelve or one in the morning, and "discovered what the downtown financial district looks like at midnight with no one in the streets and cats prowling about the garbage cans." It was, Nash would say, "a lot like Don Marquis's Mehitabel." After a year and a half and the sale of a single bond—to his godmother—Nash decided it was time to move on to a vocation better suited to his talents. By this time the interest in writing he had shown at St. George's had resurfaced. He knew that he wanted to write professionally, but how or what—and how to make a living from writing—was by no means clear. His first opportunity for professional writing of any sort involved a rather narrow speciality—streetcar advertising for the Barron G. Collier firm. It was the same firm that had once employed Scott Fitzgerald in a similar capacity, but despite that interesting heritage (unknown to Nash at the time), the position offered limited opportunity. After two years Nash was making a hundred dollars a month and not having much fun.

Despite his unpromising situation, Nash still had dreams of becoming a writer, and he shared them with his roommate, Joe Alger, who had similar aspirations. Alger had been two years ahead of Nash at St. George's and Harvard, and the two were now living in a gas-heated, cold-water flat under the Third Avenue El. After canvassing the possibilities, Nash and Alger decided to collaborate and concluded that the easiest place to start would be a book for children. The result was *The Cricket of Carador*, which they succeeded in selling to a major publisher, Doubleday, Page & Company.

The Cricket of Carador did not make a lot of money for its publisher or its authors when it appeared in 1925. Nash later wrote that the book sold fewer copies "than you could count on the thumbs of one hand. [Doubleday, Page] had a lot of copies left over that they didn't know what to do with. I believe that when all else failed they tried to trade them to Fiji Islanders for cocoanuts [sic] but the Fijis balked and held out for beads." In fact, the book does not seem to have done quite so badly, as it was still on the Doubleday annual trade list in 1927.

More important, however, the book gave Nash an entree to Doubleday and to Dan Longwell. Longwell, only a couple of years older than

Nash, had become head of the Doubleday advertising department and needed to replace a talented assistant who had just left. He offered the position to Nash, who quickly accepted. Although it required him to take a ten-dollar-per-month salary cut, and to make a "reverse commute" to the firm's offices in Garden City on Long Island, it offered him an escape from the modest niche at Barron G. Collier that he had realized was "the lowest stratum of a dying empire."

Nash soon came to have enormous respect and affection for his new boss, and Longwell, for his part, became a mentor who took every opportunity to nurture the talent that had come his way. It was the start of a relationship that would survive the departure of both men from Doubleday and continue for their entire lives. And Nash would learn lessons about marketing books that he was still putting to use decades later in dealing with the publisher of his own work.

At a tribute to Longwell at Columbia University, two years after his death in 1968, Nash reminisced that, when he joined Doubleday, Longwell was engaged in a "minor and polite battle" over a book, *The Constant Nymph*, that one of the elder members of the firm considered to be obscene. Longwell won the battle and did the advertising, and the book became a best-seller. It was a triumph that Nash enjoyed sharing, and Longwell's position on the book fit well with Nash's own views of "censorship." On a more mundane level, Nash recalled, Longwell taught him the useful knack of writing a business letter without sounding stuffy.

Nash found himself working long hours, sometimes getting home to his apartment at midnight and heading back to Garden City on the 7:49. But he didn't mind: Longwell had the ability to infuse his staff with "team spirit," creating what seemed to Nash an atmosphere comparable to "a very exciting college life." A graduate of Columbia, Longwell rewarded Nash's hard work at the office with excursions to the Columbia Club (where, Prohibition notwithstanding, an expert bartender produced old-fashioneds with an unusual recipe — scotch with a splash of soda on the top).

According to George Stevens, one of Nash's colleagues in the Doubleday advertising department, Nash was a first-class copywriter, though sometimes, perhaps, a bit too free-spirited for the tastes of senior management. Stevens recalled in particular a headline that Nash wrote for a Booth Tarkington book high on the best-seller lists: "First in New York, First in Chicago and First in the Hearts of his Countrymen." The borrowing of the salute to George Washington apparently struck one of

Nash's elders as almost scandalous. In any case, Nash soon moved beyond the confines of the advertising department, not because of any indiscretion but because Longwell recognized that he had broader talents.

On a trip to England, Longwell had discovered an association of detective story writers who gathered to discuss their work and admitted only the most respected practitioners of the genre. When Longwell returned to the United States, he persuaded Doubleday management to form a separate subsidiary, the Crime Club, that would be devoted to publishing mystery novels by the finest writers of such work. Nash became an editor of the Crime Club and worked with a number of its most prominent authors. It was a valuable experience and was probably responsible for a poem that Nash later wrote, "Don't Guess, Let Me Tell You." The poem gave a name, which became widely used, "HIBK," for the school of detective fiction made popular by Mary Roberts Rinehart and many followers:

> Personally I don't care whether a detective-story writer was
> educated in night school or day school
> So long as they don't belong to the H.I.B.K. school,
> The H.I.B.K. being the device to which too many detective-story
> writers are prone,
> Namely, the Had I But Known.

      ✻   ✻   ✻   ✻

Nevertheless, Nash was aiming higher, and by June 1929 he was able to write that "There have been some big changes at the office and I now find myself sitting firmly in a job I've always wanted—elevated above the Crime Club (which is a dear old thing just the same) and nursing all kinds of respectable books." One quite respectable book for which Nash was responsible was *Intellectual Things*, the first book of poems by Stanley Kunitz. Kunitz, later the Poet Laureate of the United States, recalls that Nash telephoned him to say how much he had enjoyed it and that Doubleday would like to publish it.

Longwell also encouraged Nash's experiments with his own writing. The year after he joined Doubleday, his humorous poem "The Bishop's Christmas Wish" appeared in *Country Life*, a Doubleday magazine. No other published work would emerge for some time, but Nash had reached the important conclusion that he simply lacked the talent to become a serious poet: "There was a ludicrous aspect to what I was trying to do; my emotional and naked beauty stuff just didn't turn out as I had intended."

As a result, he had begun to write poems that poked fun at his own unsuccessful attempts, sometimes on scrap paper folded up and tossed on the desk of George Stevens.

As Nash worked increasingly on the editorial side, he found further sources of inspiration. For one thing, work as an editor subjected him to reading a great deal of bad poetry written by others. Sometimes his exasperation overflowed: "I was miserably drowning in a liquid mass of poetry sent in [with] a written guarantee from her father and mother that if we published the book they would buy at least a thousand copies for Christmas presents, so that by unkindly stamping on it I have made at least one thousand Christmases bigger and brighter. . . ."

The example was not an isolated one. As Nash later observed, "If you have a job in an editorial office for seven years, in the course of that seven years, if you put your mind to it, you can get to read the most enormous quantity of bad poetry." Over that time, Nash's experience tended to reinforce his notion that "if somebody who knew the rules of versification, began writing bad poetry deliberately and consciously instead of unconsciously," it might "turn out to be fairly amusing." Nash also realized that he did have "this certain knack for rhyming and versification, which is something like the knack for sinking an eighteen-inch putt."

At the same time Nash discovered that there was a market for humorous poetry. Roland Young wrote a book for Doubleday, *Not for Children*, containing short verses about animals. Nash thought some of the verses were quite funny but others not up to that standard. So, as an earnest young editor trying to be helpful, he offered the author one or two of his own. Not surprisingly, Young declined the offer, but Longwell thought they were something that Nash might be able to publish under his own name. For example, "The Turtle":

> The turtle lives twixt plated decks
> That practically conceal its sex.
> I think it clever of the turtle
> In such a fix to be so fertile.

The poem made a remarkable impression on the humorist Corey Ford, who met Nash one night at Ford's favorite speakeasy, the "109," run by Jim Moriarty. This "bespectacled and modest young advertising copywriter" admitted to Ford that he dabbled in light verse. Over a drink, and after some urging, Nash recited "The Turtle." Years later, Ford could still remember the words. More important, "The Turtle" would be included in Nash's first book, *Hard Lines*, and it was followed in succeeding books by an extensive menagerie of similar poetic subjects.

Nash also claimed that a duck-hunting trip to South Carolina by Longwell and Nelson Doubleday during the same period inspired a verse called "The Hunter":

> The hunter crouches in his blind
> Mid camouflage of every kind.
> He conjures up a quacking noise
> To lend allure to his decoys.
> This grownup man, with talk and luck
> Is hoping to outwit a duck.

According to Nash, Longwell "took this very gracefully," but the story itself may involve some poetic license. The poem was not published until 1948, many years after Nash and Longwell had both left Doubleday, and it would have been quite uncharacteristic of Nash to let a publishable verse lie dormant so long. There is no doubt, however, that Nash did write a poem for Longwell, "Songs for a Boss Named Mr. Longwell." (When the poem was initially published in *Hard Lines*, the name of the boss was changed to "Linthicum," but in later collections it reverted to Longwell.)

In addition to encouraging Nash's experiments in versification, Longwell brought him together with Christopher Morley, a Doubleday author who was also an editorial adviser and consultant to the firm. Morley was a man of extraordinarily diverse literary talents and was perhaps the most widely known man of letters of his generation. In his lifetime, Morley wrote eighteen volumes of fiction, sixteen of poetry, and thirteen of essays. He was one of the original judges for the Book-of-the-Month Club and a contributing editor of the *Saturday Review of Literature*, for which he wrote a weekly column. In addition to his own work as a novelist, essayist, and poet, Morley took delight in the promotion of undiscovered or underappreciated talents: writers who benefited from his interest included William McFee, Joseph Conrad, Elinor Wylie, and Sherwood Anderson. He was, in short, a very good person for an aspiring young writer to know.

Morley's association with Doubleday had begun in 1913, when he returned from England where he had studied at Oxford and published a volume of poetry, *The Eighth Sin*. (The title of the book was taken from a passage in the letters of John Keats: "There is no greater sin after the seven deadly than to flatter oneself into an idea of being a great Poet." That was precisely the sin that Nash was determined to avoid.) Morley was able to arrange an interview with the head of the firm, F. N. Doubleday, at which Morley presented a dizzying succession of ideas for various books and projects. To gain a moment's breathing room, Doubleday interrupted: "You would have to be about ten men to successfully carry out all these plans; now if you had your chance of any job in the place, what would you choose?" Morley replied without hesitation, "Yours." Doubleday was sufficiently impressed by such confidence that Morley was given a job, albeit one with more modest responsibilities.

By the time Nash arrived on the scene, Morley was working for Doubleday only part-time, but his influence had grown with his reputation. He was also a good friend of Dan Longwell, with whom he founded the "Nassau and Suffolk County Deviled Ham and Lake Ronkonkoma Club." Nash was elected its "permanent secretary pro tem" at the first meeting on May 7, 1929. According to Nash, the club had only two rules: "One was that no member must ever go to Lake Ronkonkoma, and the other was that all meetings must take place on Doubleday time." Meetings were called whenever Morley, a notoriously bad driver, rolled up in his "uncontrollable car." Then Morley, Longwell, and Nash, along with two or three other Doubleday staff, would depart for a nearby tavern where the "real stuff" could be obtained along with sandwiches, and they would then find somewhere to eat and talk about books. The actual minutes of several meetings of the club in the summer of 1929 were taken by Nash and are now preserved at the University of Texas. Not surprisingly, perhaps, they are a bit difficult to follow, and while literary allusions abound, Nash's notes do not suggest that the "talk about books" ever became overly serious. Minutes of one of the meetings, for example, recorded the following: "Meeting unanimously endorses Thomas Nashe. His Pe wee tu witt witt juga jug is good. Chris mordantly remarks that with the contemporary Nash the jug precedes the wit. This is a good point but unkind." The club, Nash said, was a "delightful and charming thing," but one that "was never allowed to interfere with our efficiency."

Nash's friendship with Morley soon led him in another direction. In 1928, Morley and a friend, Cleon Throckmorton, a well-known architect and stage designer, had acquired the Rialto theater in Hoboken, New Jersey. In the 1860s the site of the theater had been a beer garden and dance hall, and the theater itself had a long tradition of melodrama and burlesque.

The initial concept of Morley and Throckmorton was to have a stock company that would present a new show every week or two. Over the first three months the theater mounted a number of productions, including a dramatization of Morley's own novel *Pleased to Meet You*, with incidental music by Jerome Kern. Operations, however, were marginal until December 1928, when the production of an old melodrama, *After Dark*, by Dion Boucicault, drew favorable reviews from the *New York Times*'s Brooks Atkinson and other critics. Suddenly thousands of New Yorkers were coming to Hoboken by ferry, tubes, and tunnel, and the run of the play was extended indefinitely. Morley later estimated that "Between January and May 150,000 people packed themselves into that shabby little old playhouse." Encouraged by their success, Morley and Throckmorton acquired another old theater across the street, the Lyric, and staged an elaborate production of a venerable musical drama, Charles M. Barras's *The Black Crook*. The show had originally played in New York in 1867, when it was described by a visiting Charles Dickens as "the most preposterous peg to hang ballets on that was ever seen." Nevertheless it had enjoyed a run of 474 performances and is now thought to have been the first true American musical. In Hoboken it too became a hit, despite an opening-night performance that lasted from 9 o'clock until 1:30 (cut the following night to less than three hours).

At Morley's urging, Nash made frequent visits to Hoboken, and in 1928 he co-authored a play that he hoped might be produced there. Morley expressed a cautiously favorable reaction ("Its girlish babble has a shrewd knife edge underneath") and referred it to a potential director. Soon after, Nash was dazzled by the excitement over *After Dark*. In January 1929 he wrote that he had seen the play three times and that "all of New York's intellectual leaders are flocking to it." Moreover, Nash, went on, "I now get the thrill out of meeting actors and actresses that I got five years ago from meeting authors. . . . The footlights bite in as deeply as radium; the glow just won't wear off." Nash's fascination with the theater even led him to consider the possibility of a job in Hoboken, and in February he wrote an eager letter to Morley: "Did you really mean what you said to me about crossing the river? I can't get it out of my head. Do let me know about this or I shall be in a state." The position, however, never materialized, and Nash continued at Doubleday.

Morley did recruit Nash to write an article about *The Black Crook* for publicity purposes. The article later became part of a book, *Born in a Beer Garden*, that told the history of the Hoboken theater venture. Nash's contribution was entitled "Up and Down the Amazons, or *The Black Crook* from Behind, A Travelogue." (The "Amazons" were female dancers in the show, so titled despite a setting in the Harz Mountains of Germany.) The production involved multiple costumes and elaborate staging, all described by Nash with tongue in cheek but unconcealed delight. After one scene, in which girls dressed in solemn grey dresses and black stockings suddenly began an exuberant dance, Nash exclaimed:

> Where are my Quakers now? Their faces are buried in their flying skirts; their shiny black knees dip in and out of a sea of watermelon-pink underthings that I never knew about; their tiny black toes kick at the ceiling and kick again, higher, higher and again higher, so fast my eye can scarcely follow. It is too much for one impressionable young man; I turn backstage and find myself in the midst of the Amazons. Amazons from six feet four to four feet six. My gaze runs down them like a xylophone. They wear golden helmets and carry spears; their upper persons are most snugly fitted into black and gold corselets that look like fishes' scales and follow their contours as closely; and as I look at them they begin to march. Thousands of Amazons, filling the stage from the footlights to the moonlit castle, marching, counter-marching, doubling, twisting; stepping like fusileers over the bodies of their enemies.

Clearly, Nash's backstage view of *The Black Crook* had stimulated his interest in the theater even further. While he never acknowledged it, the Hoboken experience was surely the genesis of the long-running love affair with musical theater that Nash would begin in the forties.

In the meantime, however, Nash's hopes of writing a play that might be produced at the Lyric or the Rialto were never realized. It soon became clear that it would have been a serious mistake for him to have abandoned Garden City for Hoboken. In 1930, after Hoboken audiences began to diminish and a trusted associate embezzled money from the theater company, it was forced into bankruptcy. Morley assumed personal liability for loans to the theater, and in consequence he suffered not only deep discouragement but financial hardship.

Picnics with Longwell and Morley, and jaunts to Hoboken, were not Nash's only opportunities for diversion. Nearby Roosevelt Field, where Lindbergh had taken off for Paris in 1927, was a mecca for budding aviators and onlookers. Yates Satterlee, a friend of Nash's, took him to the field one evening in September 1929 where they watched "hundreds of aviators performing against the sunset." Less than two weeks later, Nash returned to the field with his brother-in-law, Culver McWilliams, who was thinking of buying a plane. This time Satterlee, who worked for Curtis Aircraft, persuaded Nash to go up for a spin with one of the young pilots. Nash agreed reluctantly but returned saying that, while he had initially been scared nearly to sickness, he then realized that he was in the hands of an experienced aviator and had actually enjoyed it. His potential as an aviator, however, came to an abrupt end. A month later, when Nash was passing the field, he witnessed at close range the spectacular crash of a plane somersaulting onto the ground and setting fire to several houses. Miraculously, no one was killed, but Nash quickly decided that he would "wait a while before going up again." In fact, the experience left Nash with a permanently jaundiced view of aviation. *Hard Lines* would contain a poem entitled "No, You Be a Lone Eagle," which concluded:

> It seems to me that no kind of depravity
> Brings such speedy retribution as ignoring the law of gravity.
> Therefore nobody could possibly indict me for perjury
> When I swear that I wish the Wright brothers had gone in for
> silver fox farming or tree surgery.

It was a view from which Nash would not recede, even as air travel became commonplace, and it was one that in later years would greatly complicate his life.

Another occasion, the following year, brought Nash into contact with a developing technology of a gentler sort. Lowell Thomas, already an established author, was asked to audition for William Paley, president of CBS, for an evening news broadcast. Radio was still in its infancy, but it seemed an interesting opportunity to Thomas, so he cast about in various directions for "brains" to help him write a script. His friend Russell Doubleday sent over a senior editor and young Nash. According to Thomas, Nash was the only one of the several assembled talents who was able to come up with anything usable, but, as Thomas later recalled, even his witty contributions "did not prevail against the heat and acrimony generated on our memorable audition day." In the end, Thomas bought a couple of newspapers, made some notes, and proceeded extemporaneously. He got the job and went on to become the most celebrated newscaster of his day. Although

32

Nash's material was not used, he had been present at a minor historical event. Broadcasting, unlike aviation, was something to which he would return with pleasure.

Despite his extracurricular activities, Nash continued to put in long hours as a Doubleday editor. Much time was spent meeting prospective authors who had approached Doubleday with everything from vague ideas to completed manuscripts. This brought Nash into contact with a continuing parade of colorful characters, including one Charles Hedlund ("sailed before the mast, deserted the ship, hidden under a pile of fish to escape the police, worked in the diamond mines, served in Cecil Rhodes' body guard, fought against the British in the Boer war, been captured by savages in Madagascar, scooped snakes out of gold mines by the bucket full etc."). In other cases, Nash courted authors who had been successfully published, seeking to attract them to Doubleday. He eagerly pursued Thorne Smith, a highly popular author of comic novels that by the standards of the day were rather racy: "I'm lunching tomorrow with Thorne Smith, author of *Stray Lamb*, and shall make a desperate attempt to land him." Nash did land Smith and became his editor at Doubleday, a responsibility that would produce its own headaches. Other pursuits were no less eager but unsuccessful, as in the case of George S. Kaufman, whom Nash and Longwell jointly tried to recruit.

Authors who were already in the Doubleday fold frequently required entertaining or other forms of attention, particularly when they might appear restless and perhaps were looking elsewhere. One urgent trip to Canada, for example, was required to respond to grumbling by the detective writer Rufus King. ("It was lucky I went, as another publisher had been playing around Rufus and his mind was a bit unsettled; we got everything straightened out and Garden City takes the rest of the tricks.") Entertaining was sometimes strenuous, and while Nash had no aversion to partying, he was occasionally relieved to share his obligations with colleagues Malcolm Johnson and Charlie Duell: "[When author Milt Gross] turned the conversation Harlemwards, I deemed my duty to Doubleday Doran done and caught the first taxi home. I have not yet been able to find out what happened after I left; I only know that Malcolm didn't reach the office until noon the following day." Johnson and Duell were, apart from Dan Longwell, Nash's closest friends at Doubleday, and both went on to enjoy distinguished careers in publishing.

Nash continued to write some advertising copy and had the additional duties of helping promote Doubleday books with reviewers and booksellers.

The latter could be taxing: at one booksellers' party, as the martinis flowed freely, the booksellers ("these meek, pallid bankrupt little clerks") began to tell Edna Ferber what they didn't like about her latest novel. Ms. Ferber did not appreciate the criticism, and Nash found himself obliged to act as a "tactful bouncer." Despite his acerbic description of the Doubleday book-sellers, Nash worked hard at developing good relations with them. His ef-forts would later be rewarded in a way he could not have foreseen.

Finally, of course, there was actual editing. Here Nash's prize catch, Thorne Smith, presented a particular challenge. Although Nash had a strong distaste for censorship, he noted at one point that he "must go to work and edit Thorne Smith's manuscript, removing the vulgarest of the vulgarities." A month later Nash complained that Smith had disappeared, leaving him with a manuscript that needed revision of almost half. The au-thor, however, reappeared, and a few days later Nash wrote that he had spent an afternoon with Smith "going vigorously and ruthlessly over his manuscript and frightening him to death with my fierceness." Through it all, Nash and Smith became and remained good friends.

As Nash's career developed, he began to have more contact with the Doubleday family. The Doubleday firm had been founded in 1897 by Frank Nelson Doubleday. The founder used his initials "F.N.D.," which led one of the publisher's most celebrated authors, Rudyard Kipling, to dub him "effendi," the Turkish word for "chief," a nickname he would carry for his entire career. In 1922, F.N.'s son, Nelson Doubleday, had joined the firm and soon became the driving force behind its operations. By the fall of 1929, effendi, or, as Nash referred to him, "old Mr. Double-day," was in poor health. Although he had recently visited Kipling in Eng-land, he seldom came to the office; if he wanted a report on a matter, staff would be summoned to meet him at a designated roadhouse and then join him for a jaunt in his chauffeur-driven Packard. Once under way, Double-day would crouch in a corner, firing questions in a barely audible voice to listeners who were reluctant to ask, "What?"

Mrs. Doubleday, rather younger than her husband, issued command invitations to tea or other social occasions. Nash described his first such appearance:

> [T]he old lady at once took me out and demolished me at deck
> tennis. She's about sixty, her face is lined like the bottom of a
> newly raked bunker; but she's spry as a spider, and really very
> amusing and pleasant. I admired the dog . . . [and] she said they

were fond of him but not so fond as they had been of their St. Bernard that had just died. "Oh," I said brightly, "I suppose the second never is the same as the first." Just the remark that was needed considering that she is Mr. Doubleday's second wife. But the air soon cleared and I lost a dollar at bridge and we all felt better and parted friends. . . .

The younger Doubleday, Nelson, was, unlike Longwell, Morley, or even his own father, much more of a businessman than a bookman. The merger with the George H. Doran Company in 1927 had made Doubleday, Doran and Company "the largest publishing concern in the English-speaking world," and Nelson's leadership would bring the firm successfully through the depression. But Nelson was not a literary sort: "I don't read books, I sell them." For his part, Nash sometimes found Nelson a bit "rough and tumble," and despite occasional socializing, maintained a rather wary relationship with him.

By the fall of 1929, Nash's promotion from the Crime Club was only a few months old, but he and Dan Longwell were already formulating a proposal for an internal reorganization. In a letter dated October 30, Nash described having worked nine hours on a memorandum to Nelson setting forth his and Longwell's ideas. Although there is no record of Doubleday's immediate response, it appears to have been encouraging, and in early December, Nash spent an evening of business and poker at the Doubleday home that he thoroughly enjoyed. Remarking on the house, the cuisine, and the family Rolls Royce, Nash concluded, "I must say that I approve of the very rich." His approval probably ran more to the accoutrements of the rich than to the rich themselves, but a degree of fascination with wealth was something he would never entirely lose.

Nash's professional growth had been accompanied by even more important developments in his personal life. In November 1928, Nash's sister Gwen and her husband, Douglas Gorman, had invited him to a dinner-dance in Baltimore. During cocktails, Nash was introduced to a young lady, Frances Leonard, whom he immediately found to be uncommonly attractive. Leaving nothing to chance, he surreptitiously changed his dinner place card so that he might sit next to her. During dinner it appeared that the two had a number of common interests, including a shared admiration of such diverse figures as Al Smith and P. G. Wodehouse. Indeed, the conversation proceeded so amiably that Miss Leonard agreed that Mr. Nash might see her home from the party. For Ogden, it was love at first sight, but Frances had a more down-to-earth reaction: Nash had provided her with an escape from an escort who had over-imbibed and spared her the terror of a wild ride home. While she had enjoyed their dinner conversation, talking of books and politics and publishing, she had no reason to think of Nash as a serious suitor.

Nash, however, wasted little time in launching his pursuit. He wrote to Frances the following Wednesday from New York, beginning the letter "Dear Miss Leonard" but quickly adding, "Or is this formality necessary?" Nash mentioned that he had sent her two books, suggested that she ought to visit New York, and said that he hoped to see her in Baltimore over Christmas. Then he continued with an amusing account of his doings at Doubleday, including a complaint from "a gentleman named Mirza Mahmoud Kanghaphi, Page to the Mad Shah of Persia and Son of the Court Physician, threatening strangulation if his book is not advertised more sensationally," and, symmetrically enough, a letter "from the Warden of Sing Sing complaining bitterly because his book about life in the death house is advertised *too* sensationally." The letter was signed simply "Ogden."

Over the next nine months, Nash's letters continued in the same vein, telling Frances of life at Doubleday, including office politics and the odd characters he met, Morley's Hoboken venture, and visits to the Long Island homes of his sister Eleanor and his brother Ted. The letters said nothing explicit about his feelings toward Frances, but they surely left no doubt that his interest was keen. During that period, Ogden saw Frances only four times: in Baltimore on visits in December and March, in New York in April as she left for Europe, and at the family "summer camp" on Cape Cod. The end of August, however, brought a pivotal event.

Nash persuaded Frances to attend a "moveable house party" with his friends George Elliman and Charlie Duell and their dates, another couple, and, as chaperones, the Christopher Morleys. The party began on Friday, August 23, on Long Island, where Frances met Ogden's sister Eleanor, and the following day moved by motorboat and sailboat across Long Island Sound and on to the Duells' house on the Hudson.

On Saturday night, under a brilliant moon, Nash confessed his love to Frances and proposed marriage. To his delight, and perhaps astonishment, she accepted. At home the following evening, Nash could hardly believe his good fortune. He wrote Frances, begging her to tell him "that everything really happened, that it wasn't just something that I wanted so much that it crystallized in my imagination." Nevertheless, Nash did not pause to wait for confirmation before eagerly dashing off letters to Frances's parents to seek their blessing—writing to Frances's mother that evening and to her father the following day.

For her part, Frances was taken aback, and not entirely pleased, by the Nash blitzkrieg. On Monday morning, Nash received a letter from Frances that plunged him into despair and prompted a desperate plea for forgiveness: "I'm dreadfully distressed if I've made you unhappy by writing to your mother and father—of course I should have waited. I'm a selfish fool." Since Frances disliked talking on the telephone, Nash begged her to telegraph him that he hadn't "spoiled everything by rushing." By Wednesday, Nash had heard nothing from Frances, and wrote that he was "miserably nervous." Finally, on Thursday, he received a letter from her that he found reassuring ("I wanted to go shouting through the office"). Still, Frances suggested that he wait a day or two before writing her father. This puzzled Nash, since he had already told Frances that he had written her father on Monday. In fact he had received a letter from Mr. Leonard admitting that he had been surprised, "but pleasantly," and adding that he had always liked Nash and would leave everything to Frances and her mother.

Nash then received a letter from Mrs. Leonard that was even more welcoming and, in his reply, Nash seemed nearly overcome: "[P]lease don't think me impertinent when I say that as I re-read your letter I am as fortunate in finding Frances' mother as I am in finding her." Thus it appeared on the surface that Nash's impetuous correspondence with the Leonards had done no harm. The effect on Frances, however, would linger.

On the way back to Baltimore from her family's vacation home on Cape Cod, Frances stopped in New York and met Ogden's parents, who found her to be quite charming. Nash's father, who was in failing health, seemed particularly taken with his son's intended ("Father keeps telling me that you kissed him; it was like you; he was terribly pleased and moved; today he is better than he has been, and you had much to do with it"). By now, however, Frances was beginning to experience cold feet. To provide an opportunity for a little distance, she accepted an invitation to visit friends in Chicago.

Nash's letters in September reflected the doubts that Frances had expressed. He tried to accept the development calmly, with good humor, and without tempering his own ardor:

Frances, I'm not impatient. God knows the last thing I want is to have you in any way uncertain: I'll wait just as quietly as I can until you are sure of yourself; but you must allow me to love you while I wait; that's something that can't be stopped.

Don't think you can frighten me with talk about child-wives—but when you say "if I ever get married" you send the chills over me in regiments of goose-stepping goose-flesh.

Frances's confessions of doubt did nothing to dampen Nash's passion. And her August acceptance of his proposal had given him the courage to express it with all the eloquence at his command:

Whatever I do, whichever way I turn, I see only, I am reminded only, that I love you, and I love you, and I love you. It's not just simple idolatry. Of course it's instinctive, but also I've reasoned it all out, in so far as I can be at all reasonable about you. I've compared your hair and your eyes and your nose and your mouth and your figure, and your mind and your spirit and your whole self with girls who are supposed to be something oh very extra special—and always, Frances, there's only you, all that's darling and adorable, all that I've lived and hoped for. Dearest, dearest, I'm not really living when I'm away from you—only hoping, and hope is so closely bound to fear!

Wisely, Nash's ardent declarations were leavened with amusing descriptions of his daily routine, similar to those that had filled his earlier letters. In touching on his social life, so far as it might involve the opposite sex, Nash made it clear that his heart was firmly planted in Baltimore ("This evening: gaiety, Frances, Gaiety! Dinner, then theater and a debutante dance! I'm so excited about that I'd just as soon go to bed right now and have a good sound sleep").

Nash saw Frances and her parents on the weekend between Christmas of 1929 and New Year's and then returned to New York. If he was disappointed at not spending New Year's Eve with Frances, he at least had unexpected consolation—on the 31st he received a check from *The New Yorker* in the amount of twenty-two dollars for a poem he had submitted to the magazine. And he spent that evening with Malcolm Johnson working on an idea for a series of questionnaires that might be sold to *The New Yorker* and later made into a stunt book.

The close of 1929 was an extraordinarily uncertain time. The country had suffered the stock market crash in October, and though the full implications of that event were still unknown, the signs were ominous. For Nash, his personal uncertainty was greater still. He had made remarkable progress in his career at Doubleday, but the new structure that he and Longwell had proposed was still to be approved. And what of Nash's ambitions as a writer? The acceptance of his poem by *The New Yorker* was fun, but the project with Malcolm Johnson was speculative at best. Above all, what of Frances? Now that the euphoria of August had worn off, how great was the risk that she might slip through his fingers?

3

THE NEW YORKER:
IN THE BEGINNING

For Ogden Nash, the new year of 1930 began auspiciously on two counts. In the first week of January a reorganization of the Doubleday editorial department was announced, and although the scheme proposed by Longwell and Nash had been considerably modified, Nash was pleased with the result. The firm had created a New Books Department to be in charge of all books by new authors, with Nash the editor and his friend Malcolm Johnson the administrative head. Nash welcomed the new responsibility and was delighted that the new position called for him to work principally in New York and to visit Garden City only two or three times a month. The shorter commute, Nash reflected, would add three hours a day to his life.

A few days later *The New Yorker* published the poem it had purchased in December. "Invocation" poked fun at Senator Smoot of Utah, best known today for his co-authorship of the Smoot-Hawley tariff, a protectionist measure that contributed significantly to the worldwide depression of the thirties. Indeed, the *New York Times* would publish a letter from Edmund Nash later that year pointing out that the tariff "had done nothing to revive the drooping industry of the country" but had aroused bitterness abroad.

Smoot's interests in international trade were not limited to economic matters. He also championed a provision in the tariff bill prohibiting the importation of books deemed to be salacious, and to help make the point he had assembled a personal collection of such items. It was this aspect of the tariff bill that had drawn the attention of the younger Nash. Ogden had a keen distaste for censorship and had even proposed, more than half-seriously, a book to be titled "Banned in Boston," comprised of passages to which the Boston censor (then considered the nation's most vigorous) had objected. Meanwhile the Smoot proposal seemed to present a perfect target that Nash homed in on with "Invocation":

> Senator Smoot is an institute
> Not to be bribed with pelf;
> He guards our homes from erotic tomes
> By reading them all himself.
> Smite, Smoot, Smite for Ut.
> They're smuggling smut from Balt. to Butte.

    ✻   ✻   ✻   ✻

Nash did not recognize the publication of the Smoot poem as a turning point in his life. He remarked rather diffidently to Frances, "I like picking up the odd cash as well as breaking into print, which is extremely helpful to me in my profession." Still, the poem drew favorable notice, including letters of congratulation from Max Schuster of Simon and Schuster and from Theodore Morrison, editor of the *Atlantic Monthly*, who asserted that "A few more things of that kind and we should almost become a reasonable nation."

All was not well, however. Nash's successes at Doubleday and with *The New Yorker* were immediately overshadowed by alarming developments in his courtship of Frances. When Nash visited Baltimore over the weekend of January 11–12, Frances told him that she was still uncertain of her feelings and suggested that they cut back on their correspondence. Nash also learned that an old flame of Frances's (a Baltimore physician, T. I. Howen) had reappeared. This unwelcome news put Nash into a state of depression which lasted until the following Thursday, when he had revived sufficiently to write Frances ("I woke up on Monday morning with the feeling my world had collapsed; a feeling that persisted until today. Really, Monday, Tuesday and yesterday were the worst period that I have ever lived through"). On Thursday, Nash received a letter from Frances and talked with her on the phone. These contacts buoyed him somewhat, but he decided that he was sufficiently upset ("nervous, annoyed and consequently annoying") that he should not return to Baltimore that weekend.

Frances had apparently become uncomfortable with the fervor of the Nash courtship, feeling that she needed to be looked on as a mortal woman and not a goddess. Nash realized that he must adopt a slightly altered tone in his correspondence and began to insert some gentle barbs in his flowery prose.

> I adore you, I love you, I hope you are well. I'm sorry you can't see me now and that I can't talk to you, as I'm feeling thoroughly cocky and full of fighting insults which some mistaken instinct of chivalry prevents my putting on paper, while if you were here I'd take the greatest pleasure in pooh-poohing you back into your rightful lowly position in the order of things. [January 27]

> Your weekly letter arrived this morning, a day ahead of time— I hope that doesn't mean you are losing your head over me; emotion is a dangerous thing; I'd hate to see you getting involved with anyone of so many and varied interests as myself. I think perhaps some placid Republican night watchman might be better for you. [January 30]

Nash's visits to Baltimore at the end of January and in mid-February went smoothly, and relations between Nash and Frances were once again enjoyable. But Nash knew that he was still a long way from claiming what he thought he had won the previous August.

Nash had responded to the acceptance of the Smoot poem by sending *The New Yorker* two articles for publication. He also inquired, rather casually, to whom future submissions should be addressed since "I've a bit more time just now than I used to have and I'm hoping to have more stuff to market." He received a prompt reply from Katharine White, rejecting the articles Nash had sent but encouraging him to "keep at us with other stuff though and anything timely like the Smoot poem or topical material is the best of all for us."

Katharine White was to become Nash's editor at *The New Yorker*. She had come to the magazine in its very early days as Katharine Sergeant Angell, a Bryn Mawr graduate who had published articles in the *New Republic*, the *Atlantic Monthly*, and the *Saturday Review of Literature*. She soon was given a wide range of editing and writing responsibilities. As the editor, Harold Ross, relied increasingly on her sense of taste and style, she became his "one truly indispensable editor." Nash was neither the first nor the last of the talented writers Katharine White introduced to *The New Yorker*. It was her decision to buy the work of many of those who would give the magazine its distinctive character, among them Frank Sullivan, James Thurber, Clarence Day, William Maxwell, John O'Hara, John Updike, Mary McCarthy, and Marianne Moore.

Despite the encouragement from Mrs. White, Nash proffered nothing further for three months. During that period, however, he met with *The New Yorker* staff in his role as an editor at Doubleday, which published *The New Yorker Album*. In view of the importance that the magazine would soon come to have for Nash, it is ironic that he was initially unimpressed: "I went over to *The New Yorker* for a session on a new collection of their stuff. It's the dullest office in New York. I'm sure there's much more frolic-some wit in 90% of our freight yards." Correspondingly there was little charity in his reference to Katharine White's husband, E. B. ("Andy") White. Although Nash later came to regard Andy White with great affection and admiration, his first impression was distinctly negative: "a sour lit-tle bird with a bad word for everything except Berkeley Square and the large coffee cups at the Harvard Club."

In April, Nash submitted a poem and three prose pieces with a delib-erately casual note to Katharine White: "Do any of these pieces amuse you enough to make you want to buy them?" Although Nash may have con-cluded that he did not have the gifts of a classical poet, his concentration on light verse—and his own distinctive version of the genre—developed more gradually. Thus, in 1930, Nash saw verse as only one element, and not necessarily the most important, in his repertoire as an aspiring writer. In his first year as a contributor to *The New Yorker*, he made repeated submissions of humorous essays and short stories, and his correspondence is studded with references to various potential literary projects, often collaborations: a mystery play with Rufus King, a detective story with Malcolm Johnson, a novel, a play, and lyrics for a musical comedy or revue.

Mrs. White accepted the poem but rejected Nash's prose. Despite the rejection, Nash seemed encouraged, remarking that "it looks to me as if the time had come to sign up with them for some stuff." His optimism was derived largely from the lengthy critique that Katharine White had given one of his rejected pieces, a short story entitled, "Preface to a Wedding Trip." A bemused Nash observed that "I've never had such an excited and interested rejection," and, alluding to his own editorial duties at Double-day, "I've never even written one, in fact."

Mrs. White's comments on "Preface" provide a glimpse of *The New Yorker's* sensibilities in 1930. Nash's story employed a lower-class dialect in portraying the tensions between a bride and groom after a send-off by several of the groom's rather coarse friends. It was, Mrs. White said, "a most impressive piece of writing and it has made us all sit up and take notice, so to speak." Having taken notice, however, Mrs. White made it clear that the "shocking vulgarities, almost obscenities," were unacceptable. She found to be especially egregious a joking reference to a birth-control magazine and concluded, "We don't quarrel with you as to your accuracies [sic] for certainly there are people as cheap and vulgar in the world as this, but we can't print them."

As it turned out, that was not the end of the matter. In August, Nash responded to an invitation from *Vanity Fair* and stopped by their offices one day at noon. He met first with the associate editor, then the editor, and finally, as he described it, "Frank Crowninshield, the suave old Holy of Holies, sent for me and it ended up by my staying for lunch." Crowninshield and his colleagues were highly complimentary of Nash's work, and he promptly submitted to them everything *The New Yorker* had rejected, including "Preface to a Wedding Trip." The piece was quickly accepted and was published in the October issue of the magazine. After the story appeared, Nash received a flattering letter from the publisher Donald Friede of Covici, Friede: "[Y]our story took my breath away. . . ." And Dorothy Parker told Nash that the story was the best she had read in years. She had sent it on to Ernest Hemingway.

Meanwhile Nash's verse was receiving growing recognition. The second poem Nash submitted to *The New Yorker* had been eagerly accepted by Mrs. White: "Here's our check for your most amusing Spring poem. One of the funniest that has come our way. You certainly must keep at us with this sort of thing." It was published in the May 3, 1930, issue of *The New Yorker*:

SPRING COMES TO MURRAY HILL

I sit in an office at 244 Madison Avenue
And say to myself You have a responsible job, havenue?
Why then do you fritter away your time on this doggerel?
If you have a sore throat you can cure it by using a good goggeral,
If you have a sore foot you can get it fixed by a chiropodist,
And you can get your original sin removed by St. John the
    Bopodist,

Why then should this flocculent lassitude be incurable?
Kansas City, Kansas, proves that even Kansas City needn't always
    be Missourible.
Up up my soul! This inaction is abominable
Perhaps it is the result of disturbances abdominable.
The pilgrims settled Massachusetts in 1620 when they landed on a
    stone hummock.
Maybe if they were here now they would settle my stomach.
Oh, if I only had the wings of a bird
Instead of being confined on Madison Avenue I could soar in a
    jiffy to Second or Third.

Just as in the case of "Smoot," Nash failed entirely to recognize the publication of "Spring" as an important moment in his career. In a letter to Frances he had remarked disparagingly that the magazine would "run the asinine verses week after next." The poem, however, was a great success, and it was the first of Nash's published poems to employ the unique approach to spelling and rhyming that would become his trademark. As the Poet Laureate Billy Collins would observe decades later, Nash was not the first to experiment with clever or playful rhymes. Perhaps, he speculated, Nash had been influenced by Byron ("But oh ye husbands of ladies intellectual/ Inform us truly, have they not hen-pecked you all"). But Nash had carried matters a step—or several steps—further. It was, Collins said, as if Nash had "discovered a secret set of alliances in the dictionary."

Pleased with the response to "Spring," Nash sent *The New Yorker* a series of two-line poems entitled "Random Reflections." Six of them were published as a group in the July 12 issue of the magazine, including "Random Reflections: Introspection," in which he confessed, "I would live all my life in nonchalance and insouciance/ Were it not for making a living, which is rather a nouciance."

Even before publication of the "Random Reflections," another of Nash's poems had appeared in the "Conning Tower," a highly regarded literary column by Franklin P. Adams in the *New York World*. The Tower did not pay for the contributions it printed, but appearance in the column carried with it considerable prestige. As E. B. White recalled years later, "There are still plenty of writers alive today who will testify that the high point in their lives was not the first check in the mail from a publication but the first time at the top of the Tower looking down in the morning at the whole city of New York. Making the Tower was a dizzying experience." For Nash, "making the Tower" was more of a lark. On his way to work one day, he had composed a poem about Admiral Byrd, simply to tease his colleague at Doubleday, Malcolm Johnson, a great admirer of the explorer. Johnson reacted suitably, and Nash thought that was the end of it. But Dan Longwell had then taken the poem and telegraphed it to Adams, who promptly inserted it in his column. Although Nash did not submit additional poems to the *Tower*, it was not long before he ran into Adams at a cocktail party and took the opportunity to tease him for accepting verses that were imitative of the Nash style.

Longer Nash poems appeared in the July issues of *The New Yorker* and another collection of "Random Reflections" in an August issue, including "Reflections on Ice-Breaking" with Nash's unforgetttable observation that, "Candy/ Is dandy/ But liquor/ Is quicker." In the same month, however, Nash again ran afoul of *The New Yorker*'s sensibilities with a poem, "Are Sects Necessary," that mocked the condescending attitude of some Protestant clergy toward Catholicism. ("Their righteousness runs too high a steeple;/ I prefer the purple papal people.") Although Nash was a lifelong Episcopalian, the poem may have been inspired by his admiration for the leading Roman Catholic political figure of the day, Al Smith. In any event, it proved to be too risky for *The New Yorker*. As Mrs. White explained, "It is refreshing for once to have a poem that is pro-Catholic and we do agree heartily with your point of view, but Mr. Ross says he really just can't come out so wholeheartedly for the Catholic church. I wonder if you couldn't change the poem, making it against all sects and anti-everything. It is just too amusing in its rhyme and all to lose. Do try it again." Nash made no attempt to revise the poem, and it appeared unrevised in his first book, *Hard Lines*. Writing to a cousin after the publication of *Hard Lines*, Nash's father referred proudly to the book but was careful to assure his relative that Ogden did not "lack a religious tendency" but was offended by "hypocrisy, bigotry and charlatanism."

Occasional differences in taste did nothing to dampen *The New Yorker*'s growing demand for Nash's poems. Mrs. White told him that he was "fast getting to be our favorite poet" and wrote three times in June and July asking for more material. In August, Harold Ross added his own plea: "A future suggestion: Write a lot more of these verses for us. They are about the most original stuff we have had lately." Another member of *The New Yorker* staff, Raymond Holden, with whom Nash had established a personal relationship, told Nash that, though the magazine was now receiving imitations at the rate of three or four a day, he would insist on the original.

Nash credited Frances for his success. When "Smoot" was first published, he had written her that "one rejection slip is apt to discourage me unless I have you backing me up—because it is you I'm doing it for." Now, when Nash's poems were appearing regularly in *The New Yorker*, he again told Frances that she was the inspiration for his work and success. He wrote that, since he could not write poetry the equal of her beauty, he was reduced to "writing versicles that I hope will amuse you," adding that "you're really responsible for this sudden energy that's carried me headlong into *The New Yorker*—it seems to be all I can do for you."

It was inevitable that some of the verses Nash sent to *The New Yorker* would touch directly on his courtship of Frances. The clearest example was "For Any Improbable She":

What shall I do with So-and-So?
She won't say yes and she won't say no.
She tiptoes around the cunningest traps
With a smile and a murmur of Perhaps.
At nine I'm Darling, at ten I'm You—
Tell me, what is a man to do
When the lady his life is based upon
Likes to be wooed but won't be won?

    ✻   ✻   ✻   ✻

What shall I do with So-and-So?
She confesses that I am her favorite beau;
But let the topic of marriage arise
And see the astonishment in her eyes!
Why am I chosen so to be harried?
Other people have gotten married.
Is every courtship conducted thus
Or is it only confined to us?

    ✻   ✻   ✻   ✻

Frances said she liked the poem but denied that it fit her. Nash responded, shortly before the poem was published: "So you like her even though she isn't you? Of course she's not entirely not you, but she has several characteristics that you haven't. For instance, if you have ever admitted that I am your favorite beau it must have been to your diary alone. Also, I believe I have your permission to go. And I'm not sure that you like to be wooed." Even then, he could not help ending on a rapturous note: "I saw a line from Chaucer today that applies to you more closely: 'In thee magnificence assembled is.'"

Consistent with having placed the reluctant Frances on something of a pedestal, Nash's declarations of love and descriptions of her beauty had a rather literary, almost ethereal, quality. Conspicuously absent were references to physical features, other than facial, or to physical acts of love — even kisses or embraces. A rare exception was a letter describing a taxi ride on the way to the station in Baltimore. When Nash and the taxi driver fell into conversation, it developed that each had had a date with his girl that evening. The driver inquired whether Nash had gotten any lipstick on his handkerchief and, receiving an affirmative reply, offered to bet that his had more. Upon a comparison of handkerchiefs, Nash claimed, "he paid me not only the fare but a five dollar tip besides."

In early August, Nash visited Simon and Schuster for an initial meeting about a proposed book. Dan Longwell had wanted Doubleday to publish it, but Nash preferred another firm, perhaps thinking that would give the book more stature. Agreement was quickly reached, and in September, *Publisher's Weekly* reported that Simon and Schuster "had made a collection of Ogden Nash's verse from *The New Yorker* which will be published in the late fall" and would include the "celebrated poem of Senator Smoot." In fact, most of the verses that would be included in *Hard Lines* had not yet appeared in *The New Yorker*, or in many cases even been written. Under the circumstance, the publisher was placing remarkable confidence in an untested young writer.

By September, Frances was packing for a trip to Europe. Her mother had wanted to recoup from the strain of nursing her own mother through a final illness that had ended in July. Mrs. Leonard suggested that Frances come along, also seeing the trip as a chance for her daughter to decide finally whom she would marry. Their ship was to sail on October 3, and less than two weeks before, the issue still seemed very much in doubt. In a letter dated September 23, Nash wrote Frances accepting an invitation to come to Baltimore but complaining mildly about what he seemed to feel was a somewhat lukewarm tone. He added that "the problem that I spoke of yesterday namely, whether or not you are suffering from qualms, quibbles, jibes etc., remains unsolved. So my pride and common sense forbid me saying too much too nicely to you."

Somehow, however, Frances's doubts were resolved over the course of the next several days, and at dockside she gave Nash a note promising to marry him upon her return. With Frances's mind made up, the rationale for the trip, or at least her part in it, had disappeared. But too many plans had been made, and Frances was unwilling to desert her mother at the last minute. For his part, Nash was willing to submit to a delay, even of several months, if the prize was finally to be his.

> Remember that I'm giving up all the loveliness in the world for six months. Not giving it up, but rather lending it to Europe. For you are all loveliness, Frances, and I have always adored you, even in the moments when I wanted to beat you. You are romance, and daydreams made tangible, and the misty charm of far-off things made real. . . . You are beauty and enchantment and all the dear virtues; and you are going to marry me when you get back.

Two days after the sailing, Nash took Mr. Leonard to lunch at the Harvard Club and gave him a ticket for the theater. He felt amply rewarded when Leonard suggested that Frances's trip might not last the full six and a half months planned.

The abrupt rise in Nash's fortunes was further compounded when Harold Ross offered him a position at *The New Yorker*. Years later, when James Thurber was writing *The Years with Ross*, Nash told him that he had first met Ross in a speakeasy and described how the offer had come about:

> I don't need to tell you that in many ways he was a strangely innocent man and he assumed that my presence in a speakeasy meant that I was a man about town. He was, I believe, still in mourning over the departure of [Ralph] Ingersoll, who had apparently been the ultimate in men about town, and was looking for a suave and worldly editor. He hired me practically on the spot.

The early days of *The New Yorker* have been chronicled by a variety of the participants and their biographers. At the center stood Harold Ross, who had founded the magazine with the financial backing of the baking company heir Raoul Fleischmann. Although accounts differ in emphasis and perspective, there is common agreement that Ross was by temperament, manner, and background an unlikely candidate to found a magazine that would come to epitomize a witty and urbane view of the world. As Ben Hecht had put it bluntly, "How the hell could a man who looked like a resident of the Ozarks and talked like a barroom brawler set himself up as pilot of a sophisticated, elegant periodical?"

Ross was ten years older than Nash, having been born in 1892 in Aspen, Colorado. His father was an Irish immigrant and a prospector turned grocer. His mother was a schoolteacher of New England stock who had grown up on the Kansas plains. Ross's mother, much like Ogden Nash's, took an active part in his early education, supplementing his classroom instruction with her own curriculum of language and literature. Ross's formal education, however, had ended even more precipitously than Nash's when he left high school after his sophomore year to become a reporter for, and then the editor of, a newspaper in Marysville, California. Over the next six years, Ross worked as a "tramp reporter" for a variety of newspapers around the country. Then, with the entry of the United States into the world war in 1917, he enlisted in the army.

Once in the ranks, Ross maneuvered his way onto the *Stars and Stripes*, the army newspaper newly formed at the direction of General Pershing. Ross's assignment to the *Stars and Stripes* was a pivotal event that provided the first real opportunity for him to develop his talents as an editor. The paper attracted a variety of gifted writers, including Alexander Woollcott, the drama critic for the *New York Times*; Franklin P. Adams, then a *New York Tribune* columnist; and the sportswriter Grantland Rice. Although Ross never advanced beyond the rank of private, he eventually became editor of *Stars and Stripes*, supervising a staff largely comprised of his superiors in rank. After the war, Ross served briefly as editor of three different magazines (*The Home Sector*, *American Legion Weekly*, and *Judge*), but he resigned from the last, determined to found a magazine of humor and commentary that he had been formulating. After its founding in 1925, *The New Yorker* survived a beginning that was quite shaky, both editorially and financially. By 1930, however, it had become a profitable venture. It was enjoying increasing revenues, circulation, and prestige, and would soon be considered a "dream destination for writers and editors."

The speakeasy encounter between Nash and Ross was followed by a meeting in *The New Yorker* offices which came about almost as casually: "[Ross] called up and asked me to come over to see him. I needed air, so I went out for a walk, ending up in his office." This time, however, the meeting resulted in a definitive offer. Nash had reason to be tempted. Despite his success at Doubleday, he was not entirely happy there. It had taken six months for the New Books Department to be implemented, and the interval had been marked by long discussions of "office politics" with Longwell and Johnson. The very day Ross called, Nash had particular cause to be annoyed. He had signed up a celebrated aviator for a book and had found a ghostwriter who could turn one out in six days to coincide with the start of the "author's" national tour. To Nash's great irritation, however, Doubleday had summarily rejected the proposal.

Nevertheless he was determined not to make a decision while angry, and after some reflection he turned down Ross's offer. He was reluctant to write off several years' experience in publishing to go "into strange new territory on a gamble." What Nash did have in mind was to start a new publishing house with Longwell and Johnson. Between the three of them, he believed, they could control authors worth nearly half a million dollars in revenue. What they lacked was capital, which Nash hoped to raise from wealthy friends in Newport.

Despite Nash's optimism, the scheme of founding a new publishing house failed to take shape. He continued to work at Doubleday, write new verse and prose, and work with Dick Simon on preparations for his forthcoming book. In October he received a poem from Dorothy Parker, in Nashian style and sent from Chalet la Bryere in Switzerland, which Simon and Schuster promptly incorporated into its publicity for Nash's book:

> I want very much to tell you that were you on an Alp, as I'm
> You would get Ogden Nash's verses though you had to commit
>   arson or m'yh'm.
>   *   *   *   *
> I wish you all successes, in life as in lit'rature
> And I remain your respectful admirer from the very bottom of my
>   coeur.

The publication date of Nash's book was delayed until January, but by November he was thoroughly caught up in the whirl of prepublication activities. After a visit to Simon and Schuster to discuss preliminary advertising plans, he wrote to Frances in Europe that his head was swimming from the publisher's confidence in the book and their "elaborate and costly preparations" for it. He reported gleefully on being wined and dined by the publisher after his own years of entertaining others on behalf of Doubleday ("I thoroughly relish every minute and mouthful"). And he promised to send Frances a copy of the publicity photo "if it doesn't turn out too oddly."

If the final preparations for publication were not enough to think about, Nash was also having renewed discussions about possible employment at *The New Yorker*. Relations with Nelson Doubleday were still problematic. Nash had been keenly disappointed to learn from Chris Morley in October that Nelson had personally vetoed Morley's proposal to take Nash with him on a trip to England and introduce him to various literary figures. And since the plan of starting a new publishing house no longer seemed feasible, Ross's offer now had become more attractive. Coincidentally perhaps, *The New Yorker* had finally agreed to publish one of his prose submissions, a satirical piece entitled "Ziegfeld Hits Evils of Pulpit." In any case, by November 16, Nash considered *The New Yorker*'s offer an open question and wrote to Frances that he expected to make a decision within ten days. A week later, having met again separately with Raymond Holden and Harold Ross, he promised them an answer within the week, during which he planned further discussions with Nelson Doubleday. Summing it up, Nash sounded as exuberant as his father had been in writing from tsarist St. Petersburg: "I'm highly interested and quite excited about what is going to happen, but fortunately not worried, as I shall win either way. I seem to have everybody where I want them right now."

On December 3, Nash accepted the offer from *The New Yorker* for a salary of $9,100. In addition to his editorial duties, he would be given time to write material for the magazine for which he would be separately compensated and which, Nash estimated, would amount to an additional $2,000. Finally, if things worked out, at the end of the year he would be provided a large raise and a bonus of stock in *The New Yorker*. Since the basic salary was fifty dollars a week more than Nash had been making at Doubleday, he was elated at the prospect.

All the while, Nash's social life, never meager, had begun to reflect his celebrity status. Although he remained devoted to the traveling Frances, that didn't mean that he couldn't get about with a few friends. At the end of November he and Dan Longwell were invited to a country weekend with Edna Ferber. Nash, in thanks, sent Ferber some caviar and was quite charmed to receive in return a Nashian poem that concluded: "But when caviar is sent me by Frederic Ogden Nash/ I'm swept by warm emotion which is nothing short of pash." The following Wednesday he went to a party at Dorothy Parker's lasting until four in the morning and mingled with the cream of New York's wit and humor, George S. Kaufman, Marc Connelly, Robert Benchley, Alexander Woollcott, Heywood Broun,

Franklin P. Adams, Edna Ferber, and, as Nash put it, "all the rest of the luminous boys and girls." Mrs. Parker he described as "small, dark, not pretty but very attractive, and not hard, but wistful." She told Nash that he was her hero and complimented him extravagantly on the story in *Vanity Fair.* Three weeks later she called Nash and asked him to take her to Alexander Woollcott's Christmas Eve tea that afternoon. Nash not only obliged but took her to dinner and spent the evening with her. It is reasonable to speculate that, if Nash had not been so smitten with Frances, he might have briefly become one of Parker's conquests. But his enthusiasm for the woman would soon be tempered by an exasperation borne of his dealings with her as a *New Yorker* editor.

December was also marked by Nelson Doubleday's farewell party for Nash, attended by twelve of Nash's closest friends from the Doubleday office and graced with caviar, terrapin, and champagne. Nelson presented Nash with a green gold cigarette case that, Nash proudly reported to Frances, several people told him was worth between four and five hundred dollars. Nash was quite touched because Nelson, whom he had regarded as rather rough and cold-blooded, had never before sponsored such an affair. All in all, it was a heady time for a twenty-eight-year-old college dropout who could not quite believe his own good fortune. As he wrote Frances, with a rather kid-in-the-candy-store tone: "I'm riding right on the crest and am somewhat astonished and embarrassed to find myself the bright boy of the moment. I don't know how long it will last, but I'm cashing in while I can."

Early 1931 appeared to be every bit as promising as the end of 1930. *Hard Lines* was published in January—a slight volume of ninety-nine pages. Many of the poems, such as the "Random Reflections" that had appeared in *The New Yorker,* were quite short. Illustrative cartoons were provided by Otto Soglow, whose work had also appeared in *The New Yorker* and whom Harold Ross had recommended to Nash for a possible cartoon book to be published by Doubleday. Even with Soglow's cartoons, the book displayed considerable white space, but the reviews were, as Nash proudly acknowledged, "incredibly, ridiculously good." Favorable notices appeared in the *New York Times,* the *Daily News,* and the other New York papers. And William Rose Benét, writing in the *Saturday Review of Literature,* expressed the reaction of many: "There he sits the antic old philosopher, and puts down most anything that comes into his head, most of which is extremely funny and about as good a picture of his life and times as others have spent volumes on." The chorus of praise was joined even by critics better known for their unsparing dissection of literary offerings, H. L. Mencken and Alexander Woollcott. Encouraging reviews appeared not only on the East Coast but across the country—"gorgeously funny," *Omaha World Herald*; "Never have we been so generously entertained by mad verse," *Dallas News*; "Droll, pithy, pointed and rollickingly funny," *Louisville Courier Journal*; "Cherish [the book] as you would the last cob-webbed demijohn of old vintage Burgundy," *Rocky Mountain News*.

Only an occasional cautionary note was sounded. The network of friends that Nash had made during his time at Doubleday had proved to be a fertile source of prepublication endorsements, and Nash had worried that they might antagonize critics. His concern proved to be unfounded, except for one radio reviewer who "said he guessed the book must be pretty good because so many famous writers said so, but that it may be because Mr. Nash was friendly with so many famous writers." Nash noted wryly that the observation had "a good deal of truth in it."

Nash's Doubleday connection proved valuable in another respect. The Doubleday sales force produced excellent sales from the Doubleday book-stores, and a Doubleday executive wrote Nash, "The managers and shop personnel with whom you are still 110% are really the ones who deserve credit for work on the book." The first printing of 4,000 copies was largely exhausted before the official publication date of January 15, and a second printing of 3,500 went to press that morning. By the end of February, sales were still strong and the book was on every best-seller list in the country, its position varying from second to sixth.

Nash received letters of congratulation from any number of authors and writers, including Milt Gross, Stephen Vincent Benét, Nunnally Johnson, Sara Mencken, Corey Ford, Frank Crowninshield, and the cartoonist H. T. Webster. Frank Sullivan, referring to a poem that had mentioned him as well as Marc Connelly and Robert Benchley, wrote, "I will settle for two per cent of the gross for the use of my name and those of Connelly and Benchley. I control the American rights to both." But the letter that probably meant the most to Nash was from P. G. Wodehouse, whom Nash had long admired. "I simply revel in your poems," he wrote, adding, "I think the book is simply terrific and this cannot be too widely known."

Demand for *Hard Lines* was so great that Simon and Schuster jubilantly allocated fifty copies of the book to be shown in store windows attached to a lock and chain as protection for the hard-to-find volume. At the end of January they decided to double the price to two dollars. Nash, looking on from the perspective of his own professional experience, concluded that the book had become a fad: "that means it will die quickly but meanwhile it is profitable." The dimensions of the fad were illustrated by a report from a Baltimore acquaintance that she had dined in Washington, D.C., with the Nicholas Longworths and that each guest had been presented with a copy. Longworth was speaker of the House of Representatives and was married to Alice Roosevelt, daughter of Theodore. When Nash remarked grumpily to Frances that it was "the first good thing I've ever heard about Alice Roosevelt," it may have reflected the old family animus toward TR. On the other hand, when the respected poet Corinne Roosevelt, sister of the late president, complimented the book, Nash replied with a suitably gracious note ("It was good of you to write me; kind words are always pleasant, and it is seldom that they come from so distinguished a source").

Only one contretemps briefly dampened the general euphoria. Max Schuster had drafted some publicity for the book which mistakenly included an endorsement by Edna Ferber that had not yet in fact been given. As a consequence, though she was an ardent admirer of both Nash and the book, Miss Ferber was furious and wrote a stinging rebuke to Dick Simon. After prompt and suitably abject apologies, she was mollified and agreed to lend her name to the promotion of *Hard Lines*. She wrote Nash that the book was "gay and amusing, and refreshingly mad," and that she left it out "where people can—must in fact—notice." At the end of January, when she congratulated Nash on his success, she added: "I'm so glad. So it seems is everyone else. I never knew a man with so few enemies."

Nash's new job at *The New Yorker* also seemed to begin in an encouraging, albeit somewhat bewildering, fashion. He had started on December 22 after a brief vacation at the home of his sister Gwen in Baltimore. At the close of his first day he wrote Frances an enthusiastic letter, chirping about the atmosphere and the fact that no one arrived at the office until ten and that he could leave at six or seven without taking work home as he had at Doubleday. He also expressed pleasure at the idea of working for a single boss rather than a board of directors.

Ironically, one of Nash's first chores was to reject a piece, "Homage to O.N.," of which he was the subject. He explained to the writer, the poet Melville Cane, that it was too "intra-mural" in that "the magazine never recognizes that anybody writes for it. . . . There is some sort of theory that no human hands peck out the text on the typewriter, but that it's brought in late at night by brownies or something." Nevertheless, Nash said, he would make and preserve a copy for his grandchildren.

Nash soon learned that, despite his first impressions, relaxed hours were not always the rule at *The New Yorker* and that working for a single boss had its own challenges, particularly if that single boss happened to be Harold Ross. In January, he wrote:

> The day at the office was quiet enough, if you except Ross's usual blow-up. Ross, who made *The New Yorker* what it is, and who really is a genius, is probably the strangest man in the world. He comes from San Francisco where he was known as the worst ship-news reporter and the best card-shark on the West Coast. His hair sticks straight up, his teeth stick straight out, his eyes slant, and his expression is always that of a man who had just swallowed a bug. His collars flap, and he wears high shoes. Once a day at least he calls you into his office and says "This magazine is going to hell." He never varies the phrase. Then he says "We haven't got any organization. I'm licked. We've got too many geniuses around and nobody to take any responsibility." He has smoked five cigarettes while saying that. Then he takes a drink of water, prowls up and down, cries "My God" loudly and rapidly, and you go out and try to do some work.

The job that Nash had been hired to fill at the magazine was essentially to function as a deputy to Ross. Each fresh occupant of that position—and there were many—was colloquially referred to among the staff as "the new Jesus." Ross biographer Thomas Kunkel recounted that, "according to *New Yorker* lore, Nash became the twenty-fifth 'Jesus' in six years." One of his more noteworthy predecessors was Ralph Ingersoll, who had been listed as the magazine's managing editor from 1925 to 1930 while various new Jesuses came and went. Despite his value to the magazine, Ingersoll had felt consistently overworked and underappreciated. After a breakdown in 1926, he repaired to the family farm for several weeks, during which he chopped wood while chanting, "I'll never go back, I'll never go back." When he returned, he asked for a smaller salary and reduced responsibilities with a predictable result: Ross reduced his salary but not his responsibilities. Ingersoll left in 1930 to become managing editor of *Fortune*. Nash had probably been correct in thinking that Ross saw him as Ingersoll's replacement.

All that history, however, was unknown to Nash, and at the end of January he wrote Frances that he was "beginning to get a glimmer" of his role at *The New Yorker.* It was, he said, mostly to "listen to Ross's woes," but he then went on to enumerate a fairly lengthy list of specific chores. Heading the list was trying to see that Dorothy Parker wrote a piece for the magazine every week, but Nash's duties also included getting material in from the various departments (fashion, sports, theater, and so forth), handling profiles, and reading manuscripts. Interestingly, Nash concluded that there were "far too many people, doing far too little work," particularly in comparison with Doubleday where "every body does about two men's jobs."

One responsibility of his job that became increasingly difficult was trying to get his hands on Dorothy Parker's weekly contribution. Nash's letters to Frances in February chronicle a rapidly increasing frustration with Parker. It made her "wistful" mien rather less endearing:

> I didn't get away from the office till 9 o'clock this evening. I had to wait for Dorothy Parker's stuff to come in, and waiting for Dorothy Parker's stuff to come in is a full-time job. And the trouble is that when it finally does arrive it's so good that you forget how mad you were while you were waiting. It's too bad she's so absolutely irresponsible, she'll never do anything until the last minute—until after the last minute, in fact. She's worn out about eight people at *The New Yorker* so far, and bets are now being made on how long my nerves will stand up under the strain. Little do they know the training I've had. *February 13.*

> Not a very exciting day, mostly routine, with a large part of it spent on the telephone trying to find Dorothy Parker, who hides in queer places hoping that no one who wants to make her work can reach her. It's a man-killing job to force her into the theater, and another to make her read a book—and as she is reviewing books and theater it's fairly important to see that she does one or the other—perhaps both. *February 16.*

> Today's Parker episode. Her book page was due at twelve. I called her up at eleven to ask her how it was coming. "Oh," she said very sweetly, "I've got a big surprise for you. I've decided not to do it." So, what fun I had in getting a substitute page. A cooing serpent, that's what she is. *February 18*

Millions of things going wrong, including Dorothy Parker—
though I imagine it's some years since she first did. *February 19*

On the other hand, Nash had developed a growing appreciation of
Andy White. White had graduated from Cornell, where he gained his nickname from one of the University's founders, Andrew D. White. He had
been hired in 1926 at the suggestion of Katharine Angell, and within a short
time her interest became personal as well as professional. Katharine's first
husband, Ernest Angell, was a prominent lawyer whose numerous infideli-
ties had placed their marriage in serious difficulty, and when the Angells
were divorced in 1929, Katharine and Andy married a few months later.
Over time *The New Yorker* would spawn a number of office romances, but
none were more durable or as important to the development of the magazine. E. B. White was a man of many talents: essayist, humorist, poet, sto-
ryteller, and authority on language. Today he may be best remembered as
the author of two beloved children's books, *Charlotte's Web* and *Stuart Little*, and as the co-author of *The Elements of Style*, perhaps the most widely
used book on writing ever published. But he was also a vital part of *The
New Yorker* for over five decades, as an editor from 1925 to 1956 and then as
an outside contributor.

In Nash's earliest days at *The New Yorker*, he admitted to some resentment of White's status as "the super-sacred cow" of the office. Very quickly,
however, he found that White was in fact "a very nice shy young man" and
that "the hocus-pocus that surrounds him is mostly Ross's doing." After
they had grown to be friends, Nash was surprised when White told him one
day that he had written a poem about him. And he was stunned when
White recited the poem: "If I were Ogden Nash, I would marry a girl in
black taffeta/ And sit around the house all day and laffeta." Nash had promised Frances a black taffeta dress but had never spoken of it to White or
anyone else.

Just as Nash was learning his way around *The New Yorker*, Harold Ross
became seriously annoyed by an advertisement for *Hard Lines* that had appeared in the magazine. The ad was addressed to "Readers of The New
Yorker" who, it said, would be delighted that the new book by "their latest
discovery," Ogden Nash, was at the top of the best-seller lists. Ross was
concerned—not unreasonably—that this was an unfair exploitation of
The New Yorker. He wrote a furious memo to Raoul Fleischmann:

I haven't the words to register my disgust over the running of the
ad on Ogden Nash's book on Page 71 of the current issue, nor my
chagrin over the inefficiency, stupidity, perversity or whatever it is
in the business office by which, contrary to solemn and oft-
repeated assurance, all ads mentioning our contributors are to be
passed on by the editorial department. For Christ's sake if we have
no taste we might have common sense.

There is no indication that Ross ever spoke to Nash about the advertisement, or felt him to be responsible for it. Nevertheless Nash's tenure at
The New Yorker was soon to end—he left by the end of March. In later
years Nash referred to Ross's initial impression that he was a "man about
town" and reflected, without rancor, that it took less than three months for
Ross to "discover that it takes more than a collection of speakeasy cards to
make a man about town." Moreover, he said, Ross didn't need an editor as
"anything he didn't do himself was capably handled by Raymond Holden
and Mrs. White." On another occasion he put it succinctly: "Harold Ross
hired me under two misapprehensions: first, that he wanted a managing
editor, and second, that I would be a good one."

Nash's successor was James M. Cain, who would later write the classic
suspense novels *The Postman Always Rings Twice* and *Double Indemnity.*
Cain's "Gesthemane," as he would later refer to it, lasted three times as
long as Nash's, some nine months, and by all accounts Cain was far more
miserable in the position than Nash had ever been. Years later, when Cain
wrote Nash to comment on a Nash poem, he added a fascinating vignette
of the scene when he had arrived at the magazine. On his way to meet with
Ross, Cain related, he had passed Nash's office and observed that Nash was
regarding him with a "sweet seraphic smile." Nash rubbed away the smile
with the back of his hand, but it left Cain with a sense of foreboding. Indeed, he remembered the smile, he claimed, more vividly than anything
else that occurred during his tenure at the magazine.

It is probably fortunate that Nash's tenure was so short-lived. An early
termination, before disappointments and grievances could accumulate, allowed the continuation of a relationship that was founded on mutual respect. As Nash told Thurber about Ross, "He was an almost impossible
man to work for—rude, ungracious and perpetually dissatisfied with what
he read; and I admire him more than anyone I have met in professional

life. Only perfection was good enough for him, and on the rare occasions he encountered it, he viewed it with astonished suspicion." For his part, Ross would remain a lifelong admirer of Nash's verse and treasure his contributions to *The New Yorker*.

Now, however, Nash was without employment at a distinctly inconvenient time: Frances had just returned from Europe. Despite the understanding that Ogden and Frances had reached in September, the trip had produced yet another rival for Nash, and when Frances wrote in February that she had rejected the latest suitor, Nash had replied with somewhat edgy relief:

> So you've turned down le Harvard? Very good. But why do you describe him to me as red-headed and pink-eyed and dressed in a blue suit and white sneakers and then tell [Frances's cousin] Isabel that he's an attractive young man on the Riviera. You know—not jealousy, just curiosity. Not jealousy at all. At all. He's the one I wrote the verse about people who go abroad about. I hope an octopus gets him in the Mediterranean.

Having survived that final challenge, a successful conclusion to Nash's ardent courtship now seemed in sight—unless it had been derailed by Harold Ross. Nash, however, swiftly addressed the problem of his employment by negotiating a return to the world of publishing as an editor at Farrar and Rinehart. The only remaining uncertainty was Frances herself.

4

HAPPY DAYS

Even when Frances arrived home, it would have been understandable if Nash had felt a lingering doubt as to whether the long-promised wedding would at last take place. But Frances remained true to her word. The engagement was announced on March 28, 1931, and the wedding was held on June 6.

Ogden's bride was not only beautiful but intelligent, charming, and witty, and it is not difficult to understand the fascination that she held for him. At the same time Frances Leonard had a volatile nature that sometimes revealed less endearing qualities. One aspect of her complex personality was a sense of insecurity that may have derived from a somewhat unusual family background and childhood.

Frances's parents, William Wirt Leonard and Nellie Jackson Leonard, were both from families long established in Salisbury, Maryland, but having quite different traditions. Will Leonard's family were Episcopalians, and Will's father had fought with the Union Army during the Civil War. Nellie Jackson's family, on the other hand, were Southern Methodists and Southern sympathizers. Nellie's father, Elihu Emory Jackson, had made a sizable fortune in the lumber business and had later been elected governor of Maryland. Her mother, Nannie Rider Jackson, had been widely known for her elegant parties in the governor's mansion.

Although Will and Nellie fell in love during their school days in Salisbury, friction between the Leonard and Jackson families prevented their marriage until 1903, when both were twenty-eight. Two circumstances would have a pervasive influence on their marriage: the dominant personality of Nellie's mother, known in the family as Mama, and the wealth of the Jackson family. Under the circumstances, it was not surprising that Nellie would pay considerably greater deference to her mother than to her husband. Will Leonard, for his part, was a man of considerable charm with wide-ranging interests in music and art. Although he was a graduate of law school and business school, he never had a serious career in either discipline.

Maryland always remained the family home base, but the Leonards also lived for brief periods in Georgia, Florida, and Texas and traveled often to Europe. As a result, Frances's education, like Ogden's, was rather scattered. In France she had attended school at Versailles, and at home her schooling included day schools in Baltimore and a boarding school in Great Barrington, Massachusetts. She attended Vassar, largely to please her father, but left before graduating.

Despite her family's affluence and the experience of travels abroad, Frances lacked the sense of self-confidence or the sophistication that such a background might have produced. On the contrary, she regretted that her peripatetic education had cost her the opportunity to make lasting friendships. By the time she made her debut in Baltimore, the family had moved to that city, and Frances envied the girls who had lived there, and known one another, all their lives. Although her grandfather had been governor of Maryland, being from Salisbury meant that Frances did not have Baltimore roots. In the rather staid atmosphere of the city, she was an outsider who longed for nothing more than to be a "normal Baltimorean."

Another source of insecurity may have been Frances's difficulty in pleasing her father, who, she believed, favored her cousin, Isabel Jackson, a lively and attractive girl. Frances had been tall and awkward as a youngster, and even when she grew to be a strikingly beautiful young woman, her father seemed not to recognize the fact. (In a rather odd complaint, he would sometimes observe that she had "no bridge to her nose.") Frances's experience with members of the opposite sex had also not been entirely reassuring.

When she was eighteen, on a cruise with her mother, she was attracted to a young man on the ship who had become a nodding acquaintance. His reciprocal interest seemed to be confirmed when he sent her flowers. But when Frances wrote to him, at her mother's suggestion, the young man called to say, as politely as possible, that unfortunately he was already engaged. The flowers, it turned out, had been sent by Frances's mother. Two years later Frances had become engaged rather impulsively to a young man named Frank Rose, but had quickly realized that she had made a mistake. Too embarrassed to resolve the situation herself, she had prevailed upon her mother to speak to her suitor and end the relationship. Later Frances had a more serious romance with another young man, Joe Bryan. She had been very much in love with him and believed that he wanted to marry her. But after taking a trip around the world, Bryan told her that he was marrying another (even wealthier) girl. Frances was devastated.

When she rejected a Baltimore doctor in Nash's favor before departing for Europe, her decision was based at least in part upon a conviction that Ogden would never make her jealous by attentions to other women. Ironically, Nash's repeated expressions of devotion, which Frances sometimes found unsettling, may have been a deciding factor in his favor.

Although much of Nash's courtship had been at long distance, he was well aware that Frances could sometimes be quite difficult. Indeed, he had once inquired rhetorically: "Wayward Frances, wilful Frances, capricious Frances, whimsical Frances, unpredictable Frances, fanciful Frances, crotchety Frances, skittish Frances, unreasonable Frances, impervious Frances, what's to be done with you?" Still, even such moments of exasperation left his devotion undiminished, and they were no cause for hesitation in June 1931.

Before the wedding, however, Nash's euphoria was shaken by another event—the death of his father on April 27. Edmund Nash's passing was duly reported in the New York Times, and the obituary noted his descent from Abner and Frederick Nash as well as his long career in the naval stores industry. It mentioned his extensive travels abroad and the fact that his letters "presenting views on political activities in this country and Europe" were frequently published in the Times. No mention was made of the government's ruinous anti-trust suit or the successful appeal to the Supreme Court.

Although Nash had remained close to his father, the death was not allowed to delay the wedding. Ogden wrote to Edmund's cousin, Frank Johnson, that his father had urged him, only a few days before his death, not to postpone the wedding on any account, and that the last thing Edmund wrote was a list of friends to be invited. Ogden went on to explain that the church had a small side door, and a pew whose occupant could not be seen, so that his mother was planning to come. The wedding was held in Baltimore, and Nash's close friend from St. George's, the publisher Eugene Reynal, served as best man. The affair was considerably less elaborate than Edmund and Mattie's, and Harold Ross wrote his regrets that he could not be away from New York at the time. Nevertheless guests came from New York, Philadelphia, and Washington, and it was reported in the press, from as far away as Beaumont, Texas, that "So-and-So," celebrated in Nash's poem "For Any Improbable She," had finally relented and said yes.

After a brief honeymoon in Canada, Ogden returned to Manhattan and his duties at Farrar and Rinehart. The depression was deepening, and he now had the challenge of supporting a wife who had been raised in considerable comfort. (In the fashion of the day, Frances repaired to the family's summer home on Cape Cod, with Ogden commuting on weekends.) John Farrar was six years older than Nash and had been an editor at Doubleday until 1929, when he left to join with two sons of the mystery writer Mary Roberts Rinehart in forming Farrar and Rinehart. He had tried to recruit Nash to the firm in December that year, but Nash had been reluctant to leave an environment at Doubleday that seemed more secure. A year later, Nash still had reservations about Farrar, writing Frances that "He thinks the publishing business is on the road to hell, but an hour of my cheery companionship restored his optimism at the expense of mine. John is one of those nice people of whom you say 'He's a dear, but—.'" By the spring of 1931, however, matters looked quite different. Nash felt that Doubleday was increasingly beset with management problems, and while Nelson Doubleday had proclaimed at the farewell dinner that he would like to have Nash return after five years, a reappearance after only three months might have been another matter.

Once on the job, Nash immediately began to recruit authors for Farrar as eagerly as he had for Doubleday. Indeed, one of his very first targets was his recent colleague, Andy White, with whom he had lunch in early April. ("I'm trying to hook him for a book, but it hasn't jelled yet.") He was also unembarrassed about approaching Doubleday authors and soon attracted David Frome, who had written mystery novels for the Crime Club. At the same time *The New Yorker* was seeking to assure a continuing flow of material from its former editor, and Katharine White wrote Nash suggesting a weekly deadline. With the pressure of his publishing duties, Nash could not make such a commitment, but he continued to write as much as he could, with an eye not only to *The New Yorker* but to a second book, *Free Wheeling*, that was planned for later that year.

In the fall of 1931, as Nash continued to hunt for manuscripts, he received the draft of a novel from John O'Hara, whose short stories had appeared in *The New Yorker*. Nash thought that O'Hara's novel, *The Hofman Estate*, needed rewriting, but was promising. The novel was set in the Pottsville region of Pennsylvania, and Nash told O'Hara that it was "a shame to keep it so short, to overlook the opportunities for writing about a swell, small-town aristocracy." Farrar and Rinehart did not accept Nash's recommendation to give O'Hara an advance, and the novel was never published. Still, Nash's appraisal of O'Hara's potential was later vindicated by O'Hara's publication of *Appointment in Samarra* and the subsequent books in his "Gibbsville" cycle.

Another of Nash's initiatives appeared to be something of a success. A year earlier Ross had suggested to Nash that Doubleday publish a book of cartoons by the *New Yorker* cartoonist Otto Soglow (who later became the illustrator for *Hard Lines*). Ross's suggestion had not been taken up by Doubleday, but after Nash joined Farrar he carried it forward in a somewhat different form—a book of cartoons with ribald scenes and including cartoons not only by Soglow but by two other *New Yorker* cartoonists, Gardiner Rea and William Steig. It became a pet project of Nash, who selected the artists and also suggested ideas for some of the cartoons. Nash sent a copy of the book, *The Stag at Eve*, to Ross, noting somewhat sheepishly that the book was different from the one Ross had suggested, but asserting that they had "done a pretty good job that doesn't reflect discredit on anybody." He went on to note proudly that it had been enthusiastically received by booksellers and reviewers and predicted a sale of fifty thousand copies by Christmas. Ross referred the book to Raymond Holden for a recommendation, but Holden's reaction was unequivocally negative: he termed it a "bum book" that did not merit a review in the magazine. A view from the distance of several decades tends to support Holden's judgment, and suggests that Nash's sense of taste may have deserted him on this occasion. The cartoons, while hardly shocking by today's standards, seem on the whole rather sophomoric.

In any case, Nash pursued his career even as the effects of the depression grew more severe. In early 1932 he noted that Farrar's revenues were below budget, but he was heartened when the firm's accountants, who were also auditors for half a dozen other publishers, indicated that Farrar was doing better than any of their other publishing clients. In August he wrote to Frances that two new books had good advance sales and "it looks like a prosperous October." Beyond that, he added, "everything looks good and I feel swell." Nash was also keeping up his contacts at Doubleday. He rode out to Garden City to have dinner with Dan Longwell and Chris Morley and, not so incidentally, to ask Morley, one of the Book-of-the-Month Club judges, why Farrar couldn't seem to have any of its books selected by the Club.

The summer of 1932 also brought Nash an interesting task from John Farrar. While the names of Ezra Pound and Ogden Nash have seldom, if ever, been linked, circumstances brought them briefly together. Farrar and Rinehart was preparing to publish Pound's *A Draft of XXX Cantos*, and Nash was given the delicate responsibility of dealing with the often cantankerous poet. Nash did not presume to edit the *Cantos*, but he did find it necessary to ask, with evident reluctance, for one modification. The firm, Nash said, had "altered the excremental words to s--t." Nash offered to let Pound write a foreword commenting on the alteration and, ever the promoter, suggested that such a commentary "would draw much more attention to the book, and create much more discussion than would the actual use of the word." But Pound accepted the alteration, and it was decided that no explanatory foreword was required. (The precise need for the change is not clear, and it is all the more curious in light of considerably coarser language in the *Cantos* that went unchallenged; an entirely unexpurgated version was published by Farrar and Rinehart in 1934.) Nash also worked with Pound's friend and colleague, Ford Madox Ford, in marketing the book. They assembled a series of appreciative essays in a separate pamphlet, *The Cantos of Ezra Pound: Some Testimonies*, which included contributions from Ford, Ernest Hemingway, Hugh Walpole, Archibald MacLeish, James Joyce, T. S. Eliot, Edmund Wilson, and William Carlos Williams.

Soon thereafter Nash took on a far more substantive assignment. Throughout the following winter he worked, sentence by sentence and paragraph by paragraph, on the editing of a massive historical novel. The book, Hervey Allen's *Anthony Adverse*, filled a thousand pages, an unprecedented length at the time, offering minute details of the Napoleonic era. It became one of the best-selling historical novels of all time and initiated the trend toward large novels that developed during the depression years. Such books, the public discovered, could provide several weeks of entertainment, and an escape into a world of romance, all at an affordable cost. Nash and Allen became good friends, and Nash delighted in the reception of the book for what it meant not only to his firm but to the author.

Despite the popularity of *Anthony Adverse*, Farrar and Rinehart was increasingly feeling the effects of the depression—and so was Nash. By the spring of 1933 his compensation had been reduced to twenty-five dollars per week, the very salary he had earned at Barron G. Collier before joining Doubleday. For Nash, whose prospects had seemed so brilliant at the beginning of 1931, it had to be bitterly disappointing. What's more, the Nashes now had a daughter, Linell, and were expecting a second child in the fall. He needed to make a career change, but he was uncertain how to do it.

Unexpectedly, the answer came from the *Saturday Evening Post*. Having published two Nash poems in November and December 1932, and three more in early 1933, the magazine decided that it wanted to assure itself of a steady supply; and with a circulation much larger than that of *The New Yorker*, it was able to offer Nash significantly higher rates. The *Post* suggested a contract calling for Nash to submit 35 poems a year, from which the magazine would accept 25 that averaged 40 lines in length. Nash would receive $100 for each of the 25 accepted, if they were 30 lines or over, and for a poem of less than 30 lines, $2.25 a line. The proposal of an effective rate of $2.50 per line was a significant improvement over the going rate of $1.25 to $1.75 from *The New Yorker*. *The New Yorker* felt it could not match the *Post* but offered to raise Nash's rate to $2.00 per line on the condition that "we should have to reserve the right to choose at this price only the things we thought were your very best." In any case, the prime importance of the contract was not the leverage it gave Nash with *The New Yorker* but the fact that, with the guarantee of a steady stream of revenue, Nash felt he could leave Farrar and Rinehart and devote himself to writing full time.

The decision to leave Farrar and Rinehart also meant that he no longer had to bear the expense of living in New York City. A move to Baltimore seemed a natural step. In fact, by the time the contract with the *Saturday Evening Post* was in place, Frances, pregnant with the Nashes' second child and suffering from an eye infection, had returned to Baltimore with one-year-old Linell. Nash subleased their New York apartment, and until he left Farrar and Rinehart in September, he stayed at the Harvard Club (at the price, modest even for the times, of $2.75 per day). Once in Baltimore, Nash joined Frances and Linell at the spacious home of Frances's parents on Rugby Road. The second Nash daughter, Isabel, was born in September. By the end of the year, the young family had moved to their own home, a rented house at 4205 Underwood Road.

When Linell was born in March 1932, it had been perhaps sooner than Ogden and Frances might have wished. In a letter written the previous August, Nash had remarked on a visit to the Farrar and Rinehart offices by family-planning advocate Margaret Sanger and wryly observed, "I could only look at her and think 'Why couldn't you have come in June?'" Fatherhood was a new experience for a poet who, in an early verse, "Did Someone Say 'Babies'?" had seemed to view infants with a distinct lack of enthusiasm. On the other hand, Nash had been exposed to nieces and nephews and was not entirely unschooled in the arts of child-rearing. He had, after all, observed in "Pediatric Reflection":

Many an infant that screams like a calliope
Could be soothed by a little attention to its diope.

And in "The Baby":

A little talcum
Is always walcum.

When Linell arrived, it took Nash little time to make the transition to doting father. He might still claim, as he did in "Some of My Best Friends Are Children," that he was not fond of "little humans," but he then went on to explain in several stanzas why "our child is different." By the time Linell was six months old, Nash was worrying, at least poetically, about the infant boy who might turn up years later as a suitor. In "Song to Be Sung by the Father of Six-Month-Old Female Children," he contemplated various preemptive attacks against the young man, including:

I'll pepper his powder and salt his bottle
And give him readings from Aristotle
Sand for his spinach I'll gladly bring
And Tabasco sauce for his teething ring.

    *   *   *   *

The poem was published in *The New Yorker* and later drew a response from Andy White, entitled "Memorandum for an Infant Boy." White's poem was addressed to the boy "who was foully attacked by Ogden Nash in a popular magazine," and included a caution that:

My son there are things in life much higher
Than attending the daughter of a versifier.

Linell had been named for her father's aunt, Linell Chenault Rogers. Isabel was named for Frances's cousin and close friend, Isabel Jackson,

whose tragic death from meningitis had been a terrible blow to Frances.
Thus their names were not chosen for their rhyming potential. Nevertheless Linell and Isabel would share not only their father's affection but the
measure of public attention that came with being subjects of his verse.
Close together in age, they were constant companions as small children,
and since Nash worked at home, he had ample opportunity to observe and
chronicle their activities. For example, in "Rainy Day":

> Linell is clad in a gown of green
> She walks in state like a fairy queen.
> Her train is tucked in a winsome bunch
> Directly behind her royal lunch
> With a dignified skip and a haughty hop
> Her golden slippers go clippety-clop
> I think I am Ozma, says Linell,
> I'm Ozma too, says Isabel.

>   *   *   *   *

As Linell and Isabel grew up, they were in general not troubled by being depicted, occasionally by name, in their father's verse. There were,
however, exceptions such as "The Sniffle":

> In spite of her sniffle
> Isabel's chiffle
> Some girls with a sniffle
> would be weepy and tiffle;
> They would look awful,
> Like a rained-on waffle,
> But Isabel's chiffle
> In spite of her sniffle.

>   *   *   *   *

Chiffle or not, Isabel did not particularly enjoy the experience of having
people frequently say, even years later, "Oh, Isabel, you were the one with
the sniffles."

Still, neither Linell or Isabel ever felt the resentment that Nash had
wryly imagined in "My Daddy":

> I have a funny daddy
> Who goes in and out with me,
> And everything that baby does

69

My daddy's sure to see
And everything that baby says,
My daddy's sure to tell
You must have read my daddy's verse
I hope he fries in hell.

Life in Baltimore agreed with Nash. A few years later, in 1938, when he was working as a screenwriter in Hollywood, he wrote yearningly of those days in a letter to Frances: "I'm eager to get back to the 1936 pre-Hollywood routine, a good morning's work, an hour or so for lunch, and the rest of the day together." On weekends the Nashes had an active social life, principally involving Frances's family and friends, with whom Nash mixed comfortably. He also became acquainted with the Pimlico racetrack in the company of his friend, Ed Duffy, editorial cartoonist for the *Baltimore Sun*. It might be some years before Nash would become truly an adopted son of Baltimore, but meanwhile he could take periodic trips to New York to meet with editors and lunch at the Dutch Treat Club—a popular spot for editors, authors, journalists, and artists, which provided entertainment at weekly luncheons.

For Nash the early thirties in Baltimore echoed in many ways the title of his 1933 book, *Happy Days*. Yet the book included a number of poems with a distinctly darker tone that reflected some of the depression's painful realities. In Nash's case, the economics of freelance writing were a continuing challenge, but the most serious threat to his own happy days was a different sort: a growing disagreement with Frances over his drinking. Alcoholism is the occupational hazard of writers, and that was never more true than with the brilliant group who had come of age in Manhattan in the twenties in the atmosphere of ubiquitous speakeasies. It was a milieu with which Nash was well acquainted: when Prohibition ended, he remarked wistfully that he would miss the speakeasies: "After all those years of intimate and secluded sipping, I find that to order and drink in a hotel gives me the naked feeling of a scallop torn from its shell."

It was to be expected that an affectionate regard for cocktails would sometimes turn up in Nash's verse. *The Primrose Path*, published in 1935, included "A Drink with Something in It," which began:

There is something about a Martini,
A tingle remarkably pleasant
A yellow, a mellow Martini
I wish that I had one at present;

There is something about a Martini,
Ere the dining and dancing begin,
And to tell you the truth,
It is not the vermouth —
I think that perhaps it's the gin.

⁂   ⁂   ⁂   ⁂

In that same year, however, alcohol became a serious issue in the Nash household. While Nash did not allow drinking to interfere with his work, he had begun to push the term "social drinker" to its limit. Matters may have been brought to a head one evening when he and Frances attended a cocktail party at a home near the top of a very steep road. In those days, hosts were not so well aware of their responsibilities, and the Nashes were permitted to leave the party though Frances did not drive and Ogden was obviously "under the weather." Ogden got behind the wheel, but it was Frances who had to take over the steering as the car made a perilous descent to level terrain. While no damage was done, the experience left a considerable impression. That may well have been the occasion when Frances, as she once confided to Isabel, warned Ogden that if he didn't get his drinking under control, she would sleep with the next man who asked her. The threat was no doubt rhetorical, and intended to get her husband's attention, but Frances took a concrete step to address the situation. On October 19 she departed on a six-week trip to Europe with her mother, leaving Linell and Isabel in Ogden's care and giving him an ultimatum: if their marriage was to survive, he must get his drinking under control by the time she returned.

Nash's letters to Frances during her absence reveal only partially the stress that he must have felt. They tell of progress with his work, routine social activities, and how much the children and he missed her:

> The children are now asking "Where's Mummy?" several times a
> day. At least Linell asks "Where's Mummy?" and Isabel asks
> "Vare's Mummy?" I don't know how long the promise of those
> Paris dresses will keep them satisfied. Darling, I adore you, and I
> am so damned lonely. And I try to lose the loneliness in seeing a
> lot of people and the more people I see the more I ache for you.

Despite the high stakes, Nash had apparently been forced into moderation but not abstinence. In November he was dismayed to receive an angry letter from Frances, who had heard a report from someone in Baltimore of his having overindulged. He immediately sent a cable to rebut the allegation and received a conciliatory cable in reply. He then followed up with a letter: "There is one thing I must get straight. I have not once had too much to drink since you left. And I am using your standard of too much, not mine." Remarkably, he then struck a saucy and confident, even cocky, note: "So that's that and you are my girl and I worship you and if you ever again mention a possibility of our not being together forever and more than ever, I shall ruthlessly spank the most beautiful bottom in the world. Kiss me."

When Frances returned in December, she found matters resolved to her satisfaction. Many years later, Linell observed that her mother's approach to Nash's drinking might today be termed "confrontation" or "intervention." The point was, she had acted at a time when Nash "could still weigh the importance of the extra drink against its consequences—a world without Frances." Nash would continue to be an enthusiastic (and occasionally overenthusiastic) consumer of alcohol, but the habit never got out of control. And while his drinking might become an occasional source of contention, it never again threatened his marriage.

Whatever the extent of Nash's drinking in Baltimore, it did not get in the way of writing verse. His years there in the early thirties were the most productive of his life in terms of the sheer number of poems he published in magazines—125 in 1935 alone. At the same time he continued to resist being pigeonholed as a writer only of light verse, even a remarkably successful one. He made repeated experiments with other forms of writing: several short stories or essays that were published in the *Saturday Evening Post*, others that were unpublished, and the book for a show, *Family Album*, that failed to find a producer. It was verse, however, that paid the bills and supported his family. That in turn forced Nash to seek new outlets for his poems, and this created inevitable tensions, particularly with *The New Yorker*.

When Nash had first been published in the *Saturday Evening Post* in 1932, Harold Ross had not taken kindly to the competition. He had argued that Nash was better off to publish in *The New Yorker*, not only for his own satisfaction but with a view to subsequent publication of the verse in book form. Moreover, he told Nash, his "best stuff wouldn't fit into the SEP." But when Nash entered into a contract with the *Post* the following spring, Ross acquiesced—and he not only backed off a demand that all Nash's work be offered to *The New Yorker* first, but raised Nash's rate. Nevertheless, conflict was inevitable. Nash felt the strain of both the increasing demand for his work and, ironically, the fact that, however eagerly *The New Yorker* sought his submissions, he never had assurance that they would accept what he proffered:

> I wish we could agree more often about my verse, but no two people seem to be able to—the day after I heard from you that Mr. Ross would have liked to print the last *Post* poem, I got this from Lorimer [of the *Saturday Evening Post*]: "I want the sort of things you are do [sic] for the *New Yorker*."

Katharine White replied with a warm letter congratulating him on his new baby and noting that she didn't wonder that he was bewildered "as to who likes what." In only a matter of weeks, though, a major problem arose.

Nash received an agitated letter from Mrs. White asking if he had abandoned *The New Yorker* for the *New York American*, and claiming that Nash had promised *The New Yorker* the first chance at anything he did not send to the *Saturday Evening Post*. She concluded that "this isn't said as much in bitterness as in grief, and also in the belief that *The New Yorker* is really your proper medium." Nash made a plaintive response:

> I have always considered and shall always consider *The New Yorker* the proper medium for my work. I dislike seeing anything of mine printed anywhere else, but what happened to me was this—since I left publishing I found it absolutely necessary with a wife and two children on my mind to assure myself of a regular income, so that all I could do when a contract was offered me was to take it.
>
> *The New Yorker* has never wanted a contract, and as a matter of fact no matter how good a piece I wrote I have never been able to be sure *The New Yorker* would use it. This last I say neither in sorrow nor in anger. It is simply a statement of fact and is, I think, probably good editing. But now that I have to live on what I make from my writings, and I am absolutely forced to earn so much money every month, it makes things difficult for me.

Nash then disclosed that he had three contracts: the *Saturday Evening Post* for twenty-five poems, *Red Book* for twelve poems, and the *New York American* for one poem a week. He asked Mrs. White not to consider him a "renegade" until he had a chance to come up to New York to discuss the situation. Mollified, she wrote back, inviting Nash to come in for a meeting

73

and assuring him that "we don't consider you a 'renegade' but are simply grieved not to have you in the books and to see all this good stuff that is so up our street coming out elsewhere."

There is no record of what understanding, if any, Nash and Katharine White were able to reach. The next year Nash appeared only six times in the magazine and was seen predominantly in the *New York American* (fifty-two poems) and the *Saturday Evening Post* (forty-eight poems). In 1935 and 1936, however, his output in *The New Yorker* increased to nineteen poems each year. And it is clear that he never relinquished the view that *The New Yorker* was the "proper medium" for his work. Nevertheless, writing for other magazines broadened the scope of what Nash was able to do and enabled him to reach a far wider audience than he otherwise would have.

Most of Nash's poems that were initially published in magazines later reappeared in books. In the thirties this amounted to six volumes: *Hard Lines* and *Free Wheeling* (1931), *Happy Days* (1933), *The Primrose Path* (1935), *The Bad Parents' Garden of Verse* (1936), and *I'm a Stranger Here Myself* (1938). It was a substantial body of work, showing that Nash was no mere fad. Indeed, he had become the most quoted poet of the day, and had permanently altered the landscape of light verse in America.

5

WRITING LIGHT VERSE . . .
IN THE DEPRESSION

The dedication in *Hard Lines* suggested that Nash was not taking himself too seriously:

To

MRS. PARKER

MR. HOFFENSTEIN,

MR. ROGET

and

THE SWEET SINGER OF MICHIGAN,

without a complete and handy set of
whose works this book could not have
been written so quickly.

Amidst the fun, however, he would strike some serious notes.

A note of self-deprecation was found in Nash's reference to the "The Sweet Singer of Michigan." That was a sobriquet adopted by Julia Moore, a lady whose poetry was—quite unintentionally—so comically awful that it attracted a substantial following in the nineteenth century. In Nash's eyes she may have been a surrogate for all the writers of dreadful poetry whose work he had been required to read as an editor at Doubleday. No doubt a similar instinct also accounted for the nod to Mr. Roget and his *Thesaurus*. On the other hand, Nash did have genuine admiration for the work of Dorothy

Parker. Two years later, reviewing a volume of short stories, he made an observation that would be widely repeated: "To say that Mrs. Parker writes well is as fatuous, I'm afraid, as proclaiming that Cellini was clever with his hands." While Parker also had a considerable reputation for light verse, it is doubtful that her poetry had a significant influence on Nash's writing.

Samuel Hoffenstein was quite another matter. Hoffenstein was a theatrical press agent, newspaper columnist, drama critic—and poet. In 1928 he had published a book of verse, *Poems in Praise of Practically Nothing*, that became a best-seller and brought a different voice to light verse. While its diction—informal and colloquial—was "light," its tone was darker, consistently tinged with sadness and regret. The opening stanza of the title poem gave some flavor of what was to follow:

> You buy some flowers for your table
> You tend them tenderly as you're able;
> You fetch them water from hither and thither—
> What thanks do you get for it all? They wither.

To Nash, Hoffenstein's work was far more interesting than the traditional light verse that he felt was "graceful, facile and said nothing . . . like wax flowers under the bell on the mantelpiece." Nash's description might have been fairly applied to most of the verse in *The New Yorker* when his own poems began to appear there. *The New Yorker* of that day occasionally published poems by well-known poets—W. B. Yeats, Babette Deutsch, Louise Bogan, Mark Van Doren—but most of its poetry was light verse from contributors whose names and work are largely forgotten. The best known, perhaps, Margaret Fishback and Arthur Guitterman, published volumes of light verse but today are seldom read or remembered.

Hoffenstein, Nash believed, "took light verse out from under the glass bell and took it into the kitchen and the bedroom and onto the side street, into the human experience of living human beings, with a slightly cynical 'this is the way it is' approach which opened the doors wide for me." Nash once summed it up to a young (still in college) Gene Shalit: "You know, if it hadn't been for him, I would never have begun to write poetry."

Despite the dedication in *Hard Lines*, a connection between Nash and Hoffenstein did not seem obvious to most critics. One reviewer did note that Nash appeared to be a "philosophic first cousin" of Hoffenstein, but he went on to suggest that "deeper down we find more than a trace of Walt Whitman." There were at least two important differences between Nash and Hoffenstein. Hoffenstein's style was more conventional—though his poem "Promises" did provide an example of the kind of creative spelling that Nash would make his own ("You practice every possible virtue;/ You hurt not a soul while others hurtue"). As to tone, there are times when Nash's work may seem to reflect Hoffenstein's mordant perspective, but on the whole Nash is considerably more good-natured in his reflections on life's irritations and inequities. Whatever the degree of inspiration Nash derived from Hoffenstein, most critics agreed that he had "achieved the first new note in light verse that [had] come along in a long time."

Nash's early verse revealed him to be something of a rebel. In *Hard Lines* he needled prudish clergy in "Birth Comes to the Archbishop" and "The Pulpiteers Have Hairy Ears," and some of his own verses were mildly racy ("In the Vanities/ No one wears panities"). He poked fun at celebrities ranging from the health guru Bernarr Macfadden to the composer Maurice Ravel to the crooner Rudy Vallee, at the U.S. Senate, and even at his fellow man ("My fellow man I do not care for/ I often ask me, what's he there for?"). Bipartisan swipes were given to both Republicans ("Like an art lover looking at the Mona Lisa in the Louvre/ Is the *New York Herald Tribune* looking at Mr. Herbert Houvre") and Democrats ("I wonder if the citizens of New York will ever get sufficiently wroth/ To remember that Tammany crooks spoil the broth"). In Nash's second book, *Free Wheeling*, published the same year, his satirical targets were fewer but included Walter Winchell, imitators of Ernest Hemingway, and the British author J. B. Priestley. And in "Peekaboo, I See a Red," Nash tweaked the Daughters of the American Revolution:

> The results of the activities of the D.A.R. might not be so minus—
> Were the ladies not troubled by sinus.
> Alas, every time they try to put people who don't agree with them
>   on the stand as defendants
> They find themselves troubled by the sinus of the Declaration of
>   Independence.

The humorist and critic Max Eastman declared that this was more than a pun, indeed it was a "punitive expedition." Although the pun was a lame one—since sinus and signers do not have an identical pronunciation—the lameness had an added point. As Eastman explained, "one of the ways these exalted ladies are accustomed to demonstrate their elevation is by pronouncing *signers* as if it were identical with *sinus*."

The time was coming, however, for even more pointed commentary as the growing depression became the central fact of life in America. It would emerge in *Happy Days* (1933), *The Primrose Path* (1935), and *I'm a Stranger Here Myself* (1938). Nash had felt the effects of the depression firsthand in the salary reductions he had experienced at Farrar and Rinehart. And while the move to Baltimore and his success in selling his verse had provided a cushion against the harshest effects of the economic collapse, Nash's brothers, Ted and Aubrey, had lost their jobs, and his brother-in-law, Culver McWilliams, had been forced to sell his seat on the New York Stock Exchange. More broadly, the effects of the depression were all-pervasive. As it persisted, Nash became one of the humorists whose work helped to keep the country grinning whenever it could and bearing it as well as it could. Nash and his contemporaries—Robert Benchley, Dorothy Parker, James Thurber, S. J. Perelman, and E. B. White, to name a few—seldom wrote about the depression directly. But it gave context to their work. In writing about love and marriage, for example, one critic has noted that "preconceived notions of what the family is or was during the age of paterfamilias came under attack from the literary humorists no longer content to maintain the status quo in light of the turbulence of the decade." Nash probably did not view himself as attacking "preconceived notions of the family," and his reports on the war between the sexes were far gentler than James Thurber's. Still, very little of the paterfamilias remains in his sketches of family life.

Inevitably the depression bred cynicism about many of society's institutions and erstwhile pillars. Bankers were a favorite target of literary humorists, and few were more unsparing than Nash. (Nash's own attitude toward bankers may well have been influenced by the role they had played in the demise of the American Naval Stores Company.) In "Ma, What's a Banker," Nash depicted a banker sheltered from the winds of hard times:

For when he is good,
He is not very good,
And when he is bad he is horrider.
And the chances are fair
He is taking the air
Beside a cabana in Florida.
But the wailing investor, mean thing, mean thing.
Disturbs his siesta, poor thing.

   *   *   *   *

And in "Bankers Are Just Like Anybody Else, Except Richer," Nash mused on bankers' secret of success:

> Most bankers dwell in marble halls
> Which they dwell in because they encourage deposits and
>   discourage withdralls.
> And particularly because they all observe one rule which woe
>   betides the banker who fails to heed it,
> Which is you must never lend any money to anybody unless they
>   don't need it.

    *   *   *   *

Politicians and the government were another obvious target for humorists in the depression. In 1935 a Nash poem attacked the tradition of appointing the president's campaign manager to the position of postmaster general. The incumbent was James Farley; the poem was entitled "Ave Atque Farley." Katharine White thought the poem was one of Nash's best and told him that the magazine's lawyer had said that, while the poem was libelous, the magazine should take the risk of running it. She did request— and Nash agreed to—one change, deleting the word "pander" which had been seen as the most libelous word in the poem. (From today's perspective, the magazine's concerns simply show that the libel law has changed as much as social mores.)

In "One from One Leaves Two," Nash cast a jaundiced eye at the New Deal program establishing agricultural production quotas and at the growing burden of taxation. Nash's sentiments about taxes were similar to those of Will Rogers, who had asserted that the government had taxed everything but optimism. As Nash put it:

> Mumbledy pumbledy, my red cow,
> She's cooperating now.
> At first she didn't understand
> That milk production must be planned;
> She didn't understand at first
> She either had to plan or burst.
> But now the government reports
> She's giving pints instead of quarts.

    *   *   *   *

Nash's roughest attack on the economic and political establishment came in a song he wrote for performance at the Dutch Treat Club in New

York in 1933, variously titled "Pedigree," "Four Prominent So-and-So's," or "Four Prominent Bastards Are We." The song depicted, in highly colorful language, three bastards, "a banker, a broker, and Washington joker," and the fourth, "a self-appointed bastard," determined to get back what the others had taken. The song was widely circulated in typewritten form, and a somewhat expurgated version appeared in *Happy Days* (titled "Quartet for Four Prosperous Love-Children," "bastard" became "love-child" and references to rape were eliminated). A recording of the performance at the Dutch Treat Club made its way to Hollywood and resulted in a letter to Simon and Schuster from the novelist and playwright Rupert Hughes. Hughes reported that he had taken the record to a dinner at Charlie Chaplin's where Chaplin and Will Rogers insisted on playing it twice "and fair perished with laughter." Hughes further reported that Chaplin insisted on playing it for anyone who came to his house and had nearly worn it out. Hughes despaired of ever getting the record back from Chaplin and enclosed a check for another copy.

Despite the sometimes sharp edges of his verse, Nash managed to remain, at bottom, an optimist. His personal feelings were probably best expressed in "Look What You Did, Christopher!" After a highly selective "history" of the country, the poem concluded:

> The American people,
> With grins jocose
> Always survive the fatal dose.
> And though our systems are slightly wobbly,
> We'll fool the doctor this time, probly.

It is not entirely clear what Nash's personal politics were during these years. In a letter written many years later, he advised an inquiring journalist that he had cast his first vote for Al Smith and had later voted for Franklin Roosevelt. On the other hand, his verse suggested that he was not an unalloyed admirer of the New Deal, and in a 1936 letter to his mother, he had indicated that he would not vote for Roosevelt. The letter was written from Little Boar's Head, New Hampshire, where the Nashes vacationed. Little Boar's Head was also the summer home of Dr. Harvey Cushing, whose youngest daughter, Betsey, was married to James Roosevelt. Nash wrote: "I have met James Roosevelt, John Roosevelt, Franklin D. Roosevelt Jr., Mrs. James Roosevelt, Sarah Delano Roosevelt, and Kate Roosevelt. . . . All very attractive, but I am still voting twice for Landon. . . . We live on political tiptoe up here."

When Nash's 1936 letter came to the attention of Nash's daughters in recent years, it surprised them because they had assumed that their father had supported Roosevelt. They both recalled vividly an incident when a guest in the Nash home had made a highly offensive remark about the president and had been required by their father to leave at once. Nash's reaction, however, may have been driven more by respect for the office than political support for its occupant—a distinction he would feel even more sharply in the 1960s.

While Nash's verse provides an interesting perspective on the economic and political crosscurrents of the thirties, he never allowed it to be swamped by them. The bulk of his work continued to concern ordinary human foibles, his own and others', as well as excursions of pure whimsy. His experiences as a husband and a father provided a theme for many poems, some of which were collected in a 1936 book, *The Bad Parents' Garden of Verse*. The book provided a variety of "advice" to parents and children, including "A Child's Guide to Parents," which remains quite timeless:

The wise child handles father and mother
By playing one against the other.

Don't! Cries this parent to the tot;
The opposite parent asks, Why not?

Let baby listen, nothing loth,
And work impartially on both.

In clash of wills, do not give in;
Good parents are made by discipline.

  ✻   ✻   ✻   ✻

In *The Primrose Path* and *I'm a Stranger Here Myself*, Nash experimented with still another new form—somewhat bizarre stories entitled "The Strange Case of . . ." and consisting of one-line stanzas encumbered by neither meter nor rhyme. These "poems" probably exceed the most liberal definition of verse and are generally not among Nash's more successful efforts. Yet some of the stories are fun, particularly when concluded with an imaginative pun. ("The Strange Case of Mr. Fortague's Disappointment" told the story of a man who, after moving to Innisfree, became annoyed with the townspeople. At an annual clearance sale he bought a

81

fierce-looking dog to bite them. But Fortague was disappointed: "He had forgotten that a bargain dog doesn't bite.")

Nash also tried his hand at an old form, the limerick, and in "Arthur" brought to it his distinctive touch:

> There was an old man of Calcutta
> Who coated his tonsils with butta,
> Thus converting his snore
> From a thunderous roar
> To a soft oleaginous mutta.

Finally, as a counterpoint to nonsense, Nash sometimes wrote serious poems. The last poem in *Hard Lines* was "Old Men," which examined society's indifference to the elderly and concluded with the poignant lines, "People watch with unshocked eyes;/ But the old men know when an old man dies." It was, as William Rose Benét wrote in the *Saturday Review*, "a real poem, a significant thing, extremely well said." *Happy Days* included "The Beggar (after William Blake)," a poem that followed the form of Blake's "The Tiger" in depicting the condition of a beggar. It is technically a parody and hence perhaps "light," but the message is searing. Then, in 1935, Nash wrote "A Carol for Children," which concluded:

> Two ultimate laws alone we know,
> The ledger and the sword—
> So far away, so long ago
> We lost the infant Lord.
>
> Only the children clasp his hand
> His voice speaks low to them,
> And still for them the shining band
> Wings over Bethlehem.
>
> God rest you, Merry Innocents,
> While innocence endures.
> A sweeter Christmas than we to ours
> May you bequeath to yours.

More than thirty years later, on Christmas Day, 1978, the poem would be the centerpiece of the lead editorial in the *New York Times*.

By 1936, Nash had shown that he could make a living writing light verse—no mean accomplishment, especially in a period of severe economic hardship. But he was not satisfied. He still felt there were more things he could do as a writer, and if he did them, he could make more than "a living." Although Nash had been spared the worst of the depression, there is a sense in some of his poems of the financial pressures he felt personally. In "Prayer at the End of a Rope," he spoke for many of his countrymen and perhaps himself: "Oh, when the postman's whistle shrills/ Just once, Lord, let me grin:/ Let me have settled last month's bills/ Before this month's come in." So it is not surprising that when Nash was invited to come to Hollywood and try his hand at scriptwriting, he decided—just as so many celebrated writers of his generation had—to try it.

6

HOLLYWOOD BECKONS

In August 1936, Ogden and Frances set out for Hollywood and a new chapter in Nash's career. Hollywood in the thirties was an oasis of hope, providing entertainment to a depression-weary nation. It was also an oasis of prosperity for the creators of that entertainment. As one observer has noted, "By the mid-thirties nineteen of the twenty-five highest salaries in America and forty of the highest sixty-three went to film executives. Louis Mayer earned more money than any other individual in the country—well over $1 million, even in the depths of the Depression."

Writers were not as lavishly compensated as studio executives. Still, the best-paid might command five thousand dollars a week, and even those on lower rungs took in far more than they were likely to earn elsewhere. Moreover, Hollywood seemed to have an insatiable demand for writers and their products. In addition to the practical need for plots, scripts, adaptations, and lyrics, Hollywood executives seemed to crave celebrated writers for the aura of professional distinction they were thought to carry with them. By the time Nash arrived in Hollywood, he had been preceded by an impressive roster of essayists, novelists, and playwrights.

The New York literary scene had contributed Dorothy Parker, Robert Benchley, John O'Hara, Donald Ogden Stewart, Marc Connelly, and Corey Ford. Other luminaries who came and went with varying degrees of success included Thornton Wilder, William Faulkner, John P. Marquand, and F. Scott Fitzgerald. Nor did Hollywood's reach stop at the water's edge: it crossed the Atlantic to lure English writers, including Aldous Huxley,

Anthony Powell, and J. B. Priestley. What some or all of them could have told Nash was that, despite the glamour and the money, life in Hollywood could be hazardous to a writer's mental health.

One problem was the tendency to hire writers more for their names than for the suitability of their talents for screenwriting. As Neil Gabler put it in *An Empire of Their Own*: "The writer was a trinket for men of dubious breeding and culture. He was another affectation along with the race-horses, the mansions, the limousines, the tailored suits. He was a reproof of the accusation of vulgarity. 'The higher the class of talent [a producer] could tell what to do and how to do it,' Ben Hecht noted, 'the more giddily cultured he could feel himself.'"

A second problem was that, once the distinguished writers were hired, the studio often seemed uncertain as to what to do with them. The matching of writers to projects was sometimes bizarre, and teams of writers might be deployed to rewrite scripts to the point of diminishing returns and beyond. The humorist Corey Ford, Nash's sometime speakeasy companion from the twenties, had made the discovery on his tour with RKO when he was assigned to write "a grim exposé of the professional wrestling racket." Ford also recounted how William Faulkner had been assigned to write a sophisticated drama of New York society, "a background about which he knew nothing and cared less." After a brief but intense period of frustration, Faulkner simply departed for Mississippi without so much as mentioning it to his employers.

Even the icon of Nash's youth, P. G. Wodehouse, had experienced treatment he found exceedingly curious. As he wrote a London friend, "So far I've had eight collaborators. The system is that A gets the original idea, B comes in to work with him on it, C makes the scenario, D does preliminary dialogue, and then they send for me to insert class and what not and then E and F, scenario writers, alter the plot and off we go again. I could have done all my part of it in a morning, but they took it for granted that I should need six weeks."

When Wodehouse later described the system in a lengthy interview for the *Los Angeles Times*, it drew attention even on the East Coast. The *New York Herald Tribune* commented that "[Wodehouse] confirms the picture that has been steadily growing—the picture of Hollywood the golden, where 'names' are bought to be scrapped, talents are retained to be left unused, hiring [of distinguished authors] is without rhyme and firing without reason. It is indeed amazing. . . ."

If Nash had heard any cautionary tales from his predecessors, he was undeterred by them. His invitation to Hollywood came from one of its legendary figures, MGM's Irving Thalberg (who would later be fictionalized in F. Scott Fitzgerald's unfinished novel, *The Last Tycoon*). Thalberg was only three years older than Nash but had become the prince of Hollywood. He had initially been hired at Universal Pictures by Carl Laemmle (whose conspicuous nepotism later became the subject of a widely quoted Nashism: "Carl Laemmle has a very large faemmle"). Then, in 1923, at the age of twenty-three, Thalberg had gone to Metro Goldwyn Mayer where he joined Louis Mayer to form the most powerful production team in the history of the industry.

Before Nash even arrived in Hollywood, he had been given a taste of what might lie ahead. In his July 1936 letter to his mother from Little Boar's Head, he wrote: "No we are not dead or missing, only bewildered by Hollywood. Ten days ago I got a telegram ordering me to report for work, in Hollywood, on the second day following. They had promised not to send for me until September, so it was upsetting. . . . Telephone and telegraph wires have been burning up ever since, and they have finally postponed it, though threatening to repeat the command at whatever moment suits them." As it turned out, Nash left for Hollywood two weeks later.

Nash's first project, unlike Corey Ford's, had at least a plausible connection with his reputation as a humorist. He was assigned to collaborate on a screenplay with another humorist and emigré from the East Coast, S. J. Perelman. Sid Perelman, two years younger than Nash, had attended Brown University but left before graduation to become a cartoonist at *Judge*, the national humor magazine where Harold Ross was then the editor. Perelman had come to Hollywood in 1930 and had been one of the principal writers for two Marx Brothers pictures, *Monkey Business* and *Horse Feathers*. In the following years he had worked on a number of pictures and had also become a regular contributor to *The New Yorker*.

The project for Nash and Perelman was a screenplay for *How to Win Friends and Influence People*, inspired by the best-selling Dale Carnegie book. Professionally the collaboration was not a success. As Perelman put it, the film was "an expensive vehicle for Fannie Brice, Claude Rains and Esther Williams that fortunately never made it out of the garage. If it had, it would have been known as the Edsel of the entertainment industry."

Personally, however, Nash and Perelman formed an enduring friendship. Perelman later recalled the setting in which he and Nash labored as a "ramshackle structure," known officially as the "New Writers Building" but referred to by its occupants as the "Neuritis or Neuralgia Building." Nash and Perelman soon discovered that they were both devotees of Sherlock Holmes, and while vainly awaiting inspiration on the script, they began to develop an intricate quiz that might even have commercial possibilities. Other distractions were also close at hand. One was a writer across the hall who spent all day talking into the tube of a recording device while wearing "a very strange aluminum contraption, like an inverted cocktail shaker, the purpose of which was to stimulate his scalp and hopefully generate the growth of hair." Even more entertaining, Perelman claimed, was looking out the window to note the daily arrival of two of Irving Thalberg's minions sneaking into Thalberg's villa to plot the overthrow of the Screenwriters Guild.

Perelman was active in the Guild, and his wife, Laura, served on its executive board. The Guild had been formed in 1933 when screenwriters' wages had been cut, and feelings had improved little since then. The screenwriter Albert Hackett, a founder of the Guild and later a close friend of Nash's, once quipped that Louis B. Mayer had "created more communists than Karl Marx." A bitter dispute with the Guild had arisen in 1936, just before Nash's arrival, but he could have observed the comings and goings at the Thalberg villa for only a very short time: Thalberg, who had always suffered from frail health, contracted a cold over Labor Day, 1936, and died within days. Unlike his friends, Nash did not participate actively in the Guild or become involved in its politics. As he later recalled, "In my Hollywood years I was regarded as a harmless fascist, and my friends in the East dismissed me as a parlor pink."

Thalberg's death was the end of an era for Hollywood, and it briefly complicated Nash's situation: after *How to Win Friends* was abandoned, others had the task of finding a niche for his talents. The studio's deliberations resulted in a major assignment—to write the screen adaptation of a musical, *The Firefly*, that had been successfully produced on Broadway in 1912. The film was to star Jeanette MacDonald, who had already made three enormously popular films with Nelson Eddy. The very success of the MacDonald-Eddy musicals provided the inspiration for MGM to split up the team, at least temporarily, to see if they might produce two hits rather than one. As a result, Jeanette went into *The Firefly*, her first solo starring movie, while Nelson Eddy appeared in *Rosalie* with Eleanor Powell.

Nash was initially told that he could do anything he wanted and that only the music, by Rudolf Friml, would be retained. By early October,

Nash had completed a scenario set in New York in 1900. A month later he was joined by two other writers, Claudine West and Alice Duer Miller, and the setting was shifted to Napoleonic Spain. In December 1936, Nash wrote his mother, resigned but amused: "*Firefly* marches on—Jeanette MacDonald is now on the point of single-handedly driving Napoleon out of Spain, pausing only to sing 'When a maid comes knock-knock-knocking at your heart.'"

The producer of *The Firefly* was Hunt Stromberg, whom Sid Perelman had found almost as difficult to work with as he had Thalberg (he claimed that he endured Stromberg's endless story conferences by watching the producer's shoes untie themselves as he paced back and forth attempting to light his expensive pipe). Stromberg was also the producer of *Maytime*, and at one point Nash was briefly transferred from *The Firefly* to work on that film. While it does not appear that he ever suffered personally at the hands of Stromberg, one of his letters recounted sadly the experience of a fellow scriptwriter, Noel Langley, the principal writer for *Maytime*. Langley had been leaving to spend a long-anticipated weekend with the Gershwins "when Stromberg called and said he wanted him to read the play of *Pride and Prejudice* aloud to him at 3 this afternoon; really a pretty hard blow." Nash provided what consolation he could by inviting Langley to supper and a movie that night.

Ultimately the lead writing credit for *The Firefly* went to two of Hollywood's most talented scriptwriters, the husband-and-wife team of Frances Goodrich and Albert Hackett. The Hacketts were not only the writers of *The Thin Man* but had adapted *Naughty Marietta* and *Rose Marie*. Later they would also write the scripts for many highly acclaimed films, including *It's a Wonderful Life*, *Easter Parade*, and *The Diary of Anne Frank*. In a 1976 interview they recalled that they had been unable to develop a story for *The Firefly*, but that after Nash and Alice Duer Miller had written a story, they were successful in adapting it as a screenplay. In this instance, Hollywood's convoluted team system seemed to have functioned. The result, however, was not among the Hacketts' more distinguished films, and to the extent anyone noted Nash's contribution, it did not do much for his reputation. (The *New York Herald Tribune* review observed that "Mr. Nash's revamping of the original book has added nothing in the way of dramatic substance.")

Again, however, the collaboration was highly successful on a personal level. The Hacketts became good friends, and Nash once said that if it hadn't been for them, he probably would have left Hollywood. Although the Hacketts were aware of Nash's discomfort at the studio, they enjoyed his company. As Albert Hackett said, "We hung onto him. He was a great lifesaver for everybody. . . . He was lovely and amusing and fun. . . . The people who came to our house were always hanging around him." In addition to spending time with Nash socially, the Hacketts tried to look out for his interests at the studio, but they were sometimes frustrated by their friend's lack of assertiveness. As Frances Hackett put it: "At a conference, I'm a screamer, and you know, here would Ogden be, shy and silent, and you thought, 'Oh God, you are so good, you're so wonderful, you're worth all of us, why don't you yell?'" But to have done so, of course, would have been quite foreign to Nash's personality.

While *Firefly* was experiencing its several metamorphoses, Linell and Isabel traveled to California and the Nash family settled into a rented house at 348 Canyon View Drive in Brentwood Heights. It was to be the first of several rental houses that the family would occupy since, under the prevailing practice, Nash worked under a series of five-month contracts and thus felt able to enter into only short-term leases. In November he wrote to Dan Longwell, congratulating him on the first issue of *Life* magazine and noting wryly that it was "by far the most important step in the elimination of you know—words." The letter also reflected that Nash was still getting used to his new environment: "I'm still distinctly a rookie; probably need a season or two at Republic or Invincible before taking the field as a regular in this league."

In January, Nash flew home to be with his mother who had fallen into a comatose condition and was thought to be dying. Nash was a reluctant air traveler at best. Six years before, in *Hard Lines*, the verse "No, You Be a Lone Eagle" had revealed his qualms about aviation. In this case the flight would have tested the resolve of even hardier flyers. Nash described it in a letter to Frances from Cincinnati, where the plane had been grounded and the passengers advised to complete their journey by rail: "Except for the first hour last night, and about an hour today, we flew continuously through fog so thick you couldn't see beyond the wing tip. . . . I took two luminols last night, and got to sleep about twelve, waking to find that we had been on the ground for three hours at Big Springs, Texas, waiting for the fog to clear enough so we could get down at Fort Worth. The pilots are marvelously skillful; but even so, it was a bit uncomfortable. Incidentally, everybody on the plane but me was sick. I am quite looking forward to the B & O."

Ironically, by the time Nash reached Baltimore, his mother had regained consciousness and subsequently recovered. Her sudden illness was never explained satisfactorily. Nash's daughter Linell later noted that it was at that time that a nurse, Beryl Summers, was engaged and maintained a careful watch over the sedative bottles.

Nash's flight, however, had been a formative experience. Despite his understatement ("a bit uncomfortable"), his minor triumph of not having become sick was small consolation. The experience made such an impression on him that, for the rest of his life, he would never again travel by air. Even years later, when air travel had become routine, Nash was not persuaded. In "Come, Come Kerouac, My Generation Is Beater Than Yours," he insisted:

> Progress may have been all right once, but it went on too long;
> I think progress began to retrogress when Wilbur and Orville
>   started tinkering in Dayton and at Kitty Hawk, because I
>   believe that two Wrights made a wrong.

In April, Frances returned to Baltimore to visit her family and for routine trips to the doctor and dentist. Nash's letters to her equaled those of his courtship years in ardor and expressions of his unhappiness at being without her. His loneliness, however, was eased to a degree by the companionship of Linell and Isabel. He wrote Frances that they had undertaken to cheer him up one evening by role-playing: Isabel was Frances and Linell her mother, who delighted in calling him "Ogden." ("Now, Ogden, the children are asleep. We'll all go to that movie about May, and then we'll go to a ball, and after the ball we'll go to the beach and watch the moon on the water. Oh and we mustn't forget Will, must we, Ogden? But I expect Will has a key and can get in all right. Frances, don't crawl around hunting for treasure; it isn't dignified.")

Meanwhile, despite the somewhat chaotic history of *Firefly*, Nash still seemed enthusiastic about the film. He wrote Frances that filming had begun on her birthday, and that "the first rushes are magnificent." Later that month he wrote, "It's really very exciting to see all the *Firefly* costumes around. MacDonald looks very handsome, and Allen Jones not too silly." At the same time his loneliness was painfully clear: "I loathe living in the god damned vacuums. How many times have we said never again? I love you, I need you, I adore you, and I am yours for more than ever."

While Frances was in Baltimore, Nash was lining up another house. It was on Linden Drive in Beverly Hills and rather grand: five bedrooms and three maid's rooms, with a library and study, all complemented by an attractive patio, pool, and garden. It was furnished, Nash said, "as if nice people had lived in it," and rented for $750 a month. Although the Nashes leased the house for a few months, by November they had moved again to a smaller and more economical home at 733 Malcolm Avenue in Westwood. Linell Smith's principal recollection of the Malcolm Avenue house is that she was disappointed at not being allowed to swim in the basement when it filled with water during a heavy rain. She and Isabel and their nanny, Delia, were sent to a hotel while Ogden and Frances remained behind, without fresh water or electricity. Hearing that her parents had brushed their teeth in ginger ale and read by candlelight, Linell "was very envious and felt extraordinarily deprived."

The move to a smaller house may have been occasioned by uncertainty about the future, for at that point Nash did not have a film assignment. He had been reduced to sitting in the office waiting for the telephone to ring, or taking on brief projects, such as a radio sketch for Myrna Loy on the MGM Maxwell House radio program. During slow periods Nash might well have occupied himself by writing verse, but he did not. The year before, when he had completed some advertising verse for Otard Brandy, he had been looking forward to magazine work and hoping it would not cause a problem with the studio: "I'm having a slight disagreement with the studio about my right to do outside work—I think it will end happily, but if so I think maybe I'd better show up again in *The Post* and *The New Yorker*. And oh yes, Mr. Hearst wants me again, with two poems a week."

The extent to which Nash was contractually prevented from writing verse for magazines is not clear. Thirteen new Nash poems were published in 1937–1938, and all but two were written before, or just after, Nash's arrival in Hollywood. (The two, both for *The New Yorker*, were not listed in Nash's personal journal, so it is hard to say when they were written.) On the other hand, even if Nash had not been permitted to write for immediate publication, he could hardly have been constrained from writing for future publication in the privacy of his own office. In fact Nash's journal lists six poems written in April and May 1938 but never published. When he returned to Baltimore in November 1938, after his first tour in Hollywood, he blamed the Hollywood atmosphere, rather than contractual restraints, for his failure to write verse while he was not occupied with screenwriting: "I don't know why it is, but in spite of all the time they have on their hands there isn't an author in Hollywood that gets anything worth while done outside of his motion picture assignments. Maybe it's the weather, maybe it's the studio atmosphere, maybe it's just plain laziness—but the fact remains you simply don't get anything done in all those long hours you sit around waiting for the phone to ring."

For a time Nash enjoyed being in a state of comfortable and well-compensated inactivity. But it soon became monotonous. He found himself putting on weight and tried his hand at the popular pastime of badminton: "takes up a lot of time and it's healthy too." The monotony was also relieved by a circle of friends and acquaintances whom the Nashes enjoyed. In addition to the Hacketts, their close friends included Edgar Ward, who, it turned out, had been "le Harvard" whom Frances had met on her 1930–1931 trip to Europe. Ward was now living in California with his wife, the actress Jane Wyatt. Wyatt had made her film debut in *Lost Horizon* as Sondra, the beautiful European schoolteacher in Shangri-La with whom Conway (Ronald Colman) falls in love. Another friend from the East, Ben Ray Redmond, formerly with the *Saturday Review*, had migrated to Hollywood and was married to the actress Frieda Inescort.

Through the Hacketts, the Nashes met Tony and Laura Veiller. Tony Veiller was an experienced and successful screenwriter and someone to whom, along with the Hacketts, Nash could turn for professional advice. They became good friends, and on one visit to the Veiller ranch Nash's wit broke through his shyness in a quite public way. The setting was a rodeo that the Nashes attended with Laura and Tony and several other friends who were weekend guests at the Veiller ranch. The star attraction at the rodeo was a cowboy and his wife and young son, who were given an introduction that proclaimed: "This is Monty Montana who is a great example to American young men and young women. He has never smoked a cigarette, he has never touched liquor." Before he could say the next line, Ogden's voice rang out over the bleachers, "And that little boy is adopted." The incident was widely recounted and appeared in the *Hollywood Reporter*, giving Nash more local fame than his screenwriting had.

Perhaps the best known of the Nashes' Hollywood friends were F. Scott Fitzgerald and Sheilah Graham. Indeed, Nash once quipped that he was the only person to have known Fitzgerald and not written a book about it. The Nashes had been acquainted with Fitzgerald in Baltimore, and Fitzgerald had also known Frances's father, Will Leonard, through their

mutual friend, Andrew Turnbull. Fitzgerald's two earlier trips to Hollywood, in 1927 and 1931, had not been successful, and when he returned in
1937, Nash was among the familiar and friendly faces from the East that he
looked to for reassurance.

By 1937, Fitzgerald was making a serious attempt to reconstruct his personal and professional life: his wife, Zelda, was in a sanitarium; his last
book, *Tender Is the Night*, had enjoyed only modest success; and his career
as a writer was widely thought to be over. When the invitation to Hollywood came from Eddie Knopf, the story editor at MGM, Fitzgerald felt he
had been given a miraculous reprieve. He was not drinking. Anita Loos,
who had known Scott during his great days in the twenties, observed that
he had "that unhealthy humility of the reformed alcoholic." When
Fitzgerald arrived at MGM in 1937 he took lunch alone in the commissary
until the Hacketts persuaded him to join the long table known as the Writers' Table. There he joined the Hacketts, Nash, and assorted other writers,
including Dorothy Parker, George Oppenheimer, and S. J. Perelman.
Nash would later recall Fitzgerald "at lunch with his Coca Cola," where
he was "very quiet indeed but extremely attractive with a sweet nature that
came through."

Groucho Marx sometimes added a disruptive presence at the Writers'
Table. According to Nash, Marx "turned things upside down so that you
couldn't have a coherent conversation—everything had to be a joke."
Fitzgerald remained silent through Groucho's jokes and monologues, and
his silence was not appreciated. Scott and Groucho had been neighbors in
Great Neck during the party days of the twenties, but Fitzgerald now
seemed to Marx "a sick, old man—not very funny stuff."

Fitzgerald's diminished confidence ebbed still lower when Ernest
Hemingway arrived in Hollywood to raise funds for the embattled Spanish Republic. He had brought with him the final cut of a motion picture,
The Spanish Earth, that he had made with Lillian Hellman and Archibald
MacLeish. After a benefit showing attended by the Hollywood elite,
Fitzgerald gave Miss Hellman a ride to Dorothy Parker's where Hemingway and others would celebrate his success. When they arrived, Fitzgerald
did not want to go in—his relationship with Hemingway had been
strained for several years, and he did not care to face him at a time of personal failure. Hellman nevertheless bullied Fitzgerald into the house just
as Hemingway threw a glass against Parker's fireplace. Whatever confidence Fitzgerald had gathered was shattered with the glass—he stayed

only a few moments and left without speaking to Hemingway. A few days later, at the studio, he confided to Nash, "It's no use writing so long as Ernest is around."

Life was not all melancholy for Fitzgerald. He began work on the screenplay for *A Yank at Oxford* and, even more important, he met Sheilah Graham. Miss Graham was a Hollywood gossip writer whose life was perhaps more interesting than the book she wrote about it, *Beloved Infidel.* She had been born in 1904 into the lowest strata of English society as Lily Sheil. After spending much of her youth in an orphanage, she made her way to London and a job in a department store. From there her considerable beauty and native intelligence propelled her successively into marriage to Major John Graham Gillian, careers as a showgirl and a journalist for the *Daily Mail*, and, improbably enough, acceptance by London society. She came to Hollywood in 1935 as a gossip columnist for the North American Newspaper Alliance, arriving with the stage name she had used in London, fashioned from her husband's middle name and her own last name.

In 1937, Sheilah Graham ended what had become a marriage of convenience with her husband and became engaged to an admirer of long-standing, the Marquess of Donegall. On July 17 an engagement party began at her house and, when the neighbors complained of noise, moved to Robert Benchley's bungalow at the Garden of Allah. It was there that she met Scott Fitzgerald, who was occupying a nearby bungalow in the same complex. When Lord Donegall returned to London, a romance with Fitzgerald ensued, and the engagement to Donegall was terminated within weeks.

The Garden of Allah was a residential hotel and complex of bungalows that was, at various times over the years, home to a remarkable number of talented writers and actors, including, among many others, Dorothy Parker, Marc Connelly, John O'Hara, Greta Garbo, John Barrymore, Errol Flynn, and Humphrey Bogart. The Nashes were no strangers to the Garden of Allah, and Nash stayed there briefly in 1939. In a book recounting the history of the hotel, Graham included Nash among those whose presence, either as a resident or regular visitor, had prompted Fitzgerald to move there: "It would be private and yet he could, at a moment's notice, be with the people he knew—Ogden Nash, S. J. Perelman, Nat West (Sid's brother-in-law), Donald Ogden Stewart, Robert Benchley, Dorothy Parker and Eddie Mayer." Graham also recalled being with Ogden and Frances in Benchley's bungalow during the big flood of 1938. "Fitzgerald came in very excited and told us 'there are bodies floating down the river under the Warner Brothers bridge and Jack Warner's body is leading them.' Then he exploded into laughter."

A favorite pastime of the revelers at the Garden, perhaps second only to drinking, was charades. At first Sheilah Graham declined to participate. Her remarkable rise through English society had been accomplished without a comprehensive education, and she was well aware of her limitations. But Fitzgerald took on the job of tutoring her in a broad range of subjects, and Graham experienced an unusual graduation by joining Dorothy Parker's team at charades. As described by her son, Robert Westbrook:

> It was a premeditated act, carefully rehearsed, the summation of months of work. Scott had done his Svengali magic, transforming her almost into a cultured young woman. This was the test. She was nervous but he assured her that charades was nothing; her life had been a charade beyond other people's imagination. At the last moment, he spent several hours briefing her on the definition of the pronoun, because, as he told Sheilah, "at charades, they always ask, 'Is it a pronoun?'"
>
> Ogden Nash guessed almost immediately that Sheilah was acting out a period of art history, Picasso's Blue Period, and Sheilah had rarely felt so happy to be found out in her life.

Fitzgerald admired Nash's verse. In a letter to his daughter, Scottie, in 1938, he admonished her for an inferior Nash imitation that she had rendered and offered his own evaluation of his friend's technique: "Ogden Nash's poems are not careless, they all have an extraordinary inner rhythm. They could not possibly be written by someone who in his mind had not calculated the feet and meters to the last iambus or trochee. His method is simply to glide a certain number of feet and come up smack against his rhyming line. Read over a poem of his and you will see what I mean."

Fitzgerald, however, was not above his own attempts at imitation. On one occasion Scott and Sheilah had been invited to a dinner party at the Hacketts that Sheilah was very much looking forward to. At the last minute Fitzgerald was summoned to an evening conference with Stromberg, on the film *Marie Antoinette*. In order to break the news to Sheilah after they had arrived at the Hacketts', he wrote a poem in Ogden Nash style—explaining the call and that he would have to leave her alone

at the party—and read it to her. And the following day he wrote a poem
in similar style to the Hacketts by way of apology:

> Sing a song for Sheilah's supper, belly void of rye;
> Gone before the cocktail, back for the pie.
> Stromberg sent for Poppa, though Papa hadn't et,
> To do what Jesus couldn't—
> Save Marie Antoinette. . . .

On another occasion Fitzgerald autographed a copy of *The Great Gatsby*
for the Hacketts and dashed off another poem that concluded, ("Writing
this way is rash/ In the presence of Ogden Nash").

Imitation was something that Nash was forced to endure throughout
his career. It came not only from other writers but from friends and admirers and frequently from reviewers. Such imitations rarely matched the
caliber of the original. Understandably, Nash sometimes chafed at the
imitation—after all, if just anyone could produce verse in the Nash manner, it would inevitably undermine the value of his work. Ironically Nash
was, in a sense, sometimes guilty of imitating his own work. He had the
gift of coming up with rhymed couplets on the spur of the moment, to in-
scribe a book to a friend or a complete stranger, or just to amuse friends.
Inevitably his spontaneous verses varied in quality. While some appeared
as polished as any that he had labored over for publication, others were
distinctly not. Whatever their quality, they seldom failed to charm and
delight the recipient, and the Nashes' friends in Hollywood were no exception. Thus, though Nash wrote little verse for publication while in
Hollywood, he continued to scribble couplets for his own and his friends'
amusement. For Laura and Tony Veiller (pronounced "Vayay") he inscribed *The Bad Parents' Garden of Verse*

> For Laura and Tony Veiller
> To remind them of their infant
>> While far awayay.

And, later, written at a party:

> For Tony and Laura
> Good Friends from Gomorrah
>> May 24, 1938   9 p.m.

followed by

> Postscript
> Or if you're in sodom
> Call Tony and Modom
> May 24, 1938   11:20 p.m.

For his West Coast agent, Corny Jackson, Nash inscribed a book

> Better than vaccinated
> I'm Corny Jacksonated

For the Hacketts, inscribing *I'm a Stranger Here Myself*:

> Everyone in Hollywood is nothing but cod or halibut,
> Compared to Frances and Alibut.

Regrettably, Nash never focused his satirical eye on the Hollywood scene, at least for publication. Corny Jackson recalled one poem, "Oh Zanucksville," that "took Twentieth Century Fox from stem to stern and cut it to ribbons," but the only copy was lost.

Badminton, the companionship of interesting friends, and dashing off the odd couplet here and there obviously could not long sustain anyone with Nash's energy and ambition. Realizing this, the Hacketts maneuvered behind the scenes at the studio to get work for him. Nash insisted that he had not asked them to do so: "I told them not to go to any trouble on my account. After all, I'd only been in Hollywood a little over a year. I was a comparative newcomer. There were writers there who had been playing badminton for two or three years. But you know how friends are. They went right ahead with their plotting—and, sure enough, my phone finally rang."

In the spring of 1938, Nash was assigned to work on *The Wizard of Oz*. After only a month he was released and became one of more than a dozen writers whose contributions to the film went uncredited. Later that year he worked on two less memorable pictures, *Hold That Kiss* and *The Shining Hour*. He completed a screenplay for the latter film in collaboration with an experienced screenwriter, Jane Murfin. Murfin had worked on screenplays for several films, and in 1939 she would replace Scott Fitzgerald to write the screenplay for Clare Boothe's *The Women*. This time, however, the Hollywood system did not deal kindly with her work with Nash. After months of joint effort had resulted in a product that Nash felt was at least respectable, the entire script was rewritten by producer Joseph Mankiewicz in a period of twenty-four hours.

That experience was far from unique. Mankiewicz gave similar treatment to the script that Fitzgerald had written for *Three Comrades.* Fitzgerald, who had formed a strong dislike for the producer (referring to him as "Monkeybitch"), protested vigorously and in writing, but to no avail. Confrontation was not in Nash's repertoire; he licked his wounds more quietly. When he returned to Baltimore late in 1938, it was reported—with perhaps unrecognized irony—that when Nash saw the movie he was "gratified to hear quite a few lines of dialogue exactly as he had written them."

As time went on, Nash seemed less able to deal with the unique pressures of working as a scriptwriter. Linell Smith has recounted that her father was not only unhappy with his professional situation, but his health, both physical and emotional, was beginning to decline. He consistently ran a low-grade fever and once woke her mother asking frantically, "Frances, who am I?" Seeing the effect on Ogden that life in Hollywood was having, Frances urged him to give it up. This, according to Linell, gave Nash a graceful way out: "He wasn't quitting—he was doing it for mother." Years later Nash recalled that his stint in Hollywood had "almost destroyed" him. When he returned to Baltimore, his aim was to recapture his old form. He wrote to Harold Ross that he hoped to spend most of the following year "writing verse, if I haven't lost the knack." Even then he was careful not to burn any bridges, and resolved only that any future Hollywood tours would last not more than six months.

In January 1939, Ogden and Frances traveled to Europe. Although his future livelihood was uncertain, it seemed the right time for a break, particularly since the growing threat of war suggested that the opportunity might not soon come again. In March, after the Nashes returned from Europe, Ogden left for—Hollywood. This time it was not for the film studios but for a radio appearance arranged by Corny Jackson. Traveling as usual by train, Nash used the trip to write material for the radio program. But he told Frances that he was still impatient to get to work on "my own stuff" and vowed that he would have at least two good verses to show her on his return.

En route to the West Coast, Nash wrote to Frances with his usual fervor of his loneliness without her. But he had scarcely returned to Baltimore when he headed westward once again for more radio appearances on the Chase and Sanborn Hour. Frances had intended to accompany him on this trip, but became ill the day before, so Ogden was on his own again. He stayed briefly at the Garden of Allah before moving in with the Hacketts for the remainder of his three-week stay. He dined with the Hacketts, George Oppenheimer, and Scott Fitzgerald and Sheilah Graham. He also saw Joe Mankiewicz, who told Nash that in the future he wanted to make only good pictures and that he had a *good* picture in mind for him.

The invitation from Mankiewicz came the following year, in November 1940. Ogden and Frances left almost immediately, and after a week at the Garden of Allah moved to an apartment in Beverly Hills. Nash's agreement with MGM was just what he wanted: it guaranteed him five weeks of work but obligated him for no more than ten. The film was called *The Female of the Species*. As Nash wrote his friend Bruce Gould, editor of the *Ladies' Home Journal*, the plot concerned "a professor of psychology who understands women until he marries Hedy Lamarr," and added, "Shall we all not exclaim Oh boy?"

Once again, however, Nash's career as a screenwriter would go awry. Just before Christmas he came down with the flu. By year's end he felt better and wrote to Dan and Mary Longwell that he expected to finish work on the picture within weeks. But the illness continued and grew worse, and Nash's friend George Oppenheimer assumed principal responsibility for the script. (The film was issued in 1941 under the title *The Feminine Touch*, starring Rosalind Russell rather than Hedy Lamarr, and received mildly enthusiastic reviews.) Meanwhile Nash had been hospitalized and given extensive tests. Ultimately he showed positive on a tuberculin test, though his lungs were not involved and he was not thought to be contagious. Upon doctors' advice he returned to Baltimore in late February for further treatment and rest. Although he did not know it, his career as a screenwriter was over—but his best days in the world of show business were yet to come.

7

AT HOME IN BALTIMORE

In the years before World War II, Baltimore was a rather old-fashioned place, "fundamentally a city with a British background and British social customs." Baltimore Society—with a capital "S"—was defined by subtle and complex criteria, including registration at the correct stationer's shop on Charles Street. The most important factor, of course, was family. A 1968 book, *The Amiable Baltimoreans*, made the point with a story concerning one Rebecca Shippen, whose veins were said to carry the bluest blood in Maryland:

> She was sitting one afternoon with a friend over a cup of tea. "Rebecca," inquired the friend, "did it occur to you that if Our Lord had come to Baltimore we wouldn't have met him, since his father was a carpenter?"
>
> "But, my Dear," replied Mrs. Shippen, "you forget. He was well connected on his mother's side."

In Baltimore, the book observed, "it is essential to be 'well-connected' on one side or the other, if not both."

Despite her youthful regrets at not having been a native Baltimorean, Frances was herself rather well connected. She had, after all, been invited to the very exclusive Bachelors' Cotillion—the annual affair at which debutantes were presented and which gave rise to stories "of girls whose lives have been ruined and who have carried the scar to the grave because they were not invited to the cotillion." For Nash's part, his Southern background and Revolutionary War antecedents eased his own acceptance by Baltimore Society. And it didn't hurt that he was willing to contribute verse to local causes from the Children's Aid Society to the more light-hearted Turtle Derby at Johns Hopkins Hospital. The Derby, a burlesque of the Preakness, was staged each year by doctors, nurses, and convalescents at the hospital and, as an occasion of social importance, rivaled the real event at nearby Pimlico. In the spring of 1940, Nash was in the hospital for a week, being tested for allergies, and was asked if he would write a poem to help publicize the event. He requested only a pencil and paper and quickly produced a verse beginning "Oh come to the Turtle Derby/ Or is it the Turtle Darby?/ Where the terrapins leap as swiftly/ As the fingers of Senor Iturbi."

Nash had little time for elaborate socializing and was far more concerned with regaining his momentum as a writer. He did have the advantage of working in quite comfortable surroundings at the house on Rugby Road. Mrs. Leonard had given the house to Frances when she and Ogden returned from Hollywood in 1938. Although the Leonards continued to live there, it would be Ogden and Frances's home for the next several years. While the gift was to Frances, it also reflected the remarkable bond between Nash and his mother-in-law. In his rather formal way, Nash always addressed his in-laws as "Mr. and Mrs. Leonard," even as Linell and Isabel spoke to them on their own terms as "Minnie" and "Boppy." But the formality of address did not disguise the warmth of Nash's feeling for Mrs. Leonard. In 1945 he would dedicate *Many Long Years Ago* to her with a poem, "For N.J.L.," that candidly expressed his feelings:

In June of 1931
She gained a moody, broody son,
While he acquired with loud hurrah,
A calm and understanding ma.
Because she never tried to change him,
Reform, reprove or rearrange him,
But gave him only love and wisdom
And in her kingdom freedom was hisdom
In '45 he can but purr
And dedicate this book to her.

Others in the family felt that Nellie Leonard could be manipulative, and that Nash's view of her may have been, in its own way, as idealized as his vision of Frances. Nevertheless, Nash's admiration was unquestionably sincere. On the other hand, his relations with his father-in-law were not as warm, though they never approached actual conflict which to Nash would have been almost unthinkable.

The Rugby Road house was a large and attractive home. The first floor included a library paneled in wood from a colonial house on the Eastern Shore of Maryland that had once belonged to the Jackson family, and the living and dining rooms had many special fittings, including marble mantels. Nash did his writing in the library except during the war years when it was closed to conserve fuel and he was relegated to the sitting room upstairs. Still, the yellow legal pads on which he liked to write often migrated to the living room coffee table, and his notes to himself—possible subjects for future poems, intriguing rhyme combinations that might prove useful—appeared on scratch pads by the telephone or on grocery lists or old envelopes.

On the second floor, at the west end, the Nashes' bedroom suite consisted of a bedroom, dressing/sitting room, bath, and a little upstairs porch from which they could feed the birds. At the other end of a long hall was Mr. Leonard's room and bath. On the south side of the hall were Mrs. Leonard's bedroom, the bedroom shared by Linell and Isabel, and the bedroom for Delia Ratigan, who was initially Isabel's nurse and later served as a maid for both girls. Each of the bedrooms had a full bath, and three of the bedrooms (each of the Leonards' and the girls') had fireplaces. Across the hall on the second floor was an office/sewing room where Frances kept a desk and a typewriter on which she typed many of Ogden's poems. The third floor contained three maid's rooms and a playroom for the children.

The house was well staffed with servants. Both Ogden and Frances had grown up with the attendance of servants. It was a tradition they would perpetuate even after World War II, when the employment of domestic help became less common. And it endured even during the times when Nash felt financially pinched. That way of life may have been attributable not only to Nash's romanticized picture of Frances, as someone who should not be found "slaving in the kitchen," but also out of some sense of obligation. Indeed, Isabel's husband, Fred, who had also grown up in a household with a domestic staff, was struck by the fact that, unlike the tradition in his own home, the Nash servants were thought of in many ways as members of the family.

At Rugby Road, the most important servants, in addition to Delia, were Carrie Custis and Clarence Collins. Carrie, the cook, was a native of Salisbury, Maryland, who had come to work for Mrs. Leonard after her mother's death. Clarence had originally worked for the Jackson family but joined the Nashes in 1933, when Isabel was born, as cook, butler, and chauffeur. At Rugby Road he served as butler and chauffeur. Although he was handicapped in the latter role by an inability to read and the lack of a driver's license, these were deficiencies that his employers were somehow willing to overlook for many years.

The house on Rugby Road was situated on grounds that left the Nash children with memories they would carry for a lifetime. Even decades later, Linell would recall them in detail:

> The grounds were created for enjoyment. A walled flagstone terrace ran the full length of the house. In warm weather we often had breakfast there, sitting under an arbor of wisteria and climbing roses. The garden below was also walled. There was an aquamarine-tiled fish pool, replete in summer with large, lazy goldfish who, at the first touch of frost, were brought indoors in bowls for winter comfort. . . . [T]he front garden was the formal cutting garden; to the east was another enclosed yard with apple trees and several pines. To the west lay the wilder shade garden. Hundreds of my grandmother's prizewinning daffodils nodded from periwinkle-covered slopes that ran down to the end of the property. Huge oaks stood in this area as well as one cherry tree, which was solemnly covered each year with a bridal veil of cheese-cloth to save the precious crop from greedy birds.

The house and grounds became the venue for children's games in which Nash was the principal instructor: Sardines, Red Rover, Red Light, Kick the Can, and even darts and mumblety-peg. Inside the house the girls learned how to slide down the wide banister, and outside, in the summertime, they would run under the spray from underground sprinklers. Inside the house and out, the girls' companion was Spangle, a Bedlington Terrier who would make her own appearance in "Please Pass the Biscuit." ("She's as much a part/ Of the house as the mortgage/ Spangle, I wish you/ A ripe old dortgage.")

Nash also introduced the girls to two of his favorite adult sports, baseball and horse racing. He had grown up a New York Giants fan, and Baltimore did not acquire a major league team until 1954 when the St. Louis Browns moved to Baltimore and became the Orioles. Before then, however, Baltimore was represented by the Orioles of the International League, one step below the majors. Frances was also a baseball fan, and the family frequently enjoyed outings to the ballpark where Nash revealed the mysteries of recording the game's progress by his intricate notations on a score card. At home Nash taught the girls how to play the game. Linell claimed that, by the time she left for boarding school at fifteen, she "could throw a blazing fast ball, a solid curve and zinger of a slider" but admitted that her "knuckleball still left much to be desired."

An interest in horse racing was a part of the Kentucky heritage that Nash had inherited from his mother. Her tutoring had sometimes turned to horses when the lessons in Latin had been completed. Nash was not a heavy bettor, but he enjoyed trips to Pimlico. Even if the day was a financial loss, it might provide the grist for a poem, as in "Hark! Hark! The Pari-mutuels Bark":

Why in the world must the horses run?
Or if they must, through a fate unholy,
Why must some of them run so slowly?
Brothers, the country's crying need
Is horses that run at an equal speed
And a stone-dead heat on every track
And every one getting their money back.

* * * *

Frances did not particularly enjoy horse racing, but Linell and Isabel, as well as Mrs. Leonard, often accompanied Nash to the Pimlico racetrack. In Isabel's case, racing was a pastime of transitory interest, but for Linell racing and horses became a passion that would shape her adult life.

On the more intellectual side, Nash immersed the girls in words and language. Dinnertime was an occasion for word games, and after dinner Nash would read to the girls almost every evening, most often from the classics such as Dickens, Kipling, or Dumas. And he worked, gently but implacably, to instill in his daughters his own respect for the English language. If they said "Thanks," he might reply "Welks" to elicit a proper "Thank you," which would receive, in turn, a proper "You're welcome." Another solecism that Linell recalls "drove him crazy" involved the past tense of "fit." Many years later he memorialized his objection in "Laments for a Dying Language":

Those authors I can never love
Who write, "It fit him like a glove."
Though baseballs may be hit, not "hitted,"
The past of "fit" is always "fitted."
The sole exception worth a *haricot*
Is "Joshua fit de battle ob Jericho."

Linell's and Isabel's religious instruction was considerably less formal than Nash's own had been as a young man. The Nashes attended the Episcopal Church of the Redeemer, where Ogden and Frances had been married, but Linell often accompanied Delia Ratigan to the Roman Catholic services at St. Phillip's and St. James's. The services, and Delia's faith, made a powerful impression on Linell, and many years later she would become a convert to Catholicism. Even before her conversion, Linell's third daughter, Brigid, born in 1956, was named after the saint whose name Delia had taken at her confirmation.

Although the Rugby Road house provided an atmosphere of genuine warmth, it was not a home of unrelieved tranquility. There were, to begin with, tensions between the Leonards rooted not only in the dominant economic position of Mrs. Leonard but in differing interests and tastes. As Linell and Isabel grew older, they became aware that, to some extent, Mr. Leonard lived a separate life, following his interests in music and the arts. At times he maintained a separate apartment, and there were rumors of extramarital liaisons. More important were the tensions that arose from Frances's sometimes difficult personality.

Frances shared Ogden's love of words and language—they sometimes worked on the Double Crostic together, and at dinner Frances joined in the word games as well as other games involving geography or history. On the other hand, dinner was much less pleasant if something had occurred to upset Frances. She could be a witty and charming companion but also a severe critic. Her displeasure, expressed in sarcastic comments or icy silence, could dominate the table, or indeed the entire house, until her mood passed.

Growing up as children, and later as mature adults, Linell and Isabel sometimes marveled (and sometimes despaired) at their father's remarkable ability to turn the other cheek. Isabel theorized that her father had found a way of rationalizing Frances's temperament. His wife, he believed, had suffered from the attitudes of her father, who, at least in Nash's eyes, was seen as rather selfish and heartless. In consequence, he was inclined to absolve Frances for her moods and insecurities and to place the blame with Will Leonard. Nash's method of coping, and his expressed response, was simply to be very gentle and quiet and to encourage Frances to be reasonable. Whatever his rationale, Nash followed far more ably than most men could, the advice he offered in "A Word to Husbands":

To keep your marriage brimming,
With love in the loving cup,
Whenever you're wrong, admit it;
Whenever you're right, shut up.

The only known instance of Nash ever raising his voice at Frances occurred when the family was returning from a vacation on Martha's Vineyard. The regular ferry was full, but the Nashes found a boat that was large enough to take their car, with a captain willing to undertake the trip despite rough seas. As the boat made its way toward the mainland, it began to list alarmingly, and the Nashes made a hasty exit from the car in fear it might slide overboard. The dog, Spangle, however, remained in the car. Nash was then alarmed to see Frances standing on the higher side of the deck and clinging desperately to the car as if to prevent it from slipping.

"Frances, for God's sake, let go of the car," he bellowed.

"Ogden, I can't," came the reply, "Spangle is in the car." The voyage was completed without disaster, but Nash had learned, perhaps, that raising his voice wouldn't do much good anyway.

The vicissitudes of married life were a frequent subject of Nash's verses, many of which were collected in a 1964 book, *Marriage Lines*, subtitled *Notes of a Student Husband*. Although some of his attitudes now seem rather dated, Nash was a fairly evenhanded observer of the marital condition. His outlook was far gentler than, say, that of his colleague, James Thurber: it reflected no hint of misogyny but rather conveyed a sense of a bemused affection. Nash delighted in exploring a large catalogue of feminine idiosyncrasies (a wife disparaging her own appearance, shopping sprees, keeping a husband waiting, the contents of a handbag). Nevertheless he showed in "The Trouble with Women Is Men," that he could see the other side as well:

A husband is a man who two minutes after his head
    touches the pillow is snoring like an overloaded
    omnibus,

Particularly on those occasions when between the
    humidity and the mosquitoes your own bed is no
    longer a bed but an insomnibus,
    *   *   *   *

Nor can he so much as wash his ears without leaving
    an inch of water on the bathroom linoleum,
But if you mention it you evoke not a promise to
    splash no more but a mood of deep melancholium.
    *   *   *   *

Although money was frequently a concern for Nash, it was not a point of contention in the family. In addition to the gift of the Rugby Road home from her mother, Frances had an income of her own from her grandmother. Nash, however, felt very strongly that he wanted to be able to support his family and not depend on Frances. The Leonards' marriage may have been a cautionary example in that regard, but it would only have strengthened Nash's instinctive feeling. His view of the economic relationship between men and women was perhaps reflected in one of his most widely quoted couplets from "I Do, I Will, I Have":

So I hope husbands and wives will continue to debate
    and combat over everything debatable and combatable,
Because I believe a little incompatibility is the spice
    of life, particularly if he has income and she is
    pattable.

Viewed from today's perspective, Nash's observation seems rather quaint and may provoke feelings of nostalgia in some and irritation in others. But it probably reflected a consensus at a time when the stirrings of women's liberation were yet to be heard.

Although Nash's commentaries on marriage were—like much of his verse—rooted in his own experience, they dealt with problems and foibles that would be readily recognized by many readers: that was the key to his popularity with a wide audience. On the other hand, his poems occasionally seemed to speak directly to the Nash union and to do so in a more serious voice. Frances's changeable moods and Ogden's devotion were both captured in "Always Marry an April Girl":

Praise the spells and bless the charms,
I found April in my arms.
April golden, April cloudy,

Gracious, cruel, tender, rowdy;
April soft in flowered languor,
April cold with sudden anger,
Ever changing ever true—
I love April, I love you.

Whatever frustrations Nash endured, his method of coping kept his married life on a relatively even keel that allowed him to get on with his work and regain his footing as a versifier. For two years, 1939 and 1940, he failed to make any record in his personal journal of the poems he wrote, but fifty of his poems were published in magazines during that time. In 1941, despite the convalescence from his Hollywood illness—requiring self-administered tuberculin shots—Nash published another forty-two poems. For purchasers of Nash books, the author reintroduced himself in 1940 with *The Face Is Familiar*, combining poems from earlier books with new verse; it was followed in 1942 by *Good Intentions*, comprised entirely of work previously unpublished in book form. Both volumes received enthusiastic reviews, with only one or two critics reluctantly suggesting that the quality of the poems was uneven. George F. Whicher, writing in the *Atlantic Monthly*, remarked that few readers would get far in *Good Intentions* "without coming upon just the poem they would take malicious pleasure in sending to So-and-so, or more probably, Mrs. So-and-so." In the *Saturday Review of Literature*, Louis Untermeyer began by saying that some of the poems in *Good Intentions* were far from Nash's best, but he then retreated to acknowledge that "he is at his best often enough . . . [a]nd when he is at his best there is none better, none quite as good." Thus, Untermeyer concluded, the reader should ignore his initial complaint. Thomas Sugrue in *New York Herald Tribune Books* found that *Good Intentions* revealed "a more mellow personality, a less subjective approach to life, and a deadlier, deeper wit." On the whole, it was clear that Nash had recovered from the Hollywood detour with no lasting injury to his talent or reputation.

Still, he had not entirely abandoned his thoughts of show business or even the Hollywood variety of the business. In a March 1941 letter to Dan Longwell, by now an editor at *Life*, Nash asked that a forthcoming article in the magazine omit any reference to his time in Hollywood, or refer to it only in very general terms, and include "no opinions of Hollywood I may have injudiciously mumbled." The point, Nash explained, was that he wanted "to be able to go back there sometime." Meanwhile he was about to become a performer in what might be described as a form of show business.

Nash made his debut on the lecture circuit on November 10, 1941, at Clark University in Worcester, Massachusetts. The following day, the *Worcester Daily Telegram* reported that it had been quite a successful appearance: Nash, it said, had "amazed the audience with his boyish looks and manner" and "displayed a quick and infectious verbal wit." From Worcester, Nash proceeded by train to Buffalo and then to Tulsa, Omaha, Fort Worth, Decatur, South Bend, and Lewisburg before returning to Baltimore on November 28. As chronicled in letters to Frances and in a long poem to Linell and Isabel, the trip appears fairly arduous, but for the most part Nash took it in stride. His friends, who viewed him as an essentially shy man, believed that he disliked being a performer. But many experienced performers are shy offstage or off-camera, and Nash's letters from this trip and many later ones do not reveal a serious discomfort at performing. On the contrary, they offer glimpses of a performer's delight at having appeared before an appreciative audience. ("Last night turned out to be a great success, a really warm and enthusiastic audience of 1200 who laughed in all the right places.") Nash was heartened to find, in autographing books, how many people in remote areas of the country had been reading his poems for years and had become his ardent fans.

He found the people whom he met on tour to be warm, friendly, and intelligent. There were, of course exceptions—for example, Nash's host in South Bend: "Mr. F___ dumped me gruffly at the hotel, returned to guide me to the auditorium, and when all was over, walked stiffly up to me and said he had enjoyed my talk and hoped I didn't mind his having gone out in the middle of it to throw up. I said No, not at all, I hoped it wasn't anything I said, and he said No he didn't think so, probably his wife's pecan pie, good night." Another letter included a quietly hilarious account of being dragged off by a gentleman in Tulsa to visit two young ladies ("medium attractive, and not very bright") with whom they "solemnly" drank a bottle of champagne before Nash was allowed to escape—alone—to his hotel. More typical were his impressions of a teacher in Coffeyville, Kansas, whom he met on his next tour: "I have found somebody like her almost everywhere I have been and they are wonderful people doing wonderful work; very much alive, always stimulated and stimulating, with a range of interests and ideas that makes me ashamed of my own stagnant complacency."

What Nash intensely disliked about the tour was his separation from Frances. He wrote to her almost daily, sometimes twice in the same day, describing in detail the people and places he'd seen. As the trip wore on, his loneliness was increasingly evident and his expressions of devotion became even more impassioned. ("[Y]ours is the beauty few men are given to know while they are alive; it is the beauty of the charmed and unattainable and irrecoverable past.") Nevertheless, the lectures provided welcome income and helped generate book sales. They would become an important part of Nash's life for many years.

Nash had scarcely returned from that first tour when the family was stunned by the devastating news of Pearl Harbor. Like most of their countrymen, the Nashes would have little difficulty in remembering just where they were when they heard the news. Ogden and Frances had taken the girls to a noon movie, and afterward, when they had gotten in the car to return, Ogden turned on the radio. Hearing the first report, Nash said only, "Dear God," and silently embraced Frances. The children were terrified, sensing that something awful had happened, but not understanding what it was. Frances spoke to them gently and invited them into the front seat, where both parents tried to explain the dreadful news and what it might mean.

As events developed, the impact of the war on the Nash family was not as devastating as it was on many others. At age thirty-nine, with poor eyesight and three dependents, Nash was not a likely candidate for combat. On the day after Pearl Harbor, he telegraphed Archibald MacLeish, who was already serving in Washington as director of the Office of Facts and Figures, seeking advice as to how he might best contribute. MacLeish immediately telegraphed a gracious reply but provided no useful information. Nash then attempted to join the navy, possibly to serve in naval intelligence or public relations, but a series of letters to the Navy Department in Washington and to the Fifth Naval District in Norfolk, Virginia, proved fruitless. After a time he was recruited by the Treasury Department to make war bond tours and write slogans and poems for the war effort.

On the bond tours, Nash joined other well-known writers, including Edna Ferber, Fannie Hurst, Louis Bromfield, and Dorothy Parker. Some years later the *New Yorker* writer E. J. Kahn recalled a particular tour he made through Pennsylvania with Nash and Dorothy Parker: "We visited schools, mostly, and at each one each of us would give a more or less set spiel—laced, we hoped with humor, and calculated in a low-key way to

instill patriotic fervor in our auditors. After we had been to three or four institutions, we could tell pretty well when to expect our listeners to laugh;
but this did not hold for parochial schools. The kids there would not laugh
until a nun laughed."

For Nash, the depths of frustration were reached in one large city
when, after the speeches had been delivered, Nash and his colleagues sat
at a long table, prepared to autograph any savings stamps that might be
bought from an adjoining booth. On that particular evening, sales were
slower than usual, and Nash was dismayed to learn the cause: "The public apathy was due not to our collective lack of glamour but to the fact that
the handsome and spellbinding mayor had established his pitch at the
other end of the hall and was handing out autographed photographs of
himself for free."

Despite such moments, the war bond tours were less arduous than
Nash's lecture circuit and at least provided him with amusing companions.
What he found less pleasurable were his assignments from the Treasury
Department to write patriotic poems. He was quite dissatisfied with those
he managed to produce, though three patriotic poems did find their way
into *Good Intentions*. At the end of the war, Nash received a letter from
Treasury official Julian Street, expressing his personal appreciation for
Nash's various efforts and crediting him with having helped to sell $170
million in war bonds. But Nash's unhappiness with his attempts at patriotic
verse left him with an enduring conviction that he should avoid trying to
deal with serious social or political issues. ("[E]very time I try to cope with
them I find myself writing bathos, and the side I'm trying to benefit would
be better off without this twelfth man on the field.") Although his view
seemingly undervalued a number of the poems he had written during the
depression, he would continue to maintain it, with relatively few exceptions, in later years.

Nash's other contribution to the war effort was through the distribution
of his verse to the troops. *I'm a Stranger Here Myself*, *Good Intentions*, and
a 1945 book, *Many Long Years Ago*, appeared in Armed Forces Editions. Although the books were quite popular, Nash enjoyed recounting the tale of
a serviceman who reacted to one of his books by writing to the author that
"perhaps if he lived to be eighty he could find something to laugh at in it
but that thank God was still fifty-five years off." A more admiring corre-
spondent said the books were swell but asked whether Nash had written
any books on love-letter writing: "I am overseas and it is very difficult to

write love-letters with everything these days being censored." The service-man could not have known that he was writing to so eloquent an author of love letters; there is no record of how Nash replied. Even more popular than Nash's books was his caustic poem "Four Prominent Bastards." It struck such a resonant chord with the GIs that Nash felt obliged to have hundreds of copies made and sent to the troops overseas.

Frances, meanwhile, was busy with hospital work for the Red Cross while Mrs. Leonard and the children made paper flowers to sell at war ral-lies, using war savings stamps as petals. The rationing of oil brought other changes to the house at Rugby Road. The living room and library were closed off, Nash worked in the upstairs sitting room, and the piano was moved into the hall stairwell so that piano practice could continue. Spam was served and blackouts observed. Gasoline rationing interrupted the pat-tern of vacations at Little Boar's Head, and in 1942 the Nashes spent the summer at the Jackson family farm, Rider's Trust, in Maryland. Ogden in-structed the girls in fishing and canoeing. Picnic lunches were sometimes taken to the little family graveyard where Linell and Isabel quizzed their grandparents about their forebears.

Despite the pleasures of Rider's Trust, Nash found himself growing in-creasingly depressed that summer. The dark days of 1942 were—even more than the depression—simply not congenial to writing light verse, and Nash felt himself growing stale. But what else could he do? The answer would come from a quite unexpected quarter.

8

ONE TOUCH OF VENUS

The remedy for Nash's wartime blues arrived in a letter from the composer Kurt Weill, inviting him to write the lyrics for a Broadway show. Nash had never met Weill but knew of his reputation and was immediately intrigued.

Weill's legendary collaboration with Bertolt Brecht, *The Threepenny Opera*, had been unsuccessful when it was initially produced in the United States in 1933. But Weill himself had come to the United States in 1935 and, once here, had settled down to work on Broadway musicals. Although his first show, *Johnny Johnson*, had failed, the second, *Knickerbocker Holiday*, enjoyed a modest run and had introduced one of Weill's most memorable ballads, the enduring "September Song." Weill's third musical, *Lady in the Dark*, with a book by Moss Hart and lyrics by Ira Gershwin, had been a hit.

In November 1941, Irene Sharaff, the costume designer for *Lady in the Dark*, told Weill of a novella, *The Tinted Venus*, written in the 1890s by an English humorist, Thomas Anstey Guthrie, under the name F. Anstey. Weill was fascinated by the book and tried to interest Ira Gershwin in adapting it for the musical theater. The novella, he wrote Gershwin, contained a "first-rate idea for a very entertaining and yet original kind of 'opera comique' on the Offenbach line." When Gershwin was unimpressed, Weill took the idea to Cheryl Crawford who had produced *Johnny Johnson*. Crawford, who had just enjoyed a major success in producing *Porgy and Bess*, quickly came to share Weill's enthusiasm for the Anstey novella. She hired Bella Spewak to write the book and then set out to find a lyricist. She later recalled that "someone suggested Ogden Nash. An inspired idea, we thought: he had the light touch with just the right social punch. It didn't particularly bother us that he'd never done lyrics."

Within days of receiving Weill's invitation, Nash was on his way to New York, carrying his clothes in a large, stiff suitcase. It was not large in order to carry many clothes, nor stiff to protect them, Nash explained, but "because a suitcase suitable for sitting on was a valuable adjunct to wartime travel." After meeting with Weill and Crawford, Nash told them that he'd like to think it over; but when he read the novella, he quickly agreed "to give it a whirl." His adventures in Hoboken with Chris Morley had kindled a love of the theater that had never been satisfied. Early on, he had talked to Richard Simon about his interest in working on a musical, and in 1935 he had put together material for a show to be entitled *Family Album*. Nothing had come of either venture or, in the end, of Nash's painful experiences in Hollywood. Still, the allure of show business remained. And a fresh project was just what he needed to renew his creative energies.

Nash began work on the show, now titled *One Touch of Venus*, in early 1942. By the fall he was spending considerable time working with Weill in New York or traveling to Weill's home in suburban New City. He enjoyed the collaboration and found that Weill had an excellent command of English, though a noticeable accent sometimes produced amusing results. When Nash asked the name of Weill's large English sheepdog, "Voolie," came the answer.

"Voolie?" repeated the puzzled Nash.

"Named after Alexander Voollcott," explained Weill.

On another occasion, linguistic confusion produced a brief impasse between composer and lyricist. Nash was trying to come up with the words for a Weill melody and suggested a title phrase, "Love-in-a-Mist." Nash thought the phrase—the name of a flower—was a fitting description of how Venus might have felt during a romantic moment in the show; Weill responded with cryptic but implacable opposition, and the title was eventually discarded. Only later did Nash discover that the English word "mist" is also the German word for manure.

Nash was struck by Weill's ability to write music for *Venus* even as he was working on an army training film for the Office of War Information. In an article written for the *New York Times*, Nash observed that "after working some six months with Kurt Weill, I still don't know where the music comes from. He has a piano, but he does not sit at it picking out melodies with one finger; he uses it for laying his pipe on before going out to chuck pebbles at the trout in the brook that runs past his window. He does not pace the floor in a brown study humming tum-ti-tum, tum-ti-tum until suddenly he claps his brow and his face is transfigured with ecstasy as another ballad is born. Nor is he ever to be found curled up in his favorite armchair poring over a dog-eared copy of Tschaikowsky." According to Nash, Weill put in a full day at OWI, then took the Weehawken ferry to the train for an hour's ride in a non-air-conditioned smoking car, and when he finally arrived home, would go to his desk and promptly turn out an enchanting melody.

During his work with Weill, Nash returned to Baltimore as often as possible, finding that separation from Frances was as painful as ever. In an October letter he wrote to her that he was trying to write a song for Vulcan with a theme that work is not a satisfactory substitute for love. He felt so deeply on this subject, Nash wrote, that he did not know whether he would produce "a masterpiece or a mouse." In the intervals between his trips to Baltimore, and visits by Frances to New York, Nash had at least the companionship of his old friends from Hollywood, the Hacketts and the Perelmans, who were now in New York.

While the melding of music and lyrics progressed, it became apparent that another aspect of the show had serious problems. Writing again in October, Nash told Frances that he would meet with Weill the following day to discuss "the disturbing matter of the book." Four months later, in February 1943, it was clear to all that the Bella Spewak libretto was not satisfactory and that a replacement would have to be found. That gave Nash the opportunity to recruit Sid Perelman to the project. They went to work together on the book at the Harvard Club on West Forty-fourth Street. The club, where Nash was a member on the strength of his one year at Harvard, is a somewhat cavernous building whose stately dining rooms and quiet lounges have spawned countless corporate mergers. It is less well known as a birthplace of Broadway productions, but the room where Nash and Perelman holed up to rewrite the book had a fitting tradition: it was one in which Robert Sherwood had written several of his plays.

Neither the Anstey original nor the Perelman/Nash version of the Venus story was encumbered by a serious plot. Indeed, as Nash observed, it was about as substantial as *Puss in Boots*. In both versions of *Venus*, a young and naive barber inadvertently brings to life a statue of Venus by placing on the statue's finger an engagement ring intended for the barber's fiancée. This leads to a brief, frantic, and ultimately unsuccessful romance between Venus and the barber. In the Perelman/Nash version, Anstey's London barber, Leander Tweddle, became Rodney Hatch of New York City. In both versions, Venus concludes—on the basis of abundant evidence—that life with Leander/Rodney would be unbearably prosaic. For *One Touch of Venus*, however, the choreographer Agnes de Mille suggested a charming final scene: Rodney meets a new girl who looks much like a country cousin of Venus but lives in the very housing development on Staten Island to which Rodney has aspired—Ozone Heights. The curtain falls on an upbeat ending as Rodney departs with the girl on his arm.

The character of Venus created by Perelman and Nash was sophisticated and sexy. The initial choice of Weill and Crawford to play Venus was Marlene Dietrich. Miss Dietrich, however, was reluctant. Whenever Weill and Crawford came to discuss the project, she sought refuge in her favorite instrument, the musical saw. As Crawford later wrote, "I was accustomed to many varieties of eccentric behavior from stars, but I must confess that when Marlene placed that huge saw between her elegant legs and began to play, I was more than a little startled. It was an ordinary saw about five feet in height and played with a violin bow. We would talk about the show for a while, then Marlene would take up the musical saw and begin to play; that, we soon found out, was the cue that the talk was finished for the evening."

Although Dietrich finally agreed to play Venus, the agreement did not hold. She considered the Perelman-Nash script to be "too sexy and profane" and expressed concern that showing her legs on stage might offend the sensibilities of her nineteen-year-old daughter. From today's perspective, her reaction seems curious indeed and is perhaps a measure of the cultural light-years that separate us from 1943. True, Venus does get to spend one night with Rodney in a hotel room. But contrary to current fashion, their activities together are left largely to the imagination of the audience. All in all, the raciness of *Venus* the script and Venus the role would surely not cause the quiver of an eyebrow in today's audience.

After Dietrich turned down the role of Venus, several actresses were considered, including Mary Martin. Martin had made a name for herself with a single number, "My Heart Belongs to Daddy," in Cole Porter's *Leave It to Me*, and had then left Broadway to make several films in Hollywood. But she doubted she was right for the role. At this point Weill came to Nash with a new melody that, Nash said, gave him the kind of spine tingle produced by "Begin the Beguine," "Old Black Magic," and Weill's own "September Song." "If we can find the right words for it," Weill said, "I think Mary would like to sing it."

Nash believed that the entire future of the show rested in his hands and, feeling the pressure, struggled vainly to come up with the lyrics. After numerous false starts over several days, Weill came to the table where Nash was working, trying to find inspiration from the sounds of the mountain brook outside the Weill house. "Have you read *Much Ado About Nothing* lately?" Weill asked.

"No. Why?"

"There is a line in it that might help you: 'Speak low, if you speak love.' Think about it."

Nash did think about it and went on to write the lyrics for a song that would long outlive the show and become a lasting favorite, "Speak Low."

Nash was generally loath to discuss which came first, the music or the lyrics, and even resorted to double-talk to dodge the question: "[There is] a question that has been put to me by countless little old ladies between Sedgewick Avenue and 167th Street, which also happens to be the question put by me to countless little old lyricists between $1,750.00 and $5,000.00 a week before I obtained my own toehold in the trade, between Spuyten Duyvil and 57 cents an hour. Which comes first in writing a song, the words or the music? The answer, of course, is Mary Martin. Any attempt to break this answer down into A, B and C only leads to frustration and amnesia."

In the case of "Speak Low," however, Nash freely acknowledged not only that the music had come first but that its composer had helped him come up with the lyrics. Ever the avid baseball fan, Nash compared himself to a pitcher saved by a double play, "a unique double play started nearly 400 years ago by Shakespeare and completed by a tiny German emigré who knew Shakespeare better than I did."

Yet it turned out to be another Weill/Nash song that made the crucial impression on Martin. She and her husband, Richard Halliday, went to hear the score in Kurt Weill's apartment one very hot night in August. She was charmed by the music and, in particular, by Weill's rendition, "with a kind of quavery German sound," of Venus's song "That's Him." She longed to sing the song but still could not see herself as Venus. Her husband, Richard, who was enthusiastic about the role, responded in an imaginative way. He took his wife on a tour of the Metropolitan Museum where together they inspected a wide variety of Venuses: "tall ones, short ones, even one who was noticeably broad of beam." The tour proved to be just what Richard needed to persuade Mary that, even as each sculptor had a different image of Venus, she could bring her own image to the role. But Halliday went further, promising Mary that she would play Venus in the most beautiful clothes in the world. To that end he arranged, through Katherine Cornell and Guthrie McLintic, a meeting with the famous couturier, Mainbocher.

Mainbocher had never designed clothes for a theatrical production and was wary of attempting it. He had to be won over, but Martin knew how to do it: she picked up a little chair, sat down directly in front of him, and sang "right smack into those kind brown eyes." With that, Mainbocher succumbed, but only on the condition that Martin would agree to sing "That's Him" in the same way in the production—to the audience as if it were one person.

Once the book, lyrics, and score had been completed, and the cast fully recruited, it was time for rehearsal—and the inevitable conflicts and crises. Initially the principal source of contention lay in the relationship between the director, Elia Kazan, and S. J. Perelman, as well as to some extent, Nash. Kazan viewed the Perelman/Nash book as "abysmal," "foolish," and "boring." From his point of view, the solution was one that "most musicals finally come to," cutting down the dialogue scenes to move "as quickly as possible from one musical number to the next." Even as the dialogue scenes were streamlined, however, abundant sources of irritation remained. At one rehearsal, Kazan stopped the actors in mid-scene and paced up and down in deep thought for fifteen minutes. Perelman and Nash finally approached him to ask what might be the matter. After ignoring them for a few more minutes, Kazan responded that he was trying to think of some stage business for the scene. Surprised, Perelman and Nash pointed out a lengthy description of business for the scene written into the script. Kazan stared at the script and erupted: "That chicken shit? I never read that. What do you think my business is in being here? I'm the director; I have to think of the business. I never read that kind of thing!" Perelman and Nash, ever the gentlemen, retreated quietly.

Ironically, with the increasing emphasis on the musical numbers, Kazan saw his own importance diminishing and felt he had been "reduced in rank," made an "overpaid stage manager, subservient to everyone else." He concluded that "this kind of theater was another species, one for which I had no talent." Kazan's perspective was perhaps inevitable, given his background and the fact that the essence of the Perelman/Nash book was style and fantasy. As Agnes de Mille shrewdly observed: "Style is a very tricky business, and the realistic methods of the Actors Studio, in which Kazan had trained, proved no help." Kazan himself commented that he was "a mediocre director except when a play or film touched a part of [his] life experience." It is difficult to imagine that anything within the frothy confines of *Venus* had much resonance with Kazan's life.

When the show arrived for its tryout run in Boston, concerns with the book were overtaken by even more urgent problems with scenery and costumes. At a glum meeting after the first Boston rehearsal, Weill pronounced the set "a disaster." Nash supported Weill, adding, "I'm a mild, agreeable sort of fellow usually, but I think we might as well not open." The principal feature of the scenery was a permanent masking frame hung with a grey velvet drape. Everyone involved with the show, excepting Kazan and the set designer Howard Bay, considered the set hopeless. Descriptions ranged from the moderate ("the inside of a coffin," "dirigible hangar") to the anatomically rude ("an enlarged prostate gland," "testicles"). Nash and Perelman took the lead with Weill and de Mille in demanding changes in scenery and costumes and threatening to return to New York if they were not agreed to.

At Kazan's urging, a decision was made to open the show in Boston as scheduled, but after heated debate an additional $25,000 (20 percent of the total budget) was allocated for the design of new sets to be completed before the opening in New York. Cheryl Crawford viewed demands of her creative team as "a mutiny" and "blackmail" but felt that she had no choice but to accept them.

Costumes—other than Venus's Mainbocher gowns—also provoked considerable dismay. Mainbocher was put in charge of getting the other costume designers to make the necessary revisions. This proved to require a firm hand, which Mainbocher readily supplied. After one of the set designers, Kermit Love, had disappeared for forty-eight hours to produce a new nymph costume, the resulting product was summarily rejected. Mainbocher then took a bath towel and pinned it to the brassiere of the dancer who was acting as a model. "Give her breasts, give her thighs, give her a waist," he commanded. As the model stood in her improvised costume, five of the watching dancers applauded. "I think it looks like a bathing suit," Love protested. "So?" said Mainbocher. "It looks like a girl. Now get on with it."

As solutions to the scenery and costume problems were pursued, attention swung back to the book and the fact that some of the laugh lines were failing to produce laughs. At one point George S. Kaufman, who was working on another show in Boston, and who had often dropped in on *Venus*, had dinner with a member of the cast, Paula Laurence. He commented on the production to illustrate one of his favorite themes—the difference between writing and writing for the theater. Laurence, who was concerned that her own part was not getting the audience response it should, asked Kaufman to speak to Perelman and Nash and give them the benefit of his experience. Kaufman did as he had promised, but with no visible results. Perelman and Nash each took Paula aside to tell her of his talk with Kaufman, but each thought that Kaufman was talking about the other. Neither changed anything.

Although a newcomer to the theater, Nash did not limit himself to defending or revising the book or polishing his lyrics. Unchastened by Kazan's earlier rebuke, Nash and Perelman concerned themselves with various matters of stagecraft. Agnes de Mille later described her impressions of the duo. Perelman, she wrote, "was charming, brilliant and slender; a slouch made him look thicker. . . . [H]is expression alternated professorial dignity and raffishness. He spoke in a sententious monotone, and there was always a raising of the eyebrows behind the round glasses, an intake of breath and a clearing of the throat as though in preparation of a public address or a Noel Coward song." Nash, on the other hand, "appeared quieter and younger (although he was not), like a bashful and nicely reared college boy." The two, she recalled, "went around together through our rehearsals like visitors on a vacation, bubbling with curiosity and an enthusiasm which lasted a good three weeks."

If Nash's and Perelman's bubbling enthusiasm had appeared to wane, their interest in the details of the production did not. At one point, for example, they focused on the scene in which Venus makes her hated rival, Rodney Hatch's fiancée, Gloria, disappear. On their own initiative, Nash and Perelman consulted a magician to find a means of making the girl vanish from sight in full light. The magician's initial question was whether it would be necessary to use the actress a second time. He seemed quite disappointed to be told that it would be: "Pity. Because, you know, I could evolve a wonderful effect." The magician then suggested the more modest idea of a barber's chair with a trick back—the chair would revolve and Gloria would disappear into it. The cost of installing the chair was put at only five hundred dollars, and Perelman and Nash were eager to do so. Craw-ford, however, rejected the idea on grounds of safety.

Nash was also upset with the statue of Venus, calling it "An abomination! What was that fancy-pants sculptor thinking of? It in no way suggests Venus. And it is certainly unlike Mary Martin, who so far as I can tell, is a handsome woman. This thing is a monster." Cheryl Crawford, however, coolly rebuffed Nash's criticism. "Ogden," she replied, "the sculptor measured Mary's entire body, including her breasts."

A minor issue to be resolved was Mary Martin's objection to one line in the show. Although she did not, in general, have concerns about the "sexiness" of Venus, Mary was troubled by having to express an observation by Venus that "Love is not the moaning of distant violins, it's the triumphant twang of a bedspring." It was, she thought, simply too vulgar. Crawford reluctantly agreed to cut the line if anything in the audience reaction made Martin uncomfortable. As it turned out, the "roar of pleasure and delight from the audience that greeted that line opening night was so great that Mary never mentioned it again." But not everything on opening night in Boston went so well. A rather spectacular mishap occurred when Martin was unaccountably missing throughout most of the final ballet in which she played a central part. It was later learned that a stagehand had left her costume on the wrong side of the stage, requiring her to run all the way across the back of the stage, "panting and nearly naked," in order to retrieve it. Eventually such matters were sorted out, and the show moved on to the opening at New York's Imperial Theater.

Despite Marlene Dietrich's misgivings about the potential reaction of her daughter to the show, Nash's own daughters of even more tender years (Linell, eleven, and Isabel, ten), saw it without ill effect. Linell later wrote, "I can still feel the special thrill of listening to . . . songs that I had heard in the making. The next morning, when I carefully pasted the program into my theater scrapbook, I wrote beside it in my very best hand, 'This is my favorite play, I went with Mummy and Daddy and Minnie and Isabel and Mrs. Longwell.' And then I added, in parentheses 'This is *Daddy's* play.'"

More objective critics gave the show a reception that was almost as glowing. Favorable reviews appeared in the *New York Herald Tribune*, *Newsweek*, the *Daily News*, and *PM*. In general, praise was almost unanimous for Mary Martin, her Mainbocher gowns, and the Weill songs, though the humor of the book was regarded as inconsistent. This complaint could be taken as support for Kazan's appraisal. On the other hand, it might be argued that another director, better attuned to musical comedy by experience and temperament, could have been more effective in addressing the weaknesses of the book.

Lewis Nichols of the *New York Times* wrote that once again "going to the theater has become a pleasure." He found that the book by Perelman and Nash, "while not perfect throughout, is better than those of most musicals." The Weill and Nash songs, were "due for juke boxes and other fame." He correctly identified "Speak Low" as a sure hit but also remarked favorably on several other songs. Mary Martin was given special praise, as was Agnes de Mille and her premier danseuse, Sono Osato. A successful resolution of the crisis in Boston was reflected in brief but favorable references to scenery and costumes.

Nichols described Nash's lyrics as "soft and sweet" but added the comment, as cryptic as it was tentative, that the lyrics were "sometimes, perhaps, just a shade confused." Other critics were more generous. Nash's lyrics were described as "devastating" in the *New York Sun*, "smart and ingenious" in *PM*, and "smartly turned" by John Chapman in the *Daily News*. Chapman added that he had "noticed the champion lyric-turning expert, Cole Porter, cocking an attentive ear from the second or third row." Even Burton Rascoe of the *World-Telegram*, who termed the show a "disappointment," acknowledged that "there are some of the brightest and most singable song numbers you ever heard." One of the least enthusiastic reviews came from Nash's friend and former colleague at *The New Yorker*, Wolcott Gibbs. Even years later, Nash would remark ruefully on his failure to benefit from any "log rolling" from Gibbs.

On the whole, Nash's lyrics for *Venus* were clearly more successful than his contributions to the book. He had written fourteen songs for *Venus*, of which nine were essentially humorous and displayed the irony, wit, and wordplay familiar to readers of his light verse. The opening chorus of the show, set in the museum to which the statue of Venus is being delivered, is a gentle spoof of modern art with Nashian rhymes. ("Was Gauguin really in love with a rhinoceros? That's prepocerous.") It also displays Nash's flair for erudition—referring by name to thirty different painters, classical and modern, in a song of only forty-five lines.

Another song, "How Much I Love You," had originally been written as a Valentine poem to Frances. It had then been published in a somewhat different form in *The New Yorker* in 1941, and included in *Good Intentions* under the title "To My Valentine." The song and the poem employ conventional rhyming but provide a good example of another Nash technique, the unexpected and absurd comparison:

> More than a catbird hates a cat,
> Or a criminal hates a clue,
> Or the Axis hates the United States,
> That's how much I love you.
>
>   ＊   ＊   ＊   ＊
>
> As a sailor's sweetheart hates the sea,
> Or a juggler hates a shove,
> As a wife detests unexpected guests,
> That's how much you I love.
>
>   ＊   ＊   ＊   ＊

Another song, "Very, Very, Very," reflects upon the comforts of affluence and may have had origins in an earlier Nash poem, "The Terrible People," which mocked the attempts of the wealthy to belittle their advantages. Although the thrust of the song is somewhat different from the poem, one portion suggests its provenance. Thus the observation in "The Terrible People" that:

> The only incurable troubles of the rich are the troubles that
>   money can't cure.
> Which is a kind of trouble that is even more troublesome if you
>   are poor.

becomes in "Very, Very, Very":

> I've heard my gilded friends complain
> There are troubles money cannot cure,
> But a trouble is a trouble is a trouble and it's twice
> The trouble when a person is poor.

A later line

> If you live along Park Avenue
> You've dandy credit havenue

reprised one of Nash's earliest and most celebrated couplets—the rhyme of "avenue" and "havenue" in "Spring Comes to Murray Hill."

Most of Nash's humorous songs were designed to advance the story line of *Venus*, and one of them, "Wooden Wedding," supplied a crucial element of the plot. In that song Rodney describes for Venus his vision of married bliss in Ozone Heights:

> We will linger o'er the laundry,
> I'll wash yours and you'll wash mine.
> Payday will be a magic casement
> Opening on something peachy,
> Maybe a trip to Gimbel's basement,
> Or a double feature with Don Ameche.
> Waiting for our wooden wedding,
> Golly what a trail we'll leave
> Sipping Coca-Cola at the pianola
> On our wooden wedding eve.

✳   ✳   ✳   ✳

The song is followed by an Agnes de Mille ballet, "Venus in Ozone Heights," which visually depicts their life to come. The song and the ballet convince Venus that she is not at all suited for a future with Rodney.

Nash's letters to Frances before and during their marriage leave little doubt that he was an incurable romantic, and his poems often had romantic themes though generally conveyed in a lighthearted manner. Mary Martin's favorite song from the show, "That's Him," was written in that mode:

> You know the way you feel when there is autumn in the air?
> That's him . . . That's him . . .
> The way you feel when Antoine has finished with your hair?
> That's him . . . That's him . . .
> You know the way you feel when you smell bread baking,
> The way you feel when suddenly a tooth stops aching?
> Wonderful world, wonderful you
> That's him . . . That's him . . .

✳   ✳   ✳   ✳

Mary Martin sang the song in just the way she had promised Mainbocher, not only on Broadway but also, on one poignant occasion, to an audience of GIs awaiting embarkation. As Agnes de Mille described it: "It was a moment of enchanting intimacy, and the soldiers looked at her with the trust of little children. They stopped smoking. They stopped shuffling their feet and fidgeting. They stopped whistling and calling out. They forgot that tomorrow they were being shipped out. They forgot the last camp rumors and privations. They lifted their faces like babies and listened. It was the final message from their sweethearts, delicate and humorous, and brought to them by this most lovely of ladies. She whispered her last remarks, and it was as though she had her lips to each man's ear and had kissed him God-speed in token of the woman who could not."

The lyrics Nash wrote for the other romantic ballads of *Venus*, "I'm a Stranger Here Myself," "West Wind," "Foolish Heart," and "Speak Low," revealed a dimension of his talent that had gone undeveloped. Of these, the most memorable, "Speak Low," was a Hit Parade favorite for many months and today remains a popular standard. Even on the printed page, without the Weill melody, the song retains its haunting quality:

Speak low when you speak love,
Our summer day
Withers away
Too soon, too soon.
Speak low when you speak love;
    *   *   *   *

We're late, darling, we're late.
The curtain descends,
Everything ends,
Too soon, too soon.
    *   *   *   *

I wait, darling, I wait—
Will you speak low to me,
Speak love to me,
And soon?

One of the premier cabaret singers of recent years, Andrea Marcovicci, has described the song as having "what may be the most poetic lyric of the era."

On the other hand, some of Nash's humorous songs may have lost something here or there in the translation from printed verse to sung lyrics. For example, part of the fun of reading Nash's verse is seeing, as a theater audience cannot, how a rhyme is accomplished by tortured spelling. For example, in "Way Out West in Jersey":

Oh, a buckaroo from Texas
Ran for Marshal of Passaic
So much lead landed in his solar plexus
Now he rattles just like a snaic.

It is doubtful that theatergoers were able to enjoy the rendering of "snake" into "snaic" or, in other songs, to appreciate fully "Park Avenue/havenue" or "rhinoceros/prepocerous." Despite any shortcoming in the lyrics, Ogden Nash received second place for Best Lyrics in the Donaldson Awards for 1943. As Cheryl Crawford noted, that "certainly wasn't bad considering it was his first venture as lyricist and his competition was Oscar Hammerstein II who took first place."

Critics and reviewers aside, *Venus* was a solid commercial success. It ran for 567 performances on Broadway before being taken on the road. Although overshadowed by *Oklahoma!*, it was the biggest hit of the latter part of 1943 and outran *Carmen Jones*, which opened in December of that year. Unfortunately the musical went on to become an undistinguished motion picture, bereft of the principal elements that had made the show a success on Broadway. The dancing was eliminated, as were all but two of the Weill/Nash songs, and Mary Martin was replaced by Ava Gardner. Nevertheless the Broadway production had been an important milestone for many of the participants.

Cheryl Crawford later wrote that "*One Touch of Venus* made a handsome profit, and it put my early failures behind me, conclusively showing that my success with *Porgy and Bess* wasn't a onetime thing. On my own I had established myself at last." *Venus* provided Mary Martin with a return to Broadway in her first starring role. And the final scene of the show, where Martin appears as "Venus's country cousin," led directly to the role that lifted her to the heights of Broadway stardom. As she recounted in her memoir, "Oscar Hammerstein saw *One Touch of Venus*. He said that the moment he saw me enter as 'the Venus of Ozone Heights' he wanted to write a part for the innocent, eager little girl in the white-piqué blouse, pink polka-dot skirt and matching rolled-brim hat. He wrote it too—Nellie Forbush in *South Pacific* was a descendant of Venus."

The show also began a new career for the creator of Miss Martin's gowns. Building on his success in *Venus*, Mainbocher went on to do the wardrobes for Ethel Merman in *Call Me Madam*, Rosalind Russell in *Wonderful Town*, and Carol Channing in *Gentlemen Prefer Blondes*.

Venus was Agnes de Mille's first show after *Oklahoma!* She received even better notices for her ballets in *Venus* than she had in that stage classic. It not only enhanced her reputation but solidified the place of ballet in the Broadway musical. And de Mille's brilliant dancer, Sono Osato, found that her performance in *Venus* won her a leading role the following season in Leonard Bernstein's *On the Town.*

For Ogden Nash, the experience with *Venus* was a life-changing event: he became convinced that lyric writing was a natural, and potentially quite profitable, progression of his talent. Although some of the reviews of the *Venus* lyrics did not match the accolades that had generally greeted his books of light verse, it was a brilliant start for a first-time lyricist. As Nash would later recall with some wonderment, "in spite of Gibbs, the show was quite a success. It was like having gone to the race course for the first time and picked a 100:1 shot."

At the time it did not seem to have been all that difficult. While Nash had worked very hard on *Venus*, crowded theaters of applauding audiences had quickly eclipsed the memory of tensions with Elia Kazan and the despair over scenery and costumes during the Boston tryouts. Nash's friend and colleague, Sid Perelman, had a similar outlook, so it was not surprising that they were determined to find a successor to *Venus*.

9

LYRICS BY NASH

Both Nash and Perelman were eager to collaborate with Kurt Weill on another show, but soon after *Venus* opened Weill left for Hollywood to work with Ira Gershwin on an original film musical. Nash made it a point to keep in touch. He wrote Weill a long, newsy letter in December, reporting that his routine was to come up from Baltimore to New York every Monday to appear on the Guy Lombardo Show, adding that Lombardo had said on the radio that "Speak Low" was the most requested song at the Roosevelt Grill for the past month. Nash explained that his radio performances were sandwiched in between stopping to see the first act of *Venus* and returning in time for the Ozone Heights ballet. In addition, Nash had brought the children for a Saturday matinee of the show, when he "had the pleasure of watching it sitting down."

On the basis of these visits, Nash offered a detailed critique of the current performances in *Venus*. In his view, only Mary Martin's performance deserved special praise, and his remarks about several other cast members were decidedly acerbic. Still, he conceded that "the box-office would indicate that I am super-sensitive, even if not quite so much as Sid." Nash then went on to discuss a new play by Weill's friend and former collaborator, Maxwell Anderson. The real point of the letter finally appeared on the fourth page when Nash confessed that he was now "incurably stage-struck" and "impatient to start work again." He told Weill that he had been reading widely, looking for a good plot or good idea, and mentioned discarded possibilities ranging from Andersen and Grimm fairy tales to Restoration comedies and minor Elizabethan plays. Only four days later, and without awaiting a reply from Weill, Nash wrote again, reporting further on the show—Sono Osato had been out with the flu but her understudy had done very well, and the house had the "usual quota of standees" while there were reports of empty seats at *Oklahoma*. But again the real point was something else—Nash had run across a story by Edgar Allan Poe ("The System of Dr. Tarr and Professor Fether") that he thought might do. While the story was set in a lunatic asylum, which Nash deemed too macabre, perhaps it could be transformed into a "gilded sanitorium." He urged Weill to read the story if he had a chance.

In January, Nash wrote again, and after a bit more gossip about the show, suggested further possibilities for a future musical. One was *The Vicar of Wakefield* and the other a story by Stephen Vincent Benét, "which might, if the central character were changed from a country doctor to an actress or a dancer, give us a very nice framework for a show." Nash pleaded for Weill to return to the East Coast, suggesting that "it's time you and Sid and I were fighting and frolicking again."

Although Weill did come to New York in March to write a propaganda film for the Office of War Information, none of Nash's suggestions had aroused his interest. Weill decided to join Ira Gershwin in working on a musical version of a 1924 play, *The Firebrand*, and in June he returned to Hollywood. He had not, however, given up on the idea of another show with Nash and Perelman, and before leaving New York he urged them to look at other stories Anstey might have written. Weill's instinct appeared to have been rewarded when he received a telegram from Nash and Perelman on July 5, touting an Anstey novelette that, after a week's work, they found very exciting. Now Weill was interested, and he wrote to his wife, Lotte Lenya, that he had shown the telegram to Ira Gershwin with whom "it made quite an impression." Nash also followed up the telegram to Weill with a letter asking for patience before they sent him anything in writing and emphasizing how much they needed his participation: "We are terribly anxious to talk to you as we miss your advice each time we start work; we can only try to keep your precepts in mind. We know that the idea is a good one, and are hopeful that you will like our treatment."

Despite Nash's attempt at diplomacy, Weill suddenly became impatient and surprisingly irascible. After fewer than three weeks, he was furious that he had heard nothing further from Sid and Ogden and said, in a letter to Lenya, "T' hell with them!" His rage was compounded a few days later when he received a letter from Perelman in which, according to Weill, "Sid now confesses that they gave up the idea after a few sessions and didn't work at all." Nash, he fumed, is "only interested in where they could have lunch and is having a wonderful time in New York."

Nash wrote to Weill on August 27 and presented a more positive account of the summer. While he admitted that "on the surface" he and Perelman had nothing to show for their efforts, Nash said he remained optimistic, "convinced that we have an extraordinarily good idea by the tail, and one that a brief conference with you can straighten out." Nash continued with a detailed summary of the Anstey plot as modified by Perelman and himself. The story was even more fanciful—or far-fetched—than that of *Venus*. But Nash insisted that he was "violently enthusiastic over it." Perelman was equally keen "at times," Nash said, "but gets depressed with terrifying ease." Nash went on to note that he was "writing verse like mad" but would rather be working on a show. Finally, despite his professed confidence in the new Anstey vehicle, Nash brought himself to pose a crucial question: "[S]hould the book-writing scheme fall through, God forbid, do your plans still hold a place for me as a lyricist? I myself want tremendously to work with you again, but I don't know what you have in mind with Ira or others who may be on the Coast. Do let me know."

If Nash had written the letter just a week or two earlier, it would have gotten a very chilly reception indeed. As it happened, however, by the time it arrived he had been restored to Weill's good graces. The instrument of Nash's redemption was his short article in the *New York Times* describing his work with Weill in writing the songs for *Venus*. It offered a very generous and affectionate appraisal of the composer's talents, and both Lenya and Weill were delighted by it. Weill summed it up: "Ogden's article is absolutely charming and makes good for all his shortcomings."

Thus when Weill received Nash's letter, he gave it a sympathetic reading. But he saw little to recommend the new proposal and was unpersuaded by Nash's "violent" enthusiasm for it. He wrote to Lenya that he had received a "sweet and pitiful" letter from Nash, who had wasted the summer in a hot New York apartment. For Weill, though, the important point of the letter was Nash's apparent willingness to give up book-writing and concentrate on lyrics: "He asks me if I still consider him as a lyric writer for me if he forgets about writing books too and that's exactly what I wanted him to find out. I will write him that I will be very glad to work with him again as soon as I find the right book." Unfortunately, finding the "right book" would prove as elusive for Weill as it had for Nash and Perelman.

With Nash having lost interest in book-writing, Perelman soon found a new collaborator. His choice was a surprising one: his good friend of many years, Al Hirschfeld. Although Hirschfeld's theatrical caricatures in the *New York Times* were widely admired, and he and Perelman shared much the same sense of humor, Hirschfeld had no experience at all in scriptwriting. Perelman was unconcerned by that detail, and in March 1945 he wrote to a friend that he was putting the final touches on a show, later titled *Sweet Bye and Bye*, that he and Hirschfeld had turned out. He further reported that Ogden Nash would probably do the lyrics and that they would like to get Harold Arlen for the music.

Nash did agree to do the lyrics, but when Arlen was not available, Vernon Duke was chosen to do the score. Duke, who would become Nash's frequent collaborator and close friend, had a colorful background. Like Kurt Weill, he was a European emigré with classical training who had made a name as a Broadway composer. Duke, however, also continued to compose classical music under the name of his birth, Vladimir Dukelsky.

Dukelsky was the son of upper-middle-class parents in prerevolutionary Russia. His immediate antecedents were of Russian stock—and Viennese, Spanish, Lithuanian, and Georgian. According to Duke, his parents were "addicted to music in the customary manner of Russian dilettantes in comfortable circumstances," and as a boy he had shown early promise of unusual talent. He had composed a short waltz at the age of seven, and later his musical education took him to the Kiev Conservatory. In the aftermath of the Russian Revolution, however, Dukelsky was forced to leave the country with his widowed mother and younger brother. After a stay of several months in Constantinople, the family set sail for New York in 1921.

While in Constantinople, Dukelsky had been introduced to American popular music and had temporarily set aside his classical work to try his hand at songwriting. In New York he was encouraged to continue by George Gershwin, who became a close friend and a continuing source of advice. By the time Nash and Duke began work on *Sweet Bye and Bye*, Duke had firmly established parallel careers in classical composition and songwriting for stage and screen. As Duke put it, "There's my Carnegie Hall self and my Lindy's self, my Russian heritage and my American influence. Can I help it if two people happen to be in my body?"

On the classical side, Duke (as Dukelsky) had benefited from the friendship and patronage of the "three Serges"—his celebrated Russian compatriots Diaghilev, Prokofiev, and Koussevitzky. His first major success had been a ballet written in 1925 for Diaghilev's company in Paris, and his later works, including ballets, symphonies, and an opera, were given major performances in the United States and Europe. More pertinent to Nash were Duke's accomplishments in popular music. He had written "April in Paris" as well as other popular standards, including "Autumn in New York," "I Can't Get Started with You," and, from Duke's most successful Broadway show, *Cabin in the Sky*, "Taking a Chance on Love." In all, Duke seemed a splendid successor to Kurt Weill as a colleague for Nash.

The script by Perelman and Hirschfeld was at least as whimsical as the book for *Venus*. It was a lighthearted spoof of the future, set in 2076 when a time capsule is unearthed from the site of the 1939 World's Fair in New York. Nash liked the idea, and by the summer of 1945, he was brimming with enthusiasm. In a letter to Kurt Weill he wrote that the first act was now "sharp, fast and funny," and that his own songs had been praised. Still, he worried whether "things look so good right now that we will probably end up by not even getting into production."

One crucial step for any production is raising the necessary financial backing through an exhausting and seemingly endless series of auditions for prospective "angels." In the case of *Sweet Bye and Bye*, the auditions ultimately produced sufficient funds for the production to go forward—much of it contributed by friends of Nash or his brother Ted. Other obstacles, however, would abound.

While Nash had been encouraged by the progress of the show, he was soon overtaken by vexing personal difficulties. Frances had enjoyed the success of *Venus* but was not comfortable in the theatrical world. She also feared that a continuing preoccupation with show business was a dangerous distraction from Ogden's work as a poet, and that it might undermine the reputation and following he had built over many years. Nash was deeply upset by her concerns. When she complained over the telephone of his absence from Baltimore, he responded with his own *cri de coeur*.

"Darling," he wrote, "What am I to do? Am I faced with the bald alternative of having you angry and unhappy or lying down on the job? I am miserable and bewildered; deeply, deeply in love, and therefore all the more hurt and disappointed to find your hand withdrawn from me when I most need it." He could not leave New York, Nash explained earnestly, because he was in the midst of working with Vernon Duke on a song to be played the following day for Warner Bros. (who, it was hoped, might publish songs from the show and possibly invest in it). Then, appealing to Frances's pride in his work: "My heart is sore, but I think not as sore as yours would be if I took the easy road to mediocrity. I am following my road—not Vernon's, not Sid's or Kurt's or anyone else's; I am doing the work I know how to do, and doing it the best way I know how."

A subsequent letter addressed an even more sensitive issue: Frances had somehow gained the notion that Ogden had a romantic interest in Naomi Burton, a young woman employed by the Curtis Brown firm, Nash's literary agents. Nash first explained, once again, that his absence from Baltimore was unavoidable. Then, with mounting exasperation, he emphatically dismissed Frances's concern over Naomi Burton: "The only times I leave you are when I have to work, and I cannot do my work properly when I look forward all day to hearing your voice, and then find it icily sarcastic and indifferently polite. . . . I am thoroughly tired of this Naomi business; as far as she is concerned, I look on her more as a brother than a sister. . . . I am naturally proud that you should be jealous of me, but I wish to God you would realize that I don't want to sleep with Greer Garson, Rita Hayworth, Franklin Simon, Alan Collins or Naomi Burton; I just want to sleep with you."

Nash even offered to change agents, but Frances's feelings were assuaged and so drastic a move proved unnecessary. (Naomi Burton later left Curtis Brown and when, still later, she married Ned Stone, a Baltimorean who knew Frances, the Stones became welcome visitors to the Nashes' summer home in New Hampshire.) While Frances never fully shared her husband's love of the theater, she came to accept it and the absences it required. For his part, Nash's devotion to Frances never wavered. His love was movingly expressed in three poems he wrote for her in 1946: on her birthday in April, upon her discharge from the hospital in July after a hysterectomy, and in August on the anniversary of the 1929 weekend when she had accepted his first proposal. In a lifetime of letters and poems to Frances, the opening lines of the April poem "For Frances" are among Nash's more memorable:

Love is the lost dimension, a realm of time
Where seconds lag and years slip by unheeded;
The precipice to drop, the cliff to climb;

Love is to need, and needing, to be needed
It is the patient architect that builds
Misunderstandings into understanding . . .

But while the Nash marriage remained on firm ground, the underpin-
nings of *Sweet Bye and Bye* had begun to appear problematic. In January
1946, Nash wrote to Kurt Weill again, with a report that was markedly less
optimistic than his letter only six months before. It had been, Nash wrote,
"a long heart-breaking haul so far, and even now things are none too certain." He remarked ruefully that "The only winners to this point have been
the Pennsylvania Railroad, the Harvard Club and whatever hotels in New
York would condescend to shelter my carcass."

When the show opened for previews at the Forrest Theater in Philadelphia, the notices were largely unenthusiastic. This provoked consternation
among the creative team of Perelman, Hirschfeld, Nash, and Duke, all of
whom were billeted in adjoining rooms in the Warwick Hotel. Dispositions
were not improved when, through a connecting door, Perelman overheard
Duke in the next room discussing the reviews over the telephone. "Yes," he
heard Duke say, "but the music is great and I'm helping the fellows with
the book." Furious, Perelman stood by the door, where Duke would be
sure to hear him, and placed mock calls to Walter Winchell and Leonard
Lyons, explaining that Hirschfeld was helping Duke with the music—". . .
you know Al plays the piano." Duke was thoroughly taken in and immediately called Nash, saying, "These fellows are insane. They're out to crucify
me." Moments later a pajama-clad Nash confronted Perelman and
Hirschfeld, and was told the whole story. Ever the peacemaker, he insisted
they stop because, he claimed, Duke was not in good health.

After a week at the Forrest Theater, a scheduling conflict required the
production to be moved to the Erlanger Theater for a second week. According to Duke, the Erlanger was "probably the most sinister theater in
the world, situated in a street chiefly noted for cheap furniture stores."
Moreover, he observed, "The inside of the Erlanger looked like a furniture
store too—I never saw so many empty chairs in my life." Perelman believed
the show was too sophisticated for out-of-town audiences but would succeed in New York. That theory, dubious at best, was never put to the test.
A shortage of theaters in New York allowed the Shuberts to pick and
choose and they chose not to pick *Sweet Bye and Bye*. The show closed in
Philadelphia, never to be revived.

An autopsy of *Sweet Bye and Bye* would probably have revealed multiple causes of death. Although the casting was spotty, Hirschfeld believed that the music was the weakest part of the production. Duke's attempt to suggest music of the future by putting five harpists in the orchestra, he felt, just didn't work. Duke, on the other hand, believed that although the book was excruciatingly funny—especially when read by Perelman himself—it did not translate well to the stage. He also speculated that postwar audiences were not in a mood to look far into the future. Although no one was inclined to lay great blame at Nash's door, his lyrics were clearly less successful than they had been in *Venus*. Two songs from the show would survive to be recycled several years later in another collaboration with Vernon Duke, but nothing approached the magic of "Speak Low" or "That's Him."

The failure of *Sweet Bye and Bye* was a serious blow to the major participants. Perelman and Hirschfeld fled the country for a trip around the world on a writing assignment for *Holiday* magazine. On the other hand, as Hirschfeld put it, "Nash stayed here to face the music." And the music was not pleasant. The closing resulted in an estimated loss of $300,000 to the backers—many of them friends of Nash or his brother Ted. Ogden was so abashed by the failure that for a period of time he gave up his cherished visits to the Pimlico racetrack: "I felt if any of those people who backed those shows would see me at the $2 or $5 window, they might believe it was their money I was betting."

The painful experience of *Sweet Bye and Bye* did not end Nash's fascination with Broadway. Only a year later, in December 1947, he was talking with Felix Jackson, once a German playwright and now a producer, about a musical based on Emily Post's *Etiquette*. Kurt Weill was an old friend of Jackson's, and he had not only recommended Nash but had agreed to consider doing the score. That would have fulfilled Nash's desire to work again with Weill, but the project never developed, and in 1950, when he was just fifty years old, Weill died of a heart attack.

By 1948, Nash had renewed his partnership with Vernon Duke. Despite the debacle of *Sweet Bye and Bye* they had become good friends. They were in many ways an odd couple: Nash, thoroughly American, was usually shy and reserved; Duke, an international cosmopolitan, was outgoing, even boisterous. Notwithstanding their differences of background and temperament, the two held each other in high regard. In his 1955 memoir, *Passport to Paris*, Duke would write, "I still think Ogden the finest human being

I was ever privileged to know. . . . An old hand at the Gentle Art of Making Enemies, I can only marvel at the fact that Ogden hasn't a single enemy in the world: there *are* a good many people *he* doesn't like, but I've never met a man who doesn't like him." And Duke proudly quoted several affectionate inscriptions on books that Nash had given him, including "Like Kostelanetz/ and lesser planets/ I am learnon/ Fast from Vernon."

Inevitably Nash sometimes found his friend's exuberance a bit too much. He once wrote Isabel, describing a luncheon at which Duke, "rising from a surf of press clippings," had regaled him "with a detailed saga of his European triumphs, musical and amatory." This led Nash to observe a bit sourly, "I don't want him, you can have him, he's too luscious for me." On another occasion Nash wrote a rather brusque letter complaining about a late-night telephone call from Duke. He was particularly upset, he made plain, because the telephone was located at Mrs. Leonard's bedside, and the seventy-eight-year-old lady, to whom Nash had always been devoted, had been forced to climb to the third floor to summon him. As always, Nash soon relented and sent a conciliatory note: "Come, emerge from that huff; have Duke and Nash never exchanged irascibilities before?"

For their first joint effort after *Sweet Bye and Bye*, Nash and Duke took on a Broadway revue entitled *He and She*. Its creator was Ken Englund, a Hollywood screenwriter who had written a series of sketches described as "a Pandora's box of human emotions that modern Americans face today in their every day living and loving." The production was to star David Wayne and be directed by Jose Ferrer. A March 1949 article in *Life* magazine succinctly described the backers' auditions for the show: "[A] sampling of the show is given with composer Vernon Duke at the piano while Nash slouches in the corner looking unhappy and everybody else has a wonderful time." Although the accompanying photograph justified the description of Nash as "unhappy," the magazine reported that the auditions "had brought in most of the needed money." But disagreements arose between Englund and his co-producer, Stewart Chaney, and the production eventually disintegrated before it reached the stage.

Only two years later, Nash and Duke were at it again, this time with a show *Wedding Day*, written as a spoof on fashion magazines. Its opening number, "I Hitched My Wagon to *Harper's Bazaar*," delighted the editors of the magazine, who gave it prominent coverage in their pages. Although the coverage provoked considerable interest among readers of *Harper's Bazaar*, this show also fell by the wayside before reaching production.

Duke lamented that he was earning a reputation as "Broadway's No. 1 Composer of Unproduced Shows."

With serial disappointments on Broadway, Nash's thoughts turned once again to Hollywood. Remarkably undaunted by his earlier experience with motion pictures, he yearned to try again, this time not as a scriptwriter but as a lyricist. In January 1952, looking forward to a trip to the West Coast, he asked Vernon Duke to use his contacts for him. Duke eagerly accepted the assignment, and Nash was appreciative: "I am more grateful than I can say for your continued loyalty and your efforts to open the gates for me, and I hope with all my heart that it won't be too long before we can do some work together again." In Hollywood with Frances a few weeks later, Nash wrote to Isabel that Duke had given them "a vast cocktail party full of agents and producers." He was "really working like mad to get me out here."

Despite Duke's help, nothing came of Nash's foray in Hollywood, but it was not long before the two were once more at work together on a musical revue, *Two's Company*, starring Bette Davis. Miss Davis was then at one of the high points of her long film career, having been recently acclaimed for her performance in *All About Eve*, the Academy Award–winning picture of 1950. Starring in a Broadway revue, however, would require a different set of talents. She was required not only to sing, dance, and don some outlandish costumes but to appear in half a dozen sketches that put her in such varied roles as a hillbilly singer, a kitchen slattern, Sadie Thompson, and Tallulah Bankhead. It was not quite a "one-woman" show—Davis was supported by a cast of more than twenty, headed by the comics Hiram Sherman and David Burns and the dancer Nora Kaye. But Davis was the centerpiece: as one reviewer would note, Davis's name—and Davis's name alone—appeared in capital letters throughout the program.

Another prominent member of the team was the choreographer Jerome Robbins. Robbins's greatest successes lay ahead of him, but he had already established an envied reputation on Broadway. Duke, in particular, was eagerly looking forward to working with Robbins, though, as it turned out, he was to be disappointed. Despite Duke's impressive credentials as a ballet composer, Robbins insisted on having his own musical collaborator on the ballets, Genevieve Pitot. Even Nash was required to rewrite his lyrics repeatedly to suit the choreography, sometimes losing lines that he and Duke had particularly prized. In the end, Duke conceded that the ballets were brilliantly staged and danced and that "Robbins's choreography was probably the best feature in the show."

The show began its previews in Detroit on an alarming note. At the premiere performance, Miss Davis made her entrance by springing from a magician's sealed box on stage, began her first number, and promptly collapsed with "a terrific bone-jarring bang." As cast members stood by helplessly, a stagehand rushed out to drag her into the wings. Gary Merrill raced backstage, fearing that his wife had suffered a fatal heart attack. As it happened, she had only fainted, a result no doubt of the physical and emotional strain of preparing for so unfamiliar a role. Within minutes she was revived and back on stage, ready to resume and reassuring the audience by quipping, "Well, you couldn't say I didn't fall for you." Nevertheless the show had to be shut down for a week, at considerable cost, to allow Bette to recuperate, and even then new problems would emerge.

Although the reviews in Detroit were fairly good, concerns grew as the show proceeded from Detroit to Pittsburgh and then to Boston. Rumors reached New York that it was in serious trouble. With considerable doctoring, the show was deemed ready for New York, where interest in Miss Davis had produced a very large advance sale. When the show finally opened on December 15, 1952, Nash later recalled, "the critics had really been waiting for us and lit after us like Indians who'd been waiting for the covered wagon to come along. The air was thick with scalps!" Nash had once again been hopeful of some "log rolling" help from his friend and former colleague at *The New Yorker*, Wolcott Gibbs, and once again did not find it. Gibbs, Nash remembered, "called it a very disappointing evening indeed, and the least memorable part of the evening was contributed by Ogden Nash's lyrics." It seemed to Nash that in New York, "rather than rolling the log, they pick it up and drop it on your sore toe."

In fact the reviews were not altogether negative. Davis's limitations as a singer and dancer were evident, and no one suggested that musical theater was a medium she was likely to make her own. But the critics saluted her energy, determination, and good humor. By consensus, the biggest weakness of the show was her material—the sketches and, for some reviewers, the songs turned out by Nash and Duke. Bosley Crowther in the *Times* liked the ballet dancers, "especially if Vernon Duke and Ogden Nash are calling the tunes and lyrics." While he found the music "uneven," Crowther added that "Mr. Duke never lets a ballet down, and Mr. Nash always has a word for it that is pithy or humorous." Others took a dimmer view. Richard Watts in the *Post* reluctantly concluded that "neither the songs by Mr. Duke nor the lyrics by Mr. Nash are in any way worthy of the capacity of these accomplished gentlemen." And John Chapman in the *Daily News* was merciless: "[S]o far as my ear could detect, there aren't any songs even though Vernon Duke and Ogden Nash are credited with some."

Two's Company did well at the box office despite the reviews. The only threat to the health of the show was the health of its star, but that threat turned out to be very real. Davis had never fully regained her stamina after her sudden collapse in Detroit, and in New York she turned to "revivifying" injections from Dr. Max Jacobson, known to his patients as "Dr. Feel Good." In March she consulted a prominent oral surgeon, Dr. Stanley Behrman, who removed an infected wisdom tooth and then discovered a painful bone disease, osteomyelitis of the jaw, that required a serious operation. Continuation of the show was out of the question. After only eighty-nine performances, it closed.

When the show closed, Nash was in Charlotte, North Carolina, on a lecture tour, and he was not in touch with Duke for some time. In June he finally wrote Duke, recounting his activities and outlining his future plans. He observed resignedly, "I can't bring myself to contemplate any further theater venture at the moment, but passage of time may heal bruises and restore ambition to be a lesser Loesser."

Since Frank Loesser was the composer of a score of popular songs and the music for several Broadway hits, including *Guys and Dolls*, the ambition to be a "lesser Loesser" was not as modest as it might sound. In any event, the passage of time eventually did its healing work, and two years later Nash was working once again with Sid Perelman, trying to develop a show based on Perelman's adventures in East Africa and entitled *White Rhino*. That project never materialized, but Nash and Duke were soon reunited in yet another new venture, *The Littlest Revue*.

The producer of the revue, Ben Bagley, was something of a theatrical *wunderkind*. He had come to New York from Vermont at the age of nineteen and briefly held office jobs with several firms. But Bagley had a love of the theater, and after seeing an Off Broadway revue by Walter and Jean Kerr, *Touch and Go*, he concluded that he could do just as well. His first show, *The Shoestring Revue*, opened Off Broadway in February 1955 at the Phoenix Theater. Bagley was just twenty-one, but the show was well received and earned him—overnight—a reputation as a theatrical innovator with a sharp eye for talent.

A year later, for *The Littlest Revue*, Bagley once more assembled a remarkable cast that included the future stars Joel Grey and Tammy Grimes.

Despite its title, the revue had a budget four times as large as *The Shoe-string Revue*. This meant, Bagley said, that "The scenery and costumes were very elegant and at last I had the means to bring to life dreams which only money can buy." Despite the fact that Nash for the first time had more experience in the musical theater than his producer/director, there was never any question of who was in charge. Whenever Bagley asked that lyrics be rewritten, Nash complied without a murmur. He later wrote that "Bagley was a tiger when aroused and few of his colleagues dared to cross him without a chair ready to thrust in his face."

The only noteworthy conflict between Nash and the young producer arose over a song, "Blame It All on Mother," which satirized the pleas of young people in trouble who held their mothers responsible. Although Bagley thought the song had a clever idea and a clever lyric, he decided to drop it from the show when it failed to get any audience reaction. Nash was furious. "I will not tolerate this. You cut things and you don't put things into rehearsal that you say you are going to put into rehearsal and you're a young man who doesn't know what he's doing," he shouted, storming from the theater. Vernon Duke, looking on, was amazed. "Do you realize, dear boy," he told Bagley, "that Ogden has never raised his voice to anyone in the whole history of the theater, and for him to raise his voice to you is quite an honor."

Bagley did not welcome the "honor" and felt chagrined that he had provoked Nash so profoundly. The next day Nash returned and the matter was smoothed over—the song remained out of the show. Despite that brief contretemps, Bagley considered Nash a consummate gentleman and a delight to work with. He was particularly impressed by Nash's contribution to "Good Girls Go to Heaven," a song that was originally written by Sammy Cahn for *Two's Company*. The song had been the opening number of that show, but after Bette Davis suffered her collapse trying to sing it on opening night, she had insisted that it be dropped. When Bagley decided he liked the music and the idea, but not Cahn's lyrics, Nash agreed to rewrite them—even though Cahn would receive the credit and the royalties.

The Littlest Revue opened on May 22, 1956, to positive reviews. Brooks Atkinson in the *Times* applauded its "uniformly high standards of intelligence and humor" while John McLain in the *Journal American* called it a "clever, witty and effervescent musical." John Chapman in the *Daily News* pronounced the show "charming, funny and witty . . . a show of the first order" (although noting that the principal songwriters, Nash and Duke, "have their ups and downs"). The Phoenix was booked with another show in the fall, so Bagley considered moving the revue to Broadway. But converging pressures of time and money intervened, and the show was forced to close after a run that, though successful, had lasted only a few weeks.

The Littlest Revue was Nash and Duke's last collaboration and Nash's last serious attempt at lyric writing. The legacy of their partnership was a modest one, but it did yield a number of quite singable songs, most of which are found on two CDs, the original-cast album of The Littlest Revue and Vernon Duke Revisited. Both albums were produced by Ben Bagley, who for reasons of health gave up producing for the theater to become, through his record company, a curator of the lesser-known works of great Broadway composers and lyricists.

The Duke album was produced in 1970, a year and a half after the composer's death, and featured several Nash songs. Reviewing the album in the New York Times, John Wilson paid tribute to Duke—and to Nash. Duke, he noted, had been plagued by bad luck with many of the musicals he had worked on. Wilson found that the Bagley album supplied "the elusive evidence that Duke deserves the high place in the musical theater to which one instinctively assigns him." And among Duke's several brilliant collaborators, Wilson singled out Nash as one of his most effective partners:

> "Round About," which they wrote for "Two's Company" in 1953, is a gently haunting song which has been sneaking slowly toward general recognition for a long, long time. "Just Like a Man," which Bette Davis sang in that same show, is an amusing piece which shows Joan Rivers to be a surprisingly capable pseudo-vocalist, and "Low and Lazy," admirably sung by Blossom Dearie, is a slinky bit of torching that was in "Sweet Bye and Bye," a 1946 musical that closed out of town.

Despite this belated encomium, it appears that both Nash and Duke might have been better served if they had not held so loyally to their partnership. Some support for that theory was offered by Al Hirschfeld, whose own memories of Sweet Bye and Bye lingered for decades. According to Hirschfeld, the collaborators suffered from an excess of mutual esteem: "It was like an Alphonse and Gaston comedy—they were too polite to each other. Neither one really criticized the other one. Collaborators when they work have the right to say 'It's terrible, it stinks, throw it out!' Ogden would never do that. He respected Vernon, and if Vernon wrote something, he would think it was absolute genius. And if Ogden wrote something, Vernon would say 'great.' Neither would say 'Now cut it out. You can't sing that—those words are too complicated. It's all right in literature, but you can't do that in the theater.'"

Nash, of course, recognized a difference in writing for the theater and did his best to adapt: "I approached songwriting with the feeling that the impact of the composition has to be instantaneous and direct, and recognition has to be immediate. The listener has to be impressed almost immediately or else he tosses it off. If the same verse were to appear in a book or a magazine, he would have time to digest it more slowly or reread it until he got the message." The principle that Nash articulated was easier to express than to implement, and even Duke eventually conceded that Nash may sometimes have stumbled in practice. Writing some years after their collaboration had ended, Duke insisted that Nash had been the first really original lyricist to succeed Larry Hart, with Frank Loesser a close contender. But he admitted that Nash's words were difficult to set to music and lost some of their spontaneity in the process: "A line that makes you bellow when read or recited elicits a raising of the eyebrows and a whispered 'Huh? What was that again?' when sung."

One Touch of Venus may have been more successful than Nash's later shows for a host of reasons, including luck, that were unrelated to Nash's lyrics. Nevertheless it is possible that further collaboration with Kurt Weill might have given Nash the best opportunity to develop as a lyricist. Vernon Duke himself observed generously that Weill had been able to overcome the complexity of Nash's lyrics by "never get[ting] in the way of the words." He pointed particularly to "That's Him" and "The Trouble with Women Is Men" as songs from *Venus* that were successful in the theater "because the self-effacing music permitted the words to shine." Neither Duke nor his music were ever regarded as particularly self-effacing. On the other hand, Duke acknowledged that the most enduring song in the show, "Speak Low," was one "where the music predominates." That may or may not give due credit to Nash's lyrics for the song, but it also suggests that perhaps Weill—or possibly some other composer—might have pushed Nash to write more songs in the style of "Speak Low" and to rely somewhat less on the wit and wordplay that worked so well on the printed page but were difficult to transplant to the stage. Sadly, Nash's hopes for doing more work with Weill ended with the composer's death in 1950.

Although Nash failed to find a lasting niche on Broadway—to become a lesser Loesser—he never seemed to regret having pursued that elusive goal for so many years. And while he devoted enormous time and energy to the theater, as well as to writing verse and lecturing, he never forgot that he had a family to raise.

10

THE CHILDREN GROW UP

Growing up as Ogden Nash's daughters in the late forties gave Linell and Isabel their own small window on musical theater. In 1945 the family spent the summer on Martha's Vineyard (a venue where, Nash noted, the principal drawbacks were "a stony beach and fish seven days a week"). They were there because Sid Perelman was also staying on the Vineyard, and he and Nash were able to spend time together working on *Sweet Bye and Bye*. The Nash girls were fascinated to observe the show being developed and to listen to the wordplay between their father and Perelman. (Even years later Linell would recall bits and pieces, such as "No stone unturned" becoming "No tern unstoned" and then "No stern untoned.")

Vernon Duke was vacationing on nearby Nantucket, and he too turned up frequently to work with Nash on songs for the show. He returned on similar missions in succeeding summers when the Nashes had returned to Little Boar's Head on the New Hampshire coast, where they had summered since before the war. Linell and Isabel (and Frances) found Duke a bit overpowering, a larger-than-life presence with "a footfall like a tree falling in a forest." In Duke's eyes, Linell and Isabel were "two leggy daughters of the extra-awkward age, given to shrieks, whisperings and incessant beach outings."

Duke's image of the girls in summer had some resonance in a poem that Nash wrote two years later. The first stanza of "Tarkington, Thou Should'st Be Living in This Hour" reflected the parental mood that often attends the transition from child to adult:

O Adolescence, O Adolescence,
I wince before thine incandescence.
Thy constitution young and hearty
Is too much for this aged party.
Thou standest with loafer-flattened feet
Where bras and funny papers meet.
When anxious elders swarm about
Crying "Where are you going?", thou answerest "Out."
Leaving thy parents swamped in debts
For bubble gum and cigarettes.

     *   *   *   *

To Linell's dismay, the poem was published in *The New Yorker* and was quoted to her by friends on the beach.

In 1949, Ogden and Frances took Linell and Isabel on a six-week trip to France and Italy, financed by Frances's share of the proceeds from the sale of property in her mother's family. The Nashes sailed from New York on the *Ile de France*, and after arriving in Le Havre, took the train to Paris. From Paris they journeyed to Nice by train and from Nice to Genoa by private automobile—a 1935 Cadillac in which Nash was seated in the front next to the driver, an elderly Frenchman ("a sweet, thin, old veteran of 1914–18 who spoke no English but, being mutually amiable, we managed to communicate"). After spending the night in Genoa, the Nashes left by train the next day for Florence. Their stay in Florence was marked by severe intestinal illnesses that struck both Linell and Isabel and left Linell in bed for several days. As Nash wrote Mrs. Leonard from Rome, "It has been rather tough, and Frances and I felt for a little while like Florence Nightingale and Father Damien, but surely the pendulum must now swing the other way."

The passing illnesses could not spoil the trip. Nash wrote Vernon Duke from Rome: "Florence was more beautiful than any of my dreams, as was the drive through Sienna, Perugia, Assisi etc to Rome, where we are anointing our feet in antiquity." Venice was even more impressive—a high point that persuaded the Nashes to extend their stay by several days. As Ogden wrote to his mother-in-law: "We were all just in the right mood for everything that Venice has to offer, and pass the most delightful days and evenings walking, gondoling, and sitting outside in St. Mark's Square sipping coffee, Coca Cola and ices. . . . We really couldn't have done better than to save Venice for the last. The girls are enchanted by it, and we all just float around in a delightful medieval haze. It's the sort of fantastic dream city that couldn't possibly happen, but I'm glad it did."

In Paris, both girls pined for Venice and a young man they had met there and with whom they had both fallen in love. But they were distracted by sight-seeing and marathon shopping expeditions that left Nash thoroughly exhausted. ("This is the weary letter of a male who has spent 8 hours with three females on the Faubourg St. Honoré and other streets with windows on them with things in them. What is more, I spent the last 3 hours at a fashion show for jeune filles where 26 dresses were exhibited, with only one model, who, though charming, wasn't able to change costumes under 5 minutes.") The Nashes' stay in Paris ended in "a blaze of glory" with ballet, colored fountains, and fireworks at the Basin of Neptune at Versailles.

The trip concluded with Nash feeling that his family had seen and done a great deal. He foresaw correctly that memories of the trip would "recur often and for years." Apart from the many grand sights, the family had enjoyed Nash's sense for trivia, which found abundant stimuli in the unfamiliar cultures of France and Italy.

—I had forgotten the smell of French tobacco. And that automobiles in Paris climb up on the sidewalk. And that all French children speak fluent French.

—Life would be easier in both Italy and France if they printed their money on bathroom paper and put their money paper in the bathroom.

—It's an odd quirk to find that the water [in Rome] costs more than the wine.

—In Paris the English apothecaries furnish south-bound travelers with something known simply as THE MIXTURE. It is bismuth and paregoric and indispensable.

—[T]he French press . . . is full of wonderful unauthenticated horrors, couched in the most florid and ingenuous terms.

Frances, too, enjoyed the trip, though, abroad as at home, she was inclined to cast a critical eye from time to time. Nash would then take pains to reassure Mrs. Leonard with more cheerful reports:

—It was a long day and again we were tired which accounts for the tone of Frances's letter from Genoa. Things weren't really as bad as that.

Nash (front, second from right) was a board member of the St. George's literary magazine, *The Dragon*. He later credited the magazine's adviser, Arthur Roberts (back, third from right), for instilling in him a love of the English language. [*St. George's School*]

Nash (third from left) was an outstanding student at St. George's but made friends easily and had time for fun and games. [*Harry Ransom Humanities Research Center, University of Texas at Austin*]

On one of his trips to Baltimore after meeting Frances Leonard, Nash posed at the home of his sister Gwen. [*Harry Ransom Humanities Research Center, University of Texas at Austin*]

In Hollywood in January 1937, Nash worked on the script for *The Firefly*, a picture that starred Jeanette MacDonald. [*Time Life Pictures/Getty Images*]

Nash recruited his colleague from Hollywood, Sid Perelman, to co-author the book for *One Touch of Venus*, a Broadway hit that opened in October 1943. [© *Bettmann/CORBIS*]

Ogden and Frances and their daughters, Linell (front) and Isabel (back), with Frances's parents, Nellie and Will Leonard, at the family's Rugby Road home in Baltimore. They all thought this picture was far too solemn. [*Linell Smith and Isabel Eberstadt*]

In the Nash family, servants were a tradition even in times of financial strain. [*Time Life Pictures/Getty Images*]

The Nashes sailed to Europe aboard the *Ile de France* in 1949, bound for Paris, Florence, and Rome. [*Linell Smith and Isabel Eberstadt*]

Ogden and Frances (right) at the marriage of Isabel to Fred Eberstadt in 1954 in New York City. (Linell, married three years earlier, was occupied with the birth of her second daughter.) [*Isabel and Frederick Eberstadt*]

Nash enjoyed relaxing on the porch at the home in Little Boar's Head, New Hampshire, a summertime retreat for many years and later his and Frances's principal residence. [*Isabel and Frederick Eberstadt*]

Nash enjoyed wonderfully receptive audiences on the lecture circuit, but the grueling cross-country tours took a toll on his health. [*Harry Ransom Humanities Research Center, University of Texas at Austin*]

Always looking for new markets for his verse, Nash found one in 1956 with Hallmark cards. [© *Bettmann/CORBIS*]

Isabel (left) and Linell (right) delighted in the postage stamp issued
August 19, 2002, marking the centennial of Nash's birth. [*Baltimore Sun*]

—I got back in time to read Frances's letter to you and chided her for flashes of gloom, since our good hours far outnumber our difficult moments.

Abroad, as at home, Nash's admiration remained unwavering. After describing a magnificent outdoor opera set in the ruins of the Baths of Caracalla—"But you should see Frances now; she is radiant and really the most exciting thing in Rome."

Nash never set aside his professional life entirely. Crossing on the *Ile de France*, he had enjoyed the company of Bruce and Beatrice Gould, editors of the *Ladies' Home Journal*, in whose pages his work sometimes appeared, and Harry Scherman, head of the Book-of-the-Month Club. Then, in Paris, he met with Andre Kostelanetz to discuss a proposal that Nash write verses to accompany Saint Saëns's *Carnival of the Animals*. On the return trip, aboard the *De Grosse*, he wrote two poems, both of which appeared later that year in the *Saturday Evening Post*. Although neither of the shipboard verses had any connection with the trip, a third, written after his return, was inspired by his travels in continental trains. Nash, it seems, had regularly taken a seat in the compartment facing backward so that the girls could look forward. As described in "My Trip Daorba":

Indeed I am perhaps the only parent to be found
Who says Europe, or eporuE, as I think of it, the wrong way round.
I added little to my knowledge of the countryside but much to my
    reputation for docility
Riding backwards through ecnarF and ylatI.
I am not quite certain,
But I think in siraP I saw the ervuoL, the rewoT leffiE, and the
    Cathedral of emaD ertoN.
I shall remember ecnerolF forever,
For that is where I backed past the house where etnaD wrote the
    "onrefnI," or ydemoC eniviD, and twisted my neck admiring
    the bridges across the onrA reviR.
In emoR I glimpsed the muroF and the nacitaV as in a mirror in
    the fog.
While in ecineV I admired the ecalaP s'egoD as beheld from the
    steerage of an alodnoG.
So I find conditions overseas a little hard to judge,

Because all I know is what I saw retreating from me as I rode
    backwards in compartments in the niart and in carriages
    sitting on the taes-pmuj.

The verse appeared in *The New Yorker* and drew an appreciative letter from Harold Ross, couched in his characteristic blend of gruffness and warmth: "The latest verse, 'My Trip Daorba,' is one of the cleverest things I've read in many years. In general it is a privilege to be connected with the publication of your stuff."

In the spring of the following year, Linell graduated from Miss Porter's School in Farmington, Connecticut, and Isabel, having skipped a grade, graduated with her. Neither girl headed off to college. Linell had not enjoyed boarding school and was uninterested in further academics. One aspect of school that she had thoroughly enjoyed was singing in presentations of Gilbert and Sullivan, and those experiences had generated an ambition to be an opera singer. After a successful audition with Romano Romani, who had been the teacher of Rosa Ponselle, she took lessons from Romani while working as a nurse's aide at Johns Hopkins. Then, in the fall, she made her debut in Baltimore society.

Linell debuted, as her mother once had, at the Bachelors' Cotillion, and Ogden proudly did his part. Despite a a progressive muscular constriction of his fingers that gave him trouble with the tight white kid gloves, he twirled Linell around the dance floor and led her in one of the obligatory figures in which the girls were presented to the Cotillion Board. The occasion, of course, would not have been complete without a verse. In Nash's typical fashion, he saw the ridiculous amid the romantic:

LINES TO ACCOMPANY A COTILLION POSY

All of your partners are bald and married;
Some of your partners may have to be carried.
Should one expire of senile zest,
Place this bouquet upon his breast.

Isabel deferred her own debut as well as her admission to Bryn Mawr until the following year. In the meantime she traveled to Europe in the company of Nash's friend and agent, Alan Collins, and Collins's wife and daughter. The trip gave rise to an incident that would be long remembered in the Nash family. Isabel, it seems, aroused the interest of a man much older and married. Flattered by the attentions, Isabel took them seriously and was prepared, at least briefly, to reciprocate them.

When Nash learned of the matter, by a letter from Isabel, he was startled, indignant, and dismayed. The man in question, Spencer Curtis Brown, had founded the agency that represented Nash and, Nash recalled, in 1939 had made a pass at Frances in a London taxi. According to Nash, Brown had a reputation "less that of a Don Juan than of an under-the-table groper." Although the dalliance had ended by the time Nash learned of it, he took the occasion to write Isabel a letter of affectionate but serious admonition:

> Where was your sense of humor? Where was your sense of
> fastidiousness? And where, if I may use an old-fashioned phrase,
> was your moral sense? You should be intelligent enough to know
> that in various eras of history it has been fashionable to laugh at
> morals, but the fact of the matter is that Old Man Morals just
> keeps rolling along, and the laughers end up as driftwood on a
> sand bar. You can't beat the game, because morals as we know
> them represent the sum of the experience of the race. That is why
> it distressed me to find you glibly tossing off references to divorce.
> You surely have seen enough of its effects on your friends to know
> that it is a tragic thing even when forced on one partner by the
> vices of the other. Read the marriage vows again—they are not
> just words, not even just a poetic promise to God, they are a
> practical promise to yourself to be happy. This I know simply
> from looking around me.

After further admonitions, the letter turned to a report on various routine items of news from home. At the end, Nash returned to his theme, concluding with a lighter touch:

> Keep on having your gay time, but keep yourself in hand, and
> remember that, generally speaking, it's better to call older men
> Mister.
>
> All my love, Daddy.

Even today the letter stands up as a wise dose of critical judgment tempered by understanding and expressed with love, a balance not always easy to achieve.

Within a few months Linell was involved in a much more serious relationship with John Marshall Smith, whom she had met at a debutante party at the Baltimore Country Club. Johnny, tall and handsome, was nearly ten years older than Linell and a veteran of World War II. His mother was from an old Virginia family, the Pages, through whom Johnny traced his descent from Justice John Marshall, and her father had founded the Calvert Bank in Baltimore. Johnny's father, however, was a notorious womanizer whom Johnny's mother had left when Johnny was only four. Although Johnny's brother, Page Smith, had been educated at Dartmouth and would become a distinguished historian, Johnny had not attended college. When he met Linell, he was working in another Baltimore bank.

In June 1951, Linell and Johnny became engaged. Despite their difference in age, and Johnny's somewhat uncertain career prospects, Ogden and Frances approved. Indeed, Nash felt that Johnny's age was a positive factor. As he wrote Vernon Duke: "Name of prospective son-in-law, John Marshall Smith, of good Maryland and Virginia family but without a nickel—Fortunately Frances and I like him enormously. He is ten years older than Linell which is all to the good as she can do with a steadying hand, being a very immature nineteen." When the engagement was announced, *Life* magazine suggested to Nash a picture story of Linell and Johnny, accompanied by a reprise of Nash's "Song to Be Sung by the Father of Six-Months-Old Female Children" and a new verse reflecting his current sentiments. When Johnny and Linell were embarrassed by the idea, Nash negotiated to have the story focused just on the wedding day, when "the kids will be so busy they won't know a photographer from Cecil Beaton." *Life* paid Nash fifteen hundred dollars for the new verse which, as Nash wrote Dan Longwell, he would present to the bride and groom for their honeymoon.

In "Poem by the Father of the Bride, Aged 19," Nash celebrated the prospect of having for the first time some male companionship in the family:

Therefore I hail this happy anomaly,
A fellow male within the family,
And cause a daughter's wrath to bloom
By monopolizing of her groom.
Oh, let the girls get on with the trousseau,
Here's a Friday at last for Crusoe,
To chew the fat and exchange the dope with,
And a simple masculine mind to cope with.

    *   *   *   *

Nash's sentiments were understandable. Despite his patient nature, he could become exasperated with lengthy exchanges of female gossip among his wife and daughters. On such occasions he was known to "hum tunelessly, and then grind his teeth rather loudly and then begin to mutter something that sounded like 'woodchuck, woodchuck' and then suddenly say 'I can't bear it! Must change the conversation.'"

Before the wedding ceremony, Nash was more nervous than the youthful bride. On the way to the church in a limousine with Linell, he found his knees shaking, and when they arrived he felt himself slipping into shock. Linell came to the rescue, suggesting they go for a drive in one of the limousines hired for the wedding. As they briefly toured the Maryland countryside, Linell tried various ploys to relax her father, and she finally hit on a Swedish-dialect routine they had fooled around with at family parties:

> "You say to me," Linell ordered, "'Mrs. Oley Olsen, I hear your son has joined the Air Force. Is he a pilot yet?'"
>
> "Mrs. Oley Olsen," Nash repeated nervously, "I hear your son has joined the Air Force. Is he a pilot yet."
>
> "No," said Linell, "he's a yet pilot."
>
> They both started to laugh at the old family wheeze. "Back to the church," Linell quickly told the driver.
>
> At the church, Nash waited for the music and walked her to the altar without a quiver.
>
> "You're a yet pilot, old boy," he told himself proudly.

After the wedding at the Church of the Redeemer, a reception for five hundred guests was held at the Elkridge Club, where Ogden and Frances had first met. It was a grand affair, befitting the "Life Goes to the Wedding" coverage. Immediately after the wedding, Nash left on a lecture tour, but in Chicago he found the time to write to Linell, then on her honeymoon in New York. He told her that when he had left Baltimore the town was still "buzzing with complimentary talk about the wedding" and that "I think the fact that it was such a happy one must have showed through because I have never heard people speak with such genuine emotion." A year later, in her parents' tradition of wasting little time, Linell presented them with their first grandchild, Linell, who would be known in the family as Nell. Linell had talked Johnny into having a child right away, but she was disappointed when her doctor told her that she would have to give up riding the horse that Isabel had given her as a wedding present. She was amused, but not consoled, by her father's attempt at reassurance: "Well, I'm sure it's only for the first few months."

Meanwhile Isabel had dropped out of Bryn Mawr and taken courses in typing, cooking, and writing. Although her earliest writings imitated her father's verse, she had won a literary competition sponsored by *St. Nicholas Magazine* when she was nine, and her first published work, "Christmas Morning," had appeared in *Seventeen* in 1950 when she was seventeen. Nash had once, without her permission, shown some of Isabel's poems to Vernon Duke, who thought they were very good. Duke also thought that Isabel had a remarkable imagination, recalling particularly the occasion when she had told an editor of *Mademoiselle* that she had been born in Paris. When Nash had objected that Isabel had been born in Baltimore, she replied unabashed: "That's what you say, Father. I may very well have been born in Paris, for all we know." Now, as Nash described it in a letter to Duke, "She has half a novel that would knock your eye out, but she keeps tearing up 20,000 words and starting over."

In the summer of 1954, Isabel was sharing an apartment with a friend, and through her friend she met Fred Eberstadt, who was a few years older and working as a television producer at NBC. Isabel's first letter to her parents had quoted some snide remarks Fred had made, and described him as rather dreadful. So they were more than a bit startled when their next communication from Isabel, a month later in August, advised that she and Fred were engaged. Fred had attended Princeton, before and after serving in World War II, and his father was a wealthy New York lawyer and investment banker, Ferdinand Eberstadt. The senior Eberstadt was Jewish and a cousin of the financier Otto Kahn (a fact that Fred, raised an Episcopalian, had discovered only by accident when he was twenty-two). But he did have a Baltimore connection: his mother, Mary Tongue, had come from a prominent family in that city.

Given the rapid pace of events, Fred was understandably nervous at his first meeting with his prospective father-in-law. Nash had invited Fred and Isabel to dinner at the Cafe Cardinale in New York, and Fred wondered whether he might feel the sting of Nash's wit. He was on his best behavior and drank no alcohol—but he had so much coffee that his hands shook and he found himself making frequent departures for the men's room. To his relief, Nash did not make him the object of satirical remarks, and the dinner was entirely pleasant. Finally, Isabel asked her father if he wasn't going to

152

ask Fred whether he could support her. To her surprise, Nash simply brushed off the question, saying he was sure it wouldn't be a problem. In a letter to Vernon Duke, he described Eberstadt as "very bright, attractive and worldly and I think quite equipped to handle Isabel, a task I feel would be too much for most young men." Isabel's wedding was less elaborate than Linell's. It took place in the chapel of St. Bartholomew's Church on Park Avenue and was followed by a reception at the Nashes' New York apartment.

The Smiths and the Eberstadts soon gave Ogden and Frances several more grandchildren to dote on: Frances and Brigid Smith arrived in 1954 and 1956 respectively, and Nick and Fernanda Eberstadt in 1955 and 1960. Nash was delighted by his status as a grandfather. In 1953, after Nell was born, he wrote Arthur Roberts at St. George's, "I am now a grandfather; the wonderchild is a ten month old girl who keeps me in a rosy mist of simple-minded adoration." Inevitably, it would not be long before Nash was moved to reflect in verse upon the responsibilities of grandparenthood in "Come On In, the Senility Is Fine":

> [Y]ou have to personally superintend your grandchild from
>   diapers to pants and from bottle to spoon,
> Because you know your own child hasn't sense enough to come in
>   out of a typhoon.

At the same time, however, there was still a knowing eye cocked in Frances's direction:

> You don't have to live forever to become a grampa, but if you do
>   want to live forever,
> Don't try to be clever;
> If you wish to reach the end of the trail with an uncut throat,
> Don't go around saying Quote I don't mind being a grampa but I
>   hate being married to a gramma Unquote.

Being a grampa would become an important part of Nash's life over the next several years. At the same time he faced the continuing challenge of earning a living as a poet.

11

ECONOMICS OF POETRY:
SELLING THE WARES

In 1923, Robert Frost made a widely quoted observation on the economics of poets and poetry:

> Do you know,
> Considering the market, there are more
> Poems produced than any other thing?
> No wonder poets sometime have to seem
> So much more businesslike than business-men
> Their wares are so much harder to get rid of.

Some years later Ogden Nash also remarked, though not in verse, on the difficulty of earning a living from writing poetry. He noted that most poets held teaching positions and depended on universities and grants for support, and that books of poetry rarely sold more than two or three thousand copies. Such sales, he said, "don't pay for much in the way of breakfast food."

Although Nash's own situation was quite different from other poets in some respects, at bottom it was much the same. Nash's books invariably sold considerably more than two or three thousand copies. And Ogden and Frances benefited from the gift of the Rugby Road house as well as income that Frances received from a family trust. The Nashes, however, were not interested in living on breakfast food. They maintained a style of life that, while neither extravagant nor ostentatious, was by no means austere. Both Ogden and Frances enjoyed living comfortably, dressing well, traveling, and entertaining graciously. Under such circumstances, making ends meet from the income of a poet—even a very popular and highly compensated one—was, more often than not, a bit of a scramble.

Nash did not have a teaching position to fall back on, though he might have done well in such a setting. After all, his friend Sid Perelman, a gentleman of some erudition in his own right, claimed that the three most learned people he had known were Edmund Wilson, Ogden Nash, and Aldous Huxley. Nevertheless the abbreviation of Nash's formal education, as well as the style of his verse, probably made him an unlikely candidate for a place in academia, and there is no evidence that he ever considered the possibility. As a result, Nash continually felt the need to deploy his talents as fully and as profitably as possible.

Nash's financial condition was frequently complicated by a chronic inability to develop a budget and stick to it. Several years after his death, Linell and Isabel published a selection of Nash's verse under the evocative title, *A Penny Saved Is Impossible*. The title poem concluded fittingly:

> Oh, that I were not a spendthrift, oh then would my heart indeed
> be gladsome,
> Because it is so futile being a spendthrift because I don't know any
> places where thrift could be spent even if I had some.

The responsibility of providing Nash with a measure of financial stability was largely in the hands of his agents, Curtis Brown Ltd., and his principal publisher, Little, Brown and Company. At Curtis Brown, Nash was initially represented by Ray Everitt and his wife, Helen. Nash's first five books of verse were published by Simon and Schuster, but Nash grew disenchanted with their handling of his books, and when Ray Everitt left Curtis Brown to become an editor at Little, Brown, it took little persuasion for Nash to follow him there. Nash's first book for Little Brown, *I'm a Stranger Here Myself*, was published in 1938 and was dedicated to the Everitts, "whose five years of steadfast friendship, lavish cajolery and vituperative encouragement have brought it on their own heads." The book landed on the best-seller lists, and by 1939 fifty thousand copies had been sold.

Some of the success of *I'm a Stranger* may be credited to Angus Cameron who was working with Everitt at Little, Brown. Cameron felt that, while Simon and Schuster had presented Nash as a "funny man," it would be more accurate—and more effective—to portray him as a minor philosopher. Cameron's view was justified by the treatment that Nash's verse had been given by critics, and there was little difficulty in shifting the focus of advertising and promotion. To make the point, the jacket for *I'm a Stranger* even took the somewhat unusual step of quoting from the London *Times*. After noting that Nash was "a most ingenious and amusing critic of frailty and absurdity," the *Times Literary Supplement* continued: "It would be a mistake, however, to think of him merely as a funny man; like James Thurber, he has a Democritean streak which entitles him to the respect due to a philosopher, albeit a laughing one. . . ."

Ultimately *I'm a Stranger* went through thirty-five printings and became the best-selling of all of Nash's books. Nash was extremely grateful for Cameron's insight, and when Everitt, the same age as Nash, died of a heart attack in 1947, Cameron became Nash's editor.

After Ray Everitt left Curtis Brown, Nash was represented there by Helen Everitt and later by Alan Collins. Collins, like Nash, was an alumnus of Doubleday, Doran and had joined Curtis Brown as manager of its New York office in 1934. He had graduated from Williams College, received a master's from Harvard, dressed conservatively, and had a serious mien that was livened by a keen sense of humor. He purchased the agency from its London parent in 1941 and remained Nash's agent until Collins's death in 1968. Like the Everitts, Collins became Nash's personal friend, even advising him on such matters as proper tipping on a transatlantic voyage. ("On a British ship there is a little fellow who comes out of the cracks just as you are about to leave the state-room and says 'I am Boots, sir' and to him I give two dollars.") Collins, assisted by Naomi Burton, represented Nash in relations with Little, Brown while negotiations with magazines were handled by Edith Haggard and later by Emilie Jacobson. Nash was grateful to both Haggard and Jacobson for their tireless efforts at placing his poems and their encouragement when placement was difficult. He dedicated *You Can't Get There from Here*, published in 1957, "To Edith Haggard, good friend, peerless agent and brutal taskmaster, with affectionate gratitude."

In addition to representing Nash, the Curtis Brown firm served in some respects as his banker. Correspondence between Nash and Curtis Brown, and between Curtis Brown and Little, Brown over many years often dealt with Nash's requests for advances, citing various reasons, ranging from tax payments to the burden of the weekly payroll for domestic help at the Nashes' summer home in Little Boar's Head. Little, Brown valued Nash and went as far as they felt they could in accommodating his requests. Nash's editor in 1954, Jim Sherman, wrote to Alan Collins almost wistfully that he hoped Nash's account could be brought into balance so that Nash "could begin to enjoy credit balances instead of debit balances on his royalty statement." He added, however, that "we are very sympathetic with his situation and if he needs money now, we'll send it now and you will find it enclosed." Eventually Nash established a system under which all his royalties and other income were held by Curtis Brown's accounting department, run by Nellie Sukerman ("Sukie" or Sukey"). The firm then established a reserve for tax payments and disbursed an "allowance" to Nash. Even this system was far from perfect, and when Nash's income flourished, he would be dismayed to find that his good fortune had left his tax reserve seriously deficient. Transcending problems of financial management, Nash believed, was a need to find additional sources of revenue.

Under the circumstances, the attraction he felt for Hollywood and Broadway was financial as well as artistic. But his pursuit of opportunities in show business carried an inevitable risk to his work as a poet. Although Nash's ventures in the theater did not force a complete halt to his poetry, as had the earlier experience in Hollywood, they did have a measurable impact. During the years of *Venus* and *Sweet Bye and Bye*, the decline in Nash's production of verse confirmed that Frances's concerns on that score had not been groundless. In the five years from 1943 through 1947, Nash published only fifty-eight new poems—the same number he had published in 1942 alone. By 1948, however, Nash realized that he could no longer neglect his verse. In that year he published thirty-five new poems in magazines, and the following year saw the publication of *Versus*, his first collection of new verse since *Good Intentions* in 1942. Over the next several years Nash would continue to publish new verse at a fairly steady rate, resulting in two additional collections, *The Private Dining Room* in 1952 and *You Can't Get There from Here* in 1957.

When he was not distracted by show business, Nash was a highly prolific poet who wrote well over a thousand poems in his lifetime. Most of them were published initially in magazines and later republished in book form. A flyleaf in the posthumous collection *I Wouldn't Have Missed It* lists twenty-three books, exclusive of children's books, and does not include collections by other publishers such as the *Pocket Book of Ogden Nash* and the Modern Library's *Selected Verse of Ogden Nash*, or a later collection, *A Penny Saved Is Impossible*. Yet Nash sometimes had difficulty producing

verse rapidly enough to meet the public demand and his own financial re-
quirements. One solution was to publish "selections" of verse that had
been published in previous books. Thus, of the twenty-three books listed
on the flyleaf, fifteen contained poems not previously published in book
form, and seven were "collected and selected." One, *The Face Is Familiar*
(1940), was a hybrid, offering some new verse as well as previously published verse, and was also published in a low-priced edition ($1.00 rather
than $2.75) by the Garden City Publishing Company. Three of the col-
lected and selected books, *Many Long Years Ago* (1945), *Verses from 1929
On* (1959), and *I Wouldn't Have Missed It* (1975), were general; the other
four, *Family Reunion* (1950), *Marriage Lines: Notes of a Student Husband*
(1964), *Bed Riddance: A Posy for the Indisposed* (1970), and *Ave Ogden:
Nash in Latin* (1973), had specific themes, as suggested by their titles, and
were aimed at narrower audiences.

Keeping all of that straight, and determining what to market (and when
and how and by whom), was the responsibility of Little, Brown along with
Nash and Alan Collins. It was not always easy. In 1945, for example, as Little, Brown was assembling poems for *Many Long Years Ago*, they and Nash
were deciding which poems to give Bennett Cerf for his Modern Library
edition, *Selected Verse of Ogden Nash*. Not surprisingly, there arose considerable confusion in determining which poems would go in which book.
Nash had a cautious view of collections that assembled poems previously
published in book form. He worried that critics, bookstores, and the public
might react against too much reuse of his material, and some ideas for proposed books were scrapped on that ground. Too, there were inevitably concerns about intramural competition, one Nash book taking customers from
another. Thus a 1947 Little, Brown internal memorandum noted a decline
in sales of Nash books and suggested that sales were being affected by three
reprint editions then on the market—Modern Library, Pocket Books, and
the Garden City edition of *The Face Is Familiar*—and suggested that the
latter two might be taken off the market. Nevertheless the Garden City
book had one more printing the following year (for a rather grand total of
172,500 copies) and the Pocket Book was discontinued, only to reemerge in
a new edition in 1955.

The 1955 Pocket Books edition became something of a sore point with
Nash on two counts. The back cover of the book bore the phrase "The
Golden Trashery of Ogden Nashery." He inscribed one copy of the book:
"My years with Simon & Schuster were largely spent in refusing to call any

of my books 'The Golden Trashery of Ogden Nashery.' I thought when I got away from them I was safe, but look at the cover." Nash was even more perturbed by Pocket Books' choice for the poem that opened the book. "Pastoral" described a scene in a meadow and concluded with the lines: "Two cows/ Mildly mooing;/ No bull;/ Nothing doing." While the poem seems amusing and inoffensive, Nash thought it was one of the few poems he wished he had not written. It disappeared from the next edition (as did the reference to a "Golden Trashery").

Perhaps because of Nash's own background in publishing, he took a particularly keen interest in the marketing of his books. When Little, Brown published *Versus* in 1949, Nash was disappointed in both the sales and his publisher's efforts in promoting it. Little, Brown's executive vice president, Stanley Salmen, responded that advertising had been in line with sales. After Nash had fretted for several months, and discussed the matter with Alan Collins, he instructed Collins to write to Little, Brown's president, Arthur Thornhill, and advise him that Nash intended to seek a new publisher. Collins did as he was asked, in a letter dated May 11, 1950, and undertook to explain Nash's decision. Addressing the relationship of advertising and sales, Collins suggested that it was "like the chicken and egg riddle," but argued that for many books it was important to have an expenditure for advertising in excess of advance sales "to get the ball rolling." More fundamentally, however, Collins lamented that "somehow a new Nash book has ceased to be an exciting property both to Little, Brown and the book trade generally." Collins asked that Little, Brown agree to cancel unfulfilled contracts and transfer fulfilled contracts, stock, and plates.

Collins's letter produced an immediate reaction. He was invited to Boston and flew there on May 18 for a meeting with Thornhill and Cameron. In the course of cocktails and a long lunch, they assured Collins of Nash's importance to them and how much they wished to retain him as a Little, Brown author. No specific commitments were made with respect to advertising and promotion before Collins departed to catch a four o'clock plane, but he was apparently satisfied, and the crisis ended. In a follow-up memorandum, Cameron advised Thornhill that, on the way to lunch, he had suggested to Collins that the issue would not have come up "if there had not been some atmosphere in the agency favorable to its coming up," and to his surprise, Collins had agreed. The memorandum indicated that Cameron was referring specifically to Naomi Burton, but there is no other evidence of what role, if any, she had played in precipitating Collins's letter.

The May meeting did not settle matters for all time. Less than a year later, in January 1951, Collins found himself relaying a farrago of queries and complaints from Dallas where Nash was on a lecture tour. He had discovered only by accident that a bookstore in Dallas had a large supply of his books: Why hadn't he been informed? Why had there been no books at the largest bookstore in Des Moines, "where the club women were screaming and bringing up battered copies of *Hard Lines*"? He ran across a Garden City reprint of *Good Intentions* at $1.00 competing with the regular edition at $2.75: Why hadn't he been informed? Then he turned again to the subject of advertising, referring to the advertising for a book by Will Cuppy and expressing disbelief that the "the Cuppy market is bigger than the Nash market." Pleading for more advertising, Nash concluded, "Will you and Naomi please apply the harpoon before it is too late—and if they do consent to advertise, for God's sake make Denhart get some feeling of excitement and success into copy and layout." Little, Brown was able to satisfy Nash on all counts, reminding him of his agreement to the Garden City reprint several years before and describing a previously planned advertising campaign that was about to commence. The same and similar issues would arise repeatedly but would not again reach a crisis level until the late sixties.

Later in 1951, Nash experienced another change in editors at Little, Brown. It was the height of the McCarthy era, and Angus Cameron, who had been active in the Progressive party, fell victim to it. Cameron was not fired, but he received a letter from Arthur Thornhill advising him that his "outside activities" would have to be approved. Although Cameron surmised that the letter had been written by another executive, he concluded that he had to leave the firm. He would spend the next several years running a small publishing house of his own until 1959, when he joined Alfred Knopf. Although Nash did not join protests against Senator McCarthy, he supported Cameron and remained in touch with him. When Cameron joined Knopf, Nash briefly considered following him there, but he and Cameron concluded that the transfer of existing stock and contracts would be too difficult. Cameron was succeeded at Little, Brown by Jim Sherman as Nash's editor. Sherman did not have as strong an editorial background as Cameron, but Nash had never relied much on Little, Brown for "editing" anyway. More important, Sherman was known for having a sweet disposition. He respected Nash and was sympathetic to his financial needs. They got on well.

In 1953, Little, Brown published *The Private Dining Room* to the enthusiastic reviews to which Nash had grown accustomed. Charles Poore in the *New York Times* said that the book presented Nash at his best and displayed "a new grandeur in his prosody this time, a profounder understanding of the orneriness of things." *Time* observed that Nash had "provoked so many chuckles by stating good sense in metrical nonsense that many readers have never paused to appraise the discipline, economy and pungency of the Nash poem at its best." But Nash and Collins found the sales figures disappointing and raised the usual complaints about advertising, requiring Sherman to follow in the footsteps of his predecessor in assuring them of Nash's importance to Little, Brown. Ultimately sales reached only about 23,000 copies. The problem appears to have been once again Nash competing with Nash. *The Private Dining Room* was published in April, and in June the Book-of-the-Month Club announced a special promotion offering six Nash titles for $5.95. The promotion was a success: more than 60,000 sets were sold by the end of 1955, earning Nash over $17,000 in royalties. But while Nash had been grateful to Arthur Thornhill for negotiating the deal, it may be that neither he nor Collins nor Little, Brown had thought through the timing of the BOMC offer in relation to *The Private Dining Room*.

Nash and Little, Brown frequently considered ways of expanding the market for Nash's verse, and one possibility that had been recognized early on was poetry for children. After all, Nash's very first book, *The Cricket of Carador*, had been a children's book, albeit in prose. The idea of a children's book of poetry was first broached in 1942 when a Little, Brown editor put together a list of Nash poems that might be suitable for youngsters. The idea was rejected by Little, Brown's then president, Arthur McIntyre, on the grounds that very young readers would not understand Nash and that older children would appreciate more poems than were on the list. In 1947, Little, Brown did publish a number of Nash's animal poems, accompanied by Vernon Duke tunes, under the title *Musical Zoo*. Four years later the idea of a book of children's poems was revived with *Parents Keep Out: Elderly Poems for Youngerly Readers*. The book contained a number of poems from the 1942 list, as well as many others, and sold well. Nash then suggested a different idea, a children's book consisting of a single, long poem tentatively titled *The Year There Was No Christmas*. Little,

Brown immediately took to the concept and hoped to publish the book in 1952. Five years later the publisher was still hoping. In the interim they had begged, pleaded, and cajoled, but despite repeated promises Nash had never been able to finish the poem. Then, in 1957, help came from within Nash's own family.

Linell had always shown a talent for drawing and painting, and Nash invited her to do the illustrations for the book. Linell, who no longer aspired to an operatic career, had no experience in that particular type of artwork, but she quickly accepted. Spurred by her participation, Nash finally completed the book. It appeared that year under the title *The Christmas That Almost Wasn't*. Although it had stiff competition from a book with a similar theme, *How the Grinch Stole Christmas*, the Nash book was widely and favorably reviewed. The plot was succinctly summarized by the poet Lloyd Frankenberg in the *New York Times*: "Take a rollicking jolly king and his cheering subjects, add an evil nephew, bring it to a boil with assorted hags and hoodlums, create an inextricable situation, send a boy to extricate, have him meet a bad, bad bird and a good little girl and a long-dead saint." Although the book did not employ Nash's "broken-field rhythms and last-ditch rhymes," wordplay can be found here and there (the youthful heroes are named Nick and Nell, after Nash grandchildren, and the boy hopes that he will be "the Nick of time").

The following year Nash spoke to Jim Sherman about the idea of doing a children's book from a popular poem, "The Tale of Custard the Dragon," that had first appeared in *The Bad Parents' Garden of Verse* in 1936 and had later been reprinted in several Nash collections. He followed up with a letter suggesting that "if it's not carrying nepotism too far," Linell would be his first choice as illustrator. Nash pointed out that the reviews of the *Christmas* book had contained very favorable comments on her drawings. Despite those reviews, Little, Brown's editor of children's books, Helen Jones, resisted using Linell to illustrate the *Custard* books. ("Even though we don't need a name artist to go with Ogden Nash, we ought at least to have one comparably skilled in his, i.e., the artist's medium.") Her objections, however, were overruled, and in the end Jones found Linell's illustrations quite charming. Indeed, *Custard the Dragon* was such a success that it was followed by a second book, *Custard the Dragon and the Wicked Knight*, for which Jones thought the illustrations were even better.

After the *Custard* books, Linell went on to write several children's books herself, illustrating the first but taking on her own illustrator for the others. In the meantime, not to be outdone, Isabel also published a children's book in 1957, *Where Did Tuffy Hide*, inspired by time she had spent with Linell's daughter, Nell. She would publish two more children's books co-authored with Fred, and her long-awaited first novel, *The Banquet Vanishes*, in 1958.

Nash wrote another dozen children's books, and while they were always secondary to his adult verse, they came to be an important part of his work. He never criticized the Dr. Seuss books, but he made it plain that his own approach was consciously quite different. He was, he said, "violently opposed to the trend in education today of trying to suit the books to the little mind instead of letting the little mind grow as it tackles the books." Thus he did not think that children could be taught "by simply repeating hat, cat, mat, rat, vat," but believed it was necessary to "sneak a few words in on them." If children didn't know a word, Nash suggested, they could look it up or figure out its meaning from the context. Finally, after noting that children love rhythm and have a keen ear, Nash claimed he was even more careful than usual with rhythm and meter when writing for children. Although he never matched the commercial success of Dr. Seuss, he found that "with six or seven going you end up with a little steady income."

Even augmented by children's books, Nash's income from book royalties was relatively modest. In 1961, Little, Brown prepared a summary of Nash's sales and royalties since 1938, when they had become his publisher. The summary included both adult and children's books and the special editions issued by other publishers. For that twenty-three-year period, royalties were just over $200,000. It was a record that would surely have been the envy of most poets, but it was not exactly a foundation of affluence. Nash's book royalties had, of course, been supplemented by the fees from magazines that had published his work in the first instance, and by royalties from *One Touch of Venus*, but a need for additional revenue remained. Children's books were only one of the ways Nash found to diversify his writing and generate more income.

Prose was another avenue. Back in the thirties, he had written a number of humorous prose pieces, and while *The New Yorker* generally preferred his poetry, it had published several of his submissions, as had the *Saturday Evening Post*. Then, in the late forties, Nash turned again to prose of a rather different sort. In 1947 he wrote a short story, "The Other Mind Reader," and the following year "Victoria." The stories appeared respectively in *Collier's* and *Harper's Bazaar*; both were very short specimens of

163

the horror story. Although the subject matter was hardly typical for Nash, his satirical tone was recognizable. ("[Victoria] could weep over the death of a horse in a story and remain composed over the death of an aunt in the hospital; she would rather eat between meals than at them; she wrote to her parents once a week if in need of anything; and she truly meant to do the right thing, only so often the wrong thing was easier.") Despite the success of the two stories, Nash said he lacked the patience for writing fiction, a form he found more difficult than verse, and he did not pursue it. Other ventures into prose were few and far between. They included a short sketch that appeared in *The New Yorker* and light essays for *Ladies' Home Journal* and *McCall's*, but collectively they did not add much to the bottom line.

Nash suggested various explanations for his failure to write more prose. One was that he preferred verse because it provided a mask behind which he could remain concealed: "When I use this form, people can never be sure whether I'm ignorant or just pretending to be ignorant—and I'm never quite sure about that myself." The concealment, he said, enabled him to express himself without self-consciousness; in writing prose "the naked bones are there." Moreover, in writing prose Nash said he could feel E. B. White or James Thurber "looking over my shoulder for some tautology or solecism or something badly expressed." Put another way, it may be that, since Nash's verse had been so highly acclaimed, he was uncomfortable at turning out prose that, while publishable, was not exceptional.

Nash was more successful in finding unexpected places to market his verse. In 1957 he began to write greeting-card verse for Hallmark Cards. His verse was not of the sentimental variety but was clearly in his own voice. The company added appropriately whimsical illustrations to Nash's poems, and the cards became a distinctive addition to the Hallmark line. Nash, never one to waste, recycled some of his previously written verse: "More than a catbird hates a cat . . . ," originally a valentine to Frances, later a published poem, and still later a song in *One Touch of Venus*, was again revised and came full circle by becoming a Valentine's Day card. But most of Nash's material was fresh and some of it quite timely, even to the point of an occasional, not so subtle reference to the cold war. On a card depicting Christmas bells and a flying missile with a sprig of greenery and berries:

At Christmas in the olden times
The sky was filled with happy chimes.
But now the sky above us whistles

With supersonic guided missiles.
This Christmas I'll be modern, so
Here comes my guided mistletoe.

Another, more cheerful verse, seems every bit as fitting today:

How speedy is the life we're living!
Now Christmas starts before Thanksgiving!
If this continues,
By and by
We'll be singing carols in July.
Since one must keep in step somehow,
Here's *next year's* "Merry Christmas" *now!!!*

Nash's relationship with Hallmark flourished and lasted nearly ten years, during which he and Frances became personal friends of Joyce Hall and his wife Elizabeth.

In an even more commercial vein, Nash occasionally wrote verse for advertising. He admitted to no embarrassment at such exercises; on the contrary, he said he was proud of them because he thought he did them well. Some products he rejected as inappropriate, such as a constipation remedy for which his services were sought in 1956. Nash regretted having to turn down a lucrative commission, but as he wrote Alan Collins, "If they want anything on pellagra, leprosy or syphilis I'm their man, but I'm afraid constipation is eliminated, if that isn't a contradiction in terms." On the other hand, having been a heavy smoker all his life, Nash had no objection in 1953 to endorsing a cigarette in prose and verse:

I hope I'm not a crank, but I've got one foible
I don't enjoy anything unless it's enjoyable.
I don't happen to go for psychoanalysis,
But I've made my own Lucky-Strike-o-analysis,
I'm pernickety about what I like,
And for thirty years I've smoked Lucky Strike.

Nash's endorsement was sincere; he remained a cigarette smoker even as the evidence of medical risks mounted. In 1964 he published a lengthy poem in the *Saturday Evening Post* that defended smoking and brought him a flood of critical mail, but he remained unrepentant.

Less controversial products for which Nash wrote advertising copy ranged from dog food to telephone service. His most sophisticated effort was a brochure for Merrill Lynch that required some interesting revisions before it was accepted. Drawing on his brief experience as a French instructor, Nash's poem included the following couplet:

> The traveler in Paris may feel like a flutter in what the French
>   politely call *ventres de cochon glaces* but which we Americans
>   who are not such verbal Nice Nellies,
> Well, we refer to them as frozen pork abdomens, or even bellies.

When a sharp-eyed Merrill executive politely informed Nash that *carcasses de porc congelees* was "Commodity French" for frozen pork bellies, he agreed to substitute that phrase for *ventres de cochon glaces*. At that point, however, the chairman of Merrill's Board weighed in with the opinion that not very many of Merrill's customers were familiar with the commodity trading of pork bellies in any language. Nash promptly obliged by supplying two new lines:

> The traveler in Paris who may have begun to feel that an English-
>   speaking Frenchman is a myth
> Will be delighted to find that the French term for Merrill Lynch,
>   Pierce, Fenner & Smith is simply Merrill Lynch, Pierce,
>   Fenner & Smith.

The brochure was printed and distributed, and Nash earned three thousand dollars (or the equivalent of several poems published in magazines).

Writing for Hallmark and for advertisers provided welcome income but was not the only, or even the most important, of Nash's efforts to broaden his base of financial support. Even more significant were fees from the lecture circuit and from television. While Nash never considered himself a "performer," he spent a great deal of time and energy on stage or before the camera.

12

FROM RADIO TO LECTURE STAGE
TO TELEVISION

Nash's earliest opportunities as a performer came during his time in Hollywood. One of the more enjoyable aspects of that sojourn had been the opportunity to appear on two of the most popular radio programs of the day, the *Chase and Sanborn Hour*, with Edgar Bergen and Charlie McCarthy, and the *Kraft Music Hall* with Bing Crosby. The invitations to appear on those programs came after the success of *I'm a Stranger Here Myself* had enhanced the national reputation Nash had earned by his earlier books. Put another way, they had no connection with his disappointing career as a scriptwriter, except for the fact that the latter had brought him to Los Angeles, where the programs originated, and had led to his friendship with a West Coast agent, Corny Jackson.

It was Jackson who arranged for Nash's invitation to appear on the *Chase and Sanborn Hour* in March 1939. The genesis of the show, starring the ventriloquist Edgar Bergen, had occurred when Bergen appeared on Rudy Vallee's program and was an immediate hit. After Bergen had returned several times with his dummy, Charlie McCarthy, Chase and Sanborn gave Bergen his own show, beginning in May 1937. From this distance it be difficult to understand how ventriloquism translated so successfully on radio. In fact it was something of a mystery at the time, and one that has never been satisfactorily explained. Nonetheless, as one historian of the medium has summed it up, "Ventriloquism is a visual art. But in

Charlie McCarthy, Bergen had something going for him that transcended those restrictions. In the minds of millions of Americans, Charlie Mc-Carthy became a real person. His character took on three-dimensional qualities and adapted itself with particular zest to the audio format." The show leaped ahead of established competitors, including the *Jack Benny Program* and the *Eddie Cantor Show*.

In addition to Bergen and McCarthy, regulars on the show included the actor Don Ameche and the screen siren Dorothy Lamour, who were joined by glamorous guest stars. According to Corny Jackson, Nash read his poems beautifully and was a big success with the public. On the other hand, Jackson said, the cast of the show, other than Bergen, were thoroughly confused by Nash and his verse and didn't really understand what he was doing on the program. The prime example was Dorothy Lamour, who always arrived wearing a hat with a feather, stood next to Nash, and frequently leaned forward in a way that put the feather in Nash's face. Although Nash responded with verbal darts, many of them appeared to pass by unnoticed until matters came to a head one day. Miss Lamour confronted Jackson, "You and Ogden Nash have tried more goddamned cute tricks around here than anybody I've ever known, but today you've gone too far and I am not going to read that poem!" The poem in question was entitled "The Egg":

> Let's think of eggs.
> They have no legs.
> Chickens come from eggs
> But they have legs.
> The plot thickens;
> Eggs come from chickens,
> But have no legs under 'em.
> What a conundrum!

Mystified, Jackson asked what the problem was. Lamour became even more furious. "If you don't think I know what that word means—and that I'll be fool enough to say it on the air—you're crazy! I wasn't born yesterday!" Jackson wasted no time in debate or explanation, and the poem was dropped. After all, if Lamour thought a conundrum was something lewd, perhaps millions of listeners might have a similar impression.

Nash appeared several times on the *Chase and Sanborn Hour*. He did not merely turn up and read a poem or two but tried to do whatever he could to make the broadcasts entertaining. The programs were produced by the sponsor's advertising agency, J. Walter Thompson, and Nash wrote Frances before one show that he was going to their offices for a script conference. He was "eager to make this next broadcast a really good one," Nash said, because although the agency had liked the last one, he had been dissatisfied. The next day he wrote to say that he had "spent a very satisfactory four hours with the Thompson people and given them an idea or two that might work out nicely, but of course we won't know until Sunday night." Nash did not critique the next broadcast but did pass along terse appraisals of his colleagues: Bergen was "extremely nice," Ameche "very kind and helpful," and Claudette Colbert "charming." Ginger Rogers, however, he found "a great disillusion, very coarse, painted and dyed." He mentioned no friction with Dorothy Lamour (or her feather); on the contrary, he said she was "very pleasant" but "as dumb as you would imagine." As to Charlie McCarthy and Mortimer Snerd, he offered no comment.

At the end of April 1939, Nash returned to Baltimore, but in July he was back in Hollywood for an appearance on the Rudy Vallee hour, and in 1941 he was twice a guest on the *Kraft Music Hall* with Bing Crosby. Wartime travel restrictions prevented further jaunts to the West Coast, but in 1942, Nash found a regular slot on the Guy Lombardo Show broadcast from New York City. That position was arranged by Naomi Burton, who saw that, despite his previous experience, Nash was still rather shy. Accordingly she took the responsibility of protecting him from undue indignities on the show. If, for example, someone at rehearsal suggested that it might be funny if Mr. Nash would bark like a dog, Burton would rise to say, "Mr. Nash is not going to bark like a dog," and sit down again. While the Lombardo show was not in the same league with the *Kraft Music Hall* and the *Chase and Sanborn Hour*, it was a steady engagement that provided welcome revenue. Nash summed it up in a letter to Kurt Weill in December 1943, when he was leaving the show: "I have always been uncomfortable on it, largely because it could have been fairly good but wasn't, and every Monday I felt that I was making a buffoon of myself in public. However, I mustn't speak ill of it, as it did pull me through financially until Venus was able to offer me her arms."

Difficulties of wartime travel also put a crimp in Nash's activities on the lecture circuit, but by 1945 he had resumed the tours, which were organized by an agency headed by W. Colston Leigh. For a 50 percent commission,

Leigh had the ability to concoct itineraries for Nash that the latter found ambitious and frequently exhausting. While the compensation from lecturing was no match for Broadway royalties, it nonetheless came in handy. As Nash wrote Vernon Duke after the closing of *Two's Company*, "The lecturing, which I had bitterly resented in advance, turned out to be a Godsend in view of the Davis fiasco, as it brings in a few dollars." The lecture tours would occupy Nash for several weeks a year for nearly twenty years and have a significant impact on his life and health.

Always a strain, the lecture tours were less objectionable to Nash when, as the girls grew older, Frances was able to join him. One of her first trips was a five-week jaunt in 1945 with stops in Wisconsin, Michigan, Ohio, Illinois, New Mexico, California, Washington, Idaho, and back to Washington. The trip was highly successful. Books sold well after each lecture, and Nash happily gave Frances credit: "[T]he snake oil man can't sell the medicine without a pretty girl."

Although Frances was a quite private person, she acquiesced in the exposure that came with the publication of her husband's verse. In a rare interview in 1975, four years after Nash's death, she said that, in general, she was not bothered by Nash's poems that were "rude" about her. Ogden, she said, wrote about human nature, and she certainly knew she wasn't perfect. Ironically, the one poem to which she objected was one that Nash invariably read in his lectures. "I felt that he was analyzing me in that one," she explained, "because he had this timorous woman who is always screaming about gas leaks and things." The poem "I Do, I Will, I Have" was one of Nash's most popular:

> Just as I know that there are two Hagens, Walter and Copen,
> I know that marriage is a legal and religious alliance entered into
>   by a man who can't sleep with the window shut and a woman
>   who can't sleep with the window open.
> Moreover, just as I am unsure of the difference between flora and
>   fauna and flotsam and jetsam,
> I am quite sure that marriage is the alliance of two people one of
>   whom never remembers birthdays and the other never
>   forgetsam,
> And he refuses to believe there is a leak in the water pipe or the
>   gas pipe and she is convinced she is about to asphyxiate or
>   drown,

And she says, Quick get up and get my hairbrushes off the
    window sill, it's raining in, and he replies,
Oh they're all right, its only raining straight down.
    ✻   ✻   ✻   ✻

Anyone, of course, might feel some frustration at being depicted humorously in public and with no opportunity for rebuttal. And that might be
particularly true in the case of someone who, even if shy in public, was by
no means timorous at home. On the other hand, the very fact that Nash
continued to read the poem to his lecture audiences suggests that Frances
had not objected strongly.

When Frances was not able to accompany him on trips, Nash contin-
ued his practice of writing to her almost daily. (In 1951 his routinely ambitious itinerary brought her letters from cities, towns, and hamlets in Illinois,
Iowa, Kansas, Missouri, Oklahoma, Texas, Louisiana, Alabama, Florida,
Kentucky, Ohio, and Minnesota.) Nash's letters were, on the whole, mundane accounts of his travels, but they were brightened by flashes of his wit.
The weather was a frequent topic, and it sometimes rose to the occasion.
("Every demon out of the Arabian hell is howling at the windows. I have
been privileged to undergo an extra fine Texas Panhandle dust storm and
it is an experience—The wind was blowing hard when I got off the train
this afternoon; as Dean Allen, who met me was opening the car door, his
hat took off like a kangaroo and he retrieved it a hundred yards away.")
Nash also reported faithfully on the discomforts of travel, bumpy trains,
late trains, and confining quarters ("I have found an infinitesimal hotel
room here, smaller than the bathroom"). Meals were generally unexciting:
"For lunch on the B&O, chowder, chicken pie and cheese. I really wanted
apple pie for dessert, but couldn't bear to break up the c-h combination."
There were exceptions, such as the dinner in Dallas that "was royal, full of
squab, champagne, flaming desert and millionaires."

The tours took Nash to places and introduced him to people that he
would otherwise not have seen or met. His descriptions of places were sometimes charming and sometimes poignant. In Milwaukee he found architec-
ture that he knew Frances would have enjoyed: "The old part of the city is
on a bluff, and every house looks as if it had been designed by a man with a
gold watch chain, nine children and an ebullient moustache." In the flat-
lands of Texas, however, he was bothered by the houses he saw in the railroad towns: "[T]he women and even their husbands had tried hard to put up

a little white fence and do some planting. Unfortunately their neat little bungalows and yards are right along the tracks, and this is a line where diesels are only hearsay. They get to hear the romantic whistle of the steam engine, but they also get a smokestack of soot on the petunias and the drying wash."

Nash also commented by way of postcards to Linell and Isabel. A January 1951 card to Linell bearing a picture of a gushing oil well was accompanied by a fitting rhyme:

The citizens of Oklahoma
Adore this oily, rich aroma
There seems to be a well for each,
But I've got nothing but a speech.

And a card to Isabel bore this observation of architectural sociology:

As American towns and cities I wander through,
One landmark is constant everywhere I roam:
The home the Banker built in nineteen-two,
Dim neon tells me is now a Funeral Home.

Nash's celebrity sometimes brought him an interesting invitation. In Dallas, Stanley Marcus ("a delightful and I suspect brilliant guy") invited Nash to his store and promised to send him some books. Later on the same trip he visited the King Ranch, where the owner Richard Kleberg gave him an extensive tour. The highlight for Nash, a veteran devotee of Pimlico, was an introduction to the Kentucky Derby winners Bold Venture and Assault ("I took care to stroke him so I could say I had"). For the most part, however, Nash spent his time on the road in the company of quite ordinary folk: members of women's clubs (and sometimes men's), students, and faculty, and he continued to find them, as he had in his early tours, to be welcoming hosts and intelligent, appreciative audiences.

The lectures not only generated speakers' fees but helped promote sales of Nash's books, which were available after each appearance. Although Nash was happy to autograph them, he got a bit carried away on one visit to Oklahoma City. After writing a little verse in the book of the first buyer, Nash then discovered that, not surprisingly, everyone else wanted a rhyme. He ended up writing almost a hundred spontaneous verses, a considerable feat even for someone with his facility. "The effect on the public was sensational," Nash reported to Frances, "and why not? I've never been through anything like it. At any rate Oklahoma City is now mine." When Nash finally managed to free himself, he staggered wearily back to his hotel and hurriedly packed his suitcase; only later, undressing on the train, did he realize that in his haste he had left behind his dressing gown, pajamas, and slippers.

In addition to the financial benefits, Nash clearly took satisfaction from the approval of his audiences: "when things go well and people enjoy it, it's a wonderful feeling." Although there was considerable humor in his lectures, and in the verses he read, he insisted there was more to it than that. From the questions his audiences asked, and from the books they carried, he concluded that for the most part they were interested in poetry and not just humorous verse. Whatever the tastes of his audience, Nash's lectures were consistently well received. Again and again he wrote Frances of how well a lecture had gone, taking special pleasure when the audience was one about which he had been a bit wary. In Wichita he noted proudly that twelve hundred students from a municipal college, many of whom already had jobs and were not "not too interested in the liberal arts," had nevertheless been a very good audience ("so much so that when I said good night to the chairman he was rushing off to the Western Union Office to wire his delight to Colston Leigh"). And when Nash spoke to his first Christian Science audience in St. Louis, he was relieved to find them "tumultuously enthusiastic, even in spite of dandy candy and reference to such non-existent things as itching and the common cold."

Despite its compensations, the lecture circuit was an exhausting routine. In March 1951, Nash wrote Angus Cameron, "I am astonished that I have the strength to write this letter. I have been on the road for nearly 8 weeks with 2 weeks still to go, and only 4 days at home in the middle to break up the hotel rooms and Pullman-day-coach-Greyhound-bus routine." He had never had to do such things when he worked for Doubleday, Nash observed, and wondered whether he'd "better try for a spot in the book business again, and see if my old editorial and advertising sense is still there."

The threat to return to publishing was facetious, but in the summer of 1951, Nash quite seriously contemplated an equally radical change in his professional life. In August, having visited Hollywood in the spring, and with the help of Vernon Duke in meeting with various producers, he candidly expressed his hopes and concerns in a letter to Duke: "I have been taking [sic] much thought and it is my firm conclusion that in this, my crucial 49th year, Hollywood is the answer to nearly all my difficulties, and I only hope I'm not too late. I believe now that one of the great mistakes of my life was turning down an offer of $1500 a week right after Venus opened." He was, Nash said, "desperately tired of going on lecture tours and borrowing money from Curtis Brown." He did not wish to give up writing verse entirely. On the contrary, he suggested that if he could find work in Hollywood writing lyrics, preferably with Duke, it would make him both happy and rich, "and being happy, I could continue to write my verse for the *New Yorker*, my old love, which I was too jittery to do when I was out there before."

To Nash's disappointment, Hollywood failed to respond. There would be no escape from writing verse, not just for *The New Yorker* but for as many magazines as might be persuaded to publish it. Similarly, there would be no escape from the rigors of lecturing. At the same time he had been successful in finding a less arduous niche in the the rapidly developing new medium of television. He appeared as a guest on several early television programs in 1951–1952, including *Who Said That?*, *We Take Your Word*, and Ed Sullivan's *Toast of the Town*. Then, in 1953, came two significant opportunities. In June, Nash accepted an invitation to join the regular panel on a popular weekly show, *Masquerade Party*, and he would continue with it for nearly four years. The show presented celebrities who appeared in costume and very heavy makeup, each portraying a character that would through some connection, generally obscure, suggest the celebrity's identity. On one show, for example, Lauritz Melchior, an opera star from Denmark, appeared with his wife, both dressed as bakers—of Danish pastries. On the same show, Franklin Roosevelt, Jr., dressed as Mr. Hyde to suggest Hyde Park. On another show Ethel Merman was disguised as a service station attendant (pumping ethyl). And so on. It was the panel's task to identify the character being portrayed and to "peer through the goo" and guess the celebrity beneath. The master of ceremonies was the comedian Peter Donald; Nash's fellow panelists included the bandleader Bobby Sherwood and the actress Ilka Chase, and from time to time the actresses Mary Healy, Barbara Britton, and Buff Cobb.

Since the concept of the show involved wordplay, Nash seemed a natural for the panel, but the format and pace of the show did not give him much opportunity to display his talents. Nash later said that he had appeared on the show "with the cold, sweaty palms and the quivering stomach." But he regretted its eventual passing "because the weekly check was most helpful in warming the cold palms." The compensation was relatively modest ($350, later $450, for each appearance), but it compared favorably with the lecture circuit and did not, for the most part, require travel. With the children grown, in 1953 Ogden had persuaded Frances to give up the house on Rugby Road and move to an apartment on Fifty-seventh Street in New York. When the Nashes were at Little Boar's Head, however, Nash would have to make a weekly commute for his appearance.

Nash's most profitable television assignment came in December 1953 when he narrated a "Man of the Year" program for which he also wrote a song and three poems. He was paid four thousand dollars, a sum he regarded as "fabulous."

The same year brought Nash still other performance opportunities. Caedmon records issued an album of Nash reading some of his most popular verses. The album was a success, and in later years he would record more albums for Caedmon and other labels. He also made his symphonic debut in 1953, reading the verses he had written three years earlier to accompany Saint-Saëns's *Carnival of the Animals*. The idea for the verses had occurred to Andre Kostelanetz when he was conducting *Carnival* at a concert in St. Louis and noticed a complete lack of expression among the audience. This told Kostelanetz that the audience did not understand the composer's joke: the music was intended to be a series of portraits of his colleagues, depicted as various animals. Kostelanetz asked Nash to write verses to accompany the music, and when they were delivered, Kostelanetz was delighted with them, feeling that "each animal had been captured with wit and precision." The verses were not "lyrics"; they were interspersed between sections of the music. Nash admitted that when he wrote the verses he had not heard Saint-Saëns's music but merely had a list of the animals to be depicted, an idea of the tempo and mood, and the number of lines needed to fill each gap.

The verses begin with a prologue:

Camille Saint-Saëns was wracked with pains
When people addressed him as "Saint-Sains."
He held the human race to blame
Because it could not pronounce his name.
So he turned with metronome and fife
To glorify other forms of life.
Be quiet please, for here begins
His salute to feathers, furs, and fins.

There follow thirteen verses and a finale. The verses, which range from twelve lines (Fossils) to two (Mules), are inspired nonsense. For example,

Nash had written a short poem entitled "The Kangaroo" a few years earlier, and it was now expanded:

The kangaroo can jump incredible.
He has to jump because he's edible.
I could not eat a kangaroo,
But many fine Australians do.
Those with cookbooks as well as boomerangs
Prefer him in tasty kangaroo meringues.

The remaining verses were new, and Nash, never one to miss an opportunity, published several of them as poems in *The New Yorker*.

After *Carnival of the Animals* was recorded with Noel Coward reading the Nash verse, it became a perennial favorite, performed by orchestras around the country. That success led Nash into a minor subspecialty of writing other verses for Kostelanetz: *Between Birthdays* (music from Tchaikovsky's *Children's Album*), Ravel's *Mother Goose Suite*, *The New Nutcracker Suite*, and *Carnival of Marriage* (music from Saint-Saëns, Strauss, and Liszt). Nash also wrote songs for two television specials based on the music of Prokofiev and Dukas—*Art Carney Meets Peter and the Wolf* and *Art Carney Meets the Sorcerer's Apprentice*.

Nash's 1953 debut in symphonic reading took place at Town Hall in New York City; a story by Paul V. Beckley in the *Herald Tribune* was headlined "Ogden Nash, No Musician, Giving Orchestral Rendition." Nash donned white tie and tails for the occasion, telling Beckley that "I've got an elderly set," adding that he had worn it recently, "so I know it's still not got holes in it." Later Nash served as narrator on several symphonic occasions, including appearances at the New York Philharmonic Promenades for *Between Birthdays* and the *Mother Goose Suite* and readings of *Carnival of the Animals* at Tanglewood and with the San Francisco Symphony.

Despite the energy and imagination he devoted to his various collateral pursuits, the core of Nash's reputation, as well as his livelihood, continued to reside in the verse he published in magazines and books. Within that realm he continued to experiment with new subject matter and techniques.

1 3

LAUREATE OF THE AGE OF FRICTION

The opening poem in *Versus*, "I Will Arise and Go Now," became the centerpiece of an essay by the respected critic Clifton Fadiman, urging that Nash be awarded a Pulitzer Prize. The poem depicted a lama in far Tibet who leads a solitary life, untouched by modern comforts and complications. The lama lacks soap and soap operas, penicillin, Spam, Tums, Irium (a popular toothpaste ingredient), and a Philco (television set). The poem concludes with the writer deciding to join that lama.

Nash's poem, Fadiman suggested, compared favorably with a famous Wordsworth ode, "The World Is Too Much with Us." Both poets were making "the same wistful comment on modern competitive life," and Nash's verse, though funny as well as serious, would reach his audience as effectively as Wordsworth's more ornate diction had reached his. Indeed, Fadiman argued, Nash had done what Wordsworth had only talked of doing, "introducing into poetry 'familiar matters of today.'"

Much of Nash's verse had always dealt with the incidents and irritations of everyday life, and the years following World War II provided him with abundant material. They marked the beginning of an era of consumerism that has proceeded largely uninterrupted ever since. It was also, Fadiman pointed out, an Age of Friction, in which an average citizen might be less concerned with cosmic issues than with "the prospect of removing several needless yards of cellophane from ordinary objects in the course of an average working day." He dubbed Nash the laureate of the Age of Friction: "In a verse form often fittingly bumpy . . . and with the aid of a dazzling assortment of puns, syntactical distortions and word coinages, he points out that most improvements in daily living entail a tiny irritation tax." And sometimes, Fadiman acknowledged, "the tax may even become confiscatory."

Humor had always been Nash's remedy for the aggravations of daily life. If Nash was a philosopher, he was, as the *Times Literary Supplement* had noted, a laughing one. While most critics had concluded that he was more than a "mere" humorist, it had always been impossible to value his work without appreciating its humor. Now, in the late forties and early fifties, he began to feel a bit lonely. Nash had been fortunate to get his start during a golden age of wit and humor in writing epitomized by the writers who had preceded him at *The New Yorker*: James Thurber, E. B. White, Robert Benchley, Dorothy Parker, Frank Sullivan, and Corey Ford, among others. It was good company to join. In a 1939 essay in the *Saturday Review of Literature*, the poet and critic Leonard Bacon had paid tribute to the work of three "young men" whose work he admired and found different from their elders, Thurber, White, and Nash. They were a triumvirate, Bacon wrote, "disturbed by perversities in their environment which they are apt to criticize with easy irony and sharp good sense." He endorsed Thurber's definition of humor as "a kind of emotional chaos told about calmly and quietly in retrospect," and celebrated three writers who lacked a message but "whose unsystematized observations are clear, fresh, diverting and loaded for bear."

That golden era at *The New Yorker* had not lasted. Even while celebrating Thurber, White, and Nash, Bacon had noted that the magazine's "two-page outbursts" of humor, in which he had found "precious ore," now came too rarely. The chronicler of the magazine, Ben Yagoda, has pointed out that "Sterling as they were, [S. J.] Perelman and Nash stood alone in the ranks of important new *New Yorker* humorists in the thirties." The contributions of White, Thurber, Benchley, and Sullivan continued, but by the end of the thirties, times had changed. "In the words of Corey Ford," Yagoda concluded, "'the time of laughter' was over and it didn't seem likely to return."

Apart from his sabbatical ventures to Hollywood and Broadway, Nash had done what he could to perpetuate the time of laughter, but humor in *The New Yorker* was not what it had once been, and no other magazine had appeared to take its place. In 1949, Nash wrote to Harold Ross, thanking him for some kind words, and adding, "Where the hell are the young writers?

Perelman, Thurber etc. can't carry the ball forever; let's find a 30-year-old humorist." Ross replied:

> Yes, where are the young writers? The success, so-called, of this magazine is primarily a straight matter of luck. Within a year after we started we had White, Thurber, Hokinson, Arno, and within a few years more we had a lot more good people, humorists with pen, pencil and typewriter. Now, by God, a whole generation has gone by and very few more have appeared—a couple of artists and not one (or not more than one or two at the outside) humorous writers. I don't know whether it's the New Deal or Communist infiltration or the law of averages, or what, but I do know that if I'd known how little talent was going to develop I'd have got in some other line of work years ago.

In an interview with a Baltimore reporter the same year, Nash offered another theory, perhaps more plausible than Ross's, for the absence of young humorists. He speculated that movies and radio might be draining off the younger talent: "Look at any young actress who makes a hit in New York. Pfft! She's in Hollywood."

Nash had a modest view of the role of humorists, and he once cautioned against taking them too seriously. In "If Fun Is Fun, Isn't That Enough?" he wrote:

> They'll sell their birthright every time.
> To make a point or turn a rhyme.
> This motto, child, is my bequest:
> There's many a false word spoken in jest.

Nevertheless, Nash understood that when he turned to social commentary, his verse was successful precisely because of the truths it told. Such verse was far more likely to provoke readers to a nod of recognition and a smile than to audible laughter. In that fashion, Nash did what he could to apply some lubrication to the Age of Friction.

One prominent feature of the age was the wave of "gadgets," electrical and mechanical, that had found their way into his household, from automatic can openers to television sets, and the changes they had introduced. Many of Nash's specific vexations now sound rather quaint: our television sets no longer produce herringbone stripes, and we are well past the transition from manual to automatic shifts in our cars and from buttons to zippers on men's trousers. But they will have a certain resonance with anyone who has struggled to become acquainted with a newly acquired VCR or computer. And we have not yet entirely solved the problem of dealing with wondrous devices that misbehave. As Nash put it in "We Would Refer You to Our Service Department, If We Had One":

> If you want a refrigerator or an automatic can opener or a razor
> that plays "Begin the Beguine" you can choose between an
> old rose or a lavender or blue one,
> But after you've got it, why if anything goes wrong don't think
> you'll find anybody to fix it, just throw it away and buy a new
> one.
>   ✻   ✻   ✻   ✻

Consumerism meant not only "new and improved" products but new and improved advertising to sell them. Although Nash was an adjunct member of the advertising fraternity, that did not deter him from taking aim at targets of opportunity as they arose. Thus some Nash verses were inspired by advertisements for such items as cigarettes, men's suits, razors, banks, and "sleep products" (sinus mask, massaging pillow, and so forth). In "I Remember Yule," his scorn was directed at advertising in the weeks before Christmas:

> What, five times a week at 8:15 P.M., do the herald angels sing?
> That a small deposit now will buy you an option on a genuine
> diamond ring.
> What is the message we receive with Good King Wenceslaus?
> That if we rush to the corner of Ninth and Main we can get that
> pink mink housecoat very inexpenceslaus.
>   ✻   ✻   ✻   ✻

> This year I'm going to disconnect everything electrical in the
> house and spend the Christmas season like Tiny Tim and Mr.
> Pickwick;
> You make me sickwick.

Nash also continued to illuminate a variety of human frailties that vary little from age to age. He had a keen eye and ear for pretensions of various kinds. He was equally unsympathetic to people who think "that anything they have is the best in the world just because it is theirs," and to their opposite numbers who think "that anything is better than theirs just because it belongs to somebody else." Similarly, he needled both those who are always

optimistic and those who are always pessimistic. A
language made him impatient with linguistic affect
ple who, after the second martini, try speaking Frenc
ple who refer to Robert Burns as "Bobby"; others wh
fans but aficionados; and still others for whom bi
events and the stomach a tummy. Another categor
Nash canon consisted of those, young and old, who
person at the bridge table who bursts into conversatic
the purveyor of vague driving directions to a hor
houseguest who wants breakfast in bed at a quarter
of the apartment above; children who play "Cho
with fingers that are "strawberry-jammed or cranbe
Nash's minor torments (Mondays, unpaid bills, gard
have no identifiable villain but nonetheless contribu

Nash's own imperfections were now associate
older, and aging became one of his favorite topics
forty-five, he wrote "Let's Not Climb the Washingto
in which he observed that "Middle age is when yo
ple that every new person you meet reminds you
cited several other indicia, including "It is when r
enough for you to hear/ And you go to the ball gam
the umpires are getting younger every year." He c
"isn't really old, it's right on the border;/ At least un!
order." In another poem, written a few months ear
more somber note:

THE MIDDLE

When I remember bygone days
I think how evening follows morn;
So many I loved were not yet dead,
So many I love were not yet born.

Nash later wrote to Jim Sherman that he thought tl
have ever done" and expressed the hopeful opinion
live "Candy is dandy."

As years passed, other poems noted the deteriora
sight, and similar phenomena ("when I jog I joggle
dreams and ambitions was noted in "Eheu! Fugace

a L
gac
flee
in "

the
by f
as e

i
S

And
pare
pare
N
ticul
rious
migl
Nyn
on w

S

V

F
amus
preo
That
lengt
hand
in th

f Days Make." (The title was borrowed from Horace's "Eheu! fu-
Postume, Postume/ Labuntur anni," Alas, Postumus, Postumus, the
years slip by.) Then, in 1956 when Nash was fifty-four, he observed
ossing the Border," perhaps a bit prematurely:

escence begins
l middle age ends
e day your descendants
tnumber your friends.

Nash's verse, as in his life, the trials of aging were accompanied by
nor annoyances and major comforts of family life. He was intrigued
lies and family relationships, and some of his observations emerged
rams. For example, in "What I Know About Life," he noted that:

e has a tendency to obfuscate and bewilder
h as fating us to spend the first part of our lives being
embarrassed by our parents and the last part being
embarrassed by our childer.

"Father, Dear Father, Go Jump in the Lake": "It is easier for one
to support seven children than for seven children to support one
"

h's views of marriage, and of women in general and Frances in par-
remained constant. Wives and other women were somewhat myste-
eatures to be regarded with puzzled adoration. Their idiosyncrasies
e remarked upon, but with more resignation than reproach. In "The
and the Shepherd," Nash depicted the husband whose wife insists
ing ahead without so much as a backward look:

netimes he is touched and flattered by her faith in him, but
mostly he feels like Queen Victoria's chair,
ich Queen Victoria never looked at before she sat down,
Because she just knew it would be there.

nces may or may not have been the inspiration for some of Nash's
g portraits, as in "The Solitude of Mr. Powers," wherein a wife is
upied with rearranging flowers, or "How to Harry a Husband, or Is
ccessory Really Necessary?" depicting struggles with a handbag. (A
footnote in the latter poem, cataloguing the contents of a woman's
g, came from suggestions by Katharine White.) On the other hand,
poems that clearly refer to Frances expressly or by implication, the

point is Nash's love for her. These poems have a different tone and depart the field of social commentary for personal revelation: "Darling, when I look at you/ Every aged phase is new/ And there are moments when it seems/ I've married one of Shakespeare's dreams" ("Reprise"), and "There are people I ought to wish I was;/ But under the circumstances,/ I prefer to continue my life as me—/ For nobody else has Frances" ("Confessions to Be Traced on a Birthday Cake"). Nash's devotion is even apparent in the poem "Always Marry an April Girl," which provided a glimpse of Frances's changeable moods, and "Don't Be Cross, Amanda," which reflected the dismay they could provoke:

Don't be cross, Amanda,
Amanda, don't be cross,
For when you're cross, Amanda,
I feel an albatross
Around my neck, or dank grey moss,
And my eyes assume an impervious gloss.
Amanda,
Dear Amanda,
Don't be cross.

✳   ✳   ✳   ✳

Nash's role as a father inspired numerous verses as Linell and Isabel grew up, and inevitably his grandchildren made their own appearance as Nash complained about the quality of current children's books and mocked his own lapse into baby talk. In "Preface to the Past" he chronicled his progress from bachelor ("struck by affection blinding") to nervous parent of infants ("counting fingers and toes"), adolescents ("One of these days they must mature"), and brides ("They did mature") to grampa ("counting the toes on my children's children's feet"). He concluded: "Thank you, kids, I wouldn't have missed it."

The misuse of language often drew Nash's attention. Critic Louis Hasley pointed out that, while clichés had been an object of fun for many humorists, including James Thurber, Robert Benchley, and Frank Sullivan, no other writer of literary stature had taken on as many as Nash. The trick, as Nash put it in a letter to Hasley, was that "it must be somebody else's cliché and not the author's own." What that meant, Hasley elaborated, is that "the author keeps the cliché he uses from being naturally his own by a satirical, sophisticated context or by an artful alteration in its phrasing." The technique was displayed in "The Visit," in which Hasley found seventeen clichés in twenty-four lines:

> She welcomes him with pretty impatience
> And a cry of Greetings and salutations!
> To which remark, no laggard, he
> Ripostes with a Long time no see.
> Recovering her poise full soon,
> She bids him Anyhoo, sit ye doon,
> And settling by the fireside,
> He chuckles, Thank you, kind sir, she cried.
> Snug as a bug, the cup he waits
> That cheers but not inebriates.

✻   ✻   ✻   ✻

Nash's fascination with language led him to collect not only clichés but other expressions he found irritating. In "Oafishness Sells Good, Like an Advertisement Should," Nash considered the slogan "Winston Tastes Good Like a Cigarette Should":

> Like the hart panteth for the water brooks I pant for a revival of
>   Shakespeare's *Like You Like It*.
> I can see the tense draftees relax and purr
> When the sergeant barks, "Like you were."
> —And don't try to tell me that our well has been defiled by
>   immigration;
> Like goes Madison Avenue, like so goes the nation.

Apart from satire, many of Nash's poems were plainly just for fun. Besides his unique approach to rhyme and meter, various forms of wordplay were sprinkled throughout his verse. One of Nash's favorites was the pun, and a fanciful specimen might be the central point of a poem. For example, in "Medusa and the Mot Juste," his lively imagination transformed the Gorgons, monsters of classical mythology, into authors. Two of the Gorgons suggested that, since they were literary sisters like the Brontës, they could all be known as brontesauresses. But the third, Medusa, replied, "You two can do what you like, but since I am the big fromage in this family, I prefer to think of myself as the Gorgon Zola."

Other poems written for pure amusement drew on the animal kingdom. Nash's first book of verse, *Hard Lines*, had included the turtle poem, and later books followed that tradition, continually enlarging the Nash menagerie. In addition to the denizens of *Carnival of the Animals*, Nash immortalized innumerable creatures, including caterpillar, toucan, platypus, hamster, manatee, and "Ostrich":

The ostrich roams the great Sahara.
Its mouth is wide, its neck is narra.
It has such long and lofty legs,
I'm glad it sits to lay its eggs.

Still another variety of Nash "just for fun" poem is one in which the entire poem is more or less a vehicle for getting to a joke at the end, as in "So I Resigned from the Chu Chin Chowder and Marching Club":

I can tell you for a modest price
The difference between a mandarin waving his hat over a
    prostrate palanquin bearer and a mandarin sitting on a cake
    of ice.
Do you want to know, really and truly?
Well, the first mandarin is fanning his coolie.

The playful Nash also experimented with different forms. In *Versus* he included five "limicks," a limerick shortened from five lines to four. The form generated little enthusiasm from reviewers, and Nash did not return to it. But he did include four limicks in his major collection, *Verses from 1929 On*, and two were included in *I Wouldn't Have Missed It*. The Third Limick ("Two nudists of Dover/ Being purple all over/ Were munched by a cow/ When mistaken for clover") may have been inspired by a well-known rhyme of Gelett Burgess, with which Nash was often credited ("I never saw a purple cow/ I never hope to see one;/ But I can tell you anyhow,/ I'd rather see than be one"). His next collection, *The Private Dining Room*, included three limericks, beginning with: "An elderly bride of Port Jervis/ Was quite understandably nervis/ When her apple-cheeked groom/ With three wives in the tomb/ Kept insuring her during the service."

In a different vein altogether, Nash's taste for horror stories occasionally surfaced in a long poem with an eerie or even macabre tone, such as "The Wendigo" (defined in a footnote as "an evil spirit, one of a fabulous tribe of cannibals") in *The Private Dining Room*, and "The Buses Headed for Scranton" and "A Tale of the Thirteenth Floor" in *You Can't Get There from Here*. The latter poem took Nash well out of his territory, having been published initially in the *Magazine of Fantasy and Science Fiction*.

Finally, Nash occasionally found, as he sometimes had in the past, a voice in which there was little humor and whose purpose seemed not primarily to entertain. One such poem, "Exit, Pursued by a Bear," came at a time when the country had become preoccupied with the almost incomprehensible threat of nuclear conflict with the Soviet Union. Although this was hardly an apt subject for light verse, it was a fact of life that was difficult to avoid. Nash's poem was inspired by the growing movement, now nearly forgotten, to construct backyard fallout shelters and stock them with canned goods. The poem had the diction of light verse ("Chipmunk chewing the Chippendale,/ Mice on the Meissen shelf"), but it had a somber tone. The final stanza invoked the image of Jamshid, a mythical Persian king, whose people fell from grace:

Jamshid squats in a cavern
Screened by a waterfall
Catered by Heinz and Campbell
And awaits the fireball.

In another poem, "The Miraculous Countdown," Nash struck a cautiously optimistic note.

When geniuses all in every nation
Hasten us toward obliteration,
Perhaps it will take the dolts and geese
To drag us backward into peace.

The message did not go unnoticed: it was quoted by Secretary of State Dean Rusk when he gave the 1964 Hammarskjöld Memorial Lecture. (Meanwhile Nash had made a modest contribution to bridging the divide of the cold war through his verse. He learned from the Harvard Sovietologist Richard Pipes that several of his poems had been translated into Russian and had "swept the literary circles of Leningrad." His Russian translator later advised that the poems had been published in the Soviet magazine *Novyi Mir*.)

Because of Nash's unique and remarkably varied style, his verse stood somewhat apart not only from the larger world of poetry but even from other light verse. Nevertheless he was widely regarded as the foremost practitioner of that form. The poet and critic Louis Untermeyer expressed the general view when he said that Nash was preeminent among those "who blend light verse and serious thought," a group in which he included David

McCord, John Betjeman, A. P. Herbert, Phyllis McGinley, Morris Bishop, Richard Armour, William Jay Smith, and Melville Cane. In a similar listing, McCord put Nash among the small company of "living American writers who combine in high degree wit with poetry or poetry with wit . . . Robert Frost, E. B. White . . . Thornton Wilder, James Thurber, E. E. Cummings, W. H. Auden, Morris Bishop."

Nash's work was appreciated not only by the public, by critics, and by fellow spinners of light verse but by more serious colleagues. Among the first of them to take note of Nash had been W. H. Auden. Soon after coming to the United States in 1939, Auden had discovered Nash and wrote home to a friend:

> Do you know Ogden Nash, one of the best poets in America?
> This is a sample.
>> As I sit in my office
>> On 23d street and Madison Avenue
>> I say to myself:
>> "You've a responsible position, haven't you?["]

Oddly, the excerpt was quoted inaccurately: Auden ignored Nash's seminal rendering of "haven't you" as "havenue." Auden's biographer, Nicholas Jenkins, has pointed out that Auden borrowed from Nash the opening cadence to one of Auden's most famous poems, "September 1, 1939" ("I sit in one of the dives/ On Fifty-second Street"). Thirty years later Auden would arrange for Nash's participation in a major festival in London organized under Auden's aegis. Other contemporary poets who expressed their delight in Nash's work included Elizabeth Bishop, Marianne Moore, and Witter Bynner. In a 1962 letter, Moore told Nash of her pleasure in one of his books: "I thought I'd put a little mark on each page I really treasure, and they all have little marks."

Nash not only traveled in the company of serious poets from time to time, he also began to collect various honors. In 1950 he was inducted into the National Institute of Arts and Letters, an organization limited to 250 preeminent American writers, composers, painters, sculptors, and architects. The poets Robert Penn Warren and William Carlos Williams were admitted at the same time. The fiftieth anniversary dinner of the Poetry Society of America, in 1960 at the Waldorf-Astoria, was a grand affair at which a letter of congratulation from President Eisenhower was read and Marianne Moore was given the Society's gold medal. Nash was among other honorees, receiving a special citation and offering remarks from the dais that were well received. As one of the members of the Society reported candidly in a letter to another member who had missed the event: "Aside from pedestrian remarks by others on the dais, [Louis] Untermeyer was witty, Robert Graves informal and chatty, Ogden Nash light and easy, [Thomas Hornsby] Ferril, able and warm, RF [Robert Frost], his own self, unwilling to be bludgeoned into giving a reading."

Nash was the only writer of light verse who belonged to the Poetry Center in New York City, and in 1962, at the National Poetry Festival in Washington, D.C., he was the only representative of light verse to join more than thirty of the country's most distinguished poets. Appearing on the third day, immediately following Stanley Kunitz, Nash read six of his favorite poems, including "I Do, I Will, I Have," "The Private Dining Room," and "Laments for a Dying Language."

Also in 1962, Nash was elected a fellow of the Academy of Arts and Sciences along with Hubert Humphrey and Cardinal Cushing. Nash took it very much in stride, writing Dan Longwell: "It took me ten days to find out what I had been elected to. I then discovered that John Adams, John Quincy Adams, Charles Francis Adams, Roscoe Pound and Harlow Shapley had been presidents of whatever it is, so I decided to accept the honor even though it will cost me ten dollars a year. Laurels are growing more expensive."

Nash received honorary degrees from Adelphi College in 1961 and Franklin and Marshall College in 1962, and in 1964 he received the Sarah Josepha Hale Award, given annually to recognize a distinguished body of work from, or associated with, New England. Nash was notified of his selection by his old friend and colleague from *The New Yorker*, Raymond Holden, who had been instrumental in establishing the award in 1956. The first recipient had been Robert Frost; others who had preceded Nash included the poets Archibald MacLeish and Mark Van Doren and the novelists John P. Marquand and John Hersey. Recipients were required to accept the award in person and to deliver a talk. Nash qualified as a New Englander through his and Frances's regular vacationing for many years in Little Boar's Head, but just to leave no doubt, he included the following lines in his remarks: "To ensure that New England forgets me not,/ I have purchased a house and a burial plot."

Despite the respect and recognition he earned, the one honor that eluded Nash was the one for which Clifton Fadiman had "nominated" him: the Pulitzer Prize. It is not clear how keenly he might have hoped for that award, and he may well have thought it unlikely that the prize would ever be given for light verse. In a 1947 poem, "I Am Full of Previous Experience," the closing couplet was in the voice of a would-be writer of catchy newspaper headlines, but it may also have spoken for Nash himself: "No, I may never win any prizes from Mr. Pulitzer,/ But when it comes to supplying the customer with little jokes for the breakfast table I will always be in there pitching honestly and trulitzer." Nevertheless, Nash and Little, Brown had taken Fadiman seriously enough to quote his essay at length on the jacket of *The Private Dining Room*, including the wish that Nash might be "Pulitsurprised." So, when the Pulitzer Prize was at last awarded for light verse in 1961, it was a serious disappointment that it went not to Nash but to Phyllis McGinley.

Although McGinley and Nash both wrote light verse, their approaches were quite different. As a matter of style, McGinley was clearly of the school that held regularity and precision of form to be all important. While the range of her verse, in topics as well as form, was much narrower than Nash's, they shared many subjects in common, including such things as husbands, wives, and children, and the vicissitudes of middle class life. But McGinley spoke with a distinctly feminine voice as a wife and mother. In the foreword to her book, *Times Three*, that won the Pulitzer, W. H. Auden observed: "What, in fact, distinguishes Phyllis McGinley's poems from those of most light-verse poets is that no man could have written them."

Ironically, Nash had been among the early discoverers of McGinley. During his brief tenure as an editor at Farrar and Rinehart in 1933, he had been impressed with her work in *The New Yorker* and "The Conning Tower," and he wrote a highly flattering letter seeking to attract her to Farrar for a book. He called her verse "wonderful" and "the best stuff to come along in years." Warming to the subject, he continued, "You have, if I may say so, both an ear and a point of view while most of our versifiers have only one—or neither." That was high praise indeed, coming from the young poet whose own work had been so lavishly praised; but nothing came of Nash's overture.

In the ensuing years, as the reputations of both poets grew, they maintained a cordial professional relationship, speaking well of each other's published work. In 1955, however, in a remarkably candid letter to Arthur Roberts at St. George's, Nash revealed a surprising resentment. After thanking Roberts for sending him a clipping about McGinley, Nash added: "I

189

am a tolerant man; my wife has no touch of tolerance regarding Miss McG. and states loudly that the lady is a thief. I am so gentle that I simply make the mild remark that through a happy coincidence she has the same ideas I have had, a few years after mine have been published."

Given Nash's sentiments in 1955, he must have been nettled at the award to McGinley five years later. But he rose to the occasion and wrote McGinley a letter that was warm and gracious while not entirely concealing his own disappointment:

> Heartfelt congratulations, and gratitude which I am sure is shared by Morris Bishop and David McCord, for freeing light verse from the condescending pat on the shoulder. It would be disingenuous of me to deny a twinge of wistful envy, but then I am also given to gluttony and sloth and I do feel a real glow of satisfaction at having my many years' admiration of your work so happily confirmed.

McGinley responded the following day in an equally generous manner. It was not just she who had received the award, she said, but Nash and Dorothy Parker, E. B. White and Morris Bishop. Nash, she went on, was "the master of us all and deserve it far more than I do."

The decision of the Pulitzer Prize committee is perhaps not difficult to understand, even for devoted admirers of Nash. If it was something of a leap to award the prize for light verse, it might have seemed an even more remarkable leap to award it for the iconoclastic form that Nash had made his own. In any event, the decision had no perceptible impact on Nash's reputation. His next book, *Everyone But Thee and Me*, published the following year, received customarily enthusiastic reviews. Charles Poore, writing in the *New York Times*, outdid even Fadiman: "When America's turn comes again there will be many candidates for the Nobel honors—including Robert Frost, Carl Sandburg, Samuel Eliot Morison and Ogden Nash." The same book prompted Morris Bishop's observation that Nash, like Walt Whitman, had "created a new poetic form and imposed it on the world." Although the 1960s would be a time of serious worries for Nash, his failure to have won a Pulitzer (or Nobel) Prize would not rank high among them.

14

ANOTHER DAY, ANOTHER DOLOR

With the possible exception of the darkest moments of Nash's Hollywood years, the 1960s were the most troubled period in his life. And while the difficulties in Hollywood had been real, they were, for the most part, difficulties that Nash could, and eventually did, simply leave behind. This time, as Nash struggled with recurring illness, periods of depression, and personal distress at the symptoms of national turmoil, there were no ready means of escape. For the most part he kept his personal problems out of his poetry, but there were glimpses here and there. In a 1963 poem, "A Man Can Complain, Can't He?" Nash combined a takeoff of William Dunbar's lamenting line from the sixteenth century, *Timor mortis conturbat me*, with the familiar saying, "Another day, another dollar":

Between the dotard and the brat
My disaffection veers and varies.
Sometimes I'm sick of clamoring youth,
Sometimes of my contemporaries.
I'm old too soon, yet young too long;
Could Swift himself have planned it droller?
Timor vitae conturbat me;
Another day, another dolor.

If Nash was not literally "troubled by the fear of life," his dolor did appear to mount as the decade wore on, and he would have to find reserves of determination and resilience.

At the outset, Nash's most serious problems were physical illnesses. By middle age he had developed—perhaps cultivated—a reputation as something of a hypochondriac. In "When the Devil Was Sick, Could He Prove It?" he caught the spirit of the would-be patient who sees the belated appearance of a slight temperature as proof of the minor malady he had been complaining about:

> And you take a farewell look at the thermometer, and it's as good
>   as a tonic,
> Because you've got as pretty a ninety-nine point one as you'd wish
>   to see in a month of bubonic.

But just as paranoiacs may have real enemies, hypochondriacs may have real illnesses. So it was with Ogden Nash, and in the face of such illnesses he responded with good humor and sought to quiet the fears of family and friends.

Nash's career as a Hollywood screenwriter had been foreshortened by the rather mysterious ailment that forced him to relinquish responsibility for *The Feminine Touch* and return to Baltimore. After a period of treatment and convalescence, he not only resumed a normal writing schedule but for several weeks each year submitted to the rigors of the lecture circuit. As he reached his mid-fifties, though, he suffered intestinal problems that were variously diagnosed and treated: polyps, regional ileitis, enteritis, Crohn's disease. Nash's condition was at times painful, exhausting, and even embarrassing. As his daughter Linell later wrote candidly: "To a man as fastidious as my father, an ailment that made it necessary to arrange his life around the proximity of the nearest bathroom must have been an almost insufferable burden."

In February 1958, Nash entered Union Memorial Hospital in Baltimore for, as he put it, "removal of a couple of cute polyps from the lower gut." Perhaps foolishly, he returned to lecturing after only a brief convalescence. He gave four lectures in March, and on April 4 set out with Frances on a four-week cross-country tour. By mid-May, writing to his new editor at *The New Yorker*, Roger Angell, to explain a lack of new verse for the magazine, Nash observed rather wearily that for the past four months he had been either on the road or in the hospital. "I used to be able to work while traveling but the years have caught up with me and now when I have my spare time I seek not a hotel room desk but the nearest horizontal surface." Still,

Nash said, he had compiled "a very promising batch of notes" and promised his "most earnest efforts" to provide new poems.

A year later, in July 1959, after another strenuous series of tours, Nash received a blunt warning from his doctors:

> I told you at the final office visit it was obligatory for you to rest as much as possible. Under no circumstance should you undertake any lecture responsibilities.
>
> An enteritis such as this may run a very chronic kind of course with remissions and exacerbation. Fatigue and emotional tension can aggravate an intestinal difficulty such as this, and I think it essential that you avoid commitments that might make demands upon you when you are not feeling well.

Two weeks later Angell wrote to Nash, after they had met for lunch, that he had been distressed at how unwell Nash had been: "I do hope those doctors will quickly find the cause of your present affliction and will put it right immediately." Following his doctors' advice, Nash gave up his lecture tours for the balance of 1959 and all of 1960, but resumed them again in early 1961. The intestinal problems continued, but Nash soldiered on, writing and lecturing. In an April 1962 letter to Katharine White, he wrote that he had "been on the road almost continuously since early December, trapped in the most exhaustive schedule yet devised for me by my rapacious agent."

In 1963 the strain of his schedule caught up with him again, and when the restorative atmosphere of Little Boar's Head failed to revive him, he was hospitalized in Boston for two weeks in August. Immediately after emerging from the hospital, he wrote Angell to explain his silence and his condition ("Diagnosis ulcerated colitis; treatment profuse medication and strict diet and quiet"). But he insisted that he expected to be writing "after another week or so," and that he had a new funny ending for a verse he had previously submitted as well as "several other pleasant notions up my sleeve for which my presently scrawny arms leave ample room." At the same time he wrote Dan Longwell that he had canceled a schedule of thirty-five lectures.

After recovering from his illness in 1963, Nash returned to lecturing on a more limited basis. By October of the following year he felt well enough to take Frances on the trip to England they had been planning for several years. In London he was taken suddenly and violently ill. After a week of confinement to their hotel room, with constant vomiting and diarrhea, Nash consulted a second physician and was promptly admitted to the

London Clinic, where he remained for eight days. After his discharge, he and Frances made a convalescent excursion to the seaside at Brighton and remained there until their scheduled sailing on the *Franconia* at the end of November. Nash had by now lost twenty pounds, which, he said ruefully, embarrassed the tailor who had measured him before he was stricken. Still, he was cheered by the fact that the English physician who had restored him to health, Dr. Avery Jones, did not believe in highly restricted diets and "recommended any form of alcohol except beer."

The London illness again forced Nash to cancel a series of scheduled lectures, and he wrote Vernon Duke that he had "been forbidden to undertake any lectures in the future under the threat of having valuable sections of my inside removed." Nash's physical condition also precipitated a major move to escape the "smog, traffic and turmoil of New York." Ogden and Frances gave up their New York apartment for a condominium in the Cross Keys section of Baltimore, not far from their former home on Rugby Road. Thereafter they would split their time between Baltimore and Little Boar's Head, becoming residents of New Hampshire and spending approximately six months a year there.

Dividing time between Baltimore and New Hampshire seemed to agree with Nash, and by the summer of 1965 he had been restored, as he put it, "if not to youth, at least to middle age." By early 1966, however, surgery was again in sight. In January, Nash wrote to Dan and Mary Longwell and attempted to portray the prospect as brightly as possible: "I have just undergone a series of X-ray tests and am lined with barium from gullet to gutter-spout. The results show a hitch in the gut which can be corrected by surgery. The magi assure me that the job is an uncomplicated one, and without guaranteeing results seem to think my turbulent insides would begin to behave themselves, so I'm pretty sure that I'll let them open me up sometime in the late winter or early spring." To further lighten the message, he added a limerick:

> Asked a patient before appendectomy
> "What kind of a fee d'you expectomy?"
> Said the doc, "If your pulse
> Indicates the results,
> Anything but a post-dated checktomy."

A note to Vernon Duke conveyed a similar tone of optimism: "The wizards all assure me that the operation is child's play." The surgery proceeded and was pronounced a success, and in June, Nash wrote to Duke that he was beginning to experience the beneficial results: ". . . occasional relapse into the old miseries of the trots but at less and less frequent intervals, and the lassitude and exhaustion that plagued me for so many years have departed."

After the 1966 surgery Nash's health was far from robust, but it remained relatively stable for the next several years, and with one exception—a severe case of the flu in January 1968—he managed to stay out of hospitals. He published a major collection, *There's Always Another Windmill*, in 1968 and was inspired to publish another book, *Bed Riddance*, that collected the verses he had written over the years with respect to doctors, dentists, and a variety of minor maladies. The book struck a seriocomic note with its dedication to seventeen doctors, identified by name and listed alphabetically, and to the staffs of Johns Hopkins Hospital, Union Memorial Hospital, Massachusetts General Hospital, and the London Clinic, "without whom this book and its author could not have been put together." Nash's introduction to the book, however, touched only lightly on his grueling experiences of the previous decade.

> We are all obsolescent; shall I be called hypochondriac simply because I am more obsolescent than most? Torpor, lassitude and procrastination have been the least of my defects. Add to these astigmatism, dyspepsia, the common cold, dreams of falling, gout masquerading as arthritis and arthritis masquerading as gout, a gnawing suspicion that the earth is slipping from under me, and an abdominal cavity that draws surgeons as the cooling spring the hart, then try to convince me that my twisted sacroiliac is psychosomatic.

Only the extensive list of medical personnel, and rather placid reference to his "abdominal cavity," gave any hint of what he had endured.

In 1968, Nash was finally forced to accept the advice that doctors had given him nearly ten years before: he gave up the lecture circuit. Initially he was reluctant to abandon that source of income altogether, and while he did not renew his contract with the Colston Leigh agency, he signed with another firm that promised a less demanding and entirely flexible arrangement. He gave no forewarning to Bill Leigh, who was dismayed to learn of the loss of his longtime client. In this instance Nash's usually reliable sense of courtesy had been overtaken by his even stronger desire to avoid an unpleasant confrontation. When Leigh wrote to protest, Nash responded with a lengthy letter explaining his decision.

In the letter Nash referred to his past illnesses and surgery and confessed he had become "more of a semi-invalid than I care to admit." "Justly or unjustly," he believed his condition had resulted from the strain of lecturing and, in particular, from Leigh's practice of "plausibly extending one engagement into three, or three into six, or a ten-day trip into several weeks." Frances, he added, "feels this even more strongly, indeed bitterly," and concluded that her view alone would make it impossible to resume the relationship. Several weeks later Leigh responded, denying indignantly that he was responsible for any of Nash's medical problems, and the relationship ended on an unhappy note. Thereafter Nash made occasional public appearances but never again undertook a lecture tour.

His physical problems were compounded by a growing sense of unease with the world around him. By the latter sixties, national concerns over the possibility of a nuclear holocaust were by no means forgotten, but they had, in a sense, receded to the background. In their place, the Vietnam War had become for Nash, as for so many Americans, an increasingly dominant fact of life. Nash did not speak out publicly against the Vietnam War; he responded principally by exercising, with some considerable effort, his franchise as a New Hampshire voter. His private letters, however, left little doubt as to his sentiments. In 1966 he and Frances returned from New Hampshire later than usual, "having lingered to cast 2 votes that helped to defeat a retired Air Force general running for senator who stated that he could end the Vietnam War in 3 days."

Two years later Nash was excited by the candidacy of Senator Eugene McCarthy, who entered the New Hampshire primary campaigning against the war and in opposition to President Johnson. Although McCarthy did not win that primary, his strong showing was credited with influencing Johnson's decision not to seek reelection. Nash wrote to the Longwells in April 1968 that he and Frances had made an early season trek to Little Boar's Head: "We have already been there, as we took the 1200 mile round trip to vote for Senator McCarthy in the primaries." In 1952, Nash had supported Eisenhower, believing he would provide strong leadership against the Soviet threat. He had even signed a joint letter to the *New York Times* making that argument. But Nash had never been much of a cold warrior, and now he had told the Longwells, as a "discouraging afterthought," that McCarthy was the first candidate he had felt deeply about since Al Smith.

Nash supported McCarthy even to the extent of writing a poem for his campaign on the occasion of the candidate's birthday. This was a noteworthy departure from Nash's practice of avoiding serious political or social issues in his verse. It was a practice he had tried to follow ever since his unhappiness at writing verse to sell war bonds in World War II. Thus Linell believed that her father's poem for the McCarthy campaign was "stark testimony to the depths of his feeling about the direction of the nation." As it happened, the poem appears not to have been used by the McCarthy campaign, and Nash was rather hurt that McCarthy did not take note of it. The lack of an acknowledgment was particularly disappointing since McCarthy, among his other attainments, was himself a published poet. McCarthy, of course, lost the Democratic nomination. As the presidential contest between Hubert Humphrey and Richard Nixon approached election day, Nash remarked morosely that he and Frances would "spend the intervening time trying to decide which one to vote against."

Although Nash disapproved of the war, he was also offended by the rhetoric and conduct of many of its most visible and vocal opponents. He was fundamentally a patriot and someone whose values had followed the familiar trajectory of growing more conservative as he aged. Not surprisingly, he was appalled by the virulence of some of the verbal assaults and physical demonstrations against the president. It seemed to Nash that hippies, yippies, and other such protesters were "more arrogant and self-satisfied than the world they [were] bucking against." Nash's ambivalence toward the domestic wars being waged over Vietnam was reflected in an occasion involving an invitation from the White House. At a point when the Johnson administration had been besieged by attacks from a variety of prominent intellectuals and artists, Fred Eberstadt received a telephone call from Alan Jay Lerner, who inquired whether Nash, if invited, would appear at a reception at the White House. Eberstadt advised Lerner that, if Nash were invited, he would probably accept and, in any event, would do nothing, such as a public refusal, to embarrass the administration. When the conversation was reported to Nash, he expressed a fervent hope that the matter would not be pursued, and to his relief it was not.

Nash also found the mores of some of the anti-war protesters to be decidedly unattractive; on matters of drugs and obscenity, for example, he held a distinctly negative view. In 1968 he told interviewers that he had amended his most famous lines, "Candy/ Is dandy/ But liquor/ Is quicker," by adding "Pot is not." He expanded on the point, philosophically, and perhaps in defense of his own tastes, to suggest that "liquor makes its drinkers nicely social. But pot doesn't do that, I hear; it's too individual."

(There is no record of Nash receiving any letters complaining that liquor sometimes has more adverse effects than making people "nicely social," or claiming that cannabis and companionship were not inconsistent. But if he had, he would not have found them persuasive.)

Nash was also offended by the proliferation of obscenity, particularly among the youth of the counterculture. In his own youth, Nash had been a vigorous critic of censorship. Indeed, that had been the theme of his very first poem published in *The New Yorker*, "Senator Smoot." In the six-ties he did not go so far as to advocate censorship, but he freely deplored what, in the absence of censorship or other prevailing standards, had become commonplace:

> I have never found reason to resort to any of those short words which are the only relics of our Anglo-Saxon heritage that the etymologists of SDS [Students for a Democratic Society] have chosen to retain. The continual ostentatious flaunting of this shopworn terminology seems to me to demonstrate a mindless, infantile boorishness which guarantees, for any revolutionary constitution or bill of rights they eventually get around to, a more prominent place in the windows of the scruffy emporiums off Times Square than in the annals of political and social reform.

In a somewhat similar vein, Nash told Roy Newquist in 1967 that he found "the incessant, repetitious accent on sex" in current writing to be "rather dreary." He pointed out, a bit acerbically, that "There are only certain ways you can couple, after all; the variations are not infinite, though I expect any day to read a novel in which they perform while swinging on a chandelier." As an afterthought, he observed that a description of *flagrante en chandelier* might not be a bad idea: "The ultimate would have been reached and we could put an end to the whole silly business."

Nash was also distinctly unenthusiastic about the advent of Women's Liberation, though he was neither hostile nor indifferent to the interests of women. His devotion to Frances reflected an appreciation of women that, despite his teasing, was clearly evident in his verse. And he had always shown great respect for the professional abilities of the women with whom he had worked in different ways and at different times. Artistically, he had admired the very different qualities of Katharine White and Dorothy Parker. On the business side, he had honored his agents, Helen Everitt and Edith Haggard, in dedications, and in later years he valued highly the advice and support of Emmy Jacobson. Finally, he had consistently encouraged the varied interests of his own daughters, never suggesting they might limit themselves to family responsibilities.

But Nash undoubtedly felt that some aspects of the feminist movement undermined his somewhat romanticized view of women—as well as some of the feminine stereotypes he had humorously exploited. Even more, just as in the case of protesters against the war, he recoiled against what he felt to be the stridency of the more militant feminists. (He once went so far as to lump the feminist Betty Friedan with other "single-minded zealots," ranging from Robert Welch of the John Birch Society to Chairman Mao.)

Cumulatively the various strands of social unrest were deeply troubling to Nash, both personally and professionally. While no one who lived through those times could have been untouched by them, they had a specific effect on Nash in his role as a humorist and chronicler of human foibles. In the face of gaping fissures in the social order, Nash began to question the importance of his work. He grew depressed and experienced extended periods when he found he could not write. On one occasion during those years, attending a racetrack with Linell, he suddenly interrupted his handicapping of the first race and said to her, "I wonder if what I write has relevance anymore. In a world gone mad, humor may have been the first casualty of war." But it was not in Nash's nature to share depressing thoughts with his family, so he quickly changed the subject before she could reply.

Nash had made his reputation during the worst days of the depression, and on occasion his verse had reflected the agonies of that time. In those days, though, he was not only charged with youthful energy but stimulated by delight in his young family and the pleasure of being able to make a career as a writer. So the surrounding national malaise had not impaired his ability to write light verse. His personal sense of relevance was not drawn into question until World War II, and then he was rescued from gloomy introspection by the opportunity to work on *One Touch of Venus*. But in the sixties his energies were depleted, not only by the normal process of aging but by his medical problems, and this time there was no new project to inspire or provide a focus for his talents.

One of his longest periods of depression and writer's block began in the fall of 1967 and continued into the winter of 1968. In February 1968, in a poignant letter to Emilie Jacobson, Nash acknowledged that he had decided to seek professional help: "For some months now I have been suffering from an overwhelming fit of the blues which was not helped by two spells of flu and two attacks of bursitis of the knee, not to mention the death of several close friends. An apathy amounting to fear has prevented me from facing my desk, and my mind refuses to function. . . . [M]y doctor has persuaded me to talk to a psychiatrist, which I shall do next Monday and perhaps discover whether I need Geritol or just a kick in the pants. I've had dry spells before, but never one like this. You might show this letter to Sukie—otherwise it is for your eyes alone."

The decision to consult a psychiatrist was not one that someone of Nash's generation and temperament could have made easily. It must have required some arm-twisting from Nash's principal doctor, Ben Baker, and reflected the depths of Nash's own concern. His calendar for 1968 reflects that he saw a Dr. Muncie on the Monday following his letter to Jacobson, and again the following week, but records no other visit to him. According to Nash, the doctor told him that he had no serious mental problems. That diagnosis, or lack of one, appeared to cheer him. In any case, the spring brought a restoration of his spirits and a resumption of the flow of verse. By April he wrote that he was "lively as a Missouri mule and back at work," and by the end of June he had completed fourteen new verses.

In addition to facing his physical and psychological problems, Nash continually felt the need to respond to financial pressures. The abandonment of the lecture circuit resulted in the loss of significant income. Less important financially, but not insignificant, was the end of his role as a participant in *Masquerade Party*. At the same time the magazine industry, feeling the inroads of television, was contracting and providing a smaller market for Nash's verse. He took up some of the slack by doing pieces on commission and by commercial work. Still, the economics remained a challenge, and when in 1965 he was faced with a tax problem, he decided to raise cash by disposing of his papers, either by gift (which would create a charitable deduction) or by sale. After canvassing various possibilities, the choice came down to a gift to the Library of Congress or a sale to the Harry Ransom Humanities Research Center at the University of Texas. When Nash decided upon a sale, the librarian in charge of the manuscript division at the Library of Congress reacted graciously: "It was entirely creditable to exchange your cache for cash, not credit."

Nash scrambled to assemble as many of his papers as possible in order to get the best price he could. He retrieved from Linell the diary that he had kept as a young boy in Rye. In a letter to the Longwells, Nash asked to have the minute book of the "Nassau and Suffolk County Deviled Ham and Lake Ronkonkoma Club" over which Christopher Morley had presided during Nash's days at Doubleday. He noted hopefully that the minutes would be of particular interest to the University of Texas because they already had an extensive collection of Morley material. *The New Yorker* unearthed and returned to Nash, at his request, letters he had sent to the magazine over the years.

The largest single element of the papers was Nash's letters to Frances and to other members of his immediate family. Although Nash and his family had received considerable exposure as subjects of his verse, in many respects Nash was still a shy and private person. None of the letters were scandalous or lurid, but many were highly personal and this, quite naturally, caused Nash some concern. He asked for and received explicit assurances from the Ransom Center that access to the letters would be limited. That assurance, however, did not satisfy Frances. She was unenthusiastic about the sale and agreed to give up Ogden's letters to her *only* on the condition that he destroy her letters to him. As Linell put it, "She had never been a public figure; the love, the doubts, the fears, the joys that she had expressed in her letters were a private matter, shared only with him."

In the end, the Ransom Center acquired more than 2,400 manuscript pages, over half in Nash's hand, encompassing over 240 poems and 1,018 letters, telegrams, and postcards, and various works of prose. It is a trove of material for anyone interested in his life, but the benefit to Nash was rather modest: the final price negotiated was $10,000.

As Nash coped with his own problems, he maintained a strong interest in Linell and Isabel and their spouses and children. In the familiar way of families, they were a source of pride, joy, and comfort but also, at times, a cause for concern. The decade began with a frightening event—a fire, just after Christmas, 1961, in the stables at Linell and Johnny Smith's home on Coniston Road in Baltimore. The fire destroyed not only the stables but three prize horses. The loss, not covered by insurance, was all the more stunning when it was determined to have been caused by arson, but the perpetrator was never apprehended. The fire was a devastating blow to Linell, emotionally and economically. Ogden and Frances had to return to New York almost immediately to get ready for a scheduled lecture tour, but the next day he wrote Linell a long letter of advice and comfort. The letter, she later said, was "a lifeline that pulled me back to my responsibilities as a wife and mother."

Quite apart from the fire, the Coniston Road house had been a mixed blessing. Although it was a large and comfortable home, life was often rather hectic. Frances's parents lived there, the Nashes were frequent visitors, and Linell found herself as a young mother in charge of a four-generational household. Matters were further complicated by growing tensions between Johnny and Frances, when it appeared that Johnny's career in the insurance business was no longer moving ahead. Two years after the fire, Linell and Johnny gave up the house on Coniston Road and moved to a small horse farm in Sparks, a few miles north of Baltimore. Johnny would continue in the insurance business until 1968 when he decided to give it up to devote his energies to working with Linell in raising horses.

Although the responsibilities of homemaking and horse breeding limited her time for writing, between 1959 and 1963 Linell was still able to publish several children's books. Then, in 1967, after extensive research that included a trip to Poland, she published *And Miles to Go: The Biography of a Great Arabian Horse, Witez II.* This book, conceived as a children's book but published for the general trade, told the story of a stallion bred on a Polish stud farm and seized successively by the Russians and the Germans. The horse was later liberated by General Patton and sent to the United States, where it became a champion of champions. Nash was sufficiently impressed by the book that he wrote a lengthy letter in longhand to his old friend Harry Scherman, founder and chairman of the Book-of-the-Month Club, urging that the Club select it. Although the Club did not, the book went on to become a classic of its kind.

Meanwhile the Nashes remained in close touch with Isabel and Fred. Before their move to Baltimore the Nashes had often seen the young Eberstadt family for lunch or dinner, and after the move to Baltimore, there were visits back and forth as well as vacations at Little Boar's Head. By the sixties Fred had left NBC and had become a fashion photographer, working first with Richard Avedon and then operating his own studio. Although he did well in his new profession, and had inherited money from his family, the Eberstadts' finances were not always stable. In 1964, Nash wrote Isabel from London, where he was recovering from his confinement in the London Clinic, and expressed pleasure that she and Fred were "on the way to arriving at some kind of financial steadiness." Speaking with a voice chastened by experience, Nash observed that "the rags to riches life is an intolerant one," adding that he and Frances had addressed such problems in their own lives through an arrangement with Frances's "trust people" and through "Sukey at Curtis Brown [who] keeps me in line."

Isabel had continued to write. In a 1965 letter to Vernon Duke, Nash reported that she had "written a couple of extraordinarily perceptive profiles for the New York magazine of the *Herald Trib*, one of Le Roi Jones which elicited a letter from Mr. Jones threatening to cut her throat." She had also been contacted by William Shawn, Ross's successor at *The New Yorker*, and had told her father that she was well along with work on her second novel. In the same letter Nash also commented that she was "struggling to get out of the Harper's Bazaar and best-dressed-ten group," a maneuver made more difficult by Fred's work as a fashion photographer.

Two years later, pride in Isabel's work as well as any concern for the Eberstadts' financial equilibrium was eclipsed by sudden and grave problem with Isabel's health. In the spring of 1967 she was stricken by an illness that Nash described vividly in a letter to Vernon Duke: "Isabel was desperately ill and for the first ten days we thought we were going to lose her. Some toxic substance in the entire system, but centered in the kidneys. Miracle doctors with miracle machines worked their miracles, though not complete ones. She was released from the hospital after five weeks, but must return two days each week for treatment under the kidney machine." Although it was first thought that Isabel might require lifelong treatment, she made a remarkable recovery from the illness. But two years later she would experience another medical emergency that was also successfully resolved, not without causing serious concern to Ogden and Frances.

A move from New York to Baltimore and Little Boar's Head in 1965 did not immediately solve any of Nash's problems, but it would alter his and Frances's lives. Consciously or not, it became the centerpiece of Nash's strategy of survival.

15

BALTIMORE *REDUX* AND
LITTLE BOAR'S HEAD

In his youth Nash had been an enthusiastic New Yorker, once writing a poem, "I Want New York," that was exuberant in its praise of the city. Many years later, after he and Frances had moved back to New York in 1953, Nash enjoyed having at hand the theater, good restaurants, and friends who either lived in New York or visited it regularly. Now he had quite a different view. No doubt it was in part because of his age and health problems, but it also reflected the rather different place the city had become and was still becoming. In 1961, Nash wrote a poem, "Our City, Our Citizens, or Patience and Fortitude," that, in one segment, seems eerily prophetic:

> If you should happen after dark
> To find yourself in Central Park,
> Ignore the paths that beckon you
> And hurry, hurry to the zoo,
> And creep into the tiger's lair.
> Frankly, you'll be safer there.

As the poem indicates, by 1961 Central Park was no longer as safe as it had once been, but its worst days were yet to come before law and order would make a comeback in the nineties. Quite apart from issues of physical safety, New York City was then, as it is today, an expensive place to live and one where a degree of tension and stress in daily living is taken as routine.

In New York the Nashes had led an active but fairly low-key social life—far less glamorous than that of Isabel and Fred. They enjoyed the theater and two or three times a week would have dinner or cocktails with family or friends. Their social companions were a varied group: sometimes they were friends of long standing, such as the Reynals or the Hacketts; sometimes they had a connection with Nash's work, such as Alan Collins or Ned Bradford; and sometimes they were summer residents of Little Boar's Head. Frances felt limited rapport with some of Nash's associates from the worlds of writing and the theater. As a result, Nash developed something of a separate social life conducted mainly over lunch. For example, he often joined a group that met weekly for lunch at the Lobster House in New York and included Sid Perelman, Al Hirschfeld, theater critic Brooks Atkinson, and the *New Yorker* regulars Charles Addams and Joseph Mitchell.

As life in the city became more difficult, though, and with no major prospects in television or the theater, there was little reason for Nash to stay. His defection from New York in 1965 was reported in an Associated Press story that appeared in newspapers around the country. But the *New York Times* carried only a brief item, noting the warm welcome given Nash by the mayor of Baltimore, Theodore McKeldin, and quoting the poem that Nash had written in response:

Dear Mr. Mayor,
My Spirits are Gayer
Because of your letter of welcome.

It rang like a clink
Of ice in a drink
From one who has newly from Hell come.

Though others may fatten
Then thrive in Manhattan
I found it a verminous vault.

So I'm glad you don't shun
The Prodigal son
Whose heart never wandered from Balt.

Whatever the sources of Nash's disaffection with New York, "verminous vault" was a bit over the top. He might have been a bit more cautious since only the year before he had responded to a complaint by contritely retracting a long-past dig at the Bronx:

I wrote those lines, "The Bronx, No Thonx."
I shudder to confess them.
Now I'm an older wiser man,
I cry "The Bronx? God bless them."

This time there were no complaints, and Nash did retain *some* loyalty to New York. Four years later, when the "amazing" New York Mets won the Eastern Division of the National League, it warranted front-page stories in the *New York Times*, one of which was headlined by a poem that Nash wrote to celebrate the occasion.

The transition to life in Baltimore was not difficult. Ogden and Frances had made frequent visits from New York to visit the Smiths, and Nash's continuing ties to the city had been reflected in a lengthy poem, "Baltimore," that appeared in 1957 in *Holiday*. The very first week after the Nashes had moved into their new Baltimore home, Nash found time to visit Pimlico, on Monday with David Woods of the *Baltimore Sun* and on Wednesday with Linell. The Nashes' new residence was modest, far smaller than the old house on Rugby Road, their house in Little Boar's Head, or even their New York apartments on Fifty-seventh Street and later Eighty-first Street. For the first time they would be without live-in help, a fact that seemed to bother Ogden more than Frances.

Nonetheless their townhouse was comfortable and cheery. It had three bedrooms, one of which Nash used for an office; another served as a guest room for grandchildren (or, as Nash put it, "the touring midgets"). The kitchen opened onto a small garden with a dogwood tree, and the living room looked out on a terrace with dogwood, azaleas, myrtle, and laurel. When they moved in, the Nashes lacked a garden hose, so Nash wrote Dan Longwell, "I water everything each morning with a Georg Jensen silver pitcher, which should produce some aristocratic blooms." To his delight, a birdbath and a supply of birdseed attracted a variety of visitors including cardinals, catbirds, doves, blue jays, and song sparrows as well as "a horde of grackles with their camp-followers." It was, he wrote Vernon Duke, "Just enough country, just enough city for my perverse ego, which is fully at home in neither." An interviewer, finding Nash seated in a chair on his patio, "in rimless glasses, gray flannel trousers, cranberry knit shirt and a brown plaid sport coat," thought he resembled "a squire just in from a leisurely survey of his estate." Having long ago been "to the manor born" at Ramaqua, Nash had apparently retained something of that aura even in circumstances now considerably reduced.

Linell and Johnny were only twenty minutes away, which meant, as Nash said, "we can see them often without getting in their hair." Despite the concerns of both Ogden and Frances over Johnny's business fortunes, and the sometimes strained relations between Johnny and Frances, the Nashes and the Smiths frequently had dinner together at the Elkridge Club. The Smiths' two youngest children, Francie and Biddy, often spent Friday nights with their grandparents while Nell, the eldest, made visits on her own until she left for boarding school at Farmington. The Nashes also enjoyed seeing Ogden's older sisters, both of whom lived in the area. Gwen, whom Nash had been visiting when he first met Frances, had been widowed since 1945, and Eleanor had been divorced since the 1930s. From his boyhood Nash had maintained a close relationship with Gwen, to the point that Fred Eberstadt felt that, until her death in 1966, she had been Nash's "best friend." Nash was also fond of Eleanor, who at the age of seventy-two was a columnist for the *Baltimore Sun* and host of a local television show. (While Nash thought that she was "miserably underpaid," Eleanor was grateful that the paper had given her a job when she was sixty-seven and needed it.) In addition to socializing with family members, the Nashes renewed ties with a variety of old friends whom they would join for cocktails, dinner, or bridge.

Although the move to Baltimore appeared to improve Nash's physical condition, his intestinal problems again required surgery in the spring of 1966. Nash spent several weeks in Johns Hopkins Hospital, where he wrote Dan and Mary Longwell that the surgeon had "removed the kink that they tell me has been causing all my recent years of harassment." He was grateful for the support of family and friends that helped to make the experience endurable: "Children, grandchildren and friends have been wonderfully affectionate and thoughtful, and all in all I consider myself a fortunate man." Frances had stayed at an inn across the street from the hospital, so she was able to visit Ogden and read to him three times a day. Isabel came down from New York for the first several days, and Linell was a faithful visitor throughout, also organizing occasional visits by the children. Beyond that, Nash pointed out, since most of the doctors were old friends, there was no risk of being lonely. The operation was once more pronounced a success, and within a few weeks, Nash even felt strong enough for a brief visit to New York.

Once recovered, Nash was able to resume visits not only to Pimlico but to the other Maryland tracks, Laurel and Bowie. He was often accompanied by David Woods and Tom White of the *News American*. Woods and White found that on the way to the track Nash was an engaging conversationalist on a wide range of topics, but once there he was all business in the matter of handicapping. At that point Nash's principal form of communication was humming: "It was funny," White wrote. "He would bow his head low over the form, humming softly as he studied the entries. If he lost the first race, the humming would be perceptibly louder. When things were really bad, it would rise ferociously to near thunder." Happily, Nash was a fairly skilled handicapper, so thunderous humming was not often called for.

The move to Baltimore also allowed Nash to root for the Baltimore Orioles and the Baltimore Colts from close range, and when the Colts met the New York Jets in the Super Bowl in 1968, any arguable conflict of loyalties was promptly and decisively resolved in favor of Baltimore. Nash wrote several poems for a splashy *Life* cover story, explaining why the Colts would win. The poems were illustrated by photographs and took up seven pages of the magazine. Nash's prediction did not seem too risky—the Colts were favored by seventeen points. But "Broadway Joe" Namath led the Jets to a stunning upset, and Nash was required to beat a gracious retreat. The week after the game, *Life* ran a lengthy poem entitled "Prognostications Are for the Birds; Lay Off Me, Please, While I Eat My Words," that paid tribute to ". . . the playboy whiz/ Who is just as good as he says he is."

Comfortable as the Nashes were in Baltimore, the center of gravity of their lives had shifted to their home in Little Boar's Head, where they now were voting residents and spent slightly more than six months of the year. The village, a part of the Town of North Hampton, is located on the New Hampshire coast, just below Portsmouth. (The origin of the name remains obscure, but the local historical society has traced it back as far as a 1633 letter which "states in part '. . . Portsmouth runs from the harbor mouth by the sea side to the entrance of a little river between two hed lands wh[ich] we have given the name Little Bores-hed and Great Bores-hed . . .'[sic].") The Nashes had begun coming to Little Boar's Head for summers in 1934, when the trip from Baltimore by automobile might take three days and when children, servants, and other "appendages" came by train to Boston or North Hampton. The Nashes had rented various cottages, including the Cushing cottage, which had been owned by the celebrated Boston physician, Dr. Harvey Cushing, and where Eleanor Roosevelt had visited after her son James had married Betsey Cushing. (A scandal of some proportions had developed one year when James was said to have become seriously enamored with Eleanor Goldsborough, a close friend of Frances's who was visiting the Nashes.)

Linell and Isabel remembered summers at Little Boar's Head from their earliest childhood. Linell later wrote poignantly of an enchanted time, marked by Fourth of July parades, picnics, and fireworks: "It's hard to describe the feeling of that summer colony before World War II. A different time—a different world—it shimmers in the mind like a mirage." When the Nashes returned to Little Boar's Head after the war, Linell and Isabel were teenagers; Nash captured a glimpse of their world in his 1947 poem "Tarkington, Thou Should'st Be Living at This Hour." (On the other hand, various teenage pranks in the company of their friends, Kay and Isabel Hobson, such as a brief foray into stealing local signs for souvenirs, went unmemorialized. When circumstances warranted, a conference would be held with the Hobson girls' parents, Phil and Kay, good friends of Ogden and Frances, to decide upon appropriate disciplinary measures.)

By 1962 the Nashes were ready to assure that a third generation would enjoy the tradition of summer visits to Little Boar's Head. After renting houses for so many years, Ogden and Frances decided to buy with the hope that the house would serve as a summer haven for children and grandchildren. The house they decided upon, at 9 Atlantic Avenue, was next door to their most recent rental and had a similarly splendid view across the road to the beach and the ocean. Downstairs the house had a large bedroom, dining room, kitchen, and two living rooms, one of which was to be a playroom, while the upstairs offered five bedrooms. There were also living quarters with two bedrooms over the garage, and the house and garage stood on three and a half acres. The Nashes acquired the house for $25,000, with a down payment of $8,000 "and the balance through eternity to our friendly Hampton bank."

Despite the number of available rooms, none were designated as Nash's study; he worked from a long table in the living room, his back to a picture window and the view of the ocean. Despite the fact that one of the living rooms had been designated as a playroom, grandchildren regularly invaded Nash's workplace. Family members and visitors alike were surprised at the sometimes chaotic conditions under which Nash was able to do serious writing. Lewis Nichols, editor of the *New York Times Book Review*, traveled to New Hampshire in 1968 to visit with Nash after the publication of

There's Always Another Windmill. In the ensuing article, he described Nash's working environment with at least one raised eyebrow. "Most writers seek solitude for their desks," Nichols observed, "but not Ogden Nash." Nash, he continued, "obviously places five grandchildren on a par with or perhaps even ahead of his work." Linell and Isabel had grown accustomed to Nash's ability to work in a "family" setting—he had never accepted confinement to an office on Rugby Road—but for Fred Eberstadt it was a new experience. Observing Nash at work at the table, Fred assumed that his father-in-law was engaged in "busy work," paying bills or balancing the checkbook, and was astonished to find that he was actually writing verse.

Nichols also reported with mild incredulity that, since Nash was the only car driver in the family, he did the grocery shopping. In fact groceries were regularly delivered to the house, but since Nash was often the only licensed driver on hand, he did come in for more than his share of running errands. Still, there was domestic help for cooking, looking after the grandchildren, and assisting with other chores. Of these, the redoubtable Clarence was foremost. Clarence Collins had worked for the Nashes in their first home in Baltimore on Underwood Road, and in later years had filled a variety of roles for the family. At one point he had suddenly disappeared from the house on Rugby Road (in flight from Mrs. Collins, it was thought), but a few years later he had reappeared, just as suddenly, upon the Nashes' arrival at their new apartment on Fifty-seventh Street in New York. Finding Frances struggling in a sea of unopened packing boxes, Clarence immediately took charge, telling her that if she went to her room and sat down on her chaise longue, he would take care of everything.

At Little Boar's Head, Clarence lived in the quarters over the garage. There, each August on his birthday, he was the generous host of a very large party for servants, black and white, from miles around. Clarence was not only the cook but the chief operating officer of the Nash household. His authority was respected by all, from Ogden and Frances to the youngest grandchild. Fred Eberstadt remarked that Clarence was "the one person I know of who could manage Mrs. Nash." He was not without flaws: his domestic arrangements with wives and girlfriends were known only vaguely, and he was sometimes observed to have drunk too much. On one such occasion, when Clarence's serving at the dining table had clearly been impaired, Frances insisted that Ogden speak to him. Clarence was duly summoned to a private meeting but promptly deflected any criticism by saying, "Mr. Nash, I know what you are going to say to me and I don't want to hear it because I've been a lot drunker than that lots of times and you've never said a thing."

Another long-standing member of the domestic staff was Agnes Baschke, who had also been with the Nashes on Underwood Road. At Little Boar's Head she did sewing and general housework. Other help came and went. In May 1968, Nash wrote to Nell at her boarding school describing a new maid: "[She] seems willing and able to learn under Clarence's constant tutelage. . . . Her name is Armentria, but Clarence can't deal with that, so we call her Catherine."

Nash's routine was quite specific. He would have breakfast in the dining room, always dressed in a jacket, while Frances had breakfast on a tray in the bedroom. After breakfast, Nash would repair to the long table in the living room to work until eleven, when he would go to the beach to sit in the sun and take a dip in the icy New Hampshire waters, returning for a drink and lunch at the house. After lunch he would nap, then do more work, or perhaps read, before returning to the beach at four for another swim. A cocktail hour preceded dinner, and after dinner Nash would read to the children. The evening routine varied somewhat three or four nights a week when the Nashes went out with friends for cocktails or dinner or had guests in, perhaps for steaks that Nash would grill outdoors. Ogden and Frances would retire sometime before midnight, though on occasion Clarence would see Nash up and working at one or two o'clock in the morning. That was, perhaps, the time when Nash found solitude for his work if he needed it.

The Nashes' friends at Little Boar's Head consisted largely of six or eight couples who enjoyed sitting together at the beach, entertaining in each other's homes, and dining at Saunders, a small and unpretentious local restaurant renowned for its lobster. Many of the group were, like the Nashes, able to arrive before Memorial Day and remain well after Labor Day, so the Nashes did not lack for companionship during their extended season. After Phil Hobson died, Kay Hobson married Pen Higginson, and the Nashes traveled with the Higginsons in 1957 on a six-week cruise to Madeira, Casablanca, and other ports of call. Jack and Jean Lincoln were summer residents who had a home on Long Island and who had sometimes met the Nashes in New York during their Manhattan years. The group also included Matt and Becky Warren. Warren was headmaster of St. Paul's School and for several years was the summer rector at St. Andrew's Episcopal Church in the adjoining town of Rye Beach.

St. Andrew's, which was attended by most of the Nashes' friends, occupies a handsome century-old stone church building, but it operates only during the summer months. Nash was a loyal member, considerably more active in its affairs than he was in the churches that he and Frances attended in New York or Baltimore. He served on the parish committee and helped with the fund raising, even contributing a poem toward that effort in 1965:

> The parish we loved in summer
> In winter we forget
> And therefore with this message
> Is cast Saint Andrew's net
>
>   *   *   *   *
>
> The yearly cost grows greater
> The yearly yield is small
> Oh Lord who blessed St. Andrew
> Send us one shining haul.

The church and its members were by no means the only recipients of Nash's verse. For example, an invitation to a birthday celebration was in verse, concluding: ". . . you must not/ Bring flowers, liquor, or gadgets nonsensical/ Or gifts either costly or inexpensical/ I'm sitting pretty with plenty to spare/ Just a year away from medicare." And following his long-standing custom, Nash enjoyed inscribing personalized verses for friends in copies of his books. Some were better than others, but they were always treasured. For the baptism of the daughter of Robert and Kay Southworth (nee Hobson, teenage pal of Linell and Isabel) he wrote a quite flippant verse on a copy of *The Untold Adventures of Santa Claus*: "No wonder little Mary grins;/ She's been washed of all her sins./ When she leaves St. Andrew's door/ Mary plans to sin some more." The Southworths, both prominent in the church, were charmed.

The Nashes' friends at Little Boar's Head, like their friends in Baltimore, were not a particularly glamorous or literary group, but they were the sort of people with whom Frances was most comfortable. For Nash, they were companions to whom he had nothing to prove and with whom he could be entirely relaxed. While the Nashes' friends were well aware of, and respected, Ogden's "celebrity," he was mostly just another neighbor, and a particularly warm and gracious one, a peacemaker who always seemed to know how to smooth ruffled feathers when necessary. He and

Frances also enjoyed having visitors, such as Nash's sisters, or their friends from Hollywood days, Edgar and Jane Ward. When friends could not make it to Little Boar's Head, Nash stayed in touch from afar, sending long letters to Dan Longwell, Vernon Duke, and others, always on paper from the same yellow tablets that he used in writing verse.

If friends were important to Nash, the visits of children and grandchildren were even more so. He once wrote to Linell that "the whole purpose of our buying this house was to hold the grandchildren and as many of their parents as possible." And in 1963, when he wrote to Isabel expressing regret that his unplanned excursion to the hospital in Boston had caused him to miss seeing Nicky and Nenna, he noted that "actually being in the house with children means so much more than the weekly mealtime relationship." In the following years there were ample opportunities to have the children in the house, and while he sometimes found their visits tiring, he cherished them. When the grandchildren visited without their parents, his letters to Linell and Isabel reported on their activities and accomplishments and complimented their behavior. In a 1965 letter he wrote Linell proudly that "Nell ate all her lobster at Saunders last night; Biddy ate her own and half of mine." Later that summer, on August 3, he wrote Isabel that Nicky was developing a sense of humor and that "His deportment is perfect, as is his care of the Kangaroo rat." (Despite Nicky's care, the latter apparently met a sudden and untimely end; Nash's appointment calendar in the very same week bears the solemn entries: "August 5, Death of Kangaroo rat" and "August 6, Burial of Kangaroo rat.")

One year, on Nash's birthday, the grandchildren put on a play that included readings of some of Nash's own poems and some original verses as well, including:

> Our comic books and chewing gum
> Do not enhance your living room.

and

> Although half grown, we'll swear it's true.
> We're warmest when our lips are blue.

Nash not only enjoyed the performance but was entitled to claim some credit—genetic or environmental—for such rhymes.

As an occasional disciplinarian, Nash discharged his responsibility gently but firmly. Once, when all the grandchildren were visiting together, the four younger children organized a séance and charged fees for telling the fortunes of neighborhood children. Nenna brought the children into the basement under the playroom, Nick collected money, Biddy was the fortune-teller, and Francie read tarot cards. Matters got a bit out of hand in the case of one young boy who was quite convinced by the act and was eager to talk with his grandfather. He paid ten dollars for the privilege and was rewarded by seeing his hosts appear to go into trances and receive messages from the departed relative. When Nash learned about all this, he was not pleased: money was refunded, apologies were given, and it was made clear that the activity was not to be repeated. The heart of his reprimand, however, was simply to make clear his disappointment in the children.

Nell, being the eldest, led a more independent life and presented somewhat different challenges for her grandparents. By 1964 she had become aware that her grandfather was something of a celebrity who was acquainted with many interesting people. On those slender grounds she once developed the notion that he was a personal friend of the Beatles, and told several of her friends that, after a scheduled concert date in Boston, the group would be coming to visit Nash. So it came to pass that, on the day after the concert, a considerable crowd of young people gathered on the lawn in front of the Nashes' house to await the arrival of the Beatles. Recognizing some of them as friends of Nell's, Nash went to the door and told them that she had returned to Baltimore. When they said they were there to see not Nell but the Beatles, Nash assured them that the Beatles were not expected. But the crowd refused to believe Nash; they remained for several hours, and the house remained under youthful surveillance for the next few days.

Four years later, when Nell was nearly sixteen and Nash was exchanging letters with Linell, trying to arrange the schedule of summer visits, Nash let slip that, while they were eager to see Nell for as long as possible, "it is only because of her present age that we shirk the responsibility of having her here without her parents to make those difficult decisions." Anyone who has been in the position of attempting to supervise the social life of a teenager could readily sympathize with Nash, but he quickly gave in. There is no record of Linell's response, but five days later Nash was backpedaling: "We are not afraid to have Nell without a parent, but we want you for as long as you can give us, and we particularly want Johnny. Even though the water has been unusually warm this year we won't force him into it."

The comfort that Nash derived from family and friends in the sixties was crucial to his survival during that decade. Surprisingly, one of his more daunting challenges during those years was getting his verse published in the magazine that had started his career and sustained it for so many years—*The New Yorker*.

16

THE WISE OWLS OF FORTY-THIRD STREET

Throughout the late forties and the fifties, publication of Nash's verse in *The New Yorker* had remained at the heart of his professional life. From a standpoint of pure economics, revenue from *The New Yorker* was significant, but not a dominant factor. Nash had a "first reading agreement" that gave the magazine the right of first refusal for all his work except for poems that were specially commissioned by others. By the late fifties the agreement provided that Nash would be paid four hundred dollars for poems of twenty lines or more and fifteen dollars a line for shorter poems.

Although *The New Yorker*'s rates were considerably higher than those of many other publications, Nash's payment for several poems published in the magazine might be less than the fee for a single long poem commissioned by *McCall's* or *Family Circle*. Poems rejected by *The New Yorker* were more often than not published elsewhere, and there is no evidence that Nash's presence in, or absence from, the pages of *The New Yorker* affected the sales of his books. Still, publication in the magazine was of great personal importance to him, and rejections were painful. As he once explained rather fervently, "*The New Yorker* is to me what St. Paul's School, Princeton and the Ivy Club are to some of my immature contemporaries: my first patron, and I hope my continuing one."

Katharine White left the magazine in 1938 when she and Andy moved to Maine, and she was succeeded by Gus Lobrano. It took a while for Nash and Lobrano to get to know each other, but in 1944 Lobrano wrote Nash to accept a poem and added the thought that if they got together he could give Nash some "suggestions about how you might get some more money from this magazine." Nash replied promptly in the same tone—"my ears pricked up one cubit at the hint that I may be able to hornswoggle your employers out of a little more dough." But at the moment he was still preoccupied with trying to find another *One Touch of Venus* and was writing little verse. The following year, Lobrano, in frustration, wrote again: "The way it works is you send us some poems and then we either send you back the poems or keep the poems and send you a check. See?" It was not until 1947, however, that Nash was again sending in poems on a regular basis. Katharine White, who had returned to the magazine in 1943, wrote to Nash that it was "such a pleasure to be getting Nash poems again." (Despite their long relationship, it was still "Mrs. White" and "Mr. Nash," though it had been "Gus" and "Ogden" from the start.)

Lobrano had a knack of establishing friendships with his writers, who included John Cheever, Irwin Shaw, Jerome Weidman, and Sid Perelman, each of whom dedicated one or more books to him. Another Lobrano writer, Edward Newhouse, has recalled that "Gus was the person primarily responsible for making the *New Yorker* a home away from home for a lot of us. He would say 'Let's have lunch' to three people simultaneously. I'd come in for lunch and see that he'd also invited Sid Perelman and Ogden Nash, and just as Gus planned it, we became friends." For his part, Nash felt that Lobrano was a wise editor and trusted his judgment implicitly.

Harold Ross also continued to be an admirer of Nash's. In July 1947 he wrote Nash with his appreciation that Nash had agreed to the magazine's current terms:

> I am greatly pleased and enormously relieved by your acceptance of our offer, which was made after a long session of figuring with the business office. I am convinced it was as high as I could expect them to go and look the other contributors in the eye. I was nervous as a cat until I got word yesterday, because I didn't want to run this kind of magazine with you out of it. The poems of yours we have used during the last years have been a great comfort to me and a source of deep satisfaction, as well as a great asset to the magazine.

It took Nash six months to reply, but when he did, he told Ross that he intended to frame the letter. He went on to say that "you and the magazine have been more than generous to me and I assure you that I belong to you both as long as there is a rhyme left in my Eberhard Faber #2." Ross wrote again a few days later, returning some Thurberesque drawings that Nash had submitted; in an uncharacteristically tactful way, he said that while the drawings were "promising," he and Lobrano felt they were not quite usable. Ross then forwarded the correspondence to Lobrano, saying he hoped he hadn't encouraged Nash too much, and he wanted Lobrano to see Nash's "extravagant committment." He was going to keep it, Ross said, "to pull on him if necessary."

When Harold Ross died in 1951, he was succeeded by William Shawn. Although Shawn would have a long and successful career as editor of *The New Yorker*, he and Nash never developed a personal relationship. Five years later Gus Lobrano died, and Katharine White again became Nash's editor on an interim basis. (She and Nash marked the occasion by deciding that it was finally time to be on a first-name basis.) Two years later, in 1958, White was succeeded by her son, Roger Angell. Angell, then thirty-eight, had been a contributor to *The New Yorker* for several years while working as a writer and editor at *Holiday*. It had not been thought appropriate for Angell to work at *The New Yorker* while his mother remained with the magazine, but upon her retirement he was invited by Shawn to join the staff. It would be Angell's responsibility to serve as Nash's editor during the trying times of the sixties.

Angell is an urbane and soft-spoken man who remains on the staff of *The New Yorker* as a writer and editor. He is best known, perhaps, not for the many renowned writers he has edited but for his own writing on baseball, in the magazine and in several books. His essays on the sport are not only highly literate but reveal a depth of knowledge about baseball and baseball players that is respected by everyone who takes the game seriously.

Angell appreciated Nash and his work: "There was no part of himself that he wasn't able to reach as a writer. All his reading and everything about Ogden Nash that was himself seemed to come out in his verse, I thought. He was very lucky; many writers work to get to that position and don't." Nash, in Angell's view, was foremost among the many contributors of light verse to the magazine, including Phyllis McGinley and Morris Bishop. He readily understood Nash's resentment of the award of the Pulitzer Prize to McGinley: "Once again his taste was exactly right."

Angell found Nash to be a gentleman and a pleasure to work with. In this respect he stood in direct contrast with another older writer whom Angell had inherited, Nash's colleague from the thirties, James Thurber. Thurber had known Angell since he was a little boy, and that didn't make matters easier. As Angell later put it: "The reason I got Thurber was because he was so bad tempered and such a handful nobody else wanted to handle him. I discovered right away that it was not a lot of fun." Nash's temperament was quite different. Despite his own seniority and long history with the magazine, he treated Angell with respect from the outset. Although it had taken Nash more than two decades to arrive at a first-name basis with Katharine White, Nash addressed his first letter to his new editor "Dear Roger" and went on to explain that "I hope you will forgive my leaping to a first-name basis, but it seems to make my relationship with my Editor easier."

While Nash and Angell never became close friends, they enjoyed each other's company, often at lunch, preceded by a couple of cocktails, at the Ritz or the Carlton House. One common ground of writer and editor was their shared interest in baseball: while Nash was not as serious a student of the game as Angell, he was an avid and knowledgeable fan. He wrote several poems for *The New Yorker* with a baseball theme while Angell was his editor, but the one Angell recalls best, and still can quote, was written in 1957, just before his tenure began. Horace Stoneham had taken his New York Giants team to San Francisco, abandoning the Polo Grounds on Coogan's Bluff, where the team had always played. Nash's poem was accompanied by a cartoon depicting No. 24, Willie Mays, and his teammates trudging off the field for the last time:

LINES TO BE CARVED ON COOGAN'S BLUFF

The candle's out, the game is up;
Who has heart for a stirrup cup?
Farewell Giants and Horace Stoneham
De mortuis nil nisi bonum.

Nash soon recognized Angell as someone who not only appreciated his work but who could make suggestions that might improve it. On the other hand, when his verse was rejected, Nash sometimes seemed able to blame "the magazine," rather than Angell personally. In so doing he may have been aided by the fact that, though Angell and Shawn made the decisions to accept or reject, Angell's letters often suggested that the rejection reflected the "vote" of several editors who had reviewed Nash's poem. Angell never claimed to have disagreed with the consensus, but his mode of expression at least allowed the responsibility for the rejection to seem more diffuse and less personal. Nash may have been mildly deceived by this technique: he would often make rueful reference to "the board of editors," "the trustees," or the "wise owls on 43rd Street." If so, it was probably a useful deception that helped to preserve a valuable relationship.

At the most basic level, Angell shepherded Nash's poems through *The New Yorker's* legendary proofreading and fact-checking departments. Serious discussions would ensue over the addition, subtraction, or relocation of commas and quotation marks, and equally weighty matters. In addition, while one might not ordinarily think of fact-checking poetry, Nash's verse was often sprinkled with factual references, and when it was, the magazine's staff checked it to the limit—and sometimes beyond. For example, in "The Wrongs of Spring," written in early 1965, Nash began by asking "Just because I'm sixty-three/ Shall April folly forbidden be?" Angell, forwarding the author's proof with various changes, remarked: "I am convulsed to see that our checking department has indignantly pointed out that you won't be sixty-three until next August; don't let that impertinence tempt you into altering the first couplet."

Angell also attempted to assure that Nash's myriad references and allusions were not too obscure for readers of *The New Yorker*. For example, with respect to a quote that he felt readers would not recognize: "I think it would just make most of our subscribers feel uneasy and somewhat illiterate. . . ." In another case he objected that to understand a particular couplet, "one must not only remember the Frost poem 'The Road Not Taken,' but must also remember what it is about. I just don't think many of our readers could do that, which is a shame because it's a fine ending to the poem."

Angell did not, however, wish to set the standard too low. After taking an office poll and discovering that no one was entirely familiar with the phrase "prunes and prism," he conceded that it was in the dictionary and concluded that "I don't think we should make things too easy for our readers." (The phrase came from Dickens's *Little Dorrit*—"Papa, potatoes, poultry, prunes, and prism are all very good words for the lips, especially prunes and prism"—and had come to signify primness or pretension.) Angell's concerns reached the mundane as well as the literary. In "The Darkest Half Hour," Nash depicted an anxious host fretting in the half-hour before his guests arrive:

He nervously whistles a snatch from the *Peer Gynt Suite* by Grieg
And wonders if his vodka—domestic not Polish—is fit for
    compounding a White Russian or Orange Julius, a Bog Fog or
    a Palm Bay Intrigue.

The fact-checkers questioned the reference to Polish vodka, and Angell fretted a bit: "I guess the question about Polish vodka is a valid one, since I can't remember ever having seen a Polish vodka, but I see no reason why you can't use Russian or Slavic if you wish." Nash, however, held firm, and the vodka remained Polish. The files do not indicate whether the fact-checking department required recipes for the enumerated drinks.

In addition to refereeing matters of style and balancing erudition against clarity, Angell often made substantive suggestions. While Angell was later modest about his role ("I hope I wasn't too interfering"), the record of his correspondence with Nash indicates that he sometimes made significant contributions. In some instances Angell simply identified problems—rhymes that didn't seem to work or lines that were not as funny as intended—and left it to Nash to find the solution. At other times he would suggest an approach or idea that Nash would then implement. For example, "Unfortunately, It's the Only Game in Town" was a poem about the kinds of everyday predicaments in which an individual finds himself bucking the odds. Angell said he would like additional examples, and suggested the problem of deciding which lane to choose at a toll bridge, noting that he always chose the one "that includes a lady who stalls her car or else manages to drop a whole handful of coins on the road instead of in the toll collector's hand." Nash promptly obliged:

> Why when choosing between two lanes
>   leading to a highway tollhouse do I take
>   the one containing a lady who first hands
>   the collector a twenty-dollar bill and next
>   drops her change on the ground?
> Why when quitting a taxi do I invariably
>   down the door handle when it should
>   be upped and up it when it should be
>   downed?

In "We're Fine, Just Fine," Nash wrote about people whose ruddy complexions led their friends to believe mistakenly that they were in good health. He concluded with a Shakespearean reference:

> I can guess why Mr. W.H. was honored as the Sonnets' onlie
>   begetter:
> Mr. W.H. alone of Shakespeare's companions didn't slap
>   him on the back when he was feeling awful and tell him
>   he had never looked better.

Angell did not stumble over the possible obscurity of the reference to "W.H." (The title page of the Sonnets, published in 1609, contained an enigmatic reference "To the onlie begetter of these insuing sonnets Mr. W.H. all happiness. . . ." Scholars have reached no consensus as to the identity of W.H. or the reason for the dedication.) Angell did suggest that the reference to Shakespeare be expanded: "There must be some lines in one of Shakespeare's sonnets that would indicate that he didn't always feel well." Nash cheerfully agreed, saying he would "proceed to the Sonnets, a happy chore too long neglected." Three days later he had the addition:

> I share the resentment of Shakespeare, who obviously wrote
>   Sonnet CXL after an evening devoted to sack and
>   malmsey,
> And the house physician at the Globe congratulated him on
>   his healthy exterior glow, when his interior was insufferably
>   queasy and qualmsy.
> Avaunt, healthy exterior glow!
> "Testy sick men," wrote the indignant poet, "when their
>   deaths be near, no news but health from their physicians
>   know."

Nash did not appear to resent Angell's editorial suggestions and frequently acknowledged that a poem had been improved by them. He would admit to a twinge—on grounds both aesthetic and economic—when the editing resulted in the substantial shortening of a poem: "If you disagree with me on this I shall not quarrel, only sigh and give you full permission to use the scissors where you will. Sizeable cuts the reason for which I do not fully comprehend always sadden me a little, not only because I see shreds of my brain matter washed down the drain, but also because they affect the size of the check which is the pleasant concomitant of acceptance."

Angell's suggestions were generally made after a poem had already been purchased, but on occasion, purchase was contingent upon acceptable improvements. Nash welcomed changes that might lead to the acceptance of a poem that would otherwise have been rejected. In 1966 he wrote Angell, "Your letter gave me great pleasure, first, of course, because of the acceptance, and next because I thought all your suggestions for revision were much to the point, and in acting on them I think I have improved the piece. You may remember that up until 4 or 5 years ago you often made suggestions for sharpening a verse that didn't strike you as just quite right, and we were able to work together very amiably. I'd like to see the custom resumed, as I think it might enable me to appear more often in your pages." In fact, correspondence from Angell throughout the period indicates that he continued to make suggestions he thought would be helpful. The real difficulty lay with the poems he thought, rightly or wrongly, could not be salvaged.

Nash's first major disagreement with the magazine during Angell's tenure came in 1961 with the rejection of a poem, "Our City, Our Citizens, or Patience and Fortitude." In separately titled stanzas it addressed various aspects of life in New York City. The poem focused on denizens of Greenwich Village ("unkempt anthropoids"), Russian diplomats living on Park Avenue (*"la creme de la Kremlin"*), and the local weather girl (deemed a linguistic "amputator" for her nightly expression "Have a happy!") as well as the jargon of café press agents, the difficulty of hailing taxis at theater hour, and the perils of Central Park.

In rejecting the poem, Angell wrote, "Shawn feels that anything we say about our city at this late date must be impressive and entirely new, and he feels, most regretfully, that these verses do not come up to that level." Nash responded in anguish:

> In my 32 years of writing I have never protested an editor's
> decision. Disagreed with, yes; protested, no. This letter is proof
> that I am heart-sick, bewildered, frustrated. If Mr. Shawn considers
> the New York verse lacking in quality, I bow my head sadly but
> with grace; to dismiss them as trivial comments on a city whose
> greatness is compounded of a million trivialities strikes me as
> wrong-headed, and leaves me with a feeling of Where do I go
> from here? By such a standard all my work is trivial, and there is
> no justification for my feather-brained observations on our doomed
> race on its doomed planet. . . . My heart is now on the table.

Angell came back with an abject apology for his earlier letter: ". . . I can only say that it now strikes me as a stupid, hasty and uninformative letter and that I am ashamed of it." Nevertheless he adhered to the earlier position while seeking to amplify it. The objection, he explained, was to a poem that appeared to "sum up" the city. Such a piece, he and Shawn believed, would have to be of "absolutely extraordinary quality." Angell stressed, however, that the magazine would continue to welcome poems concerned with "trivialities." Finally, he emphasized his regret by offering to step aside as Nash's editor in favor of someone else at the magazine, if that were necessary to retain Nash as a contributor: "I cannot imagine this magazine without Ogden Nash; it is an impossible thought."

The episode ended when Nash replied with thanks for the consideration that had been given to his "outcry" and indicated that he now understood the magazine's position, "even if not agreeing with it." It was, he said "only the arbitrary and capricious opinion that chills my blood." And he made it clear that he did not wish to lose Angell as his editor. "The thought of being turned over to other hands than yours appalls me. I have a high regard for your opinion, understanding and friendship; high enough so that I can speak my thoughts to you when troubled. What more can a writer ask?"

Nash's relationship with Angell and *The New Yorker* continued until the day of his death—in a sense beyond, as his final poem for the magazine was published posthumously. Throughout that period, Nash's frustrations waxed and waned, but matters never again reached quite such a fevered level as they had in 1961. That was undoubtedly because Nash had concluded that, despite Angell's assurances, he was not as important to the magazine as it was to him. Moreover he would fare no better, and probably worse, with a different editor. So Nash muffled his complaints to Angell and reserved his most biting comments for his agent at Curtis Brown, Emmy Jacobson, and letters to Dan and Mary Longwell or Vernon Duke. It was a restraint he would have to exercise frequently as the decade progressed.

In some cases the cause of *The New Yorker's* rejection related to subject matter, focus, or taste peculiar to the magazine. In other instances, however, Angell and Shawn felt that a Nash poem simply wasn't funny. The view that Nash took of changes in society, creeping vulgarism, loss of manners and style, sometimes struck them as more querulous than satirical. For example, in rejecting a 1965 poem, "Never Was I Born to Set Them Right," Angell wrote that "the tone of annoyance here is so much louder and shriller here than the sound of laughter," and suggested that Nash revise. Although Nash was ordinarily amenable to revision, especially if the suggestions were specific enough to be readily implemented, this time he rebelled. He wrote Emmy Jacobson in bubbling exasperation: "I have now carefully re-read the last verse rejected by the fossilized still-pond-no-more-moving paralyzed avant-garde owls at the *New Yorker.* . . . I like it the way it is, and hope some editor who lives in the same world I do, not with one foot set in Pakistan or the Tyrol and the other in a peat bog, will see eye to eye with me." The poem appeared in the *Saturday Review* and was included in

There's Always Another Windmill. Although it objected to a variety of modern "improvements," its tone does not seem very different from many Nash poems that appeared in *The New Yorker* before and since:

> I not only like Turkish towels or a reasonable facsimile on
> emerging from the tub,
> I also like towels after washing my hands, even paper ones
> that you rip untimely from a reluctant device that
> warns you, Blot, do not rub.
> I do not like the contraptions that have replaced towels in
> every washroom from the humblest Howard Johnson
> to the haughtiest Statler or Hilton,
> Those abominations you stand cringingly in front of
> waiting for them to scorch you with a blast of air from
> a hell hotter than any imagined by Dante or Milton.

> ✻ ✻ ✻ ✻

On another occasion Nash wrote a poem for a celebration marking the ninetieth birthday of composer Rudolf Friml (who, by coincidence, had composed the score of Nash's first screenwriting venture, *Firefly*). In advance of the celebration, Nash submitted the poem to *The New Yorker*, where it was rejected. Roger Angell wrote to Emmy Jacobson that, while the poem was "exactly right for the party," it was "a little too impatient with the present" for the magazine, and that if they ran it, "we might almost seem to be ninety years old ourselves." (The poem was a great success at the party, and Nash received a poem of thank-you from ASCAP president Arthur Schwartz.)

As elderly as Nash sometimes sounded to Shawn and Angell, he was still capable of writing some mildly racy verse. When he found himself unable to write verse in his usual style, he turned to limericks. The limericks were rejected by *The New Yorker*, but were published in a new outlet for Nash—*Playboy* magazine. One of the limericks, "A Teenage Protester Named Lil," reflected Nash's somewhat jaundiced view of the mores of Vietnam War protesters:

> A teenage protester named Lil
> Cried, "Those CIA squares make me ill!
> First they bugged our martinis
> Our bras and bikinis
> And now they're bugging The Pill."

Another limerick, "A Crusader's Wife Slipped from the Garrison," was one of his favorites that he repeated in letters to friends:

> A crusader's wife slipped from the garrison
> And had an affair with a Saracen
>   She was not oversexed
>   Or jealous or vexed,
> She just wanted to make a comparison.

Although it was Nash's practice not to take on political issues in his verse, he made an exception when the controversial British philosopher Bertrand Russell called for President Lyndon Johnson to be tried as a war criminal. Nash was not a supporter of the Vietnam War, or of Johnson, but he felt that Russell had gone too far, and he responded with a "concrete" poem that followed the form and typography of the mouse's "Caucus-Race and Long Tale" in Lewis Carroll's *Alice in Wonderland*:

YOU ARE OLD
FATHER BERTRAND

> Bertrand said to
>   a lyndon his
>   eye he had pinned
>   on, "Let's
>   both go
>   to law: I
> will prose-
> cute you.
>   I do not
>   stand alone,
> but with Sartre
>   and Simone,
>   and a voluble
>   French
>   intellectual crew."
>   Said the
>   lyndon, "Dear me,
>   such a
>   trial would
>   be, with

no jury
or judge
a judicative
mess."
"We'll be
judge.
We'll be
jury,"
said
Bertrand
with fury.
"And our
verdict
has
just
been
released
to the
press."

This too failed to find favor at *The New Yorker*. Angell rejected the poem on grounds of both form and substance: "The Lewis Carroll parody is almost defeated from the start because all of us have read so many Carroll takeoffs and jokes, and the prospect of still another fills one with foreboding. At the same time, I think any comment we make about Vietnam and Johnson at this point has got to be really sharp and this doesn't say much of anything." The poem was nevertheless published in the *Reporter* magazine, and when it was included in *There's Always Another Windmill*, it was favorably noted by Eliot Fremont-Smith in the *New York Times*.

Nash's experience at *The New Yorker* in the sixties was something of a roller-coaster ride. He experienced a period of serial rejections, interrupted by occasional acceptances, in 1965 and again in 1966 after he had recovered sufficiently from surgery to resume writing. By the end of 1966, however, he was well back into form. Writing to Nash in Baltimore at the end of November, Angell expressed the hope that "this torrent of good poems will continue as soon as you are settled in." Two weeks later, after lunch with Nash in New York, he wrote to Emmy Jacobson, "Ogden did seem better and more cheerful than in years." Nash's successes continued into early 1967 when Angell wrote that Nash was entering into his Periclean era. (Nash could not resist the bait of a classical reference and replied: "In 1956, I sold 17 poems to *The New Yorker*, 10 in 1957 and 11 in 1959. What a decade. This Pericles must pull up his Chlamys" (Chlamys: *Greek Antique*, a short fine woolen mantle worn by men).

By the summer of 1967, Nash was noting in a letter to Vernon Duke that *The New Yorker* had bought only two of his last seven submissions. The close of 1967 and the beginning of 1968 marked his most severe period of depression and inability to write. He emerged, however, to produce "Who Called That Pied-Billed Grebe a Podilybus Podiceps Podiceps?" a poem that Angell received exultantly, writing to Emmy Jacobson that it was "absolutely perfect . . . his best for us in a long time." He also announced proudly that it would appear the following week in the magazine's anniversary issue—an appearance that greatly pleased Nash.

The poem was of a genre to which Nash resorted increasingly in his later years. Having written of human frailties in everyday life for nearly four decades, he now often turned to more remote targets and to wordplay derived from a variety of sources that sprang from his own erudition, imagination, and curiosity. Peculiarities of history (sometimes ancient), literature, the sciences, foreign languages (usually French), and classical mythology were fertile fields. The "Pied-Billed Grebe," for example, was a spoof of ornithologists' terminology, and in particular multiple names. It concludes with a Nashian punch line:

> Did Little Sir Echo originate the double- and triple-headed
>   terminology they stuff in us?
> How else did the eastern harlequin duck become *Histrionicus*
>   *histrionicus* and the Manx shearwater turn into
>   *Puffinus puffinus puffinus?*
> By Allah,
> I believe all ornithologists must be natives of Pago Pago,
>   Baden Baden, or Walla Walla.

Nash sold several more poems to *The New Yorker* in 1968, but 1969 was a lean year in production, partly because of an extended trip to England. More rejections came in 1970, and Nash wrote Emmy Jacobson that the most recent rejection letter "really drives me up the wall. Maybe we should sign the next offering Donald Barthelme and see what happens." And, in September, Nash guessed that his fourth consecutive rejection "sets a new record, which I suppose may be eclipsed as soon as they read the Cat poem." He fought off dejection, however, adding that "I'll try, try again and hope to send another bucket to the well before too long." The Cat poem ("High, Low the Comedy: A Winter's Tale"), a charming but rather mild effort, was in fact rejected, but Nash once again broke through with the sale of "One Man's Opiate," which featured an elaborate French knock-knock joke:

> So he said, *"Frappe, frappe,"* and the man said, *"Qui
> va là?"* and he said, *"Alençon,"* and the man said,
> *"Alençon qui?"*
> And Daniel said, *"Alençonfants de la patrie."*
> The Sartre man, himself a lacemaker, was so taken
> aback that instead of exclaiming. *"Ma fwah!"* ("My
> faith!"), *il s'écria, "Mon fwah!"* which every goose
> knows means "My liver!"
> And then threw himself into the Seine, a river.

Nash was delighted by the poem's acceptance and wrote Roger Angell with evident relief: "Indeed a red-letter day. There was a dreary spell of some months when I felt that *The New Yorker* and I had lost touch forever."

Angell was quite sensitive to the pain that repeated rejections brought, and in a 1965 letter he confided his concerns to Emmy Jacobson. He concluded with the hope that Nash would keep writing "because a sale here might lift his spirits, and that's what we all want for him." Angell's letters of rejection always included expressions of profound regret—"I know how disappointed you must be at this news (and it's sad news for us too). . ."—or hearty encouragement—"I'm quite confident that some other publication will snap it up and prove us wrong again"—or both. Angell tried to word his letters to Nash as tactfully as possible while sometimes expressing his objections more bluntly to Jacobson. Frequently the letters to Nash provided a detailed explanation for the rejections. In light of Nash's earlier complaint, the explanations were no doubt intended to demonstrate that the magazine's decision was not "arbitrary and capricious." Angell later suggested that his explanations may also have served "to assuage my own guilt about turning down Ogden Nash." In any case, Nash was little soothed by the expressions of regret ("crocodile tears") and found the explanations for the turndowns to be particularly infuriating. At one point he instructed Emmy Jacobson to "tell Roger that if he doesn't like it a simple 'sorry' will suffice."

Nash acknowledged that rapid social change had made it more difficult, and sometimes impossible, for him to write. On the other hand, he
felt that when he was able to write, his work was better than ever. Thus he
told an interviewer in 1970 that "When I was younger I had a fast ball, but
now I think I've learned my craft and it's a matter of control. I don't write
nearly as much, but I'm able to do it a little more perfectly than when I was
younger, or a little closer to what I'd like it to be." So it is not surprising that
he frequently found the reasons for rejections to be "irrelevant, picayune,
stuffy and pedantic."

Nash believed that his difficulties with *The New Yorker* were attributable
in large part to a change in the tastes of the magazine, and he took a particularly dim view of the "serious" poetry it was publishing under the poetry editor Howard Moss. He was annoyed and hurt when a 1969 anthology of *New
Yorker* poetry contained twelve poems by Moss himself and four by Nash.
Nash was supported in his views by some of his colleagues, including Sid
Perelman and the poet and humorist Richard Armour. Perelman was particularly unimpressed by the work of Donald Barthelme, which frequently
appeared in the magazine during that period, and in 1968 he wrote Nash
that "your poem in *The New Yorker* about the French ones speckling the language was a daisy. I wish they'd hang Donald Barthelme from a sour apple
tree and give you all the space he consumes." When the holiday issue of *The
New Yorker* that year included pieces by Perelman and Nash as well as their
old friend Frank Sullivan, Perelman could not resist crowing in a letter to
Nash: "Question: where were Donald Barthelme and the other kooks? Answer: where they belonged behind the arras. The devil fly away with them."

Richard Armour took a similar view of Nash's problems with the magazine and Moss: "As for *The New Yorker*, the fault is theirs—not yours. It
was never a big market for me, as it was for you, but in the period starting
in 1937 and going up to the early 1960's, I had about 100 pieces of verse in
its pages. However when Howard Moss came in as Poetry Editor and
started publishing stuff that I doubt many readers read, I was gradually
pushed out—and stopped sending. I don't even take the magazine any
more. The lightness has gone, alas." Moss was never Nash's editor, and
there is no evidence that he was involved in Nash's rejections. Nonetheless
his long tenure as poetry editor, beginning in 1950, did see a decline in the
publication of light verse in general as well as that of Nash and Armour.

Nash's disenchantment with *The New Yorker's* taste in poetry led him to
pull an odd—and oddly successful—prank, which he later described in a

letter to Vernon Duke: "[*The New Yorker*] had rejected the last four of my submissions, all of which I thought were pretty good. Meanwhile they kept printing columns of the most dreary, pretentious, portentous, solemn prose cast in the form of poetry. Thought I, 'Any damn fool can turn out that stuff by the bucketful; let's see if this damn fool can.' So, with my tongue piercing my cheek, I rapidly cooked a poetic dish a la their current favorite bards and by God they swallowed it gluttonously and called it brilliant. This little bit of backstage gossip for your ear alone; I don't want to jeopardize my relationship with the lamas of 43rd Street."

The poem, "Notes for the Chart in 306," was written in 1966, not long after Nash's surgery. It is somber and, in places, a touch macabre:

The bubbles soar and die in the sterile bottle
Hanging upside down on the bedside lamppost.
Food and drink
Seep quietly through the needle strapped to the hand.
The arm welcomes the sting of mosquito hypodermic—
Conveyor of morphia, the comforter.
Here's drowsiness, here's lassitude, here's nothingness,
Sedation *in excelsis*.

    ✻   ✻   ✻   ✻

Angell was wholly unaware that the poem had been intended as a parody. He wrote Nash that he found it "interesting and truly frightening, and the best thing of its kind about hospitals I have ever read." In fairness to Angell, the poem was effective on its own terms without regard to Nash's mischievous intentions. John Updike wrote Nash expressing his pleasure at seeing Nash's name in *The New Yorker* again "and attached to such an inventive and non-light poem." Three years later, when the poem appeared in a *New Yorker* anthology, Josephine Jacobsen wrote Nash that it was "brilliant technically, psychologically and poetically." In the end, even Nash may have taken a different view since he included the poem in *There's Always Another Windmill*, whose readers would have been quite unlikely to recognize it as parody.

Later that year Nash became so dismayed at the poetry in *The New Yorker* that he drafted a letter on the subject to Angell. The particular target for his scorn was a poem in the magazine by Robert Penn Warren. Warren's poem included a passage comparing stars to falling dandruff. To Nash, the simile was, among other things, sadly derivative of a phrase coined sometime earlier by a popular columnist who had referred to snowflakes as "God's dandruff." He concluded: "I am at last convinced that the board's rejection of many of my recent submissions is fully justified, since my minor japes stand like burnt-out matches in the face of such cosmic ludicrousness."

After reflection, Nash did not send the letter to Angell. He turned his observation to a more constructive purpose, referring to the Robert Penn Warren lines in his own new verse "A Visitor from Porlock, But, Alas, No Xanadu." (The title was taken from the account by Samuel Taylor Coleridge of being interrupted by a business caller from the nearby town of Porlock while attempting to transfer the images of a dream to a poem that later became "Kubla Khan." After the visitor left, only fragments of the dream remained.) Nash's poem recounts a visit by a tedious woman ("She is full of truisms but she is not like a truism, because a truism goes without saying, but she says without going") and recounts his musings during her stay. Following brief negotiations to find a way of putting it that would not offend the magazine's other contributor, the reference to Warren's poem was included:

> Indeed, my vagrant thoughts were many,
> And one of them lingered on the distinguished poet who recently
>   wrote that he would "dream of small white stars falling forever
>   in darkness like dandruff," and I asked myself if this phrase
>   could be a subconscious tribute to the late *Daily Mirror*'s
>   immortal bard, Nick Kenny.
>
> ❖ ❖ ❖ ❖

In letters to Emmy Jacobson, Angell insisted that the taste of *The New Yorker* had not changed and that it was still eager to publish light verse in the classic Nash mode, or even verse in new forms with which Nash sometimes experimented. More recently, though, Angell has taken a different view of the magazine during the sixties: "It sure did change. We were changed not by fiat but by our writers and the times. We became more serious, more political. All I can say is that it was inevitable and that the magazine would have died if we hadn't changed." Nevertheless he continued to disagree that Nash's rejections were attributable to the changes in the magazine.

There is probably some merit to the divergent views of both Nash and Angell. Some of the verse that Angell rejected may have been labored, querulous, or simply not up to Nash's best. On the other hand, the verse that Angell rejected generally found a home in other magazines, and it seems inescapable that changes in *The New Yorker* were, consciously or not, at least partially responsible for Nash's difficulties. A test of Nash's continuing vitality came with the publication in 1968 of *There's Always Another Windmill*. It was Nash's first collection in six years, and it contained most of the poems that Angell and Shawn had rejected.

In the months leading up to the publication of *Windmill*, Nash was quite apprehensive about how it would be received. Although he never said so, it would be surprising if his confidence had not been damaged by the mixed reception his verse had been getting at *The New Yorker*. In February, writing to Vernon Duke, he wondered "how often this old pitcher can go to the well and still draw water." As publication approached, and his nervousness increased, he sent a copy to Katharine and Andy White and received a warm and calming letter that encouraged him. Still, he confessed to Angell that "My new book will be published on Thursday and I await the event with considerable trepidation. I've had many years of kind reception, but times and taste have changed. I hardly know which to dread more—to be stepped on or to be ignored. I wish I had a thicker skin." Three days later he wrote Vernon Duke that "I fear that I have been treated generously by the reviewers for too long, and that a backlash is overdue."

Nash's fears and anxieties turned out to be unfounded. Beginning with Eliot Fremont-Smith in the *New York Times*, the book received reviews across the country that fully matched those for his previous books. If Angell and Shawn had sometimes detected a crotchety tone, it did not seem apparent to other eyes and ears. As before, reviewers applauded even as they acknowledged that Nash's work was difficult or impossible to pigeonhole. Fremont-Smith made an initial stab: "Mr. Nash is our leading nonsense versifier and revivifier, a descendant in sensibility and chutzpah of W. S. Gilbert by way of S. J. Perelman." By the end of the review, however, he did some redefining—after quoting from a poem in which Nash had decried second thoughts ("I myself am more and more inclined to agree with Omar and with Satchel Paige as I grow older/ Don't try to rewrite what the moving finger has writ and don't ever look over your shoulder"). Fremont-Smith concluded by asking the question that countless reviewers before him had asked: "Who said that Nash writes nonsense?" In a similar vein, another critic credited Nash with "some acute thoughts which compare favorably with the ideas of our current and obscurant philosophers, despite the sugar coating which deceives the surface reader." Still another compared Nash to Mark Twain, H. L. Mencken, Ring Lardner, Ambrose Bierce, and Cole Porter as an "unmatchable original."

The most remarkable aspect of Nash's success may be that he had been able to continue writing in the face of burdens imposed by age, psychological pressures, and physical illness. It is no easy thing to write humor consistently, in either prose or poetry, and it is a very difficult thing to do over four decades. It is all the more difficult in the face of recurring rejections and criticism from one's oldest and most valued outlet. Under those circumstances, the *Windmill's* warm reception was a welcome respite from Nash's running battle with the wise owls of Forty-third Street. So much of the book consisted of poems the magazine had rejected that its success could easily be seen as vindication.

Nash's relief and elation at the reviews of *There's Always Another Windmill* were quickly replaced by fury at Little, Brown. In 1961, Jim Sherman had been succeeded as Nash's editor by Larned G. ("Ned") Bradford. Bradford's responsibilities included pleading Nash's case with the Little, Brown marketing staff, supervising jacket design, and generally looking after Nash's interests within the firm. He developed a comfortable relationship with his charge, eased by lunches at Nash's favorite Boston restaurant, Locke–Ober's, when Nash was in town. But a comfortable relationship was no defense when things did not go as Nash felt they should. Nash preferred to make his complaints though Perry Knowlton, who had followed Alan Collins as head of the Curtis Brown agency.

Nash had not been happy with Little, Brown's promotion of a 1967 book, *Santa Go Home: A Case History for Parents*, and before the publication of *Windmill* he asked Knowlton to make sure that this time his publishers were prepared. Nash's apprehensions appeared well founded when the *Times's* favorable review was published and no advertising was anywhere in sight. Feeling the importance of this collection, perhaps his last, and armed with a superb review, Nash was implacable. The very day of the review, Saturday, October 26, Nash wrote Knowlton again, urging a campaign to exploit it: "The hell with false modesty now that Fremont-Smith has stated it for me—Nash for better or worse is unique and for God's sake let's go to town on that basis. I rely on you to keep a hot poker applied to the Little Brown arse."

On Sunday, finding nothing in the *New York Times Book Review*, he wrote to Ned Bradford: "this hornet is on the war path. I am angry, indignant, resentful. I feel that I have been betrayed." He did not mail the letter but sent a copy to Knowlton and telephoned Bradford the following day. Knowlton replied that publication and advertising had originally been scheduled for November, but when the publication date had been advanced to October, the advertising somehow had not. He had now been assured that efforts would be made to advance the advertising.

Nash was mollified for the moment, though he noted caustically in a letter to Roger Angell that "situations as usual with my book—magnificent reviews, no advertising, but my editor at Little, Brown has just bought a Porsche." When November 11 arrived with still no advertising in sight, it was no Armistice Day for Nash. He bypassed both Knowlton and Bradford and sent an angry telegram to Arthur Thornhill, president of Little, Brown, asserting that the publisher's "ineptness could only be deliberate" and that he felt "brutally betrayed." Thornhill replied by telegram, promising a prompt review. On the same day, Little, Brown's marketing director, Robert Fetridge, sent a letter outlining the current plans for advertising and promotion.

Nash was again somewhat calmed, but his passions were reignited by a letter from Thornhill that, ironically, had been intended to soothe Nash by apologizing for the mistake in timing and by assuring him that every effort was now being made to promote the book. Nash found the letter inadequate; its effect was precisely the opposite of what Thornhill had hoped for. Nash drafted a lengthy letter that again, on reflection, he did not send. But it was an eloquent statement of his emotions:

> Why must I remind you that I have built up a wide and responsive audience over the years, not only of readers but of critics? At the risk of being egotistical I must tell you that in Nash you have a unique author—possibly a freak, but certainly unique—widely considered a worthy successor to Benchley and Thurber, perhaps, according to some critics, even Mark Twain. Young people still read me—in the perilous and ephemeral field of humor I have held my place since 1931. I have seen no indications yet that anyone at Little, Brown recognizes these facts.

As the advertising finally began to appear, the controversy receded. Bradford was able to preserve his relationship with Nash by showing him a prescient memorandum he had written the preceding spring ("If we are perhaps beginning to take [Nash] for granted, if there is a danger of our promoting his next book routinely and perfunctorily, this is certainly the time to remind ourselves how much we would miss his periodic contributions to our list"). In the end, orders for *Windmill* were respectable, though not what Nash had hoped, given the strength of the reviews. And he continued to believe that he had been significantly hurt by Little, Brown's handling of the book. From later correspondence there is reason to believe that if Nash had done another book during his lifetime, he might well have sought a new publisher. Now, however, he turned to another front.

Even before the debacle with Little, Brown, Nash had been considering a possible change of his English publisher, J. M. Dent and Sons. In the spring of 1968, negotiations were in progress for the sale to Dent of *Santa Go Home*, but Nash's London agent, Hilary Rubinstein, was startled to find they were thinking of publishing the book for the spring and summer list of 1969. That, it seemed to Rubinstein, was a very odd time to publish a book about "Father Christmas." Knowlton at Curtis Brown agreed: "Sometimes I think they are really not very bright." He added that Rubinstein felt "a bit uncomfortable about Dent as publisher for you at all." Nash, who did not feel the kind of bond that he did with Little, Brown, said he would leave the decision to Rubinstein: "if someone else can really to do lots better, let's go."

Dent was permitted to publish *Santa Go Home*, but matters came to a head in January 1969, soon after the crisis with Little, Brown, when Rubinstein advised Dent of Nash's decision to move to another publisher, Andre Deutsch. The head of the firm, Martin Dent, immediately wrote to Nash expressing his dismay and disappointment and requesting a personal explanation. Knowlton then wrote Nash, urging him to write Dent, adding that Rubinstein hoped that Nash "will cut the umbilical cord with Dent swiftly." Thus, as in his experience with Bill Leigh, Nash was faced with the kind of unpleasant confrontation that he disliked so much and had hoped to avoid. He took pen in hand, however, and did his duty, somewhat apologetically but firmly.

Given Nash's reliance on Rubinstein, he might well have made the change in any event, but his impatience with publishers generally, as a result of the Little, Brown episode, could only have strengthened his determination to take action when he felt he could. This change, unlike the change from Simon and Schuster to Little, Brown in 1938, did not result in a dramatic growth in sales in England and the Commonwealth and Nash had probably not expected it would. But he no doubt felt some satisfaction at having taken matters into his own hands. He was, moreover, looking forward to a trip to England where he would meet his new publisher, tour the countryside with Frances, and participate in a highly publicized international poetry festival.

17

OH, TO BE IN ENGLAND

Ogden and Frances made three trips to England in the sixties. Although the 1964 trip was foreshortened by Nash's sudden illness, two later visits in 1969 and 1970 were treasured respites from the pressures and preoccupations that beset him at home. London, it seemed to Nash, was an oasis of civility in a world gone seriously awry. It was also a place where he found that his work had a surprisingly appreciative audience.

The mutual affection between Nash and the English did not spring up overnight but emerged after a rather shaky start and developed gradually over a period of years. When publication of Nash's verse in England was first proposed in the thirties, he had been skeptical, believing that many of the references in his poems would be bewildering to readers abroad. In the end, Nash had agreed, but his first English edition, *Hard Lines and Others,* which included poems from both *Hard Lines* and *Free Wheeling,* was carefully pruned to omit poems that might have been obscure (or, in a few cases perhaps, irritating) to an English audience. The initial reception for Nash's work in England did not approach the spectacular success that he had enjoyed in the United States. A copy of *Hard Lines and Others* bears a note by Nash, "As I remember, it sold some 400 copies and *The Times Literary Supplement* remarked, 'Neat ideas marred by careless rhyming.'" A copy of his second English book, *The Primrose Path,* carries a similar comment: "Another hopeful English publisher tried this one, which eventually sold less than 500 copies." By then, however, English critics had begun to develop a taste for Nash. A review in the *TLS* commented that "Mr. Nash's

verse is smooth, very careful in its craftsmanship and with its verbal inge-
nuities quietly and unostentatiously inserted." When a third publisher
brought out *I'm a Stranger Here Myself*, records later showed that 2,000
copies had been printed, of which 950 were destroyed by a bomb in World
War II. Finally, a fourth publisher, J. M. Dent and Sons, took over and
would ultimately publish 18 Nash books, including 5 children's books, until it was replaced in 1968. Although sales by Dent never reached American
levels, Nash's reputation and popularity in England continued to grow.

Nash had a keen and wide-ranging appreciation of English literary traditions. His taste encompassed not only the Romantic poets, whose work he
had once attempted to emulate, but also ran to popular prose. He was a lifelong admirer of P. G. Wodehouse and of English mystery writers—A. Co-
nan Doyle first and foremost, followed by others such as Dorothy Sayers
and Agatha Christie. His poems were frequently inspired by monuments of
English literature, and his verse included parodies of sources as diverse as
Bullfinch's *Mythology*, Aubrey's *Brief Lives*, and Blake's "The Tiger":

EPITAPH FOR AN EXPLORER

Tiger, Tiger, my mistake,
I thought you were William Blake.

Even Nash's boyhood icons were not beyond teasing. (In "Very Like a
Whale," for example, Nash took on Byron's "The Destruction of Sen-
nacherib," needling the poet on various counts, including his rhyme of
"onward" with "six hundred.")

The verses omitted from the English editions included a few that poked
fun at the contemporary English. For example:

ETHNOLOGICAL REFLECTION

The Briton regards breakfast without marmalade and kedgeree
As worse than matricide, barratry or tredgeree.

In *Free Wheeling*, a verse entitled "Scram, Lion" lavished compliments on
various institutions and personages—but as a prelude to mocking the
British use, or misuse, of American slang.

In a rather lengthy 1936 poem, "England Expects," Nash took a broad
look at various English idiosyncrasies. In his customary manner, the satire
was fairly gentle, and the poem was included in the English edition of *I'm
a Stranger Here Myself*. Many years later, at a ceremony marking the entry

of the United Kingdom into the European Community and attended by the queen and Prince Philip, the poem was chosen to be read by Judi Dench—between readings from Byron and Dickens by Laurence Olivier. As read by Miss Dench, however, the poem did omit some lines no longer fitting ("Englishmen are distinguished by their traditions and ceremonials/ And also by affection for their colonies and contempt for their colonials").

The enduring success of "England Expects" is particularly notable considering that, when Nash wrote it, he had never visited England. His only knowledge of the country was derived from reading and from English visitors passing through New York. When Ogden and Frances did visit London in 1939, on Nash's first trip abroad, he was far from a confirmed Anglophile. On that trip the Nashes first traveled to Paris, which Nash found thoroughly delightful, and then to London, which seemed clearly to take second place. A letter from Nash to Dan Longwell reported in a grumpy tone, "Actually Paris was easy but this is a hell of a city—too many English. . . ." Nash did not explain just what he had found so annoying, but with Longwell's help the trip was redeemed. Before leaving, Nash had asked Longwell for introductions to anyone he might think appropriate, including Winston Churchill (who, Nash recalled, Longwell had once said, "liked my stuff"). Longwell did provide several introductions including, if not Winston, at least his son, Randolph. That introduction proved fruitful as Churchill not only treated the Nashes to a sumptuous dinner but introduced them to A. P. Herbert, whose writing Nash admired. Herbert, in turn, took them boating on the Thames and later invoked his privileges as a Conservative M.P. from Oxford, to have the Houses of Parliament opened for a private tour. Nash wrote Longwell gratefully that his introductions had lifted their stay from "intolerable, through tolerable to enjoyable."

The Nashes' trip came only months before Germany's invasion of Poland and the declaration of war by Britain and France. There would soon be cause for grave concern as to whether the concluding couplet in "England Expects" would remain valid:

Anyhow, I think the English people are sweet,
And we might as well get used to them because when they slip
    and fall they always land on their own or somebody else's feet.

In the course of the war, Nash greatly admired Britain's courage, and the conduct of its people during those years left a lasting impression. After the war Ogden and Frances took the children to Europe in 1949, but they did not visit London until 1957. Although the weather was chilly and wet, and Nash arrived with a cold, their 1957 stay was a success from the outset. Ogden and Frances enjoyed the customary round of tourist activities: sightseeing, theatergoing, and shopping, including a visit by Nash to a London tailor. ("Monday all Ogden's suits came—terrific excitement. They are really beautiful and he is preening himself like a peacock.") The highlight of one day was afternoon tea with Malcolm Muggeridge at *Punch*. Frances had been reluctant to attend the tea but agreed to "trail along." She found to her surprise that she actually enjoyed it. Muggeridge, she reported, was "a very urbane gentleman, very different from the person I had imagined." The Nashes also saw good friends from America, the historian Samuel Eliot Morison and his wife Priscilla ("Sam has been burning up England with his opinion of the English General Staff in the last war"), and Bruce and Barbara Gould, editors of *Ladies' Home Journal*. The time in London, Frances wrote her mother, had seemed too short, but "of course the next time we went we wouldn't try to put in as much sight-seeing as well as everything else." There was no indication on this trip that either Ogden or Frances had found there to be "too many English" in London.

In the following years Nash's poems depicting the English reflected both amusement and obvious affection. At some point he took to perusing *Country Life*, and it inspired two verses that were published in *The New Yorker*. The first, "Capercaillie, Ave Atque Vaillie," arose from lengthy correspondence in the English magazine concerning the habits of a particular grouse, the Capercaillie, and its mating song ("kek, kek, kek, whoosh"), around which Nash managed to construct a poem of five stanzas. The second poem sprang from the advertisement for a farm in the valley of the River Piddle, a name Nash found irresistible and commemorated in a poem entitled "Paradise for Sale." The poem found its way back to England, where it was reprinted in a local magazine and the delighted residents responded with their own poem to Nash in a Dorset dialect ("Here be a vulcome to Ogden Nash/ His zong to our Piddle/ Did create an artvul splash").

But Nash's growing reputation in England did not rest on a handful of verses with specifically English themes. It was more to the point that the objects of his satire were freely recognizable on both sides of the Atlantic. While his verse found readers in venues as far-flung as Serbo-Croatia and Moscow, it was firmly rooted in Anglo-American culture at mid-century. As one English reviewer observed, "He turns the eye of loathing and pen of scorn on users of the fashionable cliché, television advertisers, tipping, commercialized Christmas, references to famous men by pet names, fancy salad dressings and a dozen other worthy targets."

When Ogden and Frances returned to England in October 1964, it was a trip, Nash later said, they had been anticipating and saving up for, for seven years. It was also a good time for Nash to get away, since he had just experienced the latest round of rejections from *The New Yorker.* The Nashes enjoyed the transatlantic crossing on the *Mauritania* and did not lack for company on the voyage. Alan Collins had established a bar credit for them and for a mutual friend, the English publisher Robert Lusty. Lusty and Nash had met casually several times in New York, and in the course of the 1964 trip they developed a firm friendship. As Lusty recalled many years later, "When you drink with people two or three times a day for a week, and have all your meals together, you get to know people rather well." Lusty also recalled that on that trip he came to appreciate Nash's penchant for experimenting with words, "as an artist played with sketches and a musician played with notes."

Their trip had been planned to last six weeks and was primarily a pleasure jaunt, although Nash's English publisher had also arranged to publish his latest book, *Marriage Lines*, while they were in London. The event generated considerable publicity that Nash quite relished. He wrote to Ned Bradford at Little, Brown: "My final week in London would have pleased you; I was more of a lion than I have ever been at home. From the booksellers through the press, radio and TV, everyone seemed familiar with and fond of my stuff and I was received as an old friend. Very heartening." And he wrote to Isabel that "My reception by the English has been astounding to me. . . . Very good for my always vulnerable self-esteem." It was a splendid tonic for the bruises inflicted by the "board of trustees" on Forty-third Street.

Ogden and Frances spent a weekend in Bath, with trips to Wells and Glastonbury, and enjoyed a luncheon with the Anthony Powells that had been arranged by the wife of Ambassador Bruce after a dinner at the American embassy ("Mrs. Bruce had said she was going to tell the Powells we were in Bath and then by gosh did so"). Upon returning from Bath, however, their trip was suddenly interrupted when Nash was overtaken by a violent intestinal illness that confined him to his hotel room for one week, put him in the London Clinic for a second, and sent him to Brighton to convalesce for a third. Although Nash had enjoyed the flood of media attention in London, he now felt that the attendant stress had been the cause of his illness.

By the time Ogden and Frances were able to return to London in June 1969, Nash was weary from physical ailments as well as his continuing struggles with *The New Yorker*, and he was reluctant to make the trip. Frances began to feel guilty wondering if she was both "a slave-driver and a husband-killer." She was convinced, however, that the trip would do Ogden good and insisted that they proceed, though at a slower pace than she might have preferred. Frances believed her judgment had been vindicated as soon as they were on board the *Nieuw Amsterdam* and she saw that the relaxation of life at sea had begun to have a beneficial effect.

The Nashes' ship was late in docking at Southampton, and when they arrived at the Stafford Hotel in London, well after midnight on June 7, they received distressing news. A letter from Isabel told of a mole on her instep that was malignant and would require surgery, including removal of lymph nodes in her groin. The condition had been discovered before Ogden and Frances had sailed, but Isabel had refused to tell them, fearing they might cancel the trip. Isabel's condition would have been a serious worry under any circumstances, but coming at this particular time it created a further complication. Isabel and Fred had rented a castle in Ireland for June and July with planned visits not only by Ogden and Frances but also by Linell and Johnny and their two younger children. It was now questionable whether this plan still made sense, but after a series of transatlantic conversations with both Isabel and Linell, Ogden and Frances were somewhat reassured. At Isabel's insistence, they were persuaded to continue with their tour of England and Scotland with hopes that the reunion in Ireland could take place in July, more or less as planned.

Although Nash had felt in 1964 that the stress of interviews was the cause of his sudden illness, he seemed in 1969 quite willing to subject himself once again to the attentions of the media. In the brief period when the Nashes were in London at the Stafford Hotel, before setting out for Canterbury, Nash was interviewed on television by Eamon Andrews ("A sort of combination of Hugh Downs and Ed Sullivan, but a good fellow") and received reporters and photographers from the *Standard* and the *Times* as well as a writer representing both the *Scotsman* and *House and Garden*. The flurry of attention was not only flattering but had at least one happy side effect. The manager of the Stafford, previously inaccessible, now appeared and announced that, contrary to previous advice, it would not be necessary for the Nashes to move to a smaller room for the last night of their stay. Also contrary to previous advice, accommodations at the hotel would again be available when the Nashes returned in early July. In addition to meetings with the press, Nash attended a cocktail party held by his new publisher, André Deutsch, where he found it interesting to encounter Laurie Lee as well as John Updike. He recorded the event in his diary and noted with evident satisfaction "everyone flattering and reciting my verse."

In his interviews, Nash attempted to deflect questions concerning the social and political issues at home that he found so troubling. For the British press, he allowed himself to be portrayed as something of a curmudgeon but largely avoided the overtly political. He was, for example, unenthusiastic about the forthcoming American space trip to the moon: "They're turning the moon from she into it. I don't think that's right." He insisted that the color photographs from space had proved what he had always believed: that the moon is made of green cheese. When, on a more serious note, he was asked about conditions in America, he responded rather mildly: "I'm always hopeful." On the subject of President Richard Nixon, then in office for only six months, he also tried to be positive: "He's not a truly lovable man but somewhat more admirable than Mr. Johnson. I spent four years trying to love Mr. Johnson."

At the same time Nash was outspoken at his enjoyment of being in London. He did complain that, while their hotel room used to face a blitz site that "had blackbirds singing in the ruins," it now fronted on an office block populated only by pigeons. "My wife and I are pigeon haters," he explained. But otherwise his appraisal was quite favorable: "It's so pleasant to find a prevailing courtesy. People in shops don't resent you or make you feel like an intruder, and it's nice not being called Mac or Buddy. My wife likes not being called Sister all the time."

After four days in London, the Nashes departed June 12 on a tour that would take them to Canterbury, York, and Gateshead, and then to Scotland with stops in Edinburgh, Pitlochry, Inverness, Oban, and Callender. Returning to England on July 1, they would proceed first to Winchester and then up to the Cotswolds and Oxford before returning to London on July 9. It is hard to imagine that even Frances could have wanted a more ambitious schedule or hectic pace.

Nash's letters and diary provided a detailed commentary on the quality and comfort of the accommodations at each of their stops. His attitudes were not untypical of an American visitor in England: he was inclined to delight in the scenery, revere the history, and despair of the plumbing. Along the way, Ogden and Frances visited various cathedrals and churches not only for their architectural and historical interest but with Isabel very much on their minds. In London, on Sunday, June 8, Nash's diary bore the notation, "Went for Isabel to St. Paul's—first private chapel, St. Dunstan's, then hear part of musical service." On Thursday, the day of Isabel's surgery, the Nashes arrived in Canterbury and went immediately to the cathedral "to look and to pray." They returned to await a call from Linell which came at 10:30 P.M. and advised that the operations had been completed. By Sunday they had talked to Isabel by telephone and were in York, where they attended services at York Minster. The good news continued, and on July 4 a call to Isabel established that she was home from the hospital and planning to leave for Ireland on the 17th.

A last highlight of the Nashes' tour, on the Sunday before their return to London, was a visit to Oxford led by Hilary and Helga Rubinstein. Hilary was a literary agent with A. P. Watt; he had become Nash's literary agent in London when the British agency of Curtis Brown had broken its ties with the American firm of the same name. Ogden and Frances had quickly become quite fond of both Hilary and Helga. Hilary was a graduate of Merton College (which, he told Nash, vied with Balliol for the honor of being the earliest founded at Oxford). He was initially disappointed that the medieval library, which he had wanted to show Ogden, was closed, but they were both delighted when the Fellow in charge, an old friend of Hilary's, happened by and obligingly opened it for them. Nash was fascinated not only by the old bookstalls, scholars' benches, and early manuscripts but by an account of how broken pieces of glass from chapel windows had been jigsawed together to replace library windows that had been destroyed during the war. A "final fillip" was a visit to the Max Beerbohm room. In all, the visit to the library was, Nash thought, a "great piece of luck."

The centerpiece of Nash's return to London was his appearance at the Poetry Society's Fourth Poetry International at Queen Elizabeth Hall on July 10 and 11. Nash seemed, at least outwardly, to view his participation with minimal enthusiasm. He had written to his friend Pen Higginson in July that he didn't want to do the readings but that it might help make part of the trip tax deductible. Nash's diffidence may have been attributable to some uneasiness in appearing at so highly publicized an event in the company of internationally celebrated poets. Nash's view of his own work often combined humility and pride. In the course of the same trip he told Gina Richardson of the *Daily Telegraph Magazine*, "I look on what I do as essays in verse. I wouldn't presume to call it poetry. But," he continued, "I work very hard, probably harder than most modern poets." In any case, Nash had made the commitment and was prepared to keep it.

Leaving Studley Priory on the morning of Wednesday, July 9, Ogden and Frances arrived back at the Stafford Hotel. After unpacking and a brief rest, Nash went off to a cocktail party given by the Poetry Society for participants in the festival. He joined Auden and the other poets and was amused that the photographer could not remember Auden's name and kept getting it confused with "Ogden."

The following day Nash had two more newspaper interviews and, in between, spent time arranging his verses for the reading. The roster of participants was authentically international, including, among others, Vasco Popa, Miroslav Holub, and Janos Pilinszki. It was, as the *Times Literary Supplement* observed, "a really impressive line-up." And the presence of the Americans Robert Bly and Anthony Hecht in addition to Nash, as well as the Commonwealth poets Derek Walcott and Edward Brathwaite, would "prevent the whole business from being too taxingly bilingual." When the evening program opened, however, Nash was nowhere to be seen. "We seem to have lost Mr. Ogden Nash," remarked the master of ceremonies, the producer Patrick Garland, with a melancholy wave at Nash's empty seat. Nash's tardiness was occasioned by his having attended the queen's garden party with Frances, but when the time came for him to read, he was in his place. He began by modestly declaring that in such company he felt "more than ever lower than the angels" and then proceeded with his first verse, an old favorite, "Allow Me Madam, But It Won't Help" ("Adorable is an adjective and womankind a noun,/ And I often wonder why, although adorable womankind elects to talk standing up, it elects to put on its coat sitting down").

Nash wrote in his diary that he had finished the program "satisfactorily"; the next day's entry bears the terse note "Good notices on reading." In fact his appearance seems to have been rather a triumph, underscored by comparisons with the reading given by his compatriot, Robert Bly. As the critic William J. Webb wrote, Nash's "urbane and rueful stratagems, rather than Robert Bly's gaudy blanket and hippy flutterings, were the really exotic part of this night's programme." The critic Julian Jebb offered a similar and even more vivid appraisal of the two performances:

> Having invited the audience from the back of the hall to fill the empty seats at the front, [Bly] proceeded to read. Or did he speak?

Or did he just talk? I really can't say, I was so bewitched by embarrassment. His arms flailed in tragi-comic unco-ordinated circles, strongly reminiscent of Peter Cook's imitation of Macmillan in *Beyond the Fringe*. . . . I have never before witnessed such a sustained piece of good manners from an audience — nor seen during the interval which followed a bar so besieged.

But Nash, he found, was as amusing as Bly had been painful:

The house lights were extinguished for Ogden Nash, who opened the second night's reading. His verses, so often blinkered and facetious on the page, leap to wildly funny life when accompanied by his delivery and presence. What often seem bland domestic ironies were transformed into pungent obsessional fantasies by his wandering drawl, the comic dignity of his small body.

A 1996 BBC Radio retrospective, on the twenty-fifth anniversary of Nash's death, summarized the critical assessment of Nash's contribution to the 1969 festival: "He was celebrated as a skilled technician by some, a sort of anti-technician by others, and as a well disguised moral instructor by almost all."

The Nashes left London on Monday and, after various delays, arrived early at the Russell Hotel in Dublin at 7:30 that evening. The following day, a three-hour train trip took them to Glin Castle where they were relieved to find Isabel looking frail but cheerful. The castle was comfortably furnished and well staffed, and Ogden and Frances enjoyed a relaxing week getting caught up with Linell and Johnny and Isabel and Fred and with all their grandchildren except Nell, who was traveling in Europe. Even in Glin, Nash was an object of attention from the press. In an interview with John Kelly of the *Dublin Sunday News*, "a raggedy Irish poet with great charm," Nash was joined by his eight-year-old granddaughter Nenna, who had written a poem of her own. Kelly was quite taken with Nenna, admired her poem, and wrote one of his own for her in Gaelic and English.

Under the influence of Kelly's Irish charm, Nash was more candid than he had been with the London interviewers. He admitted being appalled by current tastes in literature and the theater, especially by an apparent trend to nudity on the American stage. In 1930, Nash had written the saucy couplet "In the Vanities/ No one wears panities," but now he felt things had gone too far. Similarly, though Nash recalled that as a young man he had been considered to be something of a rebel, he was now troubled by student revolts around the world. He seemed to deplore not so much the causes they expounded as their mode of expression: "I think that they've really gone mad today. The whole thing has been reduced to the level of drivel."

The 1969 trip was such a success that the Nashes returned to England the following spring. They sailed from New York on the Queen Elizabeth II, accompanied by friends from Little Boar's Head, the Higginsons and the Bryers. The ship traveled south, stopping at St. Thomas and Barbados, before heading across the Atlantic to calls at Madeira and Lisbon. The Nashes then went on to Paris before arriving in London for a three-week stay.

While in London they took a day trip to Liss, in Hampshire, to meet Iona and Peter Opie, experts in children's rhymes and games, with whom Nash had corresponded for several years. Earlier that year Peter Opie had written Nash a letter beginning, "Dear Doctor," congratulating him, at great and rather facetious length, on having received an honorary doctorate. Nash took note of this when he inscribed his most recent book that he had brought as a present: "Pangloss, Crippen, Fell and Spock/ May properly be addressed as Doc./ Nash must be addressed alas—/ Simply as a silly ass." Ogden and Frances found both the Opies and their house charming. The latter, he wrote in his diary, was literally lined with books, with an upper room that served as an extraordinary museum of toys.

At the end of the week the Nashes departed London again for a three-day excursion to Tenby in Wales, where one of Nash's forebears had lived before sailing for America in 1720. In his later years Nash's father had been interested in tracing the family back to its roots in Wales but had not been able, physically or financially, to make the trip. Thus the 1970 trip was something of a pilgrimage for Nash. Although he discovered no traces of the ancestral Nashes, he and Frances had a splendid time walking and being driven around Tenby and its environs.

Returning to London, the Nashes attended a dinner party given by the Lustys in a private room at the Garrick Club. The guests included John Betjeman and Mary Wilson, wife of the prime minister, whose book of poems was soon to be published by Lusty's firm, Michael Joseph Ltd. Nash enjoyed Mrs. Wilson and the next day went to Hatchards book store and bought one of his own books which he inscribed for her.

Diogenes would not admire
The morals of this versifier,

Who became a man of letters
By simply stealing from his betters.
His method is to snatch and scoot;
Here's a sample of his loot.
But since your book is not yet due,
There's nothing here that's filched from you.

Not to be outdone, Mrs. Wilson replied with a verse of her own. She would save the book, the poem said, to read at night before turning out the light, "To woo oblivion with your song/ Or dream about you all night long!" When Mary Wilson's book was published, Lusty arranged to have the Nash inscription reprinted in the *New Statesmen*, where it contained a rather odd misprint—"versifier" becoming "thirsty fire." The mistake seemed only to add to the general amusement. Mrs. Wilson's book was a great success, selling, as Lusty later put it, "more than any volume of verse since Byron."

Later that year, in a radio interview in Baltimore, Nash spoke of his friend Sid Perelman, who, despairing of the turbulent times in America, had recently made a highly publicized move from Bucks County, Pennsylvania, to London. He empathized with Perelman's feeling for London: "I know what he means about London. If you want to live in a city, I think London is probably the place to live . . . there is a common courtesy that just doesn't seem to exist any more here. We've somehow forgotten it. And just shopping is a pleasure, walking around is a pleasure and there is a relaxation that we've just lost touch with here." Still, he firmly rejected any notion of becoming an expatriate: "I wouldn't consider leaving this country permanently because I'm part of it and it's part of me."

Despite his serious illness in 1964, Nash's trips to England had a positive effect. They provided welcome changes of scene, and the affection with which he was received was much needed balm to his self-esteem. Indeed, the trips may well have been a factor in helping Nash get through the sixties. In the end, he was able to resolve the doubts that had plagued him about the relevance of his work.

Two months after returning from England in 1970, Nash was invited to give the commencement address at Nell's graduation from boarding school. The address was, in a sense, his own valedictory. It gave him the opportunity not only to look back on his own lifetime of work but to reflect on the place of humor in a complex and troubled world. Humor, he said, is "hope's companion in arms," and continued:

> It is not brash, it is not cheap, it is not heartless. Among other things I think humor is a shield, a weapon, a survival kit.
>
> Not only has this brief span of ours been threatened by such perils not of our own making such as fire and flood, Tyrannosaurus Rex, the black death, and hurricanes named after chorus girls, but we have been most ingenious in devising means for destroying each other, a habit we haven't yet learned how to kick. So here we are, several billion of us, crowded into our global concentration camp for the duration. How *are* we to survive? Solemnity is not the answer, any more than witless and irresponsible frivolity is. I think our best chance lies in humor, which in this case means a wry acceptance of our predicament. We don't have to like it but we can at least recognize its ridiculous aspects, one of which is ourselves.

For his part, Nash had confronted his own "predicaments" and was now ready to look ahead.

18

THE LAST STANZA

Ogden Nash ended 1970 and began 1971 in good spirits at age sixty-eight, busy with a variety of pursuits, personal and professional. In December he and Frances gave a dinner for Nell at the Elkridge Club before her presentation at the Bachelors' Cotillion held at the Lyric Opera House. Nash wrote a poem for the occasion, expressing his delight that his debutante daughter of years before now had a debutante daughter of her own. It concluded gaily: "Off to the Lyric, child/ And give them hell."

The New Year brought greetings from Nash's colleague from the early days of *The New Yorker*, Frank Sullivan, who wrote a chatty letter enlivened by a wry commentary on activities of their mutual friends, Andy White and Sid Perelman. In a February letter to Isabel, Nash reported cheerfully on his own comings and goings, including a trip to the ballet with Linell and Johnny to see a touring company that featured a "brief if brilliant" appearance by Nureyev. His disposition had even survived the Nashes' temporary loss of help with the cooking: "Mummy and I concocted some fabulous dishes, varying from triumph to disaster and always with Mary Kitchen Roast Beef Hash to fall back on." Finally, Nash disclosed proudly that, at the cost of thirty dollars, he now owned "one-tenth of one-eleventh of a race horse in partnership with a group from the Sunpapers."

During the same period Nash had also found time to read his poetry to an unusual audience: 160 mental patients at the State Hospital in Crownsville, Maryland. As reported in the *Baltimore Afro-American*, Nash's reading was part of the "biblio-therapy" program organized by the hospital librarian and was quite warmly received. Nash read his poems for 45 minutes, and as the librarian later put it: "Most mentally ill people have short attention spans, but as Mr. Nash read to them, there was a 'silence of attention and admiration.'" After the reading, Nash visited with the staff of the hospital and received a poem from one of the patients, to whom he later wrote an encouraging note.

Professionally, Nash was busy on several fronts. Uppermost in his mind was the planning for an omnibus volume of his poetry, a comprehensive selection from his complete works. The book was tentatively titled, with a nod to Robert Frost, *The Old Dog Barks Backward*. (Frost's poem "The Span of Life" included the couplet "The old dog barks backward without getting up/ I can remember when he was a pup.") Nash was planning for publication in 1972, to coincide with his seventieth birthday, and regarded it as "the biggest thing in my career." He was interested in having a foreword done by someone of stature, and several possibilities had been considered. Nash had written Ned Bradford in the spring of 1970, suggesting John Updike since he understood that Updike "likes at least some of my verse." Updike had been contacted and had replied with a gracious note, expressing a lifelong and continuing admiration for Nash's work but declining the invitation. He pleaded the press of his own schedule and suggested that "a man's collected works are only smudged by someone else's riding along in a foreword." The poet and novelist James Dickey had then been asked, but he too declined, on the ground of his lack of expertise with light verse (he suggested Updike for the job).

Early in 1971 the name of Archibald MacLeish was suggested as a possibility to write the foreword. But, although MacLeish was a distinguished poet, both Nash and Bradford felt that someone from a later generation would be preferable. Meanwhile Nash wrote to Perry Knowlton, emphasizing the importance of the book and urging that, in light of what he felt were Little, Brown's past failures, it was not too soon to begin work on matters such as design, typography, and the jacket. The "foul-up" with respect to the advertising for *Windmill* still rankled, with Nash believing that it had cost him sales of five thousand copies in the 1968 Christmas season. That had been followed by distress over the jacket for *Bed Riddance*: it had depicted an unshaven and rather unattractive patient, and Nash had insisted on its replacement in a later printing. Nash was reconciled to using Little, Brown for the omnibus, since under his contracts with them they held the rights for publication in book form, but he wanted an advance that would be large enough to provide a measure of insurance against further mishaps. He confided to Knowlton that he was prepared to take his next collection of new verse elsewhere "unless L.B. puts as much into my work as I do." He estimated that he was two-thirds through a collection that would be larger than any since *I'm a Stranger Here Myself.*

On the magazine front, the past pattern of *The New Yorker* appeared to be repeating itself. Although Nash had been cheered by the publication of "One Man's Opiate" in December, the new year brought a new round of rejections. Nash now seemed better able to take these in stride, anticipating perhaps that rejections would sooner or later be followed by an eager acceptance. In addition, he had also found a ready outlet for many of the poems turned down by *The New Yorker*: he had reached an agreement to provide verse on a monthly basis to *Signature*, the magazine of the Diner's Club. *Signature* lacked the cachet of *The New Yorker*, but, as Perry Knowlton would point out to Little, Brown, it had an official circulation of 800,000 (as compared with 475,840 for *The New Yorker*) and reached an entirely different group of readers.

In addition to the writing and marketing of his verse, Nash had other projects under way, including yet another theatrical venture—an off-Broadway revue with his verse set to music. The title was to be one of Nash's better-known aphorisms: "Progress was all right once, but it went on too long." The show was the idea of Milton Rosenstock, a Broadway conductor and composer, who had been the conductor for the ill-fated production of *Two's Company* with Bette Davis. Although Rosenstock's credentials as a composer were rather slender, he had conducted more than twenty Broadway shows and had made numerous original-cast albums. In any event, when Rosenstock came to him with the idea in 1970, Nash liked the music he had composed for several verses and agreed to go along with the idea. Nash did not write new songs for the show but helped select additional verses to be used and made suggestions as to their presentation. The show was scheduled for a brief run at the end of March, and Nash was planning to be in New York, if possible, for a few days of rehearsal.

He was also looking forward to a series of engagements in his sometime role as a performer. He had agreed to travel to Pittsburgh in April for a reading at a poetry forum, and in June he was scheduled to appear with Andre Kostelanetz and the New York Philharmonic, narrating verses he had written on the theme of matrimony entitled "Carnival of Marriage." He had agreed to narrate the same verses for the Philadelphia Orchestra in July, and they were also to be recorded by Columbia records. Finally, if he could fit it in, there was the possibility of a trip to the Bahamas to join the Eberstadts and the Smiths. Fred Eberstadt had inherited a house in the Bahamas and was trying to figure out how Nash might get there without breaking his rule against flying.

On March 4, 1971, all of Nash's plans were suddenly put on hold when a series of x-rays, which had been thought to be routine, disclosed an intestinal condition that Nash's doctors believed required surgery. Nash briefly considered making the trip to the Bahamas for a rest before the operation, perhaps even flying to do so. In the end he decided to proceed promptly with the surgery. As in the past, he struck an optimistic note with family and friends, writing Ned Bradford that he had been through similar operations twice and remembered them as "less painful than the tests." He anticipated that he would be out of action for four to five weeks and told Bradford that any good books would be welcome. He was admitted to Union Memorial Hospital in Baltimore, where surgery was performed on March 15.

The operation was pronounced a success, and Nash was further cheered by news that *The New Yorker* had bought his most recent submission. Less than three weeks before, Angell had written a confidential and mournful letter to Emilie Jacobson speculating that "Ogden's powers are waning" and wondering what they could do about it. Once again, however, the wise owls of Forty-third Street had been confounded. In a March 19 letter, Angell began by expressing his pleasure at the news that Nash's condition had improved and the hope that he would soon be back on his feet "ready to welcome spring and the Orioles." The real point of the letter, however, was to confirm the news (previously telegraphed to Nash by Jacobson) that Angell was delighted with Nash's poem "You Steer and I'll Toot, or, All's Slick That Ends Slick." It was, he said, "top Nash—the real article and very, very welcome here," and he extended "our congratulations for this most recent masterpiece."

Addressed to Nash in the hospital, there may have been a shade of hyperbole in Angell's letter, but there is no reason to doubt that his praise was sincere and well justified. The poem concerned a young man who aspired to be a marine navigator but was singularly lacking in talent ("As a country swain on the lake in Central Park he attempted simultaneously to row and woo/ Thereby achieving temporary fame as the only adult unaccompanied by a child to ground his boat in the Children's Zoo"). The point of the poem is revealed only in the last two lines:

> You might suppose that at this point he would have ceased to
> dream of being known as Henry the Navigator II and gently
> dropped anchor.
> But he didn't, and now he is captain of a spanking new seventy-
> thousand-ton tanker.

The last couplet had, as Angell put it, "the punch of a Frazier body-blow." Coming years before the misadventures of the Exxon *Valdez*, the poem seemed even more prescient than Nash's earlier verse warning of dangers in Central Park.

Nash had little time to savor his latest success at *The New Yorker*. A new intestinal problem appeared suddenly and a second operation was performed on March 29. This time, still weak from the first surgery, Nash did not rebound strongly. On April 6, Frances wrote to Emilie Jacobson to say that Ogden was feeling low but that the doctors were not despairing. She also asked if Jacobson would handle the distribution of Ogden's complimentary tickets for Rosenstock's off-Broadway show, which was now scheduled to open on April 14 and run through the 17th. He did not wish to force any tickets on friends, Frances wrote, but they should be offered to any interested Curtis Brown personnel, to a few specific individuals, including the Hacketts and the Hirschfelds, and to actor Eli Wallach, who had filled in for Nash at the Pittsburgh poetry reading. Two days later Frances sent another letter about tickets and reported that "Ogden has been and is *very* weak—he's doing a little improving and then slipping back again, and it's constantly alarming." Because of the precarious nature of his condition, Nash had few visitors other than his children and grandchildren. One exception was Clarence, who had insisted on coming down from New York and was allowed to see Nash for a few minutes. The other was Beryl Summers, who had worked for the Nashes before World War II and had remained close to the family.

By April 15, Jacobson had heard from Frances that Nash was improved. She wrote to tell him of routine business matters but also to offer a happy report on the opening of the Rosenstock show: "Nash was undisputedly the star of 'Progress' last night. How those lyrics sparkle and delight!" But Nash's condition soon began to deteriorate, and when he showed signs of kidney failure, a decision was made to move him to Johns Hopkins Hospital for dialysis. He was admitted there on April 20. (The Johns Hopkins admissions note makes pointed reference to a lack of data from Union Memorial Hospital: "No records are available [from 15 March 1971] until 29 Mar 71. . . . I&O data post-op is not available at present nor is correlation of pre- and post-op renal status possible due to lack of data").

Doctors hoped the dialysis treatment would lead to a rapid improvement in Nash's condition, but the improvement failed to appear. Frances wrote again to Emmy Jacobson on May 4 with a gloomy report: "He is so weak that only his will is keeping him alive. No one has given up yet, but it is really touch and go." Frances also made a request for donations of blood, which Nash had required in large quantities. Ned Bradford had gotten together a group of donors, and Frances hoped that Jacobson might do the same at Curtis Brown. Emmy was happy to do whatever she could, but this time the love and support of friends and family would not be enough: Nash struggled for two more weeks but finally succumbed on May 19.

At the end, Frances, Linell, and Isabel were with him, and heard his last words: "I love you, Frances." Frances and her daughters drove home to the Nashes' apartment in silence, bound up in their own thoughts. Once there, Frances led the way into the kitchen, and in a gesture that Nash would have appreciated, found a bottle of champagne for a final toast, "To Ogden." Later that day, Frances wrote in her diary a verse from Emily Dickinson:

> The Sweeping up the Heart
> And putting Love away
> We shall not want to use again
> Until Eternity.

Memorial services for Ogden Nash were held in Baltimore, New York City, and at St. Andrew's by-the-Sea in New Hampshire, where Nash was buried. The service at St. Andrew's was conducted by Nash's old and dear friend Matt Warren, who read a poem, "I Didn't Go to Church Today," that Nash had written many years before:

> I didn't go to church today,
> I trust the Lord to understand.
> The surf was swirling blue and white,
> The children swirling on the sand.
> He knows, He knows how brief my stay,

256

How brief this spell of summer weather,
He knows when I am said and done
We'll have a plenty of time together.

Nash's poem did not do justice to his active membership at St. Andrew's, but his contributions to the church were later recognized when his image was incorporated in one of its stained-glass windows.

Although Nash had not enjoyed robust health for a number of years, he was still, at sixty-eight, relatively young and looking forward to more years of productive work. The circumstances of his death left agonizing questions that have never been fully answered and that, in some measure, still haunt his family. Was the initial operation essential, or was it something that, as one doctor later suggested, could have been postponed or possibly avoided altogether? Was Nash a victim of his own "good manners," reluctant to offend doctors who were old friends by seeking a second opinion or another venue for the surgery? Had the postoperative care at Union Memorial Hospital been adequate? Clear answers are unlikely ever to emerge. Whatever the answers, Nash had been blessed by having lived a fully productive life until the very end. He had written his last poem only days before entering the hospital, he had enjoyed a final triumph at *The New Yorker*, and, thanks to Milton Rosenstock, even his long love affair with the theater had been given a happy, albeit fleeting, reprise.

Newspaper and magazine stories reporting Nash's death recognized his passing as a major loss to both poetry and humor in America, but often had the same difficulty that reviewers had experienced in attempting to summarize or categorize his work. A front-page story in the *New York Times* was headlined "Ogden Nash, Master of Light Verse, Dies." The story recalled that "Mr. Nash was considered by many of his admirers to be a sort of Abraham Lincoln of poetry, and they called his mangled verse an emancipation proclamation for all would-be poets who harbored the illusion that poetry had to follow some strict law of rhyme and meter." It went on to point out, however, that despite unconventional rhymes Nash was a careful craftsman, and that his "long straggling lines of wildly irregular length . . . on close examination revealed a carefully thought out metrical scheme and a kind of relentless logic." The *Washington Post* called Nash a "serious man who wrote funny," whose verse had "delighted a vast audience including himself." *Time* said that "He was easily the best-known—and possibly the best—American practitioner of a subtle art that is always more serious than it seems: the writing of light verse." Nash had few peers, *Time* continued, "when it came to describing human foibles with a kind of wry delight," and he left "an affectionate and inventive verbal legacy." A fitting tribute was also paid in a resolution by the Academy of American Poets. The Academy saluted Nash for his services to it over many years and as a poet "whose delicious lines gave no idea of their intricacy or difficult meter, and whose engaging philosophy ranged over almost every human field."

The last verse that Nash wrote for *The New Yorker*, "You Steer and I'll Toot," appeared on May 29 and was introduced by a brief note in memoriam. After observing that Nash had written 353 poems for the magazine since January 11, 1930, the note continued:

> There is no way to comment adequately upon such an enormous body of joyful, surprising, pointed and always gentle poetry, and no way to express gratitude for a man who gratified four generations of readers. No way, perhaps except to run the newest and last Nash verse here and let it speak, comically and pointedly and now sadly, for all the others.

Nash's death, like that of anyone with a still active professional life, required the rearrangement of various plans. In the short run, Tony Randall was called on to substitute for Nash in his scheduled performance with the New York Philharmonic in June. He proved to be an apt choice: according to the *New York Times*, Randall performed so expertly that "not one of the fragile puns was lost in the audience laughter and applause that riddled the readings." Nash lost the chance to work on the further development of Milton Rosenstock's revue, but he would have been pleased that, under the title *Nash at Nine*, it later enjoyed at least modest success, with brief runs on Broadway starring E. G. Marshall, and in Washington, D.C., with Craig Stevens.

More important, publication of the omnibus selection of verse to which Nash had been looking forward was postponed, in part because of indecision as to who should select the contents. The proposed title of the book, *The Old Dog Barks Backward*, was used for a new collection published in 1972 that offered verse Nash had written from early 1968 through March 1971. The omnibus of Nash work was published in 1975 under the title *I Wouldn't Have Missed It*. The verses were selected by Linell and Isabel, and the foreword was written by Archibald MacLeish. W. H. Auden had been asked to write the foreword and had said he would be delighted to do so, but he died in 1973. Although Nash and Bradford had preferred someone of a later generation, the choice fell to MacLeish, who was then eighty-two.

The title of the 1975 omnibus was taken from a poem, "Preface to the Past." The poem had focused on Nash's progress from bachelor to parent to grandparent, and the concluding couplet was a fitting epitaph:

Here lies my past, good-by I have kissed it;
Thank you, kids, I wouldn't have missed it.

19

THE NASH LEGACY

During Ogden Nash's life the very breadth of his popularity sometimes seemed to overshadow the quality of his work as a poet. Could someone who was so widely read, enjoyed, and quoted, and whose work was largely humorous, actually be an important poet? Today, more than thirty years after his death, the evidence suggests that the answer is "yes."

Even now there are frequent reminders of the varied facets of Nash's work. *One Touch of Venus* is periodically revived, and "Speak Low" is heard regularly on any radio station that airs standards of the past. His verses for *Carnival of the Animals* are a perennial favorite of orchestras large and small. Nevertheless the cornerstone of Nash's reputation is the trove of more than a thousand poems that he wrote over a period of four decades. He continues to find a place at the table with his more serious colleagues. Nash was, for example, the only practitioner of light verse to be included in *Poetry Speaks*, a remarkable written and oral anthology, published in 2001, that provided on compact discs the voices of forty-two celebrated poets, from Tennyson to Sylvia Plath, reading their own work. The book also included a critique of each of the recorded poets by a distinguished contemporary poet. In Nash's case the critique was written by the Poet Laureate Billy Collins, who noted that the anthology had placed Nash "shoulder to shoulder with Langston Hughes and W. H. Auden." After analyzing aspects of Nash's work, Collins concluded:

Nash occasionally wrote serious poems, some of which give us a glimpse of a darker side, but he usually stays in his favorite poetic gear: the short, playfully rhymed, humorous lyric. . . . Nash's wild rhymes, his cavalier mishandling of prosody, and his tireless inventiveness reveal the most essential of a poet's credentials— a crazed affection for the language.

Nash's work has not only survived, there are reasons to believe it may still have contributions to make.

The state of poetry in America is the subject of frequent debates that have sometimes brought to mind the Dickensian paradox, "It was the best of times, it was the worst of times." The years after Nash's death saw more poetry being written by more poets, and published in more journals, than ever before. Funding from universities, and grants from public and private sources, made it possible for poets to live lives that, if not affluent, were surely quite comfortable in comparison with many of their predecessors. But there was another side.

In 1991, Dana Gioia wrote a provocative article, "Can Poetry Matter?" that later became the lead essay in a book of the same name. The essence of Gioia's argument was that poetry had become too inbred, written too much by academics to be read by other academics. Poetry was seldom published in magazines and newspapers with a general readership but was largely confined to specialized journals whose audiences were comprised almost entirely of other poets. The consequence, Gioia lamented, was to produce a body of mediocre poetry that tended to obscure the excellent poetry it surrounded. His principal point, however, was that by reason of its isolation, poetry had largely forfeited its role as a significant voice in American culture. It was not, Gioia said, that he sought a *mass* audience for poetry, but only a less homogeneous audience, an audience comprised of "a cross-section of artists and intellectuals, including scientists, clergymen, educators, lawyers, and, of course, writers . . . a literary intelligentsia made up mainly of nonspecialists, who took poetry as seriously as fiction and drama."

In the years since Gioia's essay there have been hopeful signs of a resurgence of poetry. Gioia himself was one of the first to find encouragement in the development of such varied forms as rap lyrics, cowboy poetry, and poetry slams. Robert Pinsky worked tirelessly to make poetry more accessible during his term as poet laureate, even making regular appearances on PBS's *Lehrer NewsHour*. Billy Collins, who served as poet laureate in 2001–2003, appears before audiences of remarkable size and diversity. Regardless, some may still argue that poetry remains at the margin of American culture, and for those who are interested in expanding the audience for poetry, Nash's life and work may offer some pointers.

It is more than a coincidence that Gioia's essay made a nostalgic, almost wistful, reference to days gone by, when "the old *New Yorker* showcased Ogden Nash between cartoons and short stories." More broadly, the paradigmatic audience described by Gioia is precisely the kind of audience that Nash was so successful in attracting. A modern poet aspiring to such an audience could do well to reflect on Nash's verse, not for the innovations of rhyme and meter—which are probably inimitable—but for the kinds of things he wrote about and the perspectives he brought to them. On the anniversary of Nash's death, Roger Angell wrote in *The New Yorker* of the myriad aspects of life in the twenty-first century that would profit from "the restorative Nashian couplet or clarifying stanza." Ogden Nash, he observed, "hasn't been around for a while, but the need for him remains steady."

Nash's career is also an enduring reminder of the importance of the oral tradition in poetry. Although he was a reluctant "performer," Nash was always highly effective in reading his verse. His readings on the lecture circuit, his recordings, and his appearances on radio and television and on the concert stage all served to enlarge the audience not only for his own work but for poetry in general. In *Poetry Speaks*, the editor Elise Paschen explained the magical qualities of the spoken word:

> Just as poetry differs from prose on the page, poems have a unique
> power when read aloud. Poets are attuned to sound as they
> "make" their poems, or in Robert Frost's words, create the sound
> of sense. Hearing poetry read aloud, the listener may glimpse the
> poet's psyche. Recited well, poetry can even mesmerize.

Not surprisingly, Billy Collins suggested that listening to Nash's poems might "restimulate the delight his poems have conveyed to so many." Even more broadly, it is possible that the success of *Poetry Speaks* might encourage the publication of similar volumes, and looking beyond CDs, one may speculate that the internet, which has already had an explosive impact on the music industry, could become a significant vehicle for spoken poetry.

Finally, there is the matter of form. Gioia's book included a chapter entitled "Notes on the New Formalism," in which he reported on a revival of poetry employing not only meter but sometimes rhyme. He placed the beginning of the revival at the end of the seventies, "long after the more knowing critics had declared rhyme and meter permanently defunct." The revival of formalism, though it remains somewhat outside the mainstream of contemporary poetry, has gained a number of adherents and shows no sign of going away. It is represented, for example, by a popular anthology, *Rebel Angels: 25 Poets of the New Formalism*, and has its own journal entitled, appropriately enough, *The Formalist*.

Ironically, the revival of formalism has some resonance with Nash's work. It is ironic because his verse, a radical departure from classic formalism, was thought by some critics to have played a part in engineering its demise. In fact, it is clear that Nash never saw himself in a battle against rhyme or meter, and he always insisted that it was important to know the rules before breaking them. As Billy Collins has pointed out, the delight of Nash's unruly lines is heightened by the echo of a conventional tetrameter or pentameter in the ear of the reader.

In the end, Nash's verse is lasting evidence that there is a place in poetry for humor, for poems that examine the contradictions of everyday life—and for rhyme and meter, even of the most unconventional sort. It is a fitting legacy and one that Nash would enjoy having left.

20

EPILOGUE: THE FAMILY

Three years before his death, Nash wrote a poem in which one stanza conveyed an image of Frances growing older, and like so much of his verse it spoke with remarkable truth:

FOR FRANCES, APRIL 12, 1968

My wife
Will be an old lady mischievous and flighty,
Will shake her gold-headed cane in the face of God Almighty.
She will be revered,
Be pampered, be boasted of, be adored and feared.
She will love a surprise, and a dry martini as well,
She will still be the girl who was borne ashore on a shell
And I'll shout, as the ivy on my stone advances,
Go to it, Frances.

After Ogden's death, Frances lived on for more than two decades until she died in 1994 at the age of eighty-eight. During that time she led an active life, with interests ranging from politics to the arts. Although she appeared to mellow in some respects, Frances remained a strong personality whose opinions on a variety of subjects were freely and sometimes sharply expressed. She continued to divide her time between Baltimore and Little Boar's Head, and in Baltimore she remained at Cross Keys until moving to a nearby retirement home in 1983. In addition to supporting a number of

Baltimore organizations in the performing and visual arts, she made a habit of small acts of very private charity. Going through her papers after her death, Linell's daughter, Frances, discovered numerous notes of thanks from individuals to whom she had given financial or other assistance.

Clarence continued to run the household at Little Boar's Head, and when he died he was buried, in accordance with his wishes, in the same plot as Nash and with a headstone identical in style to Nash's. (Frances expressed some understandable qualms at sharing the family plot in this manner, but in the end the family's collective affection for Clarence prevailed.)

Linell continues to operate the horse farm in Sparks, Maryland. It has been less profitable since changes in the tax law in the 1980s, and Linell no longer has the help of her husband, Johnny, who died of cancer in 1992. But it is a way of life she holds dear. Preoccupied with the demands of running the horse farm, Linell wrote no more books after *And Miles to Go* in 1967. In the late eighties, however, she found the time to edit *Loving Letters*. The book is a selection of her father's letters accompanied by a biographical commentary that provides the kinds of reflections and insights that could have come only from a daughter of Ogden Nash.

Linell's children all live in the Baltimore area. The eldest, Linell ("Nell"), is a feature writer with the *Baltimore Sun*. Her husband is director of the Baltimore Choral Arts Society, and they have a daughter, Miranda (a pseudonym for Frances in "A Lady Thinks She Is Thirty"). Frances lives in Sparks and helps Linell run the horse farm while holding down an outside job; she also takes the lead in exploring opportunities for marketing Nash's work. Linell's youngest daughter, Brigid ("Biddy"), is on the staff of U.S. Senator Paul Sarbanes. She is married to an artist, and they have two children.

Isabel and Fred Eberstadt continue to live in Manhattan. Isabel's writing career was derailed in 1967 by her illness. In 1980 she resumed writing and in 1983 published her second novel. The book, *Natural Victims*, drew on Isabel's experiences in avant-garde theater in the seventies as well as her acquaintance with figures prominent in New York society. Meanwhile Fred continued to work as a photographer but also became a writer for *Vogue*, and he later made another, quite remarkable career change. After suffering from severe depression, and having found dramatic relief through cognitive behavioral therapy, Fred was so impressed with that method of treatment that he obtained the necessary education and training to become a therapist, and still maintains a practice in New York today.

The Eberstadts' older child, Nick, became an expert in demographics, a field in which he has written several books. He lives in Washington, D.C., with his wife and four children. He is a resident scholar at the American Enterprise Institute and has also served on the faculty of the Harvard School of Public Health. The youngest of Nash's grandchildren, Fernanda ("Nenna"), has perhaps gone the farthest in advancing the family literary tradition by writing four well-received novels. In a 1997 interview, Nenna recalled the influence of her grandfather, of playing word games with him and of being in love with words, "wanting to swallow the dictionary." A review of her 2003 novel, *The Furies*, saw her prose as "taut, fresh and vividly descriptive." The reviewer compared her observant eye to Tom Wolfe's—but a comparison to her grandfather might not have been amiss. Nenna lives in France with her husband and two children.

Nash's children and grandchildren have taken diverse paths and lead quite different lives. Nash, however, would be proud of them all—and pleased to count the toes of each new great-grandchild.

TABLE OF POEMS

THE FOLLOWING IS A TABLE OF POEMS by Ogden Nash that were quoted in the text at the pages indicated. For poems that appeared in more than one book, only the most recent are shown. The titles below correspond to the last published version and may vary slightly from what is shown in the text. Publication information for books is found in the Bibliography, and publication information for poems not included in a book is found in the Notes for the text where the poems are quoted or cited.

BIBLIOGRAPHY

I. BOOKS BY OGDEN NASH OR TO WHICH HE CONTRIBUTED

A. Prose

The Cricket of Carador, with Joseph Alger. Garden City: Doubleday, Page & Co., 1925.

Born in a Beer Garden, with Christopher Morley and Cleon Throckmorton. New York: The Foundry Press, 1930.

B. Original verse

Hard Lines. New York: Simon and Schuster, 1931.

Free Wheeling. New York: Simon and Schuster, 1931.

Happy Days. New York: Simon and Schuster, 1933.

The Primrose Path. New York: Simon and Schuster, 1935.

The Bad Parents' Garden of Verse. New York: Simon and Schuster, 1936.

I'm a Stranger Here Myself. Boston: Little, Brown & Co., 1938.

The Face Is Familiar. Boston: Little, Brown & Co., 1940.

Good Intentions. Boston: Little, Brown & Co., 1942.

Versus. Boston: Little, Brown & Co., 1949.

The Private Dining Room. Boston: Little, Brown & Co., 1953.

You Can't Get There from Here. Boston: Little, Brown & Co., 1957.

Everyone But Thee and Me. Boston: Little, Brown & Co., 1962.

Santa Go Home: A Case History for Parents. Boston: Little, Brown & Co., 1967.

There's Always Another Windmill. Boston: Little, Brown & Co., 1968.

The Old Dog Barks Backward. Boston: Little, Brown & Co., 1972.

C. Collected and selected

The Ogden Nash Pocket Book. New York: Pocket Books, 1944.

Many Long Years Ago. Boston: Little, Brown & Co., 1945.

The Selected Verse of Ogden Nash. New York: Modern Library, 1946.

Family Reunion. Boston: Little, Brown & Co., 1950.

Verses from 1929 On. Boston: Little, Brown & Co., 1959.

Marriage Lines: Notes of a Student Husband. Boston: Little, Brown & Co., 1964.

Bed Riddance: A Posy for the Indisposed. Boston: Little, Brown & Co., 1970.

Ave Ogden: Nash in Latin (Translated by James C. Gleason and Brian N. Meyer). Boston: Little, Brown & Co., 1973.

I Wouldn't Have Missed It. Boston: Little, Brown & Co., 1975.

A Penny Saved Is Impossible. Boston: Little, Brown & Co., 1981.

D. Verse for children

Ogden Nash's Musical Zoo, with tunes by Vernon Duke. Boston: Little, Brown & Co., 1947.

Parents Keep Out: Elderly Poems for Youngerly Readers. Boston: Little, Brown & Co., 1951.

The Christmas That Almost Wasn't. Boston: Little, Brown & Co., 1957.

Custard the Dragon. Boston: Little, Brown & Co., 1960.

A Boy Is a Boy: The Fun of Being a Boy. New York: Franklin Watts, 1960.

Custard the Dragon and the Wicked Knight. Boston: Little, Brown & Co., 1961.

The New Nutcracker Suite and Other Innocent Verses. Boston: Little, Brown & Co., 1962.

Girls Are Silly. New York: Franklin Watts, 1962.

A Boy and His Room. New York: Franklin Watts, 1963.

The Adventures of Isabel. Boston: Little, Brown & Co., 1963.

The Untold Adventures of Santa Claus. Boston: Little, Brown & Co., 1964.

The Animal Garden. New York: M. Evans & Co., 1965.

The Cruise of the Aardvark. New York: M. Evans & Co., 1967.

The Scroobious Pip, by Edward Lear and completed by Ogden Nash. New York: Harper & Row, 1968.

E. Theater

One Touch of Venus, with S. J. Perelman. Boston: Little, Brown & Co., 1944.

F. Edited by Ogden Nash

Nothing but Wodehouse. Garden City: Doubleday, Doran & Co., 1932.

The Moon Is Shining Bright as Day: An Anthology of Good-humored Verse. Philadelphia: J. B. Lippincott, 1953.

I Couldn't Help Laughing: Stories Selected and Introduced by Ogden Nash. Philadelphia: J. B. Lippincott, 1957.

Everybody Ought to Know: Verses Selected and Introduced. Philadelphia: J. B. Lippincott, 1961.

G. Interview

Conversations. Interview by Roy Newquist. New York: Rand McNally, 1967.

Note: The books by Ogden Nash listed above do not include foreign editions and single poems published in pamphlet form. For citation of additional books by Ogden Nash, see George Crandell, *Ogden Nash: A Descriptive Bibliography* (Metuchen, N.J.: Scarecrow Press, 1990).

II. LETTERS OF OGDEN NASH

Loving Letters from Ogden Nash: Selected and Introduced by Linell Nash Smith. Boston: Little, Brown & Co., 1990.

III. SECONDARY SOURCES, A SELECTIVE LIST

A. Bibliography

Crandell, George. *Ogden Nash: A Descriptive Bibliography*. Metuchen, N.J.: Scarecrow Press, 1990.

B. St. George's School

Taverner, Gilbert. *St. George's School, A History*. Newport, R.I.: St. George's School, 1987.

C. New York, Garden City, and Hoboken

Allen, Frederick Lewis. *Only Yesterday*. New York: Harper & Row, 1957.

Wallach, Mark I., and Jon Bracker. *Christopher Morley*. Boston: Twayne Publishers, 1976.

D. *The New Yorker*

Kinney, Harrison. *James Thurber: His Life and Times*. New York: Henry Holt, 1997.

Kunkel, Thomas. *Genius in Disguise: Harold Ross of The New Yorker*. New York: Random House, 1995.

Thurber, James. *The Years with Ross*. Boston: Little, Brown & Co., 1959.

Yagoda, Ben. *About Town*. New York: Scribner, 2000.

E. Hollywood

Gabler, Neil. *Empire of Their Own*. New York: Anchor Books/Doubleday, 1988.

Latham, Aaron. *Crazy Sundays*. New York: Viking, 1971.

Westbrook, Robert. *Intimate Lies*. New York: HarperCollins, 1995.

Fitzgerald, F. Scott. *The Letters of F. Scott Fitzgerald*. Ed. Andrew Turnbull. New York: Charles Scribner's Sons, 1963.

F. Baltimore

Beirne, Francis A. *The Amiable Baltimoreans*. Hatboro: Tradition Presss, 1968.

G. Musical theater

Crawford, Cheryl. *One Naked Individual: My Fifty Years in the Theatre*. Indianapolis: Bobbs-Merrill, 1977.

De Mille, Agnes. *And Promenade Home*. Boston: Little, Brown & Co., 1977.

Duke, Vernon. *Passport to Paris*. Boston: Little, Brown & Co., 1955.

Herrmann, Dorothy. *S. J. Perelman.* New York: Putnam, 1986.

Leaming, Barbara. *Bette Davis.* New York: Simon and Schuster, 1992.

Martin, Mary. *My Heart Belongs to Daddy.* New York: William Morrow and Co., 1976.

Sanders, Ronald. *The Days Grow Short: The Life and Music of Kurt Weill.* New York: Holt, Rinehart and Winston, 1980.

Symonette, Lys, and Kim H. Kowalke, eds. and trans. *Speak Low: The Letters of Kurt Weill and Lotte Lenya.* Berkeley: University of California Press, 1996.

H. Literary criticism

Amis, Kingsley, ed. Introduction to *The New Oxford Book of English Light Verse.* New York: Oxford University Press, 1978.

Auden, W. H., ed. Introduction to *The Oxford Book of Light Verse.* Oxford: Oxford University Press, 1938.

Baker, Russell, ed. Introduction to *The Norton Book of Light Verse.* New York: W. W. Norton, 1986.

Gates, Robert A. *American Literary Humor During the Great Depression.* Westport, Conn.: Greenwood Press, 1999.

Harmon, William. Introduction to *The Oxford Book of American Light Verse.* New York: Oxford University Press, 1979.

MacLeish, Archibald. Introduction to *I Wouldn't Have Missed It,* eds. Linell Nash Smith and Isabel Eberstadt. Boston: Little, Brown & Co., 1975.

NOTES

NOTES ON ABBREVIATIONS AND
PRINCIPAL LOCATIONS OF UNPUBLISHED SOURCES

1. Letters from Ogden Nash (ON) to Frances Leonard (FL), later Frances Leonard Nash (FLN), to Linell Nash Smith (LNS) and Isabel Nash Eberstadt (INE), and to other members of the Nash family are in the Nash Collection at the Harry Ransom Humanities Center, University of Texas, Austin, TX (HRC).

2. Letters from ON to Dan Longwell (DL) and Dan and Mary Longwell (D/ML) are in the Longwell Collection, Rare Book and Manuscript Library, Columbia University, New York, NY (Longwell Collection).

3. Letters from ON to Alan Collins (AC) and Emilie Jacobson (EJ) are in the Curtis Brown Ltd. Collection, Rare Book and Manuscript Library, Columbia University, New York, NY (Curtis Brown Collection).

4. Letters from Nash to Kurt Weill (KW) are in the Kurt Weill Collection, The Yale Music Library, New Haven, CN (YML).

5. Letters between ON and Harold Ross (HR), Katharine White (KW), Roger Angell (RA), and other personnel of *The New Yorker* are in *The New Yorker* Collection at the New York Public Library, New York, NY (NYPL).

6. Copies of the letters from ON to Vernon Duke are in the private papers of LNS.

7. Letters between ON and personnel of Little, Brown and Company are in the files of the company, Boston, MA (Files of Little, Brown).

8. Interviews of Nash friends and family by Nash's friend, David Woods (DW), are on tape recordings and transcripts in the Nash Collection at the Dartmouth College Library, Hanover, NH (Dartmouth).

9. The manuscript by Dorothy Holland (Holland Ms.) is in the Nash Collection at Dartmouth (Dartmouth).

10. The manuscript by LNS (Smith Ms.) and the travel diaries of Ogden Nash in 1969 and 1970 are in the private papers of LNS.

1. THE EARLY INFLUENCES

page

7 Nash's first book of poetry: Ogden Nash, *Hard Lines* (New York: Simon and Schuster, 1931).

7 "disputes about inheritance": INE, letter to the author.

8 "by painful experience": *Dictionary of North Carolina Biography* (Chapel Hill: University of North Carolina Press, 1991), 4:357. Other information concerning Abner Nash, Francis Nash, and Frederick Nash is from ibid., 356–360.

9 "from stragglers and looters": quoted in Roy Newquist, *Conversations* (Chicago: Rand McNally, 1967), 260.

9 Story of the family silver: Smith Ms.

9 "quite a trip isn't it": Edmund Nash to Henry Kollock Nash, 28 November 1882, HRC.

9 "the chief business in life": Edmund Nash to Mary Simpson Nash, 4 February 1884, quoted in Holland Ms., 81.

10 Information concerning the Chenault family: Holland Ms., 108–121, and Charlton Rogers, Jr., *The Descendants of Etienne Chenault*, privately published and provided to the author by Charlton Rogers III.

10 Tutoring by Nash's mother: Newquist, *Conversations*, 261.

11 "many years of abounding prosperity": Edmund Nash to his children, 25 March 1915, HRC.

12 Nash's move to Ramaqua: Shirley Watkins Steinman, taped interview by DW, Dartmouth.

12 Life at Ramaqua: Aubrey Nash, interview by DW, Dartmouth.

12 "references to the Edmund Nash family": Marcia Dalphin, *Fifty Years of Rye* (Rye, N.Y.: Rye Chronicle Press, 1955), 21–22. The book was made available by the Rye Historical Society.

12 Nash pranks: Aubrey Nash, interview by DW, Dartmouth; Daisy Gordon Lawrence to ON, undated, HRC.

13 Ambition to be a racing driver: ON to EJ, memorandum, October 1970, Curtis Brown Collection.

13 First taste of "the good life": Aubrey Nash, interview by DW, Dartmouth.

13 "her mother's strong right arm:" Linell Smith ed., *Loving Letters from Ogden Nash* (Boston: Little, Brown, 1990), 8.

14 "is always anxious on her behalf": quoted by Ogden Nash, "Lecture at University of North Carolina," tape recording, University of North Carolina Library, Chapel Hill.

14 "at others it is hot and kind": quoted in Smith, ed., *Loving Letters*, 10–13.

15 "things were not as they used to be or should be": quoted in Newquist, *Conversations*, 260.

15 Trial of American Naval Stores: Clippings from the *Savannah Morning News* and the *Savannah Press* describing the trial and its aftermath are maintained in the American Naval Stores Scrapbook at the Georgia Historical Society in Savannah.

15 "surprise and disappointment": *Savannah Morning News*, 15 May 1909.

15 "the business world with which they deal": *Savannah Press*, 15 May 1909.

16 Suspension of operations of American Naval Stores: *Savannah Weekly Naval Stores Review and Journal*, 22 March 1913, 20.

16 The government would "not pursue a phantom": Ibid., 29 March 1913, 16.

16 Convictions reversed: *Nash v. United States*, 229 U.S. 373 (1913).

17 "They never considered that they had a strong case": *Savannah Weekly Naval Stores Review*, 14 June 1913, 29.

17 Mr. Loder's ghost: Shirley Watkins Steinman, interview by DW, Dartmouth.

18 "Latin, a language I've found very useful": quoted in Newquist, *Conversations*, 260; letters from Nash to his mother are in the private papers of LNS.

18 Note to Nash's editor: ON to RA, 17 May 1965, NYPL.

19 Tutoring by Nash's mother: Newquist, *Conversations*, 261.

19 Activities at Ramaqua: Ogden Nash, Diary, HRC.

19 "The Scrappy U.S. Sammy": Enclosed in a letter from Edmund Nash to George Baldwin, 2 August 1917, Baldwin Papers, University of North Carolina.

20 "The future is full of promise": Edmund Nash to his children, 25 March 1915, HRC.

20 Auchincloss contributions to St. George's: Gilbert Y. Taverner, *St. George's School, A History: 1896–1986* (Newport: St. George's School, 1987), 52.

20 "support of the War by the boys and Masters": ibid., 54.

21 "love for the mother tongue. . .": ON to Arthur Roberts, 18 January 1968, files of St. George's School. Newport, R.I.

21 "would rather be a good bad poet than a bad good poet": quoted in G. P. Hunt, "Poet Laureate of the Colts," *Life*, 13 December 1968, 3. Or as Nash put it less modestly on another occasion, "a great bad poet," quoted in Smith, ed., *Loving Letters*, 17.

22 "make do for four years at Harvard": ON to Arthur Roberts, 18 January 1968.

22 "totally out of character for the man": Taverner, letter to the author.

22 "Head of the French Department many years later": George Wheeler to Dale Donaldson, 12 February 1963, files of St. George's School.

2. GETTING STARTED

23 "unspeakable practice of petting and necking": Frederick Lewis Allen, *Only Yesterday* (New York: Harper & Row, 1957 ed.), 89–91.

23 "lining the streets of the forties and fifties between Fifth and Sixth Avenues": Marion Meade, *Dorothy Parker: What Fresh Hell Is This?* (New York: Penguin Books, 1987), xviii.

23 "academic pomposity in books and in life": Allen, *Only Yesterday*, 230–231. Members of the Round Table: Meade, *Dorothy Parker*, 75.

24 "a lot like Don Marquis's Mehitabel": quoted in Newquist, *Conversations*, 261.

24 "the Fijis balked and held out for beads": quoted in George W. Crandell, *Ogden Nash: A Descriptive Bibliography* (Metuchen, N.J.: The Scarecrow Press, 1990), 4.

25   "the lowest stratum of a dying empire": Ogden Nash, "Reminiscences of Dan Longwell from Doubleday to *Life*," Address to the Friends of the Columbia Library, 4 February 1970, Longwell Collection.

25   Experience with Longwell: Nash, "Reminiscences of Dan Longwell."

26   Stevens recollection: George Stevens, "Ogden Nash: A Memoir," *Saturday Review*, 19 June 1971, 19.

26   "nursing all kinds of respectable books": ON to FL, 28 June 1929, *Loving Letters*, 32.

26   Kunitz recollection: Stanley Kunitz, telephone interview by the author.

26   "just didn't turn out as I had intended": quoted in Newquist, *Conversations*, 263.

27   "one thousand Christmases bigger and brighter": ON to FL, 1 October 1929, HRC.

27   "sinking an eighteen-inch putt": Ogden Nash, "Lecture at University of North Carolina," University of North Carolina Library.

28   Ford recollection: Corey Ford, *The Time of Laughter* (Boston: Little Brown, 1967), 59.

29   Morley background: Mark I. Wallach and Jon Bracker, *Christopher Morley* (Boston: Twayne Publishers, 1976), 13–29.

29   Lake Ronkonkoma Club: Nash, "Reminiscences of Dan Longwell"; "Minutes of the Nassau and Suffolk County Deviled Ham and Lake Ronkonkoma Club," HRC. The quotation of Thomas Nashe (1567–1601) was imprecise. Nashe wrote:

> "Cold doth not sting, the pretty birds do sing
> Cuckoo, jug-jug, pu-we, to-witta-woo.
> —*Summer's Last Will and Testament* [1600]

Thus, the jug preceded the wit for Nashe as well as Nash.

30   The Hoboken Theater: Christopher Morley, Cleon Throckmorton, and Ogden Nash, *Born in a Beer Garden* (New York: Foundry Press, 1930), 11–56; Wallach and Bracker, *Christopher Morley*, 21.

30   "the glow just won't wear off": ON to FL, 2 January 1929, HRC.

30   "I shall be in a state": ON to Morley, 18 February 1929, Haverford College Library.

31   "over the bodies of their enemies": Nash in Morley, Throckmorton and Nash, *Born in a Beer Garden*, 82–83 .

31   Morley financial difficulties: Wallach and Bracker, *Christopher Morley*, 19–20.

32   "wait a while before going up again": ON to FL, 28 November 1929, Smith, ed., *Loving Letters*, 71–72.

32   "our memorable audition day": Lowell Thomas, *Good Evening Everybody* (New York: William Morrow, 1976), 309.

33   "snakes out of gold mines by the bucket full etc.": ON to FL, 11 September 1929, Smith, ed., *Loving Letters*, 52.

33   "a desperate attempt to land him": ON to FL, 9 January 1930, HRC.

33   "Garden City takes the rest of the tricks": ON to FL, 20 November 1929, HRC.

33 "until noon the following day": ON to FL, 7 July 1930, Smith, ed., *Loving Letters*, 94. Malcolm Johnson became executive vice president of the publishing firm of D. Van Nostrand Company and served as president of the American Book Publishers Council; Charles Duell became a founder of the publishing firm of Duell, Sloan and Pearce.

34 "meek, pallid bankrupt little clerks": ON to FL, 25 March 1930, HRC.

34 "the vulgarest of vulgarities": ON to FL, 19 October 1930, Smith, ed., *Loving Letters*, 115.

34 "frightening him to death with my fierceness": ON to FL, 19 November 1930, ibid., 120.

34 Jaunt with F. N. Doubleday: ON to FL, 16 September 1929, ibid., 55.

35 "we all felt better and parted friends": ON to FL, 15 September 1929, ibid., 53.

35 "I don't read books, I sell them": www.hwwilson.com/Currentbio/baseball.

35 "I approve of the very rich": ON to FL, 12 December 1929, HRC.

35 Meeting Frances Leonard: Ogden Nash, *Marriage Lines* (Boston: Little Brown, 1964), xi–xii.

36 Reaction of Frances Leonard: Smith, ed., *Loving Letters*, 24.

36 The letter was signed simply "Ogden": ON to FL, 21 November 1928, ibid., 24–26.

36 "it crystallized in my imagination": ON to FL, 25 August 1929, ibid., 39.

37 "I'm a selfish fool": ON to FL, 26 August 1929, HRC.

37 Nash was "miserably nervous": ON to FL, 28 August 1929, HRC.

37 "I want to go shouting through the office": ON to FL, 29 August 1929, HRC.

37 "as fortunate in finding Frances's mother as in finding her": ON to Mrs. William Leonard, 1 September 1929, Smith, ed., *Loving Letters*, 48.

37 "you had so much to do with it": ON to FL, 12 September 1929, HRC.

38 "something that can't be stopped": ON to FL, 16 September 1929, Smith, ed., *Loving Letters*, 54.

38 "regiments of goose-stepping goose-flesh": ON to FL, 19 September 1929, ibid., 56–57.

38 "hope is so closely bound to fear": ON to FL, 20 September 1929, ibid., 58.

38 "have a good sound sleep": ON to FL, 23 December 1929, ibid., 77.

38 Nash's New Year's Eve: ON to FL, 1 January 1930, ibid., 78.

3. *THE NEW YORKER*: IN THE BEGINNING

40 Shorter commute to Garden City: ON to FL, 5 January 1930, Smith, ed., *Loving Letters*, 79.

41 "helpful to me in my profession": ON to FL, 1 and 16 January 1930, ibid., 78.

41 "become a resonable nation": Theodore Morrison to ON, 23 September 1930, HRC.

41 "I have ever lived through" and "consequently annoying": ON to FL, 16 January 1930, Smith, ed., *Loving Letters*, 80–81.

42 "order of things": ON to FL, 27 January 1930, ibid., 82.

42 "might be better for you": ON to FL, 30 January 1930, ibid., 85.

42 "have more stuff to market": ON to Middleton, undated, NYPL.

42 "the best of all for us": KW to ON, 8 January 1930, NYPL.

42 Katharine White at *The New Yorker*: Thomas Kunkel, *Genius in Disguise: Harold Ross of the New Yorker* (New York: Random House, 1995), 142; Scott Elledge, *E. B. White* (New York: W. W. Norton, 1984), 182.

43 "90% of our freight yards": ON to FL, 30 December 1929, HRC.

43 "coffee cups at the Harvard Club": ON to FL, 26 March 1930, ibid.

43 "make you want to buy them": ON to KW, 5 April 1930, NYPL.

43 "never even written one, in fact": ON to FL, 18 April 1930, HRC.

44 "take notice, so to speak" and "we can't print them": KW to ON, 16 April 1930, NYPL.

44 "staying for lunch": ON to FL, 6 August 1930, Smith, ed., *Loving Letters*, 103.

44 "took my breath away": Donald Friede to ON, 26 September 1930, HRC.

44 Nash story sent to Hemingway: ON to FL, 4 December 1930, Smith, ed., *Loving Letters*, 125.

44 "this sort of thing": KW to ON, 16 April 1930, NYPL.

45 "the asinine verses week after next": ON to FL, 18 April 1930, HRC. Because of its innovative form, "Spring" has often been cited as Nash's first poem for *The New Yorker*. The error was perpetuated by Archibald MacLeish in his foreword to the posthumous collection of Nash's poems, *I Wouldn't Have Missed It*.

45 "alliances in the dictionary": Billy Collins, National Public Radio broadcast, "The Connection," 13 August 2002.

46 "a dizzying experience": E. B. White, "Notes and Comments," *The New Yorker*, 2 April 1960, quoted in Elledge, *E. B. White*, 100.

46 Admiral Byrd poem: ON to FL, 24 June 1930, HRC.

46 Nash teases Adams: ON to FL, 8 December 1930, ibid.

46 "Do try it again": KW to ON, 17 July 1930, NYPL.

46 "hypocrisy, bigotry and charlatanism": Edmund Nash to Francis Nash, 7 February 1931, Francis Nash Papers, Southern Historical Collection, University of North Carolina.

46 "our favorite poet": KW to ON, 24 June 1930, NYPL.

46 "most original stuff we have had lately": HR to ON, 6 August 1930, ibid.

47 Holden comment: ON to FL, 30 July 1930, Smith, ed., *Loving Letters*, 102.

47 "it is you I'm doing it for": ON to FL, 1 January 1930, ibid., 78.

47 "all I can do for you": ON to FL, 7 July 1930, ibid., 95.

48 "'in thee magnificence assembled is'": ON to FL, 25 July 1930, ibid., 101.

48 "a five-dollar tip besides": ON to FL, 8 September 1930, HRC.

48 "celebrated poem of Senator Smoot": ON to FL, 16 September 1930 (enclosure), HRC.

48 "too much too nicely to you": ON to FL, 23 September 1930, ibid.

49 "marry me when you get back": ON to FL, 3 October 1930, Smith, ed., *Loving Letters*, 109.

49 "hired me practically on the spot": James Thurber, *The Years with Ross* (Boston: Little, Brown, 1959), 123.

50 "sophisticated, elegant periodical": Kunkel, *Genius in Disguise*, 89. See generally: Thurber, *The Years with Ross*; Elledge, *E. B. White*; Linda H. Davis, *Onward and Upward: A Biography of Katharine S. White* (New York: Harper &
Row, 1979); Harrison Kinney, *James Thurber: His Life and Times* (New York:
Henry Holt, 1997); Ben Yagoda, *About Town* (New York: Scribner, 2000).

50 Ross career: Kunkel, *Genius in Disguise*, 13–44, 45–70, 88–91, 185; Kinney,
Thurber, 324–327.

50 Offer from Ross: ON to FL, 8 September 1930, Smith, ed., *Loving Letters*, 108.

51 Plan for new publishing house: ON to FL, 16 September 1930, HRC.

51 "bottom of my coeur": Dorothy Parker to ON, 28 October 1930, HRC; advertisement, *Saturday Review of Literature*, 17 January 1931, 544.

51 "elaborate and costly preparations," "every minute and mouthful," and "turn out
too oddly": ON to FL, 16 November 1930, Smith, ed., *Loving Letters*, 119.

52 Veto of Morley proposal: ON to FL, 10 October 1930, HRC.

52 "where I want them right now": ON to FL, 26 November 1930, Smtih, ed., *Loving Letters*, 121.

52 Offer from *The New Yorker*: ON to FL, 3 December 1930, ibid., 123–124.

52 "nothing short of pash": quoted in ON to FL, 22 December 1930, ibid., 129.

53 "all the rest of the luminous boys and girls" and "not hard, but wistful": ON to
FL, 4 December 1930, ibid., 124.

53 Christmas Eve: ON to FL, 25 December 1930, HRC.

53 "cashing in while I can": ON to FL, 8 December 1930, Smith, ed., *Loving Letters*, 125.

54 Review excerpts compiled by Simon and Schuster, HRC.

54 "a good deal of truth in it": ON to FL, 18 January 1931, ibid.

54 "credit for work on the book": R. C. Cedric to ON, 9 March 1931, HRC.

54 "American rights to both": Frank Sullivan to ON, 2 January 1931.

54 "cannot be too widely known": P. G. Wodehouse to ON, 9 March 1931, HRC.

55 "meanwhile it is profitable": ON to FL, 23 January 1931, ibid.

55 "ever heard about Alice Roosevelt": 22 February 1931, ibid.

55 "so distinguished a source": ON to Corinne Roosevelt, 27 May 1931, Houghton
Library, Harvard University, Cambridge, Mass.

55 "can—must, in fact—notice": quoted in ON to FL, 5 January 1931, Smith, ed.,
Loving Letters, 138.

55 "a man with so few enemies": Edna Ferber to ON, 28 January 1931, HRC.

56 "brownies or something": ON to Melville Cane, 13 January 1931, Papers of
Melville Cane, Rare Book and Manuscript Library, Columbia University, New
York.

56 "try to do some work": ON to FL, 5 January 1931, Smith, ed., *Loving Letters*, 139.

56 Ingersoll at *The New Yorker*: Kunkel, *Genius in Disguise*, 193; Kinney, *James
Thurber*, 344.

57 "everybody does two men's jobs": ON to FL, 31 January 1931, Smith, ed., *Loving
Letters*, 150.

57 "the training I've had": ON to FL, 13 February 1931, ibid., 155.

57 "one or the other—perhaps both": ON to FL, 16 February 1931, ibid., 156.

57 "that's what she is": ON to FL, 18 February 1931, ibid., 158.

58 "since she first did": ON to FL, ibid., 159.

58 See generally, Elledge, *E. B. White*.

58 "all day and laffeta": quoted in ON to FL, 6 February 1931, Smith, ed., *Loving Letters*, 152.

59 "might have common sense": HR to Raoul Fleischmann, 17 February 1931, NYPL.

59 "handled by Raymond Holden and Mrs. White": quoted in Thurber, *Years with Ross*, 123.

59 "that I would be a good one": Newquist, *Conversations*, 263.

59 "a sweet seraphic smile": James Cain to ON, 26 January 1967, HRC.

60 "with astonished suspicion": Thurber, *Years with Ross*, 123.

60 "octopus gets him in the Mediterranean": ON to FL, 10 February 1931, Smith, ed., *Loving Letters*, 154.

4. HAPPY DAYS

61 The sources for the background of Frances Leonard are Smith, ed., *Loving Letters*, 23, and interviews of LNS and INE by the author.

63 "what's to be done with you": ON to FL, 24 August 1930, HRC.

64 Nash wedding: Smith, ed., *Loving Letters*, 165–166; *New York Times*, 7 June 1931; HR to Mr. and Mrs. Leonard, 22 May 1931, NYPL.

64 First offer from Farrar: ON to FL, 5 December 1929, HRC.

64 "'He's a dear, but—'" ON to FL, 27 October 1930, ibid.

64 "it hasn't jelled yet": ON to FL, 13 April 1931, HRC.

64 Katharine White suggestion: KW to ON, 16 April 1931, NYPL.

65 John O'Hara novel: Matthew J. Bruccoli, *The O'Hara Concern* (New York: Random House, 1975), 78–80; *Selected Letters of John O'Hara*, Matthew J. Bruccoli, ed. (New York: Random House, 1978), 54.

65 *The Stag at Eve*: ON to HR, 19 November 1931, with handwritten notes of HR and Raymond Holden, NYPL.

66 "and I feel swell": ON to FLN, 20 June 1932, HRC.

66 Dinner with Longwell and Morley: ON to FL, 12 July 1932, ibid.

66 "actual use of the word": ON to Ezra Pound, 19 October 1932, Beinecke Library, Yale University, New Haven, Conn.

66 Unexpurgated version: Humphrey Carpenter, *A Serious Character: The Life of Ezra Pound* (Boston: Houghton Mifflin, 1988), 512.

66 Ford pamphlet: ON to Ford Madox Ford, 26 August 1932, Kroch Library, Cornell University, Ithaca, N.Y.; Carpenter, *A Serious Character*, 486.

66 *Anthony Adverse*: Edgar Ward, interview by DW, Dartmouth; obituary of Hervey Allen, *New York Times*, 29 December 1949.

66 Nash delighted: ON to FLN, 13 July 1933, HRC.

66 Nash compensation: Smith, ed., *Loving Letters*, 178.

67 "your very best": HR to ON, 30 May 1933, NYPL; see also memorandum, HR to Bellamy, 24 May 1933, ibid.

67 Move to Baltimore: Smith, ed., *Loving Letters*, 178–180; ON to FLN, 17 July 1933, HRC.

68 "have come in June": ON to FLN, undated, probably 17 August 1933, HRC.

68 "daughter of a versifier": E. B. White, *The Fox of Peapack and Other Poems* (New York: Harper and Brothers, 1938).

70 "scallop torn from its shell": quoted in Leslie Frewin, *The Late Mrs. Dorothy Parker* (New York: Macmillan, 1986), 222.

71 Nash drinking: LNS and INE, interviews by the author.

71 "the more I ache for you": ON to FLN, 27 October 1935, Smith, ed., *Loving Letters*, 187.

72 "your standard of too much, not mine" and "Kiss me": ON to FLN, 19 November 1935, HRC.

72 "a world without Frances": Smith, ed., *Loving Letters*, 182.

73 "you are do [sic] for the New Yorker'": quoted in ON to KW, 5 October 1933, NYPL.

73 "as to who likes what": KW to ON, 9 October 1933, ibid.

73 "your proper medium": KW to ON, 28 November 1933, ibid.

73 "makes things difficult for me": ON to KW, 3 December 1933, ibid.

74 "coming out elsewhere": KW to ON, 8 December 1933, ibid.

74 Nash poems in magazines: Crandell, *Ogden Nash*, 255–289.

5. WRITING LIGHT VERSE . . . IN THE DEPRESSION

76 "clever with his hands": Ogden Nash, "The Pleasure Is Ours," *Saturday Review of Literature*, 4 November 1933, 231.

76 "They wither": Samuel Hoffenstein, "Poems in Praise of Practically Nothing," *in* Gene Shalit, ed., *Laughing Matters* (New York: Barnes and Noble, 1993), 240–241.

76 "under the bell on the mantelpiece": quoted in Newquist, *Conversations*, 268.

76 "opened the doors wide for me": ibid.

76 "have begun to write poetry": quoted in Shalit, ed., *Laughing Matters*, 239.

76 "a trace of Walt Whitman": Lisle Bell, "Verses That Click," *New York Herald Tribune Books*, 18 January 1931.

77 "come along in a long time": "Ogden Nash, a Nonchalant Rhymester," *New York Times Book Review*, 25 January 1931.

77 "as if it were identical with *sinus*": Max Eastman, *Enjoyment of Laughter* (New York: Simon and Schuster, 1936), 120.

78 "the turbulence of the decade": Robert A. Gates, *American Literary Humor During the Great Depression* (Westport: Greenwood Press, 1999), 56.

79 Katharine White on Farley poem: KW to ON, 2 December 1935, NYPL.

80 "and fair perished with laughter": Rupert Hughes to Simon and Schuster, 17 October 1933, HRC.

80 Nash voting: ON to John Goodspeed [August 1965], HRC.

81 "We live on political tiptoe up here": ON to Mrs. Edmund Nash, 20 July [1936], private papers of LNS.

81 Nash reaction to offensive remark: LNS and INE, interviews by the author.

6. HOLLYWOOD BECKONS

84 "depths of the Depression": Neil Gabler, *Empire of Their Own* (New York: Anchor Books/Doubleday, 1988), 316.

85 "the more giddily cultured he could feel himself": quoted in ibid., 325.

85 "the professional wrestling racquet": Ford, *Laughter*, 151.

85 "I should need six weeks": quoted in Sheridan Morley, *Tales from the Hollywood Raj* (New York: Viking, 1983), 87.

85 "It is indeed amazing": quoted in ibid., 88.

86 "a very large faemmle": quoted in ibid., 58.

86 "at whatever moment suits them": ON to Mrs. Edmund Nash, 20 July 1936, private papers of LNS. It is not clear what show Nash was referring to, but it may have been *Family Album*.

86 Perelman background: Dorothy Herrmann, *S. J. Perelman* (New York: Papermac, 1988), 45–111.

86 "Edsel of the entertainment industry": S. J. Perelman, "Cloudland Remembered," *Film Comment* (Film Society of Lincoln Center), vol. 14, no. 2 (March–April 1978), 25.

87 "Neuritis or Neuralgia Building": ibid. At a meeting of the American Academy of Arts and Letters held after Nash's death, Perelman also provided an amusing account of his collaboration with Nash. Proceedings of the Academy, Second Series, No. 22, New York, 1972. In that account, Perelman said he had not met Nash until 1937 in the MGM caffeteria.

87 "more communists than Karl Marx": quoted in Gabler, *Empire*, 322.

87 "dismissed me as a parlor pink": ON to John Goodspeed [August 1965], HRC.

87 *The Firefly* File, MGM Collection, University of Southern California, Los Angeles.

88 "knock-knock-knocking at your heart": ON to Mrs. Edmund Nash, undated, private papers of LNS.

88 Stromberg story conferences: Herrmann, *S. J. Perelman*, 115–116.

88 "really a pretty hard blow": ON to FLN, 17 April 1937, HRC.

89 Hacketts' recollection: Albert and Frances Hackett, interview by DW, Dartmouth.

89 "hanging around him" and "why don't you yell": ibid.

89 "a regular in this league": ON to DL, 25 November [1936], Longwell Collection.

89 "looking forward to the B & O": ON to FLN, 20 January 1937, HRC.

90 Illness of Nash's mother: Smith Ms.

90 "It isn't dignified": quoted in ON to FLN, 9 April 1937, HRC.

90 "yours for more than ever": ON to FLN [April 1937], HRC.

91 "as if nice people had lived in it": ON to FLN, 22 April 1937, HRC.

91 "felt extraordinarily deprived": Smith Ms.

91 "two poems a week": ON to Mrs. Edmund Nash, undated, private papers of LNS.

92 "waiting for the phone to ring": *Baltimore Sunday American, Green Spotlight Magazine*, 27 November 1938, 10.

92   "and that little boy is adopted": quoted in Laura Veiller Rivkin, interview by DW, Dartmouth.

93   "the reformed alcoholic": quoted in Robert Westbrook, *Intimate Lies* (New York: HarperCollins, 1995), 31.

93   "sweet nature that came through": quoted in Aaron Latham, *Crazy Sundays* (New York: Viking, 1971), 8.

93   "not very funny stuff": ibid.

94   "so long as Ernest is around": quoted in ibid., 21.

94   Sheilah Graham background: Westbrook, *Intimate Lies*, 54–90.

94   "Dorothy Parker and Eddie Mayer": Sheilah Graham, *The Garden of Allah* (New York: Crown, 1970), 59.

95   "exploded into laughter": ibid., 59–60.

95   "found out in her life": Westbrook, *Intimate Lies*, 286.

95   "you will see what I mean": F. Scott Fitzgerald, *The Letters of F. Scott Fitzgerald*, ed. Andrew Turnbull (New York: Charles Scribner's Sons, 1963), 24–25.

96   "save Marie Antoinette": quoted in Westbrook, *Intimate Lies*, 287.

96   "In the presence of Ogden Nash": David L. Goodrich, *The Real Nick and Nora* (Carbondale, Ill.: Southern Illinois University Press, 2001), 122.

97   Nash couplets: quoted in Laura Veiller Rivkin, Cornwell Jackson, and Albert and Frances Hackett, interviews by DW, Dartmouth.

97   "my phone finally rang": quoted in *Baltimore Sunday American, Green Spotlight Magazine*, 27 November 1938, 10.

98   Nash and Mankiewicz: Latham, *Crazy Sundays*, 121–122.

98   "as he had written them": quoted in *Baltimore Sunday American, Green Spotlight Magazine*, 10.

98   "doing it for mother": Smith, ed., *Loving Letters*, 192.

98   "haven't lost the knack": ON to HR, undated, NYPL.

98   "my own stuff": ON to FLN, 18 March 1939, HRC.

99   Mankiewicz comment: ON to FLN, 11 April 1939, Smith, ed., *Loving Letters*, 204.

99   "exclaim Oh boy": ON to Bruce Gould, 25 November 1940, Special Collections, Princeton University Libraries.

99   Expecting to finish work: ON to D/ML, 30 December 1940, HRC.

99   Nash treatment: Smith, ed., *Loving Letters*, 206.

7. AT HOME IN BALTIMORE

100   "one side or the other, if not both": Francis A. Beirne, *The Amiable Baltimoreans* (Hatboro, Pa.: Tradition Press, 1968), 284–287.

101   "As the fingers of Senor Iturbi": quoted in Daniel H. Labby, M.D., letter to the author.

101   Nash relations with Leonards: Smith, ed., *Loving Letters*, 318; LNS, interview by the author.

102   Description of Rugby Road house: Smith, ed., *Loving Letters*, 207–210.

102   Nash servants: INE and FE, interviews by the author.

103 "save the precious crop from greedy birds": Smith, ed., *Loving Letters*, 210.

104 "left much to be desired": ibid., 211.

105 LNS, interview by the author.

106 Ferry trip: LNS interview by the author.

109 "go back there sometime": ON to DL, 11 March 1941, Longwell Collection.

109 Letters describing lectures: ON to FLN, 11, 13, 15, 16, and 25 November 1941, Smith, ed., *Loving Letters*, 214–223; ON to FLN, [25 November 1941] and 7 February 1942, HRC.

109 "his wife's pecan pie": ON to FLN, 25 November 1941, Smith, ed., *Loving Letters*, 222.

109 "medium attractive and not very bright": ON to FLN, 15 November 1941, ibid., 218.

109 "my own stagnant complacency": ON to FLN, 7 February 1942, HRC.

110 "unattainable and irrecoverable past": ON to FLN, 27 November 1941, HRC.

110 News of Pearl Harbor: Smith, ed., *Loving Letters*, 223.

110 Nash attempts to serve: ibid.; MacLeish to Nash, telegram, 8 December 1941, HRC.

111 "would not laugh until a nun laughed": E. J. Kahn, *About* The New Yorker *and Me* (New York: G. P. Putnam's Sons, 1979), 229.

111 "photographs of himself for free": Ogden Nash, "Words to Fit the Music," in *My Most Inspiring Moment*, Robert Fitzgibbon and Ernest V. Heyn, eds. (Garden City: Doubleday, 1965), 119.

111 Street letter: Julian Street to ON, 29 January 1945, HRC.

111 "twelfth man on the field": quoted in Newquist, *Conversations*, 269.

111 "still fifty-five years off" and "being censored": ON to "Mr. Shaw," 15 February 1945, Library of Congress.

112 "Four Prominent Bastards" sent to troops: Ogden Nash, interview [interviewer unidentified], 27 May 1970, Nash Collection, Dartmouth.

112 Wartime life: Smith, ed., *Loving Letters*, 224, 229.

8. *ONE TOUCH OF VENUS*

113 "on the Offenbach line": Ronald Sanders, *The Days Grow Short: The Life and Music of Kurt Weill* (New York: Holt, Rinehart and Winston, 1980), 322.

114 "he'd never done lyrics": Cheryl Crawford, *One Naked Individual: My Fifty Years in the Theatre* (New York: Bobbs-Merrill, 1977), 117.

114 "adjunct to wartime travel": Nash, "Words to Fit the Music," 118.

114 "named after Alexander Voollcott," quoted in ibid.

115 "dog-eared copy of Tschaikowsky": Ogden Nash, "Lines from a Lyricist at Bay," *New York Times*, August 20, 1944.

115 "a masterpiece or a mouse": ON to FLN, 14 October 1942, Smith, ed., *Loving Letters*, 230.

115 "the disturbing matter of the book": ON to FLN, 13 October 1942, HRC.

115 Nash and Perelman at the Harvard Club: Dorothy Herrmann, *S. J. Perelman* (New York: Simon and Schuster, 1986), 148.

116 Plot of *Venus*: Agnes De Mille, *And Promenade Home* (Boston: Little Brown, 1958), 90; Sanders, *The Days Grow Short*, 327.

116 "talk was finished for the evening": Crawford, *One Naked Individual*, 118.

117 "Mary would like to sing it": Nash, "Words to Fit the Music," 121.

117 "Think about it": ibid., 122.

117 "frustration and amnesia": Nash, "Lines from a Lyricist at Bay."

117 "better than I did": Nash, "Words to Fit the Music," 122.

117 "with a kind of a quavery German sound": Mary Martin, *My Heart Belongs to Daddy* (New York: William Morrow, 1976), 108.

118 "those kind brown eyes": ibid., 110.

118 "from one musical number to the next": Elia Kazan, *A Life* (New York: William Morrow, 1988), 234.

118 "I never read that kind of thing": quoted in Crawford, *One Naked Individual*, 128–129.

118 "for which I had no talent": Kazan, *A Life*, 234.

119 "proved no help": De Mille, *And Promenade Home*, 90. Miss de Mille's reference to Kazan's background was imprecise. In the thirties Kazan had acted at New York's Group Theater, along with Lee Strasberg, Clifford Odets, and Stella and Luther Adler. He was a founder of the Actors Studio in 1947.

119 "a part of [his] life experience": Kazan, *A Life*, 234.

119 "might as well not open": quoted in De Mille, *And Promenade Home*, 94.

119 "testicles": quoted in Crawford, *One Naked Individual*, 130.

119 "get on with it": quoted in De Mille, *And Promenade Home*, 105–108.

120 Kaufman advice: Crawford, *One Naked Individual*, 134.

120 "lasted a good three weeks": De Mille, *And Promenade Home*, 72.

120 "evolve a wonderful effect": quoted in Crawford, *One Naked Individual*, 135–136.

121 "including her breasts": quoted in ibid., 133.

121 "never mentioned again": ibid., 131–132.

121 "This is Daddy's play": quoted in Smith, ed., *Loving Letters*, 3.

122 Wolcott Gibbs's reaction: Nash, "Lecture at University of North Carolina."

122 The Opening Chorus and the other quoted songs are from S. J. Perelman and Ogden Nash, *One Touch of Venus* (Boston: Little, Brown, 1944).

125 "the woman who could not": De Mille, *And Promenade Home*, 208–209.

126 "who took first place": Crawford, *One Naked Individual*, 139.

126 "established myself at last": ibid., 144.

126 "descendant of Venus": Martin, *My Heart Belongs*, 114.

127 "picked a 100:1 shot": Nash, "Lecture at University of North Carolina."

9. LYRICS BY NASH

128 "Watching it sitting down": ON to Weill, 18 December 1943, TYML.

129 "a gilded sanitorium": ON to Weill, 22 December 1943, ibid.

129 "fighting and frolicking again": ON to Weill, 19 January 1944, ibid.

129   "it made quite an impression": Weill to Lenya, 7 July 1944, Lys Symonette and Kim H. Kowalke, eds. and trans., *Speak Low: The Letters of Kurt Weill and Lotte Lenya* (Berkeley: University of California Press, 1996), no. 319.

129   "you will like our treatment": ON to Weill, 7 July 1944, TYML.

130   "'T' Hell with them": Weill to Lenya, 26 July 1944, Symonette and Kowalke, eds., *Speak Low*, no. 332.

130   "having a wonderful time in New York": Weill to Lenya, 4 August 1944, Symonette and Kowalke, eds., *Speak Low*, no. 339.

130   "Do let me know": ON to Weill, 27 August 1944, TYML.

130   "makes good for all his shortcomings": Weill to Lenya, 24 August 1944, Symonette and Kowalke, eds., *Speak Low*, no. 353.

131   "as soon as I find the right book": Weill to Lenya, ibid., no. 359.

131   Perelman on *Sweet Bye and Bye*: S. J. Perelman to J. J. Kapstein, 16 March 1945, Prudence Crowther, ed., *Don't Tread on Me: The Selected Letters of S. J. Perelman* (New York: Penguin, 1988), 60.

131   "dilettantes in comfortable circumstances": Vernon Duke, *Passport to Paris* (Boston: Little, Brown, 1955), 8.

131   "happen to be in my body": ibid., 177.

132   "not even getting into production": ON to Weill, 24 July [1945], TYML.

133   "the best way I know how": ON to FLN, 17 October 1945, Smith, ed., *Loving Letters*, 236.

133   "I just want to sleep with you": ON to FLN, [October 1945], HRC.

133   "For Frances," Smith, ed., *Loving Letters*, 237. The poem was not published during Nash's lifetime.

134   "shelter my carcass": ON to Weill, 24 January 1946, TYML.

134   "out to crucify me": Hirschfeld, interview by the author.

134   "so many empty chairs in my life": Duke, *Passport to Paris*, 436–437.

135   "stayed here to face the music": Al Hirschfeld, interview by the author.

135   "their money I was betting": quoted in "Ogden Nash," Associated Press Biographical Service, no. 3772, 1 October 1952.

135   Weill and Felix Jackson: Weill to ON, 19 December 1947, TYML.

136   "doesn't like him": Duke, *Passport to Paris*, 431–432.

136   "Fast from Vernon": quoted in ibid.

136   "too luscious for me": ON to INE, 14 March 1948, Smith, ed., *Loving Letters*, 242.

136   "exchanged irascibilities before": ON to Duke, 20 August 16, private papers of LNS.

136   "everyday living and loving": Producers' Prospectus, Curtis Brown Collection, Columbia.

136   "has a wonderful time," and "most of the needed money": *Life*, 7 March 1949, 19–20.

137   "Composer of Unproduced Shows": Duke, *Passport to Paris*, 473.

137   "do some work together again": ON to Duke, 10 January [1952], private papers of LNS.

137   "to get me out here": ON to INE, 25 February [1952], ibid.

137   "best feature in the show": Duke, *Passport to Paris*, 481.

138   "I didn't fall for you": quoted in Barbara Leaming, *Bette Davis* (New York: Simon and Schuster, 1992), 255.

138   "thick with scalps" and "they drop it on your sore toe": Nash, Lecture at University of North Carolina.

139   Davis treatment: Leaming, *Bette Davis*, 255–256.

139   "a lesser Loesser": ON to Duke, 12 June [1953], private papers of LNS.

139   *White Rhino*: Perelman to Leila Hadley, 17 June 1955, Crowther, ed., *Don't Tread on Me*, 170.

139   Bagley career: Ben Bagley, interview by the author; "Ben Bagley, 64; Produced Off Broadway Hits," *New York Times*, 27 March 1998.

140   "to thrust in his face": Ben Bagley, jacket for *The Littlest Revue*, compact disc PSCD-112.

140   "doesn't know what he's doing": quoted by Ben Bagley, interview by the author.

140   "quite an honor": quoted by Bagley, ibid.

141   "a 1946 musical that closed out of town": John S. Wilson, "Unlucky Shows but Good Music," *New York Times*, 25 April 1970.

142   "you can't do that in the theater": Hirschfeld, interview by the author.

142   "until he got the message": quoted in Everett S. Allen, *Famous American Humorous Poets* (New York: Dodd, Mead, 1968), 93.

142   "What was that again? when sung": Vernon Duke, *Listen Here!* (New York: Ivan Obolensky, 1963), 267.

10. THE CHILDREN GROW UP

144   "fish seven days a week": ON to DL, 29 June 1945, Longwell Collection.

144   "no stern untoned": quoted in Smith, ed., *Loving Letters*, 234.

144   "incessant beach outings": Duke, *Passport to Paris*, 433.

145   "we managed to communicate": ON to Mrs. Leonard, 12 August 1949, HRC.

145   "swing the other way": ON to Mrs. Leonard, 17 August 1949, Smith, ed., *Loving Letters*, 249.

145   "anointing our feet in antiquity": ON to Duke, 20 August 1949, private papers of LNS.

145   "but I'm glad it did": ON to Mrs. Leonard, 24 August 1949, HRC.

146   "change costumes under 5 minutes": ON to Mrs. Leonard, 30 August 1949, Smith, ed., *Loving Letters*, 253.

146   "basin of Neptune at Versailles": ON to Mrs. Leonard, 5 September 1949, HRC.

146   "French children speak fluent French": ON to Mrs. Leonard, 6 August 1949, ibid.

146   "put their money paper in the bathroom": ON to Mrs. Leonard, 12 August 1949, ibid.

146   "bismuth and paregoric and indispensable": ON to Mrs. Leonard (postcard), 25 August 1949, ibid.

146 "costs more than the wine": ON to Duke, 20 August 1949, private papers of LNS.

146 "the most florid and ingenuous terms": ON to Mrs. Leonard, 30 August 1949, Smith, ed., *Loving Letters*, 253.

146 "weren't really as bad as that": ON to Mrs. Leonard, 12 August 1949, HRC.

147 "outnumber our difficult moments": ON to Mrs. Leonard, 21 August 1949, ibid.

147 ON to Mrs. Leonard, 1 September 1949, ibid.

148 "publication of your stuff": HR to ON, 25 October 1949, NYPL.

148 Linell's activities: LNS, interview by the author.

148 "bouquet upon his breast": quoted in Smith, ed., *Loving Letters*, 262.

149 "All my love, Daddy": ON to INE, 19 October 1950, Smith, ed., *Loving Letters*, 260–261.

150 Background of John Smith: LNS, interview by the author.

150 "a very immature nineteen": ON to Duke, 18 June 1951, private papers of LNS.

150 "won't know a photographer from Cecil Beaton": ON to DL, 12 September 1951, Longwell Collection.

150 "masculine mind to cope with": Ogden Nash, "Poem by the Father of a Bride, Aged 19," *Life*, 29 October 1951, 133.

151 "Must change the conversation": quoted by INE, video tape of BBC program "A Golden Trashery of Ogden Nashery," 1976.

151 Conversation with Linell: unidentified magazine clipping, private papers of LNS.

151 "speak with such genuine emotion": ON to LNS, October 1951, private papers of LNS.

152 "only for the first few months": LNS, interview with the author.

152 "born in Paris for all we know": Duke, *Passport to Paris*, 433.

152 "20,000 words and starting over": ON to Duke [1954], private papers of LNS.

152 Eberstadt background: FE, interview with the author.

152 Dinner at the Café Cardinale: ibid.

153 "too much for most young men": ON to Duke, 9 September 1954, private papers of LNS.

153 "rosy mist of simple-minded adoration": ON to Arthur Roberts, 18 July 1953, private papers of William S. Rogers.

11. ECONOMICS OF POETRY: SELLING THE WARES

154 "harder to get rid of": Robert Frost, *New Hampshire* (Hanover: New Directions Press, 1951).

154 "in the way of breakfast food": Newquist, *Conversations*, 266.

155 Perelman on Nash: Crowther, ed., *Don't Tread on Me*, xviii.

156 Cameron as Nash editor: D. Angus Cameron, interview by the author.

156 "to him I give two dollars": AC to ON, 4 September 1964, Curtis Brown Collection.

157 "you will find it enclosed": James Sherman to AC, 25 March 1954, Files of Little, Brown.

157 Nash finances: ON to AC, 9 July 1964, and ON to Edith Haggard, 1 July [1962], Curtis Brown Collection.

157 Record of verse published: Crandell, *Ogden Nash*, 64–118, 304–337.

158 Little, Brown memorandum: A.R.M. to Arthur Thornhill, 15 July 1947, Files of Little, Brown.

159 "but look at the cover": quoted in Crandell, *Ogden Nash*, 123.

159 Nash dislike of "Pastoral": James Sherman to Freeman Lewis, 17 February 1955, Files of Little, Brown.

159 "the book trade generally": AC to Arthur Thornhill, 11 May 1950, ibid.

159 "favorable to its coming up": AC to Arthur Thornhill, 18 May 1950, ibid.

160 "excitement and success into copy and layout": quoted in AC to Stanley Salmen, 24 January 1951, ibid.

160 Cameron and Nash: AC, interview by the author.

161 "the orneriness of things": Charles Poore, *New York Times*, 9 April 1953.

161 "the Nash poem at its best": *Time*, 13 April 1953.

162 "the Nick of time": Lloyd Frankenberg, "Father Nash's Mother Goose," *New York Times Book Review*, 10 November 1957, 39.

162 "if it's not carrying nepotism too far": ON to James Sherman, 6 January 1958, Files of Little, Brown.

162 "the artist's medium": Helen Jones to James Sherman, memorandum, 14 January 1958, ibid.

162 Jones's approval: 20 January 1961, ibid.

163 "a little steady income": quoted in Newquist, *Conversations*, 269–270.

163 Little, Brown Summary, Memorandum, 8 November 1961, Files of Little, Brown.

164 "the wrong thing was easier": Ogden Nash, "Victoria," *Harper's Bazaar*, April 1948, 161, 196.

164 "something badly expressed": quoted in Patricia Baum, "A Visit with Ogden Nash," April 4, 1968, unidentified clipping, Nash Collection, Dartmouth.

164 Hallmark verses: Files of Hallmark Cards, Kansas City, MO.

165 "a contradiction in terms": ON to AC, 19 July [?], Curtis Brown Collection.

165 "I've smoked Lucky Strike": Advertisement, *New York Times*, 21 July 1953.

165 Defense of smoking: Ogden Nash, "The Kinsey Report didn't upset me, either," *Saturday Evening Post*, 14 March 1964; Nash, "To Those Readers Who Were Good Enough to Write Me About 'One Man's Cigarettes,'" undated, HRC.

166 Merrill Lynch correspondence: Janet K. Low to EJ, 24 June and 8 September 1965, and Janet K. Low to ON, 7 October 1965, Curtis Brown Collection.

12. FROM RADIO TO LECTURE HALL TO TELEVISION

168 "particular zest to the audio format": John Dunning, *Tune in Yesterday* (Englewood Cliffs, N.J.: Prentice-Hall, 1976), 125–126.

168 "wasn't born yesterday": Cornwell Jackson, interview by DW, Dartmouth; Smith, ed., *Loving Letters*, 203–204.

169 "won't know until Sunday night": ON to FLN, 11 April 1939, Smith, ed., *Loving Letters*, 204.

169 "As dumb as you would imagine": ON to FLN [18 April 1939], HRC.

169 "not going to bark like a dog": Naomi Burton Stone, interview by the author.

169 "able to offer me her arms": ON to Kurt Weill, 18 December 1943, TYML.

170 "brings in a few dollars": ON to Duke, 12 June [1953], private papers of LNS.

170 "sell the medicine without the pretty girl": ON to DL [1945] from Lewiston, Idaho, Longwell Collection.

170 "always screaming about gas leaks and things": videotape of BBC program "A Golden Trashery of Ogden Nashery" (1976), private papers of LNS.

171 "and he retrieved it a hundred yards away": ON to FLN, 4 May 1950, Smith, ed., *Loving Letters*, 258.

171 "smaller than the bathroom": ON to FLN, 4 October 1950, HRC.

171 "flaming desert and millionaires": ON to FLN, 25 January 1951, ibid.

171 "an ebullient moustache": ON to FLN, 8 October 1950, ibid.

172 "petunias and the drying wash": ON to FLN, 3 May 1950, Smith, ed., *Loving Letters*, 257.

172 Postcards: ON to LNS, postcard, 22 January 1951, and ON to INE, postcard, 9 March 1951, ibid., 271, 278.

172 "I suspect brilliant guy": ON to FLN, 25 January 1951, HRC.

172 "so I could say I had": ON to FLN, 28 January 1951, Smith, ed., *Loving Letters*, 274.

172 "Oklahoma City is now mine": ON to FLN, 23 January 1951, ibid., 269.

173 "wire his delight to Colston Leigh": ON to FLN, [3 May 1950], HRC.

173 "and the common cold": ON to FLN, 9 March 1951, Smith, ed., *Loving Letters*, 278.

173 "advertising sense is still there": ON to AC, 6 March 1951, Files of Little, Brown.

174 "when I was out there before": ON to Duke, August [1951], private papers of LNS.

174 Masquerade Party: videotape, Museum of Broadcasting, New York City.

174 "warming the cold palms": quoted in Margaret McManus, "Ogden Nash," *Providence Journal TV Weekly*, 5 April 1959.

175 Nash compensation "fabulous": ON to Duke, 29 November [1953], private papers of LNS.

175 Kostelanetz's idea for *Carnival*: Andre Kostelanetz, in collaboration with Gloria Hammond, *Echoes, Memoirs of Andre Kostelanetz* (New York: Harcourt Brace Jovanovich, 1981), 226–227.

176 "still got holes in it": Paul V. Beckley, "Ogden Nash, No Musician, Giving Orchestral Rendition," *New York Herald Tribune*, 10 December 1953.

13. LAUREATE OF THE AGE OF FRICTION

177 "introducing into poetry 'familiar matters of today'": Clifton Fadiman, *Party of One* (Cleveland: World Publishing, 1955), 66–67.

178 "tax may even become confiscatory": ibid., 69.

178 "loaded for bear": Leonard Bacon, "Humors and Careers," *Saturday Review of Literature*, April 29, 1939, 3–4.

178 "didn't seem likely to return": Yagoda, *About Town*, 116.

179 "a 30-year-old humorist": ON to HR, 7 November 1949, NYPL.

179 "some other line of work years ago": HR to ON, 14 November 1949, NYPL.

179 "She's in Hollywood": quoted in *Baltimore Sun*, [April] 1949, private papers of Linell Nash Smith.

181 "outlive 'Candy is Dandy'": ON to Sherman, 24 February 1955, Files of Little, Brown.

183 "not the author's own": quoted in Louis Hasley, "The Golden Trashery of Ogden Nashery," *Arizona Quarterly* 27 (Spring 1971), 247.

186 Hammarskjold Memorial Lecture: Madeline S. Patton to ON, 13 January 1964, Curtis Brown Collection.

186 "swept the literary circles of Leningrad": Richard Pipes to ON, 1 November 1962, HRC.

186 Soviet magazine *Novyi Mir*: Irene Komarova to ON, 12 February 1963, ibid.

186 "light verse and serious thought": Louis Untermeyer, *The Pursuit of Poetry* (New York: Simon and Schuster, 1969), 217.

187 "W. H. Auden, Morris Bishop": David McCord, "A Cache of Ogden Nash," *New York Times Book Review*, 9 June 1959.

187 Auden borrowing from Nash: Nicholas Jenkins, "Goodbye, 1939," *The New Yorker*, 1 April 1997, 88, 94.

187 "'a responsible position, haven't you'": quoted in W. H. Auden to Mrs. Dodds, 1939, Auden letter quoted in Bodleian Library to the author, 25 April 1997.

187 "they all have little marks": Marianne Moore to ON, 7 February 1962.

188 "bludgeoned into giving a reading": Isidore Salomon to Katharine Biddle, 23 January 1960, Biddle Collection, Georgetown University.

188 National Poetry Festival: program of the National Poetry Festival, 1962, and sound recording of the Festival, Library of Congress.

188 "growing more expensive": ON to DL, 23 May 1965, Longwell Collection.

188 "a house and a burial plot": Evan Hill, "The Literary Scene in Newport, New Hampshire," *Boston Globe*, August 17, 1975.

189 "no man could have written them": W. H. Auden, Foreword, in Phyllis McGinley, *Times Three* (New York: Viking Press, 1960), x.

189 "have only one—or neither": ON to McGinley, 8 May 1933, McGinley Collection, Syracuse University, Syracuse, New York.

190 "after mine have been published": ON to Arthur Roberts, 23 December 1955, private papers of William S. Rogers.

190 "so happily confirmed": ON to McGinley, 2 May 1961, HRC.

190 "far more than I do": McGinley to ON, 3 May 1961, ibid.

190 "Samuel Eliot Morison and Ogden Nash": Charles Poore, "Books of the Times," *New York Times*, 30 October 1962.

190 "imposed it on the world": Morris Bishop, "Beau Nash at His Best," *New York Times Book Review*, 11 November 1962, 10.

14. ANOTHER DAY, ANOTHER DOLOR

192 "almost insufferable burden": Smith, ed., *Loving Letters*, 301.

192 "polyps from the lower gut": ON to DL, 20 January 1958, Longwell Collection.

193 "most earnest efforts": ON to RA, 12 May 1958, NYPL.

193 "not feeling well": Dr. Phillip Wagley to ON, 14 July 1959, Curtis Brown Collection.

193 "put it right immediately": RA to ON, 30 July 1959, NYPL.

193 "my rapacious agent": ON to KW, 23 April, [1962], Mariam Coffin Canaday Library, Bryn Mawr College, Bryn Mawr, Pa.

193 "arms leave ample room": ON to RA [26 August 1963], NYPL.

193 Lectures canceled: ON to DL, 27 September [1963], Longwell Collection.

194 "any form of alcohol except beer": ON to LNS, 25 November 1964, Smith, ed., *Loving Letters*, 314.

194 "turmoil of New York": ON to Duke, 4 March 1965, private papers of LNS.

194 "at least to middle age": ON to Duke, 4 June 1965, ibid.

194 "'post-dated checktomy'": ON to D/ML, 10–14 January 1966, Longwell Collection.

194 "the operation is child's play": ON to Duke, 23 February 1966, private papers of LNS.

195 "for so many years have departed": ON to Duke, 2 June 1966, ibid.

195 "sacroiliac is psychosomatic": Ogden Nash, *Bed Riddance* (Boston: Little, Brown, 1968), 3.

196 "strongly, indeed bitterly": ON to W. C. Leigh, 13 November 1968, Curtis Brown Collection.

196 Leigh response: W. C. Leigh to Nash, 12 December 1968, ibid.

196 "end the Vietnam War in 3 days": ON to Laura and Allan Rivkin, 13 December 1966, Dartmouth.

196 "Senator McCarthy in the primaries": ON to D/ML, 3 April 1968, Longwell Collection.

197 "the direction of the nation": Smith, ed., *Loving Letters*, 324.

197 "which one to vote against": ON to Duke, 16 September 1968, private papers of LNS.

197 "world they [were] bucking against": quoted in Mohammed Rauf, Jr., "Nash the Versifier," *Baltimore News American*, February 16, 1968.

197 White House invitation: FE, interview by the author.

197 "it's too individual": quotes in Alden Whitman, "For Nash, Candy Is Dandy, but Dated," *New York Times*, 5 December 1968.

198 "political and social reform": Ogden Nash, Commencement Address, Miss Porter's School, June 1970, private papers of LNS.

198 "whole silly business": quoted in Newquist, *Conversations*, 267.

199 "the first casualty of war": quoted in Smith, ed., *Loving Letters*, 323.

200 "for your eyes alone": ON to EJ, 1 February 1968, Curtis Brown Collection.

200 "back at work": ON to D/ML, 2 April 1968, Longwell Collection.

200 "cash, not credit": David C. Mearns to ON, 28 February 1968, HRC.

201 Request for minutes: ON to D/ML, 29 November 1966, Longwell Collection.

201 "shared only with him": Smith, ed., *Loving Letters*, vii–viii.

201 HRC Collection: George W. Crandell, "'A Good Bad Poet': The Ogden Nash Collection," *Library Chronicle of the University of Texas at Austin*, New Series no. 16 (1981), 64.

201 Price of collection: Lew David Feldman to ON, 11 February 1967, Dartmouth.

201 "as a wife and mother": Smith, ed., *Loving Letters*, 302.

202 Move to Sparks: LNS, interview by the author.

202 Nash letter to Scherman: ON to Harry Scherman, 11 December 1966, Curtis Brown Collection.

203 "more prominent than in Herald Trib credits": ON to INE, 19 November 1964, private papers of INE.

203 "best dressed ten group": ON to Duke, 4 June 1965, private papers of LNS.

203 Isabel's illnesses: Smith, ed., *Loving Letters*, 322–323, 327.

15. BALTIMORE *REDUX* AND LITTLE BOAR'S HEAD

205 Lunch at the Lobster House: Al Hirschfeld, interview by the author.

205 "never wandered from Balt.": quoted in "New York City to Nash? 'Balt.' Is More a Smash," *New York Times*, 30 July 1965.

206 "God bless them": quoted in "Contrite Poet Gives a Cheer for Bronx on Golden Jubilee," *New York Times*, 24 May 1964.

206 Nash poem on Mets: Lawrence Van Gelder, "Victory Stirs a Controlled Joy in City," *New York Times*, 25 September 1969.

206 "some aristocratic blooms": ON to DL, 7 May 1965, Longwell Collection.

206 "at home in neither": ON to Duke, 4 June 1965, private papers of LNS.

206 "survey of his estate": Louis G. Panos, "Ogden Nash Makes a Dash," *Cedar Rapids Gazette*, 28 June 1966.

207 "without getting in their hair": ON to DL, [23 May] 1965, Longwell Collection.

207 "a fortunate man": ON to D/ML, 17 March 1966, Longwell Collection.

208 "to near thunder": Tom White, "Fast Wit on the Mile Track," *Baltimore News American*, 23 May 1971.

208 Nash on Baltimore Colts: Ogden Nash, "Colts Is the Name, Football's the Game," *Life*, 13 December 1968, 75.

208 "'as good as he says he is'": Ogden Nash, "A Poet's Lament," *Life*, 24 January 1969, 1.

209 History of Little Boar's Head: *First Report of the Historic District Commission of the Village District of Little Boar's Head*, 7 July 1994.

209 James Roosevelt and Eleanor Goldsborough: LNS, interview by the author.

209 "in the mind like a mirage": Smith, ed., *Loving Letters*, 180.

209 Teenage pranks: Katherine Hobson Southworth, interview by the author.

209 "friendly Hampton bank": ON to INE, 31 July 1962, private papers of INE.

210 "even ahead of his work": Lewis Nichols, "An American Notebook, Muse at Home," *New York Times Book Review*, 24 November 1968.

211 "you've never said a thing": quoted by INE, interview with the author.

211 "so we call her Catherine": ON to Linell (Nell) Smith, 23 May 1968, private papers of LNS.

211 Nash routine: Clarence Collins, interview by DW, Dartmouth.

212 "one shining haul": Ogden Nash, Untitled, in R. A. Southworth, *A History of St. Andrew's By-the-Sea* (Rye Beach: St. Andrew's Church, 1993).

212 "a year away from medicare": quoted in Mrs. G. L. Redmond to the author, 28 March 1996.

212 "to sin some more": Robert and Katherine Southworth, interview by the author.

213 "as many of their parents as possible": ON to LNS, 20 July 1968, private papers of LNS.

213 "more than the weekly mealtime relationship": ON to INE, 10 September 1963, private papers of INE.

213 "and half of mine": ON to LNS, 12 July 1965, private papers of LNS.

213 "the Kangaroo rat": ON to INE, 3 August 1965, Smith, ed., *Loving Letters*, 316.

214 Fortune telling: Brigid Robins and Frances Smith, interview by the author.

214 The Beatles: Linell (Nell) Smith, interview by the author.

214 "those difficult decisions": ON to LNS, 20 July 1968, private papers of Linell Nash Smith.

214 "won't force him into it": ON to LNS, 25 July 1968, ibid.

16. THE WISE OWLS OF FORTY-THIRD STREET

216 First Reading Agreement: Agreement, 6 January 1958, NYPL.

216 "my continuing one": ON to RA, 25 August 1966, ibid.

217 "money from this magazine": GL to ON, 26 January 1944, ibid.

217 "a little more dough": ON to GL, 2 February 1944, ibid.

217 "send you a check. See": GL to ON, 4 January 1945, ibid.

217 "getting Nash poems again": KW to ON, 11 April 1947, ibid.

217 "we became friends": quoted in Yagoda, *About Town*, 162.

217 "a great asset to the magazine": HR to ON, 16 July 1947, NYPL.

217 "a rhyme left in my Eberhard Faber #2": ON to HR, 16 January 1948, ibid.

218 "pull on him if necessary": HR to GL, undated, ibid.

218 "taste was exactly right": RA, interview by the author.

219 "it was not a lot of fun": ibid.

219 "relationship with my editor easier": ON to RA, 12 May 1958, NYPL.

219 "*De mortuis nil nisi bonum*": Ogden Nash, "Lines to Be Carved on Coogan's Bluff," *The New Yorker*, 28 September 1957, 33.

220 "altering the first couplet": ON to RA, 2 February 1965, NYPL.

220 "uneasy and somewhat illiterate": RA to ON, 15 May 1959, ibid.

220 "fine ending to the poem": RA to ON, 12 April 1959, ibid.

220 "*too* easy for our readers": RA to ON, 15 March 1960, ibid.

221 "Slavic, if you wish": 25 November 1966, ibid.

221 "in the toll collector's hand": RA to ON, 4 January 1965, ibid.

222 "didn't always feel well": RA to ON, 4 January 1967, ibid.

222 "chore too long neglected": ON to RA, 6 January 1967, ibid.

222 "concomitant of acceptance": ON to RA, 4 March 1967, ibid.

223 "more often in your pages": ON to RA, 5 September 1966, ibid.

223 "gratitude is unbounded": ON to RA, 24 February 1961, ibid.

224 "an impossible thought": RA to ON, 28 February 1961, ibid.

224 "What more can a writer ask": ON to RA, 1 March 1961, ibid.

224 "sound of laughter": RA to ON, 19 April 1965, ibid.

224 "see eye to eye with me": ON to EJ, undated, Curtis Brown Collection.

225 "ninety years old ourselves": RA to EJ, 26 November 1969, HRC.

227 "doesn't say much of anything": RA to EJ, 26 September 1966, NYPL.

227 "as you are settled in": RA to ON, 25 November 1966, ibid.

227 "more cheerful than in years": RA to EJ, 6 December 1966, ibid.

228 "pull up his chlamys": ON to RA, 24 January 1967, ibid.

228 Submissions to *New Yorker*: ON to Duke, 31 August 1967, private papers of LNS.

228 "his best for us in a long time": RA to EJ, 12 February 1968, NYPL.

228 "and see what happens": EJ to ON, 13 August 1970, Curtis Brown Collection.

229 "to the well before long": ON to EJ, 2 September 1970, ibid.

229 "lost touch forever": ON to RA, 30 October 1970, NYPL.

229 "turning down Ogden Nash": RA, interview by the author.

229 "a simple 'sorry' will suffice": ON to EJ, 6 October 1965, Curtis Brown Collection.

230 "what I'd like it to be": tape recording of radio interview, Baltimore, 1970, private papers of LNS.

230 "all the space he consumes": Perelman to ON, 10 September 1968, HRC.

230 "devil fly away with them": Perelman to ON, 5 January 1969, ibid.

230 "lightness has gone, alas": Richard Armour to ON, 14 September 1970, private papers of LNS.

231 "lamas of 43rd street": ON to Duke, 2 June 1966, ibid.

231 "about hospitals I have ever read": RA to ON, 23 May 1966, NYPL.

231 "inventive and non-light poem": John Updike to ON, 29 June 1966, HRC.

231 "psychologically and poetically": Josephine Jacobsen to ON, 19 December 1969, ibid.

232 "cosmic ludicrousness": ON to RA, 2 August 1966 (unsent), HRC.

232 "if we hadn't changed": RA, interview by the author.

233 "still draw water": ON to Duke, 26 February 1968, private papers of LNS.

233 "had a thicker skin": ON to RA, 20 October 1968, NYPL.

233 "Nash writes nonsense": Eliot Fremont-Smith, *New York Times*, 26 October 1968.

234 "deceives the surface reader": H. L. Rosofsky, *Library Journal*, 1 November 1968, 4147.

234 "unmatchable original": Tom Yarborough, *St. Louis Sunday Post-Dispatch*, 10 November 1968.

234 "the Little Brown arse": ON to Knowlton, 26 October 1958, Curtis Brown Collection.

235 "I have been betrayed": ON to Bradford [27 October 1968] (unsent), enclosed in ON to Knowlton, 28 October 1968, ibid.

235 Knowlton explanation: Knowlton to ON, 28 October 1968, ibid.

235 "brutally betrayed": ON to Thornhill, telegram, 11 November 1968, Files of Little, Brown.

235 "recognizes these facts": ON to Thornhill, 26 November 1968 (unsent), HRC.

236 "contributions to our list": Bradford Memorandum, 25 April 1968, enclosure to Bradford to ON, 5 December 1968, HRC.

236 "not very bright": Knowlton to ON, 22 March 1968, Curtis Brown Collection.

236 "do lots better, let's go": ON to Knowlton, 16 May 1968, ibid.

236 Termination of Dent: Martin Dent to ON, 7 January 1969, Knowlton to Nash, 15 January 1969, and ON to Dent, 23 January 1969, HRC.

17. OH, TO BE IN ENGLAND

238 Publication in England: Crandell, *Ogden Nash*, 13, 31, 50 *et seq.*

240 Reading by Judi Dench: Program, *Fanfare*, Royal Opera House, 3 January 1973, private papers of LNS.

240 "too many English" and "through tolerable, to enjoyable": ON to DL, 20 February 1939, Longwell Collection.

240 Wartime Britain: Two of the writers Nash had worked with in Hollywood on *Firefly* contributed to memorable films celebrating the British war effort: Claudine West won an Academy Award for *Mrs. Miniver*, and Alice Duer Miller wrote a sentimental narrative poem *White Cliffs of Dover* which enjoyed phenomenal success in both Britain and the United States before becoming a motion picture.

241 "like a peacock": FLN to Mrs. William Leonard, 22 May 1957, HRC.

241 "person I had imagined": FLN to Mrs. William Leonard, 26 May 1957, ibid.

241 "as well as everything else": FLN to Mrs. William Leonard, 31 May 1957, ibid.

241 "an artvul splash": James Stern et al. to ON [August–September 1959], HRC.

242 "other worthy targets": *Times Literary Supplement*, 13 November 1953.

242 "a musician played with notes": Robert Lusty, interview by DW, Dartmouth.

242 "very heartening": ON to Bradford, 20 November 1964, Files of Little, Brown.

242 "vulnerable self-esteem" and "by gosh did so": ON to INE, 19 November 1964, Smith, ed., *Loving Letters*, 313.

243 "a husband killer": FLN to EJ, 3 June 1969, Curtis Brown Collection.

243 Isabel's illness: Smith, ed., *Loving Letters*, 327.

244 "reciting my verse": Travel Diary, 11 June 1969, private papers of LNS.

244 "trying to love Mr. Johnson": Sydney Edwards, "Mr. Nash Stays Inside His Oyster Shell," undated, [*Evening Standard*], private papers of LNS.

244 "called Sister all the time": ibid.

244 Visiting cathedrals: Travel Diary, 8 and 12 June, 4 July 1969.

245 Visiting Oxford: ON to INE, 6 July 1969, Smith, ed., *Loving Letters*, 338; Travel Diary, 6 July 1969. Nash's travel diary correctly refers to Balliol as the rival of Merton as the oldest college at Oxford. Both were founded ca. 1264, while New College, inexplicably referred to in Nash's letter to Isabel, was not founded until 1379.

246 "harder than most modern poets": quoted in Gina Richardson, "Nonsense with a Conscience," *Daily Telegraph Magazine*, 7 November 1969.

246 "getting it confused with 'Ogden'": Travel Diary, 9 July 1969.

246 "too taxingly bilingual": *Times Literary Supplement*, 10 July 1969.

246 "lost Mr. Ogden Nash" and "lower than the angels": quoted in William J. Webb, "Poetry International," *Guardian*, 11 July 1969.

247 "dignity of his small body": Julian Jebb, "Poetry International '69, (London) *Sunday Times*, 13 July 1969.

248 "the level of drivel": John Kelly, "Just an Old Fashioned Poet!" *Sunday Press*, 20 July 1969.

248 "simply as a silly ass": Travel Diary, 19 April 1970.

249 "filched from you": ON to Mary Wilson, private papers of LNS.

249 "volume of verse since Byron": Robert Lusty, interview by DW, Dartmouth.

249 "it's part of me": Ogden Nash, tape recording of radio interview, December 1970, private papers of LNS.

250 "one of which is ourselves": Commencement Address at Miss Porter's School, June 1970, private papers of LNS.

18. THE LAST STANZA

251 "And give them hell": Ogden Nash, "Tale of Two Debutantes," Smith, ed., *Loving Letters*, 352–353.

251 Sullivan letter: Frank Sullivan to ON, 9 January 1971, private papers of LNS.

251 "group from the Sunpapers": ON to INE , Smith, ed., *Loving Letters*, 353–354.

251 Bibliotherapy program: "Crownsville Group Hears Ogden Nash," *Baltimore Afro-American*, 13 February 1971.

252 "'attention and admiration'": Eloise Richardson, statement, Nash Collection, Dartmouth.

252 "at least some of my verse": ON to Bradford, 20 March 1970, Files of Little, Brown.

252 "riding along in a foreword": John Updike to Bradford, 25 May 1970, ibid.

252 Dickey suggestion: James Dickey to Bradford, 19 June 1970, ibid.

253 "as much into my work as I do": ON to Knowlton, 25 January 1971, Curtis Brown Collection.

253 *Signature* circulation: Knowlton to Frederick E. Hill, 2 November 1972, Files of Little, Brown.

253 Rosenstock show: Milton Rosenstock, interview by DW, Dartmouth; ON to INE, 28 February 1971, Smith, ed., *Loving Letters*, 353.

253 Nash plans: ON to Bradford, 10 January 1971, Files of Little Brown; INE, interview by the author.

254 "less painful than the tests": ON to Bradford, 5 March 1971, Files of Little, Brown.

254 "most recent masterpiece": RA to ON, 19 March 1971, NYPL.

255 Frances's letters: FLN to EJ, 6 and 8 April 1971, Curtis Brown Collection.

255 Visits by Collins and Summers: Clarence Collins and Beryl Summers, interviews by DW, Dartmouth.

255 "lyrics sparkle and delight": EJ to ON, 15 April 1971, Curtis Brown Collection.

256 Admission Note, Johns Hopkins Hospital, provided to the author by Dr. Phillip Wagley, at the request of LNS.

256 "really touch and go": FLN to EJ, 4 May 1971, Curtis Brown Collection.

256 "I love you Frances": quoted by LNS, interview by the author.

256 "To Ogden": FLN, LNS, INE, quoted in Smith, ed., *Loving Letters*, 355.

256   Dickinson poem: Frances Smith, interview by the author.

256   Nash memorial service: Smith, ed., *Loving Letters*, 357.

258   "almost every human field": Mrs. Hugh Bullock to LNS, 19 November 1971, private papers of LNS.

258   "for all the others": *The New Yorker*, 29 May 1971, 92.

258   "applause that riddled the readings": Donal Henahan, "Verses of Ogden Nash in Musical Setting," *New York Times*, 4 April 1971.

19. THE NASH LEGACY

261   "crazed affection for the language": Billy Collins, "Ogden Nash," in Elise Paschen and Rebekah Presson Mosby, eds., *Poetry Speaks* (Naperville, Ill.: Sourcebooks, 2001), 157

261   "as seriously as fiction and drama": Dana Gioia, *Can Poetry Matter?* (St. Paul, Minn.: Graywolf Press, 1992), 1, 17.

262   "poetry can even mesmerize": Elise Paschen, "Introduction," in Paschen and Mosby, eds., *Poetry Speaks*, xiii.

263   "meter permanently defunct": Gioia, *Can Poetry Matter?*, 31.

20. EPILOGUE: THE FAMILY

264   "Go to it, Frances": Ogden Nash, "For Frances, April, 12, 1968," Smith, ed., *Loving Letters*, 326.

266   "swallow the dictionary": quoted in Marjorie Kaufman, "Opening a Window to the Inner Souls of Artists, in a New Novel," *New York Times*, 4 May 1997.

266   "taut, fresh and vividly descriptive": Bruce Bawer, "For Richer, for Poorer, *New York Times*, 14 September 2003. Bawer continued: "Like Tom Wolfe, Eberstadt is a precise and witty observer of life in Manhattan, where 'murderously ambitious 26-year-olds' sip cocktails at midtown hotel bars while pianists play 'Miss Otis Regrets,' where uptown 'power nannies' mind their 'power babies' and slouching 'teenage gods' (à la T. J. Eckleburg in 'Gatsby') look down on Times Square from billboards, clothed and unclothed in Calvin Klein underpants and Calvin Klein undershirts . . . moony, slack-jawed, affectless."

INDEX

A NOTE ON THE AUTHOR

Douglas Parker was born in Chicago and studied at Cornell University and the Cornell Law School before practicing law in New York and Washington, D.C. He specialized in corporate litigation and also served in the Office of Counsel to the President and later in the Department of Housing and Urban Development. After retirement, and with the encouragement of the Nash family, he began research for this book. He is married and lives in South Orleans, Massachusetts, on Cape Cod.